YALE PUBLICATIONS IN RELIGION, 11

DAVID HORNE, EDITOR

PUBLISHED UNDER THE DIRECTION OF
THE DIVINITY SCHOOL

ENGLAND'S
EARLIEST PROTESTANTS

1520-1535

by William A. Clebsch

GREENWOOD PRESS, PUBLISHERS
WESTPORT, CONNECTICUT

Library of Congress Cataloging in Publication Data

Clebsch, William A
   England's earliest Protestants, 1520-1535.

   Reprint of the ed. published by Yale University
Press, New Haven, which was issued as v. 11 of Yale
publications in religion.
   Bibliography: p.
   Includes index.
   1. Reformation--England. I. Title. II.   Series:
Yale publications in religion ; 11.
[BR375.C58 1980]   280'.4'0942   80-15226
ISBN 0-313-22420-X (lib. bdg.)

Reprinted with the permission of Yale University Press.

Reprinted in 1980 by Greenwood Press, a division of
Congressonal Information Service, Inc.
88 Post Road West, Westport, CT 06881

Printed in the United States of America

10 9 8 7 6 5 4 3 2 1

To Wilhelm Pauck
and to the memory of Olga C. Pauck
this book is gratefully dedicated

Preface

The wise man to whom this book is dedicated has identified
the genius of England's official Reformation as the settling of
religion around the ruling idea of the divine right of kings.
His insight brightly illumines the interpretation of the thought
and work of men like Cranmer and Jewel and Hooker. More
than that, it teased me to ask whether any English theologian
raised the option of a reformed Christianity ruled by some
other theological theme, prior to the attack on religious roy-
alism under Elizabeth I. English religious writings that originated between 1520 and 1535 provided data from which to
answer my question in the affirmative. For these writings debated the viability of a Christianity that combined justification
by faith with thoroughgoing moralism—a combination which
relied on Luther but also repudiated him, and one that has empowered the Puritan forces in English-speaking religion down
to yesterday. My seemingly simple question found a complex
answer.

This book poses the question, surveys those data, and for-
mulates that answer. Its primary intention to be a chapter in
the history of Christian thought leads naturally to a strong
bibliographical interest, for it tells a story of theological conflict that employed literary weapons. The conflict raged over
issues that the disputants took to be fundamental—the nature
of God and of man and of their relations. To simplify the
identification of the parties, I have called them "Protestants"
and "Catholics" in the loose, common-sense, modern meanings
of the terms. The names they called each other may be historically more accurate and certainly are more vivid. The conflict
took men on both sides to their death, but for them death was

no defeat. Perhaps in their kind of conflict there is no defeat, but only the victory of a steady conscience. Men on all sides won that.

So many persons and institutions aided my work that I can neither name them all nor confidently choose the prominent ones for mention.

A faculty fellowship from the American Association of Theological Schools, a sabbatical leave and a later grant from the Episcopal Theological Seminary of the Southwest, and a grant-in-aid from the Henry E. Huntington Library and Art Gallery enabled me to reach and read sources in far-flung collections; to the Trustees of these institutions I am grateful. The staffs of the Cambridge University Library (especially the Anderson Room), of the Folger Shakespeare Library, and of the Huntington Library served me with competence and patience that shall not be forgotten.

For several years my friend, Dr. Peter N. Brooks, of St. Paul's School, London, has repeatedly given help, counsel, and encouragement. My stay at Cambridge was made happy by Professor Charles F. D. Moule of Clare College and by Canon M. A. C. Warren of Westminster Abbey. Mr. J. B. Trapp of the Warburg Institute, University of London, read the typescript and gave good advice. Professors Hans W. Frei and Jaroslav J. Pelikan of Yale University fostered my work at critical junctures. My colleagues on the faculty of the Seminary of the Southwest assisted in numerous ways, and I am especially indebted to Mrs. Madelyn Kennedy, typist extraordinary. Mrs. Martin Price, of New Haven, and David Horne, editor of Yale Publications in Religion, exorcised from the typescript a legion of demons.

Even while acknowledging these heavy debts and more, I claim the book, errors and all.

I thank these publishers for permission to quote at length from their publications: the Cambridge University Press for excerpts from *The New Testament Translated by William Tyndale, 1534,* edited by N. Hardy Wallis, and from *Studies in the Making of the English Protestant Tradition,* by E. Gordon Rupp; the Stanford University Press for excerpts from *Henry VIII and Luther,* by Erwin Doernberg; the Society for

Promoting Christian Knowledge for excerpts from *William Tyndale,* by J. F. Mozley; the Oxford University Press for excerpts from *The Beginning of the New Testament Translated by William Tyndale 1525,* a facsimile with introduction by Alfred William Pollard, and from *English Literature in the Sixteenth Century Excluding Drama,* by C. S. Lewis; and the University of Pennsylvania Press for excerpts from *The English Primers (1529–1545),* by Charles C. Butterworth. Like these, less extensive quotations from other books are acknowledged in footnotes and bibliography.

Those who mostly and finally prove my dependence upon others are my wife, Betsy, and our son, William Ernst, and daughter, Sarah Elizabeth; their constant cheerfulness made the going good.

W. A. C.

Austin, Texas
May 1964

CONTENTS

ABBREVIATIONS

AM   *The Acts and Monuments of John Foxe,* ed.
                            J. Pratt, 4th ed. 8 vols. London, The Religious
                            Tract Society, 1877.

Cologne Fragment   *The Beginning of the New Testament Translated by William Tyndale 1525. Facsimile* [of *STC 2823*] *of the Unique Fragment of the Uncompleted Cologne Edition,* intro. by A. W. Pollard, Oxford, Clarendon Press, 1926.

DNB   *Dictionary of National Biography,* ed. L. Stephen and S. Lee, 63 vols. London, Smith, Elder, 1885–1900.

1534 NT   *The New Testament Translated by William Tyndale 1534. A Reprint of the Edition of 1534 with the Translator's Preface & Notes and the variants of the edition of 1525,* ed. N. H. Wallis, Cambridge University Press, 1938.

Five Books   *William Tyndale's Five Books of Moses, Called the Pentateuch, Being a Verbatim Report of the Edition of M.CCCCC.XXX. Compared with Tyndale's Genesis of 1534 . . . with Various Collations and Prolegomena,* ed. J. I. Mombert, New York, Anson D. F. Randolph, 1884.

LP   *Letters and Papers, Foreign and Domestic, of the Reign of Henry VIII,* ed. J. S. Brewer and J. Gairdner, 21 vols. London, 1862–1908. References are to numbered documents.

Ned. Bibl.   *Nederlandsche Bibliographie van 1500 tot 1540,* ed. W. Nijhoff and M. E. Kronenberg, 3 vols. 's-Gravenhage, Martinus Nijhoff, 1923–61.

PS *1*
William Tyndale, *Doctrinal Treatises and Introductions to Different Portions of the Holy Scriptures,* ed. H. Walter, Parker Society, 1848.

PS *2*
William Tyndale, *Expositions and Notes on Sundry Portions of the Holy Scriptures, together with The Practice of Prelates,* ed. H. Walter, Parker Society, 1849.

PS *3*
William Tyndale, *An Answer to Sir Thomas More's Dialogue, The Supper of the Lord . . . and Wm. Tracy's Testament Expounded,* ed. H. Walter, Parker Society, 1850.

STC
A Short-Title Catalogue of Books Printed in England, Scotland, & Ireland and of English Books Printed Abroad 1475–1640, ed. A. W. Pollard, G. R. Redgrave, et al., London, The Bibliographical Society, 1926.

WA
D. Martin Luthers Werke. Kritische Gesammtausgabe, ed. J. K. F. Knaake, G. Kawerau, E. Thiele, et al. *Werke,* vols. 1 ff. in process; *Die Deutsche Bibel,* 12 vols.; *Tischreden,* 6 vols.; *Briefwechsel,* 11 vols. Weimar, H. Bohlau, 1883–

Whole workes
The Whole workes of W. Tyndall, John Frith, and Doct. Barnes, three worthy Martyrs . . . collected and compiled in one Tome togither, ed. John Foxe, London, John Daye, 1573 [1572]. (*STC* 24,436; separately paginated for Tyndale, and for Frith and Barnes.)

Workes
The Workes of Sir Thomas More Knyght, sometyme Lord Chauncellour of England, wrytten by him in the Englysh tonge, ed. W. Rastell, London, 1557. (*STC* 18,076)

1. Prologue

EFORMS have been as frequent as revolutions have been rare in the history of Christianity in England. Certainly revolutions have not been unknown. The Roman mission led by Augustine of Canterbury at the end of the sixth century, the Norman conquest in the later eleventh century, the explosions of the seventeenth-century civil war, interregnum, and commonwealth, and the multifarious movements in church, state, and education during the middle third of the nineteenth century all created discontinuities that tore religion and changed religious thought. In contrast with these, the Protestant Reformation of the sixteenth century, so decisive and swift in its transformation of Germany and Switzerland, dealt gradually and rather gently with the English. This Reformation began seeping into the English Church through the thought of biblical humanists like Desiderius Erasmus and John Colet, who taught a new view of the Bible at Oxford and Cambridge from the beginning of the century. Eight decades later vernacular scripture and worship had long prevailed, monasteries had been dissolved, doctrine had been revised, and ecclesiastical authority lodged in a national Church and Crown; yet a comprehensive, uniform religion still united England's diverse populace and extensive regions.

Between 1500 and 1580, when that unity began to dissolve, distinct waves of church reform successively lapped at the edges of English religion, none quite inundating the Church but none receding without having changed the shoreline. After the biblical humanists, and in continuing debt to them, came a group of more radical men, genuine Protestants who sought from their situation in exile on the Continent to summon the English Church to repentance and reform by the rule of the pure gospel found in the letter and word of scripture. This movement began in 1520 and lasted for fifteen years. After 1535 a national church was concentrated in the Crown as its head, accepting mildly Protestant principles for reasons of politics that were variously understood by Thomas Cromwell and Stephen Gardiner. Subsequently under the boy-king, continental Protestantism directly fashioned English religion by enshrining its teachings in authorized formularies of worship in 1549 and 1552. After Mary Tudor's efforts to place England under Tridentine papalism failed, her half-sister by compromise achieved a comprehensive church at once loyally national, traditionally catholic, theologically humanistic, and doctrinally protestant. Elizabeth's settlement lasted almost a generation.

Of all these waves of reformation in England, the least understood and the most misunderstood is the second, spanning the time that elapsed between Luther's appearance before the imperial diet at Worms and the execution of the two leading champions of English Catholicism, Thomas More and John Fisher. During these years the earliest English Protestants, as distinguished from humanistic advocates of reform like Colet, lived, labored, and most of them died in the attempt to reform religion under the criterion of an essential gospel made available to all in vernacular scriptures. The leaders of this movement lived in exile on the Continent, where they drank in Swiss and German religious thought, where they wrote a large and baffling corpus of polemical and hortatory literature, and whence they smuggled their translated biblical selections and their disputatious tracts across the channel to their fellow countrymen.

The ensuing chapters describe and appreciate those men, and sort and assess the writings that from 1520 through 1535 aimed at transforming Christianity in England. Apart from the translation of the New Testament by William Tyndale and his helpers, these years yielded no theological classic in English. None of the men involved, either on the Protestant or Catholic sides, ranks as a theologian of the first class. Nevertheless, England's earliest Protestants and their books stamped

English-speaking Christianity with a concern that persists and prevails even in our day—a concern for morality as the clue to theology and the core of religion.

Under severe handicaps, living in hiding, hounded by ecclesiastical, imperial, and royal authorities, these men blended the salient insights of biblical humanists and continental Protestants into a moralistic theology and a scriptural religion designed to appeal to England's liberal intellectuals no less than to common men and women still attached to old Lollardy. Their interest in reforming religion caught fire from the flame of Martin Luther's new teachings. It fed on the fuel of Christian humanism's dedication to the Bible as the fountain of Christianity, the source of the *philosophia christi,* and the articulation of God's rules for righteousness. They wanted to burn out the dross of the Catholic Church in England. But their monarch, and the hierarchy that he increasingly persuaded to do his bidding, determined throughout this period to let no such spark touch the tinder of English life and thought. These Protestants repeated their professions of loyalty to country and prince, even though the prince relentlessly opposed them by fusing intense territorialism with conservative Catholicism into benevolent despotism over all life. For Henry VIII, who at the beginning of the period became defender of the old Catholic faith as part of the defense of the old royal power, always defended whatever faith he authorized in order to strengthen the royal power he exercised. How could such a monarch be persuaded that a movement widely thought to be directed by an apostate monk of Wittenberg, and broadly understood as anarchical and revolutionary, might increase the wealth of his realm, materially, politically, culturally, or spiritually? To detach their religious program from the unhelpful name and fame of the Lutherans, and to present it at once uncompromised and appealing to the Crown, posed politically subtle and theologically complicated problems for the early English Protestants. Regardless of the King, however, small but important audiences responded to and applauded the program.

Even while Henry VIII was revealing the folly of Luther's errors, scholars in both English universities were studying the ideas of the Wittenberg professor. First at Cambridge emerged a band of dons who discussed and assessed the rediscovered gospel. Soon a similar secret group, in some ways an offshoot of the Cambridge clique, established itself in Cardinal Wolsey's own new collegiate foundation at Oxford. Available evidence indicates that these scholars in the early 1520s perceived no great differences between the renaissance advocacy of church reform and the new Wittenberg theology. Nevertheless they spread through the universities an awareness of and a considerable interest in Luther and other emerging Reformation champions on the Continent, especially as these men propounded novel and cogent interpretations of biblical passages long left as dry husks under traditional scholia and glosses.

Stimulated by the biblicism of the previous generation's humanists, remnants of John Wycliffe's old reforming movement in England rallied to the Protestant emphasis upon the faith of the believer. Late Lollardy provided the early English Protestants with ready and tenacious devotees among the common folk; indeed certain cherished religious and theological themes of these Lollards shaped the content of many a Protestant paragraph, and the rediscovered gospel was made to appeal to the predilections of the "known men." From the outset English Protestantism was shaped by the waning Wycliffites whom it engulfed.

Luther's own theological discoveries arose out of the late medieval monastic religiosity that nurtured him and against which he revolted. Naturally English monastic life became an arena for the reception of his teachings, and in fact several Protestant leaders and writers were recruited from monasteries. The prior of the Cambridge house of Luther's own order of Augustinian Observants was the man who first publicly voiced Protestant principles in that university. The Franciscans at Greenwich supplied some poetical propagandists. A prior of Reading and some monks at Bury St. Edmunds played secondary but not minor roles in creating and circulating proscribed English Protestant writings.

Certain ranks of London society nursed the infant movement. There, as well as in such famous Lollard centers as Norwich, congregations of "the Brethren"—men and women who under whatever threatened punishment refused to desert their religious duty of reading and teaching vernacular scriptures—held clandestine meetings to sustain and to spread what they took to be biblical Christianity. Some professional men of Protestant persuasion, notably lawyers, lent the evangelical enterprise social dignity, adeptness at advocating misunderstood causes, and intellectual ability. The merchants who managed England's brisk trade with Hanseatic and other European ports were mostly in London, and many of them smuggled proscribed religious books into, and convicted heretics out of, England. Tradesmen dealt in contraband books—especially, after 1525, the several printings of the New Testament in English—not only for profit, itself probably commensurate with risk, but out of a conscientious profession of Protestant faith. Proscription of books and measures for extirpating them were designed to apply particularly to London, yet in London these books became increasingly available. Some were read in the royal palace.

Altogether the labors and achievements of the earliest English Protestants, involving as they did a variety of persons and classes, comprise a long chapter in English social history, even in so brief a period as 1520 to 1535. The episodes, attitudes, and circumstances of all these supporters of the movement are fascinating, but they reveal less about the theological character of the movement than do its literature and the intellectual processes of the men who wrote it. To be sure, these leaders themselves represented the wide range of their support. From each center of Protestant interest in England came one or more literary leaders. Cambridge was directly represented by Robert Barnes and George Joye. John Frith had been a key figure in the group of Protestants at Wolsey's college in Oxford, and he established intimate liaison between the exiled writers and the Brethren at home. William Tyndale seems to have belonged to both universities; he began his literary activity under the auspices of gentry in Gloucestershire and London. Simon Fish, who made invaluable contributions by writing and translating, was a London lawyer. Greenwich Franciscans William Roy and Jerome Barlowe versified Protestant ideas in a memorable form long influential among common people at home. Protestantism appealed also to men of rank; although these were of minor importance in the production of Protestant literature, they grew numerous later in the period, and some of them became chieftains of the English reformation in the later Henrician and the Edwardian periods.

As the early English Protestant writers represented several English traditions and institutions, so they made varying contributions and espoused differing theological positions. Certainly their finest and most widely heralded monument is the English translation of the entire New Testament achieved by Tyndale—aided, and at times (as he thought) hampered, by Roy, Joye, and Frith. This project occupied the early months of Tyndale's thirteen-year stay on the Continent; it had been substantially completed by late 1525 or very early 1526. The revision that he eagerly invited and boldly promised at the time of original publication became less attractive as years passed; Tyndale put out a new version only in 1534 and 1535, and then under certain duress. From the Old Testament he translated the first five books and other significant portions. In pursuing his vocation as translator Tyndale surmounted the successive obstacles of relying on inadequate assistance, of moving from place to place, of hiding from church authorities, of losing by shipwreck his books, manuscripts, and notes, and of seeing almost an entire edition of the New Testament destroyed. These obstacles were significant for Tyndale's theological development; they impressed upon him the difficulty of obtaining a Bible-reading church in England, and this prompted him to search for keys by which to unlock the true meaning of scripture. The theme of how rightly to understand a book that failed to be its own interpreter pervades not only his prologues and prefaces to biblical books but also all his expository and most of his controversial writings. Tyndale lived as he died, that scripture might be available in his mother tongue, yet each year saw him the more definitely insisting that scripture be illuminated by his own theological lights.

Frith, a young and winsome man, was prematurely launched upon his Protestant career by persecution under Wolsey; persecution under Sir Thomas More prematurely ended that career. His finely trained mind and his humbly aggressive spirit merged to make a more consistent, and more consistently theological, literary corpus than any of his fellow-workers achieved. That is not to say that Frith was a speculative or systematic theologian. In all his extant writings he aimed either to dispute the Catholics or to bolster the Brethren. But even while pressing theological attacks against the two most potent features of contemporary Catholic religion, purgatory and the mass, Frith had always in mind not to vanquish his enemies but to praise his creator and redeemer. His brief life bore literary first fruits that, had they ripened and increased, would have placed him in the very front line of sixteenth-century theologians.

By education and rank Robert Barnes, who openly demanded church reform at Cambridge late in 1525, stood highest among the earliest English Protestants, but he so hankered for royal patronage for his reforming ideas that he trimmed his theological sails to the shifting winds of Henry VIII's ecclesiastical policies. Barnes was the first prominent English clergyman to be condemned, however unjustly, for Lutheran leanings, and after his escape he showed promise of devoting his learning to uncompromised reformation goals. Sensing the political realities of the day more keenly than most of his contemporaries, Barnes dared only one adamant opposition to the known religious convictions of his prince—in demanding authorization of vernacular scriptures. His considerable versatility at presenting plans more to the King's liking failed to win the royal commission he wanted until Henry's international policy, guided by Thomas Cromwell, needed persons capable of negotiating on a friendly basis with the evangelical princes of Germany. Despite minor advancements Barnes finally fell athwart of the reactionary religious policies of Henry guided by Stephen Gardiner, and in 1540 was burnt at the stake. Only the men who were more adept even than Barnes at sensing and adjusting to Henry's ecclesiastical whims—men like Thomas Cranmer and Hugh Latimer—survived to blend together royal church and biblical religion in some such manner as Barnes advocated.

George Joye was early apprehended at Cambridge, and docketed for trial along with the notable Thomas Bilney; Joye's literary activities until 1540 ran to liturgy. Working from various Latin texts, Joye translated large portions of the Bible

into English, selecting mainly the Old Testament writings
that were commonly used in private, monastic, and public worship. Two different Psalters, from Latin translations by Martin
Bucer and Huldreich Zwingli, the prophetic books of Isaiah
and Jeremiah (including Lamentations), and much of the other
wisdom literature, Joye turned into English. He compiled and
published the first two printed English Primers, and produced
a highly Zwinglian and very practical treatise on the sacrament of the altar. It was Joye who undertook to revise Tyndale's 1526 New Testament for printing in August 1534, a
deed that drew down the ire of the great translator and forced
him to bring out his own long-promised revision. Like Barnes,
Joye returned to England during the half-decade when Henry
haltingly tolerated Protestant emphases in his royal church,
but when the reaction came, Joye once more fled to the Continent and outlived all his earlier co-workers. Although overshadowed by Tyndale as a translator and later eclipsed by
Cranmer as a liturgist, Joye's work in both these realms was
appreciable and enduring.

There were other less important literary figures—the rhyme-
makers Roy and Barlowe, the pamphleteer Fish, and, toward
the end of our era, a number of translators, editors, and publishers of Protestant and biblical-humanist tracts. Although
none of these men became prominent in the coterie of English
Protestants under persecution, together their writings established significant guidelines for later theological and religious
developments.

Although the first and most famous literary achievement of
the English Protestants—the vernacular New Testament—
bore the date 1525–26, its production and the host of writings
defending and explicating it cannot be understood without careful regard to the posture taken by England's officialdom as
they went about rejecting Luther's teachings. Therefore the
story of the initial espousal of Protestantism by Englishmen
begins at the year 1520 and focuses first upon the derision with
which England's Church and Crown regarded Luther's theological eruption. After the appearance of the English New
Testament, Protestant writings in the common tongue were
for a brief time mostly translations of exegetical and exposi-

tory tracts by Luther. The heyday of hopes and activities by the men under study came just after Wolsey had been relieved of the enormous power he had long exerted over ecclesiastical and political affairs; it lasted until More's assiduous program against heretics took effect. Between 1528 and 1531, volume, unanimity, and theological clarity characterized the English Protestant writings that poured from Antwerp and other continental presses. By the end of 1531, however, More's resistance proved less penetrable than Wolsey's had been, and the company of exiles in Antwerp, until then led by Tyndale, dispersed as each member struck out upon what seemed to him the most promising or the conscientiously necessary path of thought and action.

As the English Protestant leaders turned toward expressing individual convictions, their theological and religious divergences grew into open controversies over the manner of the presence of Christ in the Supper and the meaning of justification by faith, as well as over less than cardinal teachings. Frith's course led back to England, where he briefly rallied the Brethren to defy More's stern policies and where he earned the reward of imprisonment and death. From the Tower of London issued his small but admirable stream of writings, as theocentric as any of Luther's, yet more directly dependent upon Johannes Oecolampadius of Basel than upon any other continental reformer. Joye's inclinations led him to admire, emulate, and translate Zwingli of Zürich and to find in Zwingli's thought a theological basis for his liturgical interests. Tyndale embarked upon the most distinct of these individual approaches by ever more blatantly interpreting Christianity as a system of rewards and punishments for moral actions. Although not alone in favoring this line of thought, he expressed it unmistakably and impressed it upon the 1534 revised New Testament; thus he became the real if unacknowledged founder of the type of English-speaking Christianity that is commonly called Puritan.

By the end of 1535 an entire English Bible was circulating openly if still illegally, and Protestant books in mild profusion came off London presses. Catholicism's stanchest and ablest defenders in England, More and Fisher, had met martyrs'

deaths for objecting to the way their erstwhile ally the King
had consolidated under his headship a Church whose hierarchy
owed fealty to him and not to the Pope. These developments,
symbolizing other kindred ones, indicate that the English Reformation was well begun, although some time would elapse
before Bible and common worship should be authorized in the
common tongue. Even then, as the closing years of Henry's
reign showed, the one unalterably secure element of church
reformation was the principle of royal headship. Yet from
1535 onward Protestant principles gradually altered traditional practices and teachings in the Church in England until,
under Edward VI, a Protestant religion prevailed, only to
suffer temporary eclipse under Mary Tudor and then permanent, if partial, victory under Elizabeth I. Although English
Protestantism had not won all by 1535, the year marks the
transition to an era in which royal headship functioned as the
mechanism for making changes in the Church. With that principle secure, Henry needed no longer to persecute Protestants,
and Protestants needed no longer to suffer exile and depriva-
tion for their faith (save under Mary).

The ensuing chapters trace the ideas and deeds of the leading men of English Protestantism during that initial and most
difficult time, 1520 to 1535, when the fountain of faith was a
banned Bible, and when the gospel rediscovered by Luther rallied Englishmen to martyrdom.

2. England's Initial Repudiation
of Luther

WHEN the Protestant teachings of Doctor Martin Luther of Wittenberg were officially branded a threat to the conscience of Catholic Christians, the English Crown and Church sprang obediently to attention. Examination of the danger, however, almost automatically ended the alert. So obviously had the heretic advanced his errors that they seemed to lack the insidiousness of subtlety. To the Pope's order that Luther be damned, the realm of course complied. King, chief prelate, and leading scholar quickly, as they thought, dispelled the danger by branding it as insane and by calling it impotent. They took their intense loyalty to the Church as warrant for their estimate of its enemy's strength. They lost no time, but they spent no great energy. England's Church was strong, her faith secure. If the empire must settle a number of accounts with the Saxon, at home Luther's lies would be exposed, his books burned, his religion castigated by the labors of the legate *a latere,* of the learned John Fisher, and of the theologically minded monarch himself.

The bull of Leo X, *Exsurge, Domine* (June 15, 1520), commanded that Luther's books, containing forty-one heretical articles alleged against him, be sought out and destroyed; it met an enthusiastically obedient servant when it came into the hands of Thomas Cardinal Wolsey, papal legate in England. Even a month before the bull was promulgated, Erasmus reported to Oecolampadius in Basel that Luther's books were about to be burnt in England.[1] Before the year was out a public

1. *LP, 3,* 1, no. 810.

burning of Protestant books had been held at Cambridge, probably at the west door of Great St. Mary's Church, as well as
at other places in the realm.[2] By the following March the Pope
had commended Wolsey for his prohibition of Luther's writings, encouraging Wolsey in his plan for a public demonstration during Ascensiontide 1521.

Luther's writings had been staple items, though not best-
sellers like the books of Erasmus, in the 1520 trade of John
Dorne, bookseller at Oxford; especially popular was Luther's
treatise on the power of the Pope.[3] Wolsey's sensitivity to Englishmen's interest in Luther cannot be accurately assessed, for
his haste in implementing official church policy against the
heresiarch may have been due more to his ambition than to
his awareness of actual danger.[4] At any rate, he arranged for
a demonstration on May 12, 1521, at Paul's Cross, at which
Luther's writings were burnt and John Fisher, bishop of
Rochester, preached a sermon damning the new heresies. The
papal bull condemning Luther's teachings was ten months old
when the demonstration occurred, but the Edict of Worms,
which commanded enforcement by the sword, was barely
drafted and not yet signed; that Edict, drawn up on May 8,
1521, and signed May 26, 1521, took effect at the expiration of
the safe conduct which had been guaranteed Luther for his
journey to Worms and home again. By May 12 Luther was
lodged at Wartburg Castle in the safekeeping of his "kid-
napers."

The English Cardinal received disturbing news on the very
day that the Edict of Worms was signed; for William Warham, archbishop of Canterbury, then informed Wolsey that he
had in hand letters from Oxford reporting that University to
be "infected with Lutheranism, and many books forbidden by
Wolsey had obtained circulation there." Warham regretted

---

2. W. D. Bushell, *Church of St. Mary the Great* (Cambridge, 1948), p. 93.
3. *Day-book of J. Dorne, bookseller in Oxford, A.D. 1520,* ed. F. Madan (Oxford, 1885). See also H. Bradshaw, *A Half-Century of Notes on the Day-Book
of John Dorne* (Cambridge, 1886), and F. Madan, *Supplementary Notes . . .*
(Oxford, 1890).
4. See A. F. Pollard, *Wolsey* (London, 1929, 1953), p. 126.

that a few "incircumspect fools" drew the whole University under suspicion, and he hoped for a quiet examination of the matter.[5]

Once the public demonstration was over and Fisher's sermon issued, Wolsey's zeal for destroying bad books waned. Two plausible reasons appear. First, the antiquated English law under which such publications might be seized, Arundel's Oxford Constitutions of the early years of the previous century, had been designed to halt the copying, distributing, and reading of manuscript Lollard tracts—a menace more easily regulated than the flow of books from Europe's many printing presses. Second, Wolsey's attempt to collect a sizable subsidy for the Pope during 1522–23 would suffer if Protestantism's progress in the land were known; during these years continental Protestants were devising church reforms and were recruiting followers from among scholars and peasants. Thus in spite of book-burnings in England during 1520–21, Protestant books seem to have circulated widely in London, Oxford, and Cambridge.

Only in the autumn of 1524 another concerted effort arose to stanch the flow of heretical literature into England. Cuthbert Tunstall, bishop of London, on October 12, 1524, called several booksellers to his palace and warned them against the illegal (but lucrative) traffic. If they handled imported books, they must submit all recent titles to Wolsey, Warham, Fisher, or Tunstall before parting with them. Although Tunstall seems to have assumed that sufficient restraints were being exercised to suppress manufacture of such books at home, just a year later John Gough and Wynkyn de Worde would find themselves under suspicion of heresy for translating and printing John Ryckes' *The ymage of loue* (*STC* 21,473). But a decade was to pass before writings and translations by Protestants issued openly from English presses.[6]

5. *LP, 3,* 1, no. 1193.

6. A. W. Reed, "The Regulation of the Book Trade before the Proclamation of 1538," *Transactions of the Bibliographical Society,* Old Series, *15* (1920), 162 ff.

John Fisher versus Luther

Despite Wolsey's vacillating, England's early repudiation of Luther and his ilk was swift and sweeping. As soon as Luther was officially condemned by the Diet of Worms, English loyalty to the Pope was publicly demonstrated. Before the summer reached its height, Church, Crown, and scholarship asserted the realm's subservience to the traditional religious order of Catholicism. England's two primates on May 12, 1521, dignified with their presence a throng gathered at Paul's Cross to witness the burning of Luther's heretical books.

To preach at the service and to bespeak English ecclesiastical rectitude, Wolsey chose the bishop of Rochester. Court favorite through the patronage of Lady Margaret, Countess of Richmond, Fisher had been elevated to the episcopate in 1504; more important was the prominence he enjoyed as humanist and scholar. Building on the foundation of a distinguished career at Cambridge as teacher, scholar, proctor, then chancellor, Fisher succeeded to the headship of English scholars on the death of John Colet. He stood well prepared, by means of learning and letters serving the single cause of Church and God, to refute the Wittenberg heresy. But he hated Wolsey's yearning for a church glorified by worldly riches and power. As learned humanist and leading English theologian of his day, Fisher was rumored to be the real author of King Henry's book against Luther. Even without that to his credit he stands as the chief literary defender of the English Church against the new Protestant religion, until More entered the fray in 1528 as polemicist against Tyndale.

Fisher was to compose many more anti-Protestant books, developing his defense of the Catholic cause and sharpening his attack upon the Protestants through a body of writings which comprises the best theology produced in England during the years 1520–27: *Assertionis Lutheranae confutatio* (1523); *Sacri sacerdotii defensio contra Lutherum* and *Defensio Regie assertionis contra Babylonicam captiuitatem* (1525); the vernacular sermon of 1526, preached at yet another book-burning service arranged by Wolsey; and *De veritate corporis et sanguinis Christi in Eucharistia* (1527), attacking the eucharistic

scripture itself repudiated such a single-minded appeal. Had not Jesus' injunction "Ye shall also bear witness, etc." warned that scripture was incomplete without the testimony of unwritten apostolic tradition and without subsequent statements of fathers and doctors and councils under the leading of God's spirit? Contravention of these traditional authorities showed Luther to have been possessed by a spirit other than the spirit of truth. To be sure, extrascriptural authorities were in Fisher's view fallible, but their fallibility did not justify Luther's dismissing them wholesale. Luther's admirers had defended him on the basis of his learning in the Bible, his courage before human tribunals, and his zeal for the spread of his gospel; Fisher saw these very attributes as marks of all heretics and servants of antichrist.

Fisher took Luther with a theological seriousness far surpassing that displayed by King Henry's book, which Fisher certainly praised and possibly wrote. Yet in spite of compelling homiletical logic and of pertinent employment of Bible and fathers, he probed the issues only a little more deeply than the royal diatribe. Henry's book took Luther's position to be so palpably wrong that it needed only to be described in order to be exposed as erroneous. Fisher's sermon reached the central point of the Reformation, justification, as Henry's book did not, but it handled that issue on the assumption that the Catholic Church enjoyed a reservoir of good will and credence deeper and broader than it actually had. The fact that as a leading English prelate Fisher set his face against certain ecclesiastical abuses made for no rapport with a reforming heretic. The great Erasmus, Fisher's friend and fellow scholar, was at this juncture confessing that, whatever else must be said, Luther's attacks on the Church might help to purify it. Even that far Fisher did not go. The German was a stubborn heretic; nothing from his pen might be endorsed, no point granted, no protest attended, no common interest recognized—none of these, at least, in the context of dealing with Luther qua heretic. That the Church might well stick to its spiritual business, that scriptures might well be held in very high esteem and interpreted according to their leading literal sense, that the tight grip of the schoolmen on theology might well be loosened—

Fisher left these points of agreement between early Protestants and Christian humanists completely unacknowledged. Commissioned not to assess but to condemn, he fulfilled his task. All that he left unsaid in favor of Luther and against contemporary church abuses indicates that the heat of controversy evaporated much of his humanism from his theological writings. An editor of his English works noted exaggeration in his attacks upon justifying faith, since Fisher's personal view of the matter was much closer to that of Luther than the commissioned sermon confessed: "The faith which he disparages . . . has nothing in common with Luther's *Glaube,* inseparable as that is from hope and love, and by inherent necessity fruitful in good works." [8] Personal integrity is not to be impeached by arguments from silence, but the fact remains that Fisher's sermon addressed the controversy instead of the issue at hand. That Fisher took Luther's errors to be apparent shows at once his stern loyalty to the Church which had anathematized them and, as the event would prove, his faulty polemical judgment.

The 1521 sermon seems to have been published in London by Wynkyn de Worde in the same year. Its reception as the first English refutation of Luther is attested by the fact that it was soon offered to scholars in a Latin translation by Richard Pace, then a reader in Greek at Cambridge and soon to become a negotiator in Wolsey's unsuccessful campaign for the papacy; the Latin version was one of the very few books to be printed at Cambridge during this period. Although Fisher's arguments were greatly expanded in his subsequent Latin writings against the reformers, the fact that this sermon was in the vernacular and that it set the style of his later arguments makes the piece especially interesting. For Fisher stood virtually alone as an English theologian producing scholarly refutations of Luther during the critical years 1520–29. King Henry's tract followed in July 1521. Two years later More published, under the pseudonym William Ross, a long and tendentious entry into the fight between Luther and Henry. Only with the appearance of More's *Dialogue,* in the writing since March 7, 1528, but published only in June 1529, was Fisher's defense of Catholicism assisted by a major theological libellus from the hand of a fel-

8. Mayor, p. xxii.

low Englishman. It must be noted that, excepting the publication of Tyndale's New Testament in 1525–26, hardly any Protestant writings appeared in English until 1528. By concentrating on the points at issue between Luther and Henry VIII and on the eucharistic position set forth by Oecolampadius, Fisher dealt with prevalent issues and left to one side others that had concerned him as a humanist. From the standpoint of the English hierarchy, these problems posed by the Wittenberg theology challenged the whole of western Christendom generally, not Christianity in England specifically; in defending Catholicism Fisher was only one of many Latin authors.

HENRY VIII'S ASSERTION

Some two months after the publication of Fisher's sermon of 1521 against Luther, and hardly before Luther himself was accustomed to his "captivity" at the Wartburg, Henry VIII published his *Assertio septem sacramentorum aduersus M. Lutherum* (*STC* 13,078), the second anti-Protestant libellus, and the first in Latin, to be printed in England. Theologically amateurish but historically momentous, the book immediately earned Henry's papal title and ultimately prejudiced all attempts at alliances between Henry and the evangelical estates of Germany.

Discussion of the tract's historical significance has overshadowed the perhaps unanswerable question of its actual authorship as well as the easier matter of assessing its theological worth. Rupp thought it "probable that the royal author had considerable assistance from More, Fisher and Lee and that the texts of Scripture, the linguistic evidence from Hebrew and Greek, the patristic citations and much of the argument were supplied by others." [9] Luther later stung Henry with the charge that the book was ghost written. Both Fisher and More during their lifetimes were credited with having written the work, and, indeed, it was they who carried on the argument after Luther's 1522 *Contra Henricum Regem Angliae*—More with the 1523 pseudonymous book and Fisher in the same year

9. E. G. Rupp, *Studies in the Making of the English Protestant Tradition* (London, 1947, 1949), p. 90; for Rupp's comment that the contemporary "John Barlow was very sceptical about the King's share" in the work, see p. 90 n.

with his *Assertionis Lutheranae confutatio*. Not until 1526
did Henry re-engage the argument with Luther, and then in
the underhanded way of pretending that Luther had recanted
his earlier opinions. Regardless of the question of authorship,
the tract bore the royal name; Henry never disowned it, not
even when to have done so became expedient. The spiritualty,
the temporalty, and the masters and doctors of the universities
learned from the start that their prince stood strong, and for
a time unwavering, in the faith of the fathers. The tract's own
introduction professed the chief motive of preserving religious
uniformity as instrumental to social and political unity.

The book's obviously small theological merit did nothing
to diminish its power, shared with that of Fisher's sermon, to
establish the grounds and the form of Catholic polemics in
England throughout the first era of the Reformation. The endeavor was to expose and publicize the doctrines and doings of
Luther that all might conclude his self-evident error and damnation—on the whole, a not too intelligent and a dreadfully
risky strategy in religious controversy. Henry undertook to
reveal Luther's alleged destruction of the entire sacramental
system of Christianity by his 1520 treatise *De captivitate babylonica ecclesiae*. Had any scholar in England been curious about
this work of Luther but feared to read a proscribed writing,
Henry's *Assertio* bid fair to inform him! Henry was so thoroughly convinced of the self-evidence of Luther's errors that he
hastened to disseminate them in the reformer's own words. For
Luther to attack the contemporary practice of indulgences
meant that a common monk called the unspotted Pope and his
predecessors religious impostors! All pastors who administered
indulgences were tacitly accused of fraud! How were one man's
fulminations to be compared with traditional practice buttressed by the dominical grant of power to bind and to loose
sins? Luther's challenge to the Pope's authority appeared ludicrous to the Scotist argument that if the Pope could and did
exercise dominion over the Church then he was entitled to do
so; Luther's rebellion against authority constituted in his own
case witchcraft and in that of his followers idolatry. Henry
thought Luther's arguments that Christ had instituted three

but not four other of the Church's sacraments really destroyed all sacraments.

Henry paid great attention to the sacrament of the altar. Utraquism on Luther's ground absurdly demanded imitating every feature of the Last Supper. To deny transubstantiation was to flaunt authority, tradition, and reason. Luther exposed the falsity of his own position by allowing his followers to choose their own explanation of the manner of presence in the Supper. By teaching that the official Church's position *might* be believed according to Luther and *must* be believed according to the Church, Luther gave the lie to his own explanation, which he allowed *might not*—and the Church commanded *must not*—be believed.

Luther's understanding of the mass as testament and promise instead of work and sacrifice most offended Henry. Here the two were at loggerheads without misunderstanding. But on the issue of faith and works in justification Henry, like Fisher before him, showed either unwillingness or inability to understand Luther's juxtaposition of grace and merit, testament and contract, gift and achievement; for the rest of his life Henry remained unteachable on this subject even by so gifted and trusted a tutor as Cranmer. To Henry's mind, perhaps as nimble and certainly as stubborn as his adversary's, Luther concocted unreal problems by posing the testamentary and sacrificial aspects of the mass as alternatives. Whatever Christ accomplished and bequeathed as a commemoration of that accomplishment, every authorized priest possessed power to repeat; the first Supper as beneficial to a few souls argued its repetition as beneficial to many. Thus early was posed the irreconcilable difference between the reforming of the humanists and the reforming of what were to be known as Protestants, a difference to be made abundantly clear in the 1524–25 controversy between Luther and Erasmus. Henry with the humanists looked at the picture of Christ with reverence and submission; so in their way did Luther and his followers. But to Henry that picture necessitated a church presenting to its creator an improved mankind, while to Luther it mirrored a God who concomitantly presented judgment and mercy to a judgment-deserving and mercy-needing mankind. Across this gulf, Luther appeared to Henry more frivolous than frightening, more deluded than dangerous; diabolical, yes, but only in his refusal to come to his senses and confess the Church's self-evident truth as preferable to his self-evident error. Laughingly, Henry taunted his opponent to claim "that he is more careful about *Faith,* than ever any man before him was"—an encomium that has come to be bestowed upon Luther by Catholics, Protestants, and humanists alike.[10]

Henry lamented Luther's magnifying the significance of baptism to the detriment of penance, because this exaggerated faith and played down good works. Henry was perplexed that Luther granted broad spiritual liberty to Christian men while counseling temporal obedience to the ruler—must not liberty in one realm beget libertinism in the other? Henry saw penance as personally and socially useful, therefore deserving more emphasis than Luther granted. Henry did not take with full seriousness Luther's discussions of contrition, confession, and satisfaction, because he could not believe that any man took seriously the injunction that literally all sins must be confessed. Henry defended confirmation on grounds of tradition and the Church's inspiration, against Luther's foolish stand on *sola scriptura*. He adduced traditional arguments regarding holy matrimony as a sacrament. On the point of holy orders Luther seemed to subvert stable society: that all Christians were priests was as false and dangerous a lie as that all Christians were kings. With regard to extreme unction Luther seemed mad because he rejected the apostolic authority of the Epistle of James in order to cut away the ground of this sacrament.

Henry's *Assertio* attained immediate fame among scholars and churchmen, a fame won by its royal authorship in spite of its dubious religious worth and scant theological merit. Alongside the masterfully subtle refutation of Luther by Johann Eck of Ingolstadt, the book pales into puerility. In comparison with the thorough work of Cochlaeus, who resolved with equal fervor that the faith should be defended and that its preserver should be Cochlaeus, Henry's piece was fragmentary. But it was direct, simple, terse. It identified the leading points of the

10. *Assertio Septem Sacramentorum . . . ,* tr. "T.W." (London, 1687), p. 47.

opponent, surrounded them by a wall of derision buttressed occasionally by sharp logic and familiarity with authorities, then
claimed jubilantly that the enemy was imprisoned. After a few
years Henry learned that Luther was doing more than (to use
Henry's figure) venting wind; if the charge of airiness must fall
on one of the contestants it is Henry, not Luther. Luther's
arguments against Catholicism mustered such support that even
Henry would soon find many of them expediting his repudiation
of papal control over England's Church. After a decade and a
half Henry came to prize nothing about his book save the title
that it earned him. In the meantime the *Assertio* gained an influence that surpassed its intrinsic value, as it helped set the
pace for ultimately unsuccessful English Catholic defenses.

3. New Aggressions and Defenses, 1525-1526

URING the first half of the 1520s England encountered the Reformation movement as a participant in Catholic Christendom. Save for Fisher's 1521 sermon there had been no publishing in the vernacular on the Reformation. Evidence abounds to indicate that English scholars, especially at Cambridge, read Luther's writings sympathetically, yet the official policy of Realm and Church explicitly supported the papacy. King Henry's *Assertio* and Wolsey's growing dominance over ecclesiastical affairs made it plain where England and the Church in England stood. The year 1525 brought sudden and significant shifts in circumstances, both within the Reformation movement on the Continent, and with particular regard to its impact in England.

Luther during that year took bold steps to distinguish between the religious movement into whose leadership he had been thrust and the various social and intellectual movements with which it might have become confused. In 1525 the evangelical princes formed the league of Torgau to defend their right to disregard the Edict of Worms in their own territories. The German mass was instituted in Wittenberg. Thomas Münzer led his peasant followers in the bloody assertion of their rights, and Luther separated himself and his followers from such *Schwärmer* as Münzer and Andreas Karlstadt. The same year brought to public attention the controversy between Erasmus and Luther over free will, symbolizing the breach between Christian humanism and Protestantism. Within the ranks of the more conservative reformers who eschewed social

24

radicals such as Münzer, major differences in theology and ecclesiology began to appear by 1525, especially in the controversy over the Eucharist. By this date the Reformation movement was deeply entrenched in certain German and Swiss duchies and cantons, showing itself as too potent a force to be stopped by the enforcement of an imperial edict against one rude monk.

Probably as early as 1525 there circulated in England manuscript copies of Johann Bugenhagen's famous letter to the English—the first appeal to English Christians to join the Protestant movement. Bugenhagen rejoiced "that in England as in other countres the ioyfull message of the glory of God was . . . well taken of dyuerse." Yet he lamented the probability that many would hold back from the cause when they heard false rumors and accusations against the reformers circulated by enemies of the gospel. The Reformation taught only one article: Christ is our righteousness; when Christ is received by faith, his righteousness becomes the righteousness of the believer; such a good tree can bear only good fruit. True believers among the English must beware lest they be put off from this saving faith by the baseless lies of those who accused the reformers of all manner of license. So argued the little letter of Pomeranus.[1]

Bugenhagen's appeal coincided with a remarkable heighten-

1. *A compendious letter which Jhon Pomerane . . . sent to . . . Englande* (n.pl., 1536; *STC* 4021). The original was dated early 1525 by O. Vogt, ed., *Dr. Johannes Bugenhagen Briefwechsel* (Stettin, 1888), p. 583; the letter may have been put into English by Tyndale, and copies made for circulation in England; Cochlaeus printed a Latin refutation of the letter in 1526. Probably in the same year—see E. F. Rogers, "Sir Thomas More's Letter to Bugenhagen," *The Modern Churchman*, 35 (1946), 350–60—Sir Thomas More composed his *Doctissima simul ac Elegantiss. D. Thomae Mori Clarissimi Viri Epistola, in qua non minus pie quam facete respondet Literis cuiusdam Pomerani, hominis inter Protestantes nominis non obscuri* (More, *Correspondence*, ed. E. F. Rogers, Princeton, 1947, pp. 323–65); More's letter was published in the 1568 Louvain edition of his works. More argued that Luther's gospel would have no support in England because of its evil fruits, such as the peasants' war, strife between people and their priests, iconoclasm, breaking of vows of celibacy, destroying the sacraments, and so forth; furthermore Bugenhagen, according to More, had no idea how thoroughly Catholic was the king of England. E. G. Rupp, *Studies*, p. 12, suggests, with J. F. Mozley, *William Tyndale* (London, 1937), pp. 54 ff., that the English version of Bugenhagen's letter was the first book published, in 1526, by the Brethren in England.

ing of activities among English Protestants. The small group
of Lutheran sympathizers at Cambridge dared give public
utterance to their convictions. On the Fourth Sunday in Advent,
December 24, 1525, Robert Barnes, prior of Augustinian Friars
in Cambridge and a leading figure in the circle of scholars who
discussed the rediscovered gospel at White Horse Tavern,
preached in St. Edward's Church a paraphrase of Luther's
postil for the day. Although evidence is far from conclusive, it
is possible that on the same day Hugh Latimer also preached
on reformation themes at Cambridge.[2] What Latimer may
have said can only be surmised from secondary testimony about
him, but Barnes left detailed accounts of his reformatory
preaching on this occasion.

A much more arresting development for English Christianity
in 1525 was the printing by Peter Quentel in Cologne, near the
end of the year, of the first sheets of William Tyndale's and
William Roy's English translation of the New Testament.
While it is uncertain whether copies of this edition reached
England during that year, certainly the untiring Cochlaeus
had notified the authorities of this new danger to ecclesiastical
security. Unless the Protestant sympathizers in Cambridge
were somehow ignorant of the activities of Tyndale on the
Continent, the surmise seems warranted that the offering of an
English New Testament and the public call for church reform
by Barnes were not only coincident but concerted endeavors.

Upon learning of the appearance of an English New Testament, Wolsey quickly made plans for another public demonstration of the loyalty of England to the papal cause. That
Barnes came to be involved in this demonstration puzzled him
no little, and recent interpretations of data make clear that his
involvement was in fact quite accidental. Wolsey's scheme for
the demonstration was communicated to the King through John
Longland, Bishop of Lincoln, who in early January 1526 was at
Eltham with Henry. Wolsey's communication is lost, but Longland's reply is extant.[3] Longland relayed Henry's full approval

2. A. G. Chester, *Hugh Latimer Apostle to the English* (Philadelphia, 1954),
pp. 22 ff.

3. Longland to Wolsey, early January 1526, abstracted in *LP, 4,* no. 995;
printed in H. Ellis, ed., *Original Letters Illustrative of English History* (3
vols. London, 1824), *1,* 179–84. The relevant passage was quoted, the documents

of the plan to hold a book-burning service. Books by Luther or his followers were to be gathered both by secret search and by proclamation demanding that their owners surrender them. The owners were to abjure. Merchants and stationers were bound not to import or circulate any such books. The King himself suggested that Fisher was "moste meete to make that sermond" at the service, "bothe propter auctoritatem, gravitatem, et doctrinam personae," according to Longland's letter. Wolsey set the date of Quinquagesima Sunday, February 11, 1526, for the service at St. Paul's Cathedral. At eight o'clock in the morning the cathedral was thronged. Wolsey had ordered a special scaffold over the stairs, on which he sat "with six-and-thirty abbots, mitred priors, and bishops, and he, in his whole pomp, mitred . . . sat there enthronised, his chaplains and spiritual doctors in gowns of damask and satin, and he himself in purple; even like a bloody Antichrist." A new pulpit had been erected also on the top of the stairs. During the service and sermon "great baskets full of books" stood before the dignitaries, and these were burnt during the proceedings. While Fisher preached, Barnes and the merchants who were made to abjure were commanded to kneel down begging forgiveness from the Church and the Cardinal. Wolsey departed in pomp before the end of the book-burning.[4]

FISHER'S SECOND SERMON

The involvement of Barnes and the merchants in this affair will receive attention later; of immediate interest is the sermon. Fisher appraised as very serious the danger in which England stood before its then ecclesiastical enemies, and again he skirted the rather large area of mutual interest between humanists and reformers. On this occasion Fisher, by royal appointment, was to refute Luther, the Lutherans, and their sympathizers as well as all their writings and books and their influences within the realm.[5]

discussed, the letter properly dated January 5, 1525/6, and the incident accurately recounted by A. G. Chester, "Robert Barnes and the Burning of the Books," *Huntington Library Quarterly, 14* (1951), 211–21.

4. *AM, 5,* 418.

5. Longland to Wolsey, January 5, 1525/6, quoted by Chester, pp. 215 f.: "contra Lutherum, Lutherianos, fautoresque eorum, contra opera eorum et

Fisher offered the sermon in printed form because noise during the service had left many unable to hear him, according to a preface which also revealed that Fisher in 1526 had become agitated by the danger of Lutheranism to the English Church. The preface, but not the sermon itself, expressed the Bishop's conviction that efforts in the style of his 1521 sermon and his ensuing Latin writings against Luther must be abandoned. The heresy now seemed too insidious to be discredited simply by mouthing the madness of its author. Fisher realized that heresies, like weeds, sprang up and flourished easily and naturally of their own accord, whereas true religion, like good herbs, required careful and daily cultivation. Between the lines, he hinted that not all the clergy in England were ardent gardeners bent on raising good herbs. Admitting that his sermon no more than scratched the surface of the issue posed by the Reformation, Fisher made a remarkable offer to his readers. If anybody scrupled over the truth of the Catholic position as he had set it forth, the learned and famous prelate would converse with such a person privately, confidentially, and as long as was required "that either he shal make me a Lutheran/ orels I shall enduce hym to be a catholyke." [6] The offer voiced misgivings as to the decisiveness with which the preacher presented his case.

Even while reckoning Luther's teachings weightier and more appealing than they had seemed in 1521, Fisher confidently prescribed that the utter blindness of these heresies could be cured only through their espousers' abject submission to the Church as true light of the world. To be sure, Wolsey had designed the service to make just that point, but many might have been led to re-assess Protestantism by the events of that day

libros, et contra inducentes eadem opera in regnum . . . ," ran the bill of particulars for the sermon. The date on which the sermon was preached is certain, but some question remains as to how soon thereafter it was printed. Apparently there were two editions, both from the press of Thomas Berthelet in London. *STC* lists only one, no. 10,892, from the press of Berthelet but dated [1528?]; but the existence of two editions, one without authorization and the other *cum privilegio regali,* has been noted and the conclusion drawn that both were probably published at the time that Berthelet fell under censure for his publishing activities, in the spring of 1526. See Reed, "The Regulation of the Book Trade," passim.

6. Fisher, *A sermon had at Paulis (STC* 10,892), [Aiiij]ʳ.

at St. Paul's. Nearly forty prelates and church dignitaries sat
on one scaffold to preside over the submission of merely five
merchants and one Augustinian prior kneeling on another scaffold; between them stood baskets of books far less plentiful
than should have been collected by Wolsey's agents.

The preacher was as near the height of his homiletical per-
suasiveness as he was near the apex of his brilliant career. Quite
apart from its being addressed to the most burning theological
issue of the day, the sermon was masterful in its prose and
vivid in its allegorical explanations of scripture. Recounting
from Luke 18 the healing of the blind man by the roadside,
Fisher rendered his Latin text (verse 42): "Open thyn eies/
thy faith hath made the safe." The crowd going before Jesus
represented the Jews who lived before his advent and knew him
in expectation. Those behind who saw his truth clearly were the
Catholic Church. The blind man was the heretic—of that or
any other age—solitary, unseeing, sitting by the roadside instead of marching heavenward, separated from all the people
of God. His cure was the only cure for heretics: to hear the
voice of the Church, to cry out for mercy, to be commanded
to be brought to the truth as Wolsey had ordered the heretics
there present, to join the throng, to assent wholly to the teaching of the Church. In its truest meaning, the text would read:
"The faith of *the* churche (whiche by thyne assent is made thy
faith) doth make the safe." [7] Specifically referring to Luther's
heresy, Fisher argued that not *fides* but *fides tua,* as the text had
it—which was to say, faith not as *fiducia* but as *assensus*—was
the means of salvation. Here Fisher showed that he understood
the central point of Luther's teaching on faith. But he supposed that Luther's day-to-day preaching led people to think
that saving faith was readily available and not necessarily connected with good works, while Luther's theological writings
made saving faith too difficult for anybody to accomplish.
On the latter point Fisher quoted accurately from Luther's
Operationes in Psalmos.[8] For Fisher, faith was, objectively
speaking, a gift from above; yet only by a work of assent might
it become *fides tua* and thus be of saving efficacy. The Turk

7. Ibid., B^r, C^r.
8. Ibid., C^r; cf. *WA,* 5, p. 206, lines 38–41.

possessed faith in God but not true faith; the heretic professed belief in God and in Christ but did not make this true faith his own faith. Only in the company of the Catholic Church, entered by making that Church's faith wholly *fides tua*—that is to say, by assent—was justification to be found.

For the rest Fisher was strictly polemical, arguing out each of his points. By denying that all approved doctors and fathers had taught true faith, Luther denied Christ's promise to be with his Church. Because Luther asserted a truth against the Church's truth he denied the spirit of God, whose truth was by definition single. Luther and his followers thereby excluded themselves from the Church and thus from salvation. Lutherans broke monastic vows for carnality; thus among them there were no fruits of good living which God required of his people.

Despite its chasing down allegorical blind alleys, the sermon was pertinent and complete, although Fisher lamented that the occasion precluded systematic treatment of all the salient points of Luther's heresy. He praised the Church's mercy and power in healing the abjurers. He spoke ably to the germane issue of faith and good works as related to justification. He demonstrated the inner logic by which the Catholic Church had determined that Lutherans were heretics to be reconciled only by absolute submission. The Church owned truth and light, therefore she must compel those without to come in, must demand that the blind be brought to sight. On the fringes of the argument were the usual inconsequential invectives: God's truth equaled the dogma of the Church; Luther and his followers were abominable heretics in all that they wrote, dangerous revolutionaries, and detesters of cardinal virtues like chastity and virginity.

Fisher's participation in the vernacular theological arguments of his day ended with the 1526 sermon, but for one further contribution. On June 28, 1532, William Rastell published Fisher's *Two fruytful sermons* (*STC* 10,909) on Matthew 5:20; the second part of the first sermon set forth the view of purgatory that John Frith later attempted to refute in a long treatise. Otherwise these sermons avoided the great theological conflicts of the day, preferring to dwell at length

on contrasts between the life of the kingdom of heaven and
the life of this earthly kingdom.

Fisher's 1521 and 1526 sermons were the original vernacular
expressions of official ecclesiastical and doctrinal policy of the
English Throne and Church. Because the early English Protestants wanted to force the consideration and practice of religion into the vernacular, first by translating the scriptures and
then by debating matters of church reform in the common
tongue, Fisher's enunciations of policy were crucial not only
to the Protestants but also to Fisher's successor. Since Henry's
Assertio had addressed itself specifically to Luther's sacramental views, Luther himself answered it in a hot exchange of
pamphlets and letters exposing the King's amateur status as a
theologian. It remained for the English Protestants to debate
the accusations lodged against the Reformation position by
Fisher's two sermons, and, subsequently, by More's protracted
essays. Thus Fisher established the terminology, chose the
ground, and set the tone for the doctrinal and ecclesiological
debates which were the substance of the English Reformation
before the "King's matter" became prominent.

Central to all these debates was the place of faith and works
in the justification of sinners before God. The reformers
thought justification by faith the most profound, the most obvious, and the most misunderstood of their tenets; English
Protestants followed suit until Tyndale revised his teaching on
justification in the early 1530s. Correlative to that doctrine
was the question of the authority of the Church, on the basis
of a multiform tradition, over against the authority of the
scriptures—or, as Luther would have it, of the word of God
which was mirrored by the scriptures. Fisher dealt with these
topics, as well as subsidiary questions, in both the vernacular
sermons and in his Latin writings: clerical celibacy as the mark
of a spiritual estate distinct from that of laity; the nature of
the Church as essentially hierarchic or laic; the necessity of
good works both to Christian life and to social order; church
control over the entry of souls into eternal bliss, either direct or
via purgatory; the right to read scripture in the common
tongue; the veneration of saints and images as efficacious to

the religious life; the capacity of the human will to move toward salvation under God. Fisher treated these points as a
conservative Catholic, unseasoned by humanism save with respect to style of presentation. Just these points were to be
contested by Tyndale, Frith, Barnes, Joye, and Roy; just these
points were to be rebutted again and again by Fisher's successor.

MORE'S LATIN LIBELLI

Between the two occasions on which Fisher stated in English
the case for Catholicism, several important theological writings were being produced in Latin by Englishmen. One writer
of such works steadily gained prominence and eventually earned
Fisher's mantle as official Catholic polemicist in the common
tongue. That was Thomas More, whose reply to Bugenhagen's
letter of 1525 had confidently scoffed at the notion that the
future of England's religion lay with the Protestants. Like
Fisher, More was a king's man until that commitment clashed
with his higher persuasion as a pope's man.

Whatever More's role may have been in the composition
and revision of King Henry's *Assertio,* the book struck him
as an excellent model for repudiating the Protestant position,
which had claimed his attention from the outset. Early in
1518 More had learned from Erasmus of Luther's Ninety-five
Theses.[9] More undoubtedly familiarized himself with Luther's
famous 1520 treatises, especially *De captivitate babyolonica
ecclesiae.* To Henry's denunciatory approach More coupled
Fisher's appeal to patristic sources, particularly St. Augustine,
to undermine the Wittenberger's arguments. In 1523 More
published at Pynson's press in London, under the pseudonym
William Ross, a scholarly tract against Luther's answer to
Henry's *Assertio.* Hardly rivaling the broad scholarship of
Fisher's defense of Henry, More proved himself a capable
amateur theologian and polemicist. The title he gave to the
work, after the manner of the day, summarized its contents:
*Ervditissimi viri Guilelmi Rossei opus elegans, doctum, fes-
tiuum, pium, quo pulcherrime retegit, ac refellit insanas Lutheri*

9. Erasmus to More, March 5, 1518, *Opus Epistolarum Des. Erasmi Roterodami,* ed. P. S. Allen et al. (11 vols. Oxford, 1906–47), *3,* no. 785.

calumnias: quibus inuictissimum Angliae Galliãq regem Henri-
cum eius nominis octauum, Fidei defensorem, haud literis minus
q̃ regno clarum, scurra turpissimus insectatur: excusum denuo
diligentisistime, digestumq̃ in capita, adiunctis indicibus opera
uiri doctissimi Ioannis Carcellij (*STC* 18,089). The preface
was signed October 15, 1523.

The writing that brought forth More's four-hundred-page
mountain of prose was Luther's quite occasional *Contra Henricum Regem Angliae* (1522). Chapter by chapter, word by
word, More plodded through Luther's terse reply to the King.
There was hardly a sentence of Luther's book that More failed
to quote; he cited *in extenso* Henry's points which gave rise to
Luther's answer, and indulged his liking for quotations by citing
long sections of Luther's *De captivitate,* against which Henry
had originally written. This technique of argument once again
awarded Luther wide dissemination of his views.

Much the same manner of argument dominated More's second venture into scholarly theological disputation. More presumably composed his answer to Bugenhagen in 1526, but it
seems to have been published no earlier than 1568. Again a
thin little letter evoked a fat reply. More's ferocity in deriding
the Lutheran position summoned no originality. All he said,
Fisher had already said more sympathetically and More would
later say more persuasively. A modern admirer of More has
characterized his letter to Bugenhagen as "easy and popular"
in style, containing some "scurrilous" passages and invectives
against the persons of married ex-monks "too bitter and scath-
ing to quote." [10] The evangelicals vainly hoped for followers
in England, More said, where the King would ever defend the
Catholic Church as it had been known and revered for a thous-
and years. He imagined continental "cacangelists" (bad-news-
men) as evil and arrogant, living licentiously, destroying religion at their whim, imagining a God so capricious as to damn
the evil and withhold rewards from the virtuous. He ridiculed
the *sola fide* teaching of the reformers as rationalization for
theological antinomianism and personal license. More was hot
against Luther for the curtness of his reply to Henry, and for
his cudgeling of Erasmus in the 1524–25 dispute on the free-

10. Rogers, "Sir Thomas More's Letter to Bugenhagen," p. 351.

dom of the will; in both exchanges More judged his friends the victors. As More had rallied in 1523 to the personal defense of his prince against Luther's theological onslaughts, it was Erasmus whose person and reputation he defended in the letter to Bugenhagen. More seized the occasion to vaunt the humanist's church loyalty.

However learned in fact the reformers may have been, More contended against Bugenhagen that they were miserably unscholarly. Whether they were single or married, More, the model husband, saw them as sexually indulgent and degenerate. All evidence to the contrary notwithstanding, he pictured Protestants as detesting Church and holy tradition because they appealed first or only to scripture. Never had a reformer, as More saw it, criticized a real ecclesiastical abuse or proposed a sensible purgation of religious practice; they only blasphemed what was holy. Reformers almost by definition reasoned illogically, beguiling the simple with the mere appearance of rationality. On all these points More blistered his enemies. What he did not reveal was an intelligent understanding of their teachings and their appeal.

While the substance of More's anti-Protestant Latin works drew heavily on Henry's *Assertio,* which he received as a normative English religious statement on all the issues of the Reformation, his style emulated that of his German opposite number, Cochlaeus, another advocate of the papacy whose fervor precluded his understanding of the issues. The reply to Bugenhagen bore More's own name, perhaps indicating a pride of work not felt for the pseudonymous piece. Boiled down to essentials, the answer to Bugenhagen crowed the absurdity of England's adopting the evangelical position, since Englishmen knew the results of Luther's gospel as peasant uprisings, the setting of people against their priests, iconoclasm, battles and wars, the breaking of sacred vows of celibacy, the destruction of the sacraments. All might know the folly of Bugenhagen's hopes by remembering the complete dedication to the Catholic cause of the King of England.

Fisher, More, and King Henry found but minor assistance in the Latin war of words against the Germans. In 1523 when

Luther's devastating response to the King's book was circulating widely, the royal printer Pynson issued two works by one Alphonsus de Villa Sancta dealing directly with reformation problems. These were *De libero arbitrio, aduersus Melancthonem* (*STC* 24,728) and *Problema indulgentiarum* (*STC* 24,729).[11] An able Oxford divine, Edward Powell (Powel), contributed to the discussion of the Reformation with his *Propugnaculum summi sacerdotii euangelici aduer. M. Lutherum,* published in 1523 (*STC* 20,140). Powell by then was a doctor of divinity of some standing; later he opposed the King's divorce. Although condemned for treason when he refused to take the oath attendant to the Act of Succession in 1534, Powell's life was spared until the reaction under Stephen Gardiner; in 1540 he was burnt at Smithfield alongside the Protestant Robert Barnes, and was lauded by a 1548 pamphlet lampooning the religious policy which made fellow martyrs of loyal Catholics and loyal Protestants—*The metynge of Doctor Barnes and doctor Powell at Paradise Gate* (*STC* 1473).

More remains second only to Fisher as a fashioner of Latin libelli against Luther and his circle. He was commissioned by Bishop Cuthbert Tunstall of London in 1527 to write similarly in the vernacular. Long before that Henry had referred to More's judgment a copy of Luther's letter to the King written in early September 1525, and just a year later Wolsey was corresponding with More about the advisability of sending German princes the King's reply without adjoining the copy of Luther's letter.[12] Henry had turned to More, not to the cardinal, for advice on this crucial matter, and Wolsey was piqued. Before December 1526 the exchange of letters between reformer and king had been printed in Latin, and another edition swiftly followed early in February 1527 (*STC* 13,084–85). Perhaps as early as 1526 but possibly as late as 1528 these

11. "Villa Sancta, Alphonsus de" is the *STC* entry. The British Museum *Catalogue* lists him as "Bishop of Scopelos" and as the reviser of a 1518 edition of "F. G. de Rubione . . . Disputatorum . . ." I have been unable to find in Bodleian Library catalogs an entry bearing out the *STC* location of 24,729 at the Bodleian.

12. Wolsey to More, late September 1526, in More, *Correspondence,* pp. 365–68 and 368 n.

letters appeared in English. At any rate, the new seriousness with which the Lutheran threat was viewed in England after 1525 enlisted More's talents as well as Fisher's.

THE ROYAL CORRESPONDENCE

The exchange of correspondence between Luther and Henry in 1525–26 forges another link in the chain of evidence marking a powerful Protestant bid for English support. Luther began the exchange on the basis of an untrustworthy rumor. The exiled King Christian II of Denmark had reported to the Saxon court that the King of England leaned toward the evangelical position. Christian suggested that an apology from Luther to Henry might heal the widely publicized breach between them and make Henry's path toward Protestantism easier. Luther was skeptical but allowed himself to be persuaded to write an uncharacteristically meek letter. Another rumor had reached Luther, to the effect that Wolsey no longer enjoyed Henry's favor.[13] False information aroused vain hopes. Genuinely submissive, Luther blamed his earlier curt answer to Henry on the instigation of his advisers who disliked Henry. He blamed Henry's own book on Wolsey, saying, "I haue by credyble persons ben enformed/ that the boke made out agaynst me in the name of your highnesse/ is nat the kynges of Englande as crafty Sophisters wolde it shuld seme." Those responsible for Henry's *Assertio* slandered the King, "especially aboue other/ that monster & commen hate of god and men/ the car-Cardynall [*sic*] of yorke/ that pestylence of your realm." In gratitude for Henry's reported advocacy of the gospel Luther was willing to "prostrate my selfe with these letters/ vnto the fete of your highnesse/ as humbly as I can deuyce." The reformer offered, for the King's forgiveness, to "make out another booke/ and therin vnsay my former writynge/ & nowe on the contrary syde/ honoure the name of your highnesse."

Cleverly Luther proposed that he might apologize openly to Henry, yet he stuck fast to his own convictions about gospel, Pope, and religion. Quoting the second Psalm Luther explained

13. See E. Doernberg, *Henry VIII and Luther* (Stanford, Calif., 1961), pp. 49 ff. and passim; Luther's letter is printed in translation ibid., pp. 50–53; this author suggested that Vives may have written Henry's reply.

the raging of princes and emperor against him, marveling at
the miracle by which Henry came to favor the gospel, praying
God "that he so worke with my words/ that the kynge of
Englande may be made shortly/ the perfyte discyple of Christ
and professour of the gospell/ and finally/ most benigne lorde
vnto Luther." The rapprochement which Luther yearned for
and which he promised humbly to welcome remained entirely
on Luther's religious terms. As usual with the Wittenberger,
personal considerations gave way to theological matters. That
never happened to Henry.

The King tarried long before replying. The eventful year
that elapsed witnessed wide distribution at home of the English New Testament of Tyndale, the necessity of investigating
the universities because of the Lutheran leanings of their members, and another public display of the fidelity of England to
the Pope by means of burning Protestant books, including the
New Testament. From Henry's standpoint Luther's side did
anything but wait patiently and expectantly for his answer;
aggression against the religion of the realm came swiftly. Luther's letter went to More for comment and judgment. Wolsey
pleaded that the King's reply be printed with the full text of
Luther's impertinence, and a fine edition was prepared for presentation to European princes, followed by a plain edition from
Pynson's press. Just when the English translation came out is
not definitely known, but it certainly appeared by 1528, probably in 1526.

Henry's preface, addressed to all the King's "faythfull and
welbeloued subiectes," ran to twice the length of Luther's whole
letter; the whole irate reply took eleven times the verbiage
of the note it answered. The duty of a king included protecting
his subjects from heresy, especially of the sort which, like
Luther's, summarized most old heresies and added grievous
new ones. Henry thought he had won the earlier controversy
with Luther handily, but now the heresiarch dared to write and
print this letter. Men born in England had been seduced into
Luther's sect and had wrongly translated the New Testament
into English. Rankled by these new attempts to pervert the
faith of his subjects, Henry had authorized the translation of
the correspondence. When the realm was rid of religious un-

rest, there would be time for an authorized translation of scriptures. That much Henry conceded in the preface.

Claiming that Luther's letter of September 1525 was received only on March 20, 1526, the King rehearsed all that Luther had said, in order to refute it point by point; the style of the answer fully accords with that consistently employed by More in all his religious libelli. Stung by Luther's attribution of the *Assertio* to others, probably Wolsey, the King proudly claimed the book as his own. Henry, smarting under Luther's accusations against the Cardinal, praised Wolsey for his great contributions to the welfare and orthodoxy of the kingdom. The only English espousers of Luther's gospel were "one or two Freres apostataes/ ron out of our realme/ raignyng in riote & vnthriftye lyberte with you"; were there more of the same, England would be well rid of them if they fled to Luther. Henry was insulted by Luther's arrogance in reporting that the King recently inclined to the gospel, because the true gospel had always been the chief matter of his study; he would not repudiate the firm belief of the old fathers for the new railings of the German.

A licentious life, as Henry saw it, gave the lie to all Luther's teaching, "for the folly of your flesshe/ ye beyng a Frere haue taken a Nonne: & nat onely vyolate her . . . but also which moche worse is/ haue openly maried her/ & by that menes openly abuse her in synne." Because of personal irresponsibility, demonstrated by Luther's having broken his monastic vows, nothing that the reformer wrote might be taken as an honest representation of his teachings. Let Luther protest his respect for the institution of matrimony ever so much, his own marriage to Katherine von Bora showed the world that he practiced what he seemed to preach, a licentious lusting after the flesh so shameful as to demand the cloak of a theology concocted from justification by faith alone. As Henry portrayed his enemy, the teaching abnegated all morality, Luther's assertions to the contrary notwithstanding. A hastily mixed salad of citations from scripture and from Luther's writings set before the reader a choice between the deadly poison of Protestant antinomianism and the delectable diet of Catholic morality. Luther lied equally when in his little letter he claimed to "bylde vpon your faithe obedience towarde gouernars." Henry castigated Luther for denying the freedom of the human will to save itself in the sight of God, for thereby Luther impugned the justice of God as that attribute was understood and taught by the Church.

Henry distastefully entered the debate with such an opponent. To protect his people against Luther's lies and licentiousness he answered the 1525 letter, but he vowed never again to stoop to dispute with such a fellow. The King's subjects were to know under his royal authority that Luther actually taught against all the sacraments of the Church, that he damned priestly chastity, denied the sacrament of holy orders, robbed the people of the mass, made women into confessors and ministers of the sacraments, impugned the virgin mother of Jesus, blasphemed the cross of Christ, taught that there was no purgatory, and so forth. The justice of Luther's condemnation as heretic Henry accepted not on the basis of his doctrine but because it was holy Pope and cardinals who condemned him, emperor and princes who undertook to enforce the ban against him. Henry would have none of Luther's offer to prostrate himself before the King of England, but counseled that

> ye prosterne your selfe/ nat at my fete/ but at goddes/ and with his grace . . . ye do endeuer your selfe to applye the fredome of your wyll . . . to the callynge for entre and encreace of grace. And thervpon/ that ye so laboure and enforce your selfe to worke with all/ *that* ye maye fyrst puttyng from you/ and sendyng in to some Monastery/ that sely wretched woman/ somtyme the spouse of Christ: Whom ye to youre bothe dampnatyon/ abuse in synfull lechery/ vnder the pretext of laufull matrimony: than by all the dayes of your lyfe/ to mourne/ bewayle/ and lament/ the manyfolde heresyes that ye haue fallen in: the Innumerable heape ofharmes/ that your yuell doctryne hath done/ the piteous distruction of all those bodies/ whom your yuell incytatyon hathe caused to be slayne.[14]

14. *A copy of the letters wherin . . . Kyng Henry . . . made answer unto . . . Luther (STC* 13,086–87); the foregoing quotations, in order, from [Aix]ᵛ–[Ax]ᵛ, [Axii]ᵛ, Aiiʳ, [Bvi]ʳ, [Bxii]ʳ–Cʳ, [Dv]ʳ, Fiiiᵛ–[Fiv]ʳ.

The fact that the King's book labored the point of advising Luther to recant, and connected this pious sentiment with Luther's offer to apologize to Henry for his earlier book, led many in Germany and England to think that Luther had offered to abjure his teachings. Polemicists against him made the most of the misunderstanding. Cochlaeus wrote a preface to Henry's reply to Luther and printed the book in Cologne, claiming that Luther offered to recant. Jerome Emser of Saxony published Luther's letter in Latin and in German, interpreting it as a proposal that the reformer would recant. Luther set the matter straight with a tract not replying to Henry's accusations but denying that he had ever offered to retract his teaching. But these continental controversies over the matter had little or nothing to do with the progress of Protestantism in England during the years after the exchange of letters.

The publication of this correspondence by Henry, first in Latin and then in translation, marks yet another assertion of the King's steadfast adherence to Catholicism and to all conservative causes. Ironically enough, the very man who advised him concerning the publication of these letters was the one he would accuse in 1534 of having done him disservice by instigating the whole controversy with Luther—Thomas More. But in 1526 Henry still bore proudly the title *defensor fidei* and understood the latter word in the fully papal sense; nobody should rob him of the credit of having written the *Assertio*, as long as credit indeed attached to it. When the King fell prey to the lechery of which he accused Luther, More was damned for having led his king to an assertion of papal supremacy—despite the fact that More had warned Henry against possible complications and implications of this very assertion.

Fisher's 1526 sermon and Henry's 1526 correspondence became the major vernacular appeals for Catholic steadfastness during the days when the English New Testament was first circulating in England. Fisher's contribution at least wore the graceful cloaks of a felicitous style and an allegorical mode. Henry's letter by contrast was drably clad. Both together molded subsequent anti-Protestant polemics, especially those of More. Because Luther had been declared a heretic, his teachings were erroneous, Henry argued. Or was it Henry? More hewed to the line laid down by his rather ineffectual proposition throughout his career as a theological tractarian, and there is not a word in the royal letter that might not have flowed from the knight's pen. Fisher saw somewhat more clearly the need to show that Luther's teachings were erroneous in order to demonstrate that Luther was a heretic. Not so More, and not so Henry.

By the end of 1526 the Protestants had seized the offensive in England. Arrayed against them were king, cardinal, and the clerical and lay deans of letters. The Church and the Realm had not budged from their wonted papalism. Yet the argument raged just where the Protestants wanted it—in the common tongue. The King's case for the old religion had been submitted not only to the learned and the nobility but to the poor commons who might read it or have it read to them. The very words of the New Testament on which the Protestants thought all their arguments turned had penetrated the vernacular in print and would spread fast by word of mouth. Luther's books had long before been set ablaze at the universities and at Paul's Cross, but now the very word of God itself had been burnt by the prelates in St. Paul's Cathedral. Fisher had been made to sense the real and present threat of Protestant appeal throughout the land. Book merchants underwent punishment for their trade as well as for their convictions. A reformation plea had rung from at least one Cambridge pulpit. The confidence that earlier stirred King and Church, and belatedly also More, to gloat over the steadfastness of England's Catholic commitment, passed to the Protestants, for the latter believed that the word of God would spread of its own accord once it, and the discussion of it, entered the common tongue.

4. The Career of Robert Barnes

URING the years between John Fisher's English sermons against Luther, Bishop Cuthbert Tunstall of London more than once reported to Wolsey the infiltration of Luther's teachings into the university at Oxford. The far more widespread regard for Luther among a circle of teachers and scholars at Cambridge came later to the attention of the authorities, only after a major Protestant coterie had arisen there. In the early sixteenth century Cambridge was a port for channel-going vessels and a terminal of trade with Hanseatic ports; there Luther's writings were readily available to, and by 1525 well known by, a circle of men who gathered for meetings and discussions of reformation topics at the White Horse Tavern. The possibility of listing "some fifty or sixty members of the University who might have been of their company" has been noted, including Shaxton, Crome, Forman, Lambert, Mallory, Frith, Bilney, Arthur, Paget, Taverner, Cranmer, Heath, Parker, May, Latimer, Ridley, Bale, Fox, and Day—a fair roster of subsequent leaders of England's church reform.[1] When, late in 1525, this group determined to make a public statement of their views regarding the Reformation and the Church in England, the person to whom the rôle of spokesman fell was Robert Barnes, D.D., prior of the Augustinian house at Cambridge. Thus among the early English Protestant writers whose works are preserved to us, Barnes first emerged as an open advocate of Reformation principles.

Whether he was chosen because of his prominence as a doctor of divinity, his membership in the monastic order that had

1. Rupp, *Studies,* p. 19.

produced the stir at Wittenberg, or his intellectual and theological prowess, we can only guess. Concerning Barnes' life before his emergence as a Reformation spokesman there remain scraps of information preserved by his friend John Bale and his admirer John Foxe. Born near Lynn in Norfolk about 1495, he became a novice at the Augustinian house in Cambridge at an early age, probably about 1511–12. He studied at the University of Louvain, probably 1514–21. As a promising young scholar it is not improbable that he heard Luther explain his theology at the general chapter of Augustinians meeting in Heidelberg in 1518; regardless of that surmise it seems certain that he learned in Louvain about the cause célèbre of his order. In 1522 or 1523 he returned to Cambridge, apparently as prior, and was incorporated in that university as bachelor, then as doctor, of divinity. Cambridge counted Barnes a champion of new learning, for he brought from Louvain an interest in classical Latin authors. Yet he was not of the humanistic avant-garde. Although he and Erasmus were at Cambridge at the same time, his writings show no trace of his having known Greek, much less Hebrew. After casting his lot with the reformers he preferred Tyndale's English New Testament to the Vulgate, but he demonstrated a broad acquaintance with some of the Latin fathers, doctors, schoolmen, and canonists. Although he probably could converse in German—in order to be the jolly table companion and houseguest that Luther and Bugenhagen reported him to be—he neither translated works of others from German into English nor his own from Latin or English into German. Despite his protestations that he cared little for the study of canon law he disputed on this subject in all his writings. He knew the church fathers largely through contemporary catenae. Barnes seems to have brought from Louvain to Cambridge neither a commanding distinction in scholarship nor special familiarity with Luther's works, but rather an interest in classical antiquity.

As nearly as Foxe's often telescoped chronologies can be stretched out to span known events, Barnes came in 1523 to know Richard Bayfield, a monk of the abbey at Bury St. Edmunds, and later converted Bayfield to the evangelical convictions for which he was burnt at Smithfield in 1531. Barnes himself is reported to have been converted to the new gospel by Thomas Bilney of Cambridge, who was arrested in 1527 and martyred at Norwich on August 19, 1531. To assist with the education of his charges at Cambridge, Barnes had brought from Louvain a scholar and helper, Thomas Parnell; together they focused students' attention on Terence, Plautus, and Cicero, and they sided with the humanists in concentrating upon the text of Paul's epistles and in disregarding medieval glosses and scholastic harmonizations. Barnes represented the same emphases in the university. George Stafford was examined by Barnes when he stood for the degree of bachelor of divinity in 1524, and the revolutionary approach to the Bible which Barnes employed in the examination caused commotion among the doctors present. But, as Foxe told it, only under the influence of Bilney did Barnes "see his inward and outward idolatry" and become "converted . . . wholly unto Christ." [2]

SERMON AND TRIAL

On Christmas Eve, 1525, in St. Edward's Church at Cambridge Barnes preached a sermon attacking the ecclesiastical evils and abuses of the day. According to Foxe he "postilled the whole epistle, following the Scripture and Luther's Postil." This succinct description of the sermon furnishes the only evidence that the sermon was a Protestant theological utterance. Less than six years later Barnes published a lengthy reply to twenty-five articles extracted from this sermon and alleged against him as heretical at his examination in February 1526.

2. *AM, 5,* 414 ff. and passim; Foxe, together with University records, has provided the biographical data about Barnes employed by several modern writers: J. Gairdner in *DNB;* Rupp (an original but not wholly reliable resifting of the evidence); N. H. Fisher, "The Contribution of Robert Barnes to the English Reformation" (unpublished thesis, University of Birmingham, 1950); N. S. Tjernagel, "Dr. Robert Barnes and Anglo-Lutheran Relations, 1521–1540" (unpublished dissertation, State University of Iowa, 1955); W. Dallmann, *Robert Barnes* (3rd printing, St. Louis, after 1917); Doernberg, *Henry VIII and Luther.* For the period 1525–34 Barnes supplied much personal information in his writings, but these data are accessible only in original sources. For the trial and abjuration of Barnes early in 1526 the best account is by Chester, "Robert Barnes and the Burning of the Books," which shows in detail that the book-burning service was arranged prior to Wolsey's knowing of Barnes' "heresy"; Barnes himself gave two quite different accounts of the sermon and trial in the 1531 and 1534 editions of his *Supplication.*

Nearly a decade after the event, Barnes greatly elaborated his recounting of the hectic few weeks which the sermon inaugurated for him, and this later account, self-justifying, alleging harsh and unfair treatment, found its way into the 1572 edition of Barnes' works. Taking the 1531 version of the incident at face value, we get a very clear picture of those portions of the sermon which were offensive, and these had little or nothing to do with Luther. Barnes himself admitted that "in those artycles that were agenst the bysshops they did great dylygence and in the most parte of them getheryd they mi very trew sentence and myne awne wordes as concerninge those thinges that made agenst the bysshops/ though in those thinges they left out vncheritablye/ those words that made for my declaration andalso for the probacion of my saynge/ The which I haue also here lefte ought alonly addying the articles as they layd them agenste me." [3]

The articles themselves were not specifically Lutheran. An enthusiastic and bold Lollard might have said them all. For that matter, most of the points had been scored a generation earlier by Dean John Colet of St. Paul's in his famous sermon before Convocation. In summary, Barnes contended that Christians were no more bound to serve God on Sunday or holy days than on any other day; that in his time nobody dared preach the gospel for fear of being accused of heresy; that contemporaneous executions of "heretics" (in England at the time that meant Lollards) made true martyrs of the gospel; that Christians broke their profession when they entered pleadings before the law against one another; that God's law forbade bishops to hold jurisdiction over more than one city, much less over a whole country; that scripture gave no precedent for church officials to hold great temporal possessions; that the bishops stood in apostolic succession to Judas as rich men, not to the other apostles as preachers of the gospel; that God's law granted no secular power to bishops; that those pricked by the sermon were Pharisees who inwardly knew the sermon to be true; that bishops and prelates followed the false prophet Balaam by riding upon the common folk as asses; that the prelates set up an idol called Baal Peor; that blessings which should be

3. *A supplicatyon* . . . (*STC* 1470), xxxiiijᵛ–xxxvʳ.

bestowed freely by servants of Christ were sold for money; that bishops would sooner part with a benediction than with a half-penny; that the sale of pardons was fraudulent; that absolution *a poena et culpa* was unwarranted and pretentious; that bishops prohibited discussion of episcopal and papal powers; that to excommunicate four times yearly was contrary to God's law; that bishops grasped for mitres and rings but gave nothing to the poor; that their mitres came from the Jews' bishops not from Christ; that the two horns of the mitre signified the devil; that they carried staffs but were not shepherds to the flock; that prayers were unavailing unless said piously.

Throughout the sermon Barnes appealed to scripture as judging ecclesiastical practices, and pleaded for inward faith as essential to religion instead of external forms. Both these points were, of course, germane to the Reformation protest against church abuses of the day. But no point in the articles derived from Luther more than from Wycliffe or Hus or Colet. Not even the Erasmian demand for scripture in the vernacular —which Luther had accomplished for Germany and which Tyndale was then accomplishing for England—was touched by Barnes in this sermon. It will be seen that Barnes adopted specifically Lutheran views when he visited Wittenberg later on. But if his 1525 sermon was in fact for the circle at "Little Germany" a "public manifesto of their views," [4] they had adopted very little of the German reformer's teaching.

Barnes quickly found himself in trouble with the university authorities over the sermon. He was charged with twenty-five points of heresy—not, be it noted, with Lutheranism as such —and silenced from further preaching by the vice-chancellor of Cambridge; there ensued weeks of debate over the articles. Toward the end of January 1526 he refused to subscribe to the recantation with which he was presented, and appealed his case to the judgment of the whole university. At this point Barnes quite fortuitously fell into a web of events that made him seem the leading Lutheran of the land. Some weeks earlier Wolsey had made plans to display England's religious loyalty by burning Luther's books and having Lutheran heretics pub-licly abjure. Early in February Wolsey learned of the proceed-

4. Chester, p. 212.

ings against Barnes at Cambridge. On Tuesday, February 6, agents of the Cardinal rode into Cambridge and Barnes was arrested by a Master Gibson. The agents began a sudden search for proscribed books in the rooms of Cambridge scholars who were Barnes' friends and associates. But some thirty suspects were tipped off to the search by the president of Queens', Dr. Forman. When the sergeant-at-arms, the vice-chancellor, and the proctors searched the rooms they knew precisely where to look for books, so well had informers done their jobs. But new hiding-places had been found, and the search proved futile. Next day, the only prize carried away to London was Barnes himself.

The Cardinal examined Barnes on Thursday, February 8, having been assured by his secretary, Stephen Gardiner, and Master Foxe, master of the Wards, that he would find the culprit learned and reformable. The mild Wolsey asked Barnes if scripture did not provide better subjects for sermons than that of a cardinal's ecclesiastical raiment; he thought the sermon better suited to stage than to pulpit. Barnes stood on scripture, conscience, and the old doctors, and proposed to dispute the articles made against him, handing Wolsey six sheets of paper on which he had outlined his position. Further exchanges led to Wolsey's demand that Barnes submit to the office of *legatus a latere,* and when Barnes refused Wolsey threatened the full extent of the law and the closest examination of Barnes' learning. Overnight Barnes prepared his defense with the aid of three amanuenses, among them Miles Coverdale. Saturday at Westminster chapterhouse he appeared for trial before a commission headed by the bishop of Bath, John Clerk. Also standing trial were four Steelyard men, Helbertus Belendorp, Hans Rensell (Reusell), Hans Ellerdorpe, and Henry Pryknes. On Saturday Barnes disputed his points, and at the end, on the advice of Gardiner and Foxe, chose to abjure rather than burn. Penance was to kneel during Fisher's sermon at St. Paul's the following day, Sunday, February 11, 1526, and to carry a fagot in procession around the church.

The entire proceeding mystified Barnes. When he was snatched from the jurisdiction of the vice-chancellor of Cambridge to that of the lord chancellor of the realm, his protest against the worldliness of the Church became a declaration of heresy. The whole thing struck him as incomprehensible injustice, made ludicrous by the fact that the bishop of Rochester preached "agaynst Lutherians as though they had conuicted me for one: The which of truth, and afore God, was as farre from those things as any man could bee, sauing that I was no tyrant, nor no persecutour of Gods worde." [5]

After recantation Barnes was committed to the Fleet, at liberty to see his friends. In August 1526 he was placed in the care of the Augustinian friars in London as a house prisoner, under which arrangement he enjoyed sufficient freedom to sell one John Tyball a copy of Tyndale's New Testament translation for three shillings twopence; the transaction took place within a half-mile of Bishop Tunstall's palace just a month before Tunstall forbade the circulation of this book in his diocese.[6] From London Barnes was transferred to his order's house at Northampton where he learned from one Master Horne that his fate was to burn. With that informer's assistance he schemed to escape. Leaving behind a letter to Wolsey telling where he had gone to drown himself, and another to the mayor saying that on his body would be found a parchment sealed in wax warning all men to submit to Wolsey, Barnes fled in plain clothes to London whence he shipped for Antwerp "and so to Luther." [7]

By Barnes' own account two and three-quarters years passed in prison. Reckoning on that basis, he arrived in Antwerp at the end of 1528. But "and so to Luther" was a slow progress. By the summer of 1530 he was a guest in the house of Bugenhagen in Wittenberg—but only on June 20, 1533, was entered in the matriculation book of the University of Wittenberg, "D. Antonius Anglus Theologiae Doctor Oxoniensis"; Melanchthon's marginal note explains that this was Barnes.[8] To

5. *Whole workes* (*STC* 24,436), p. 225.
6. J. Strype, *Ecclesiastical Memorials* (Oxford, 1822), *1*, i, ch. 8 and appendix; see also R. Demaus, *William Tyndale. A Biography* (London, 1871), p. 157, citing: Harleian MSS., no. 421.
7. *AM*, *4*, 419 and passim.
8. *Album Academiae Vitebergensis*, ed. C. E. Foerstermann (Leipzig, 1841), *1*, 149, cited by P. Smith, "Englishmen at Wittenberg in the Sixteenth Century," *English Historical Review*, *36* (1921), 423; Smith thought Barnes must have

cover Barnes' activities during 1529 and early 1530 the supposition has been advanced that he may have been in Hamburg.[9] In the Hanseatic cities were merchants responsible for
sending Reformation writings to England; Barnes might have
known about them from the Steelyard men with whom he
bore the fagot in 1526. But Foxe had Barnes in Antwerp just
when English translations of Luther's writings by William
Roy and John Frith were being published there.[10] Wherever
he may have been, more probably Antwerp than Hamburg,
Barnes was busily becoming the advocate of Luther's teachings
which Fisher had prematurely accused him of being.

BARNES IN EXILE

At Christmas 1525, Barnes offended the church by a sermon alleged to contain twenty-five assertions of the evil of ecclesiastical, and especially episcopal, worldliness. His first extant published work appeared in 1530, containing nineteen
articles of belief, each supported by scriptural and patristic
citations, all definitely informed by the theological position of
Luther and his followers. Set forth with a preface by his friend
Bugenhagen, the work was pseudonymously signed "Antonius
Anglus," the name by which the Wittenbergers knew Barnes for
the rest of his life. The little book, published by "J. Clug:
Witebergae" in 1530, was entitled, *Sentenciae ex doctoribus
collectae, quas papistae ualde impudenter hodie damnant.* Although these articles were published in English only in the 1572
collection of Barnes' works, during Barnes' lifetime they enjoyed three printings in Bugenhagen's German translation, two
in 1531 and another in 1536. Latin reprintings occurred in
1555 and 1567 editions of Barnes' *Lives of the Popes,* and also
in 1558 as emended by Eberhart Haberkorn. The original
Sentenciae were headed by certain specifically Lutheran affirma-

been married by this time, on the basis of an extant letter of 1533 conveying
greetings to "Antonius Anglus and his wife," but in November 1534 Barnes
specifically denied this and called Aepinus to witness.

9. Mozley, *William Tyndale,* p. 150 n.; but Mozley failed to distinguish between the 1531 and 1534 versions of Barnes' *Supplication,* and the references
to Hamburg occur only in the later edition as accounting for later activities.

10. See my article, "The Earliest Translations of Luther into English,"
Harvard Theological Review, 56 (1963), 75–86.

tions, and only incidentally touched on the points of Barnes'
1525 sermon:

> (1) *Sola fides iustificat.* (2) *Mors Christi satisfecit pro
> omnibus peccatis non tantum pro originali.* (3) *Prae-
> cepta dei sunt impossibilia nobis ex nostris viribus.* (4)
> *Liberum arbi. ex suis virib. non posse non peccare.* (5)
> *In omni opere bono iustus peccat.* (6) *Quae sit vera ec-
> clesia, et vnde cognoscitur.* (7) *Claves ecclesiae sunt
> verbum dei.* (8) *Concilium potest errare.* (9) *Omnes
> tenentur communicare sub utraque specie.* (10) *Licet
> sacerdotibus nubere.* (11) *Constitutiones humanae non
> obligant conscientiam ad peccatum.* (12) *Confessio auri-
> cularis non est de necessitate salutis.* (13) *Monachi non
> sunt laicis sanctiores propter cucullum aut locum.* (14)
> *Ieiunium christianorum non est in delectu ciborum scitum.*
> (15) *Christiano omnis dies est sabbatum, non solum
> septimus hebdomadae dies.* (16) *Iniusta excommunicatio
> papae non laedit excommunicatos.* (17) *In sacramento
> altaris est verum corpus christi.* (18) *Sancti non sunt in-
> vocandi pro mediatoribus.* (19) *De origine missae et
> omnibus eius partibus.*[11]

To support each assertion Barnes collected brief scriptural
and patristic citations, proving his new position on the grounds
he had chosen in his abortive self-defense before Wolsey—the
Bible and the old doctors. But the position, on the whole, was
explicitly Lutheran. Moreover, except for the carefully reasoned defense of the right of all Christians to read scripture in
familiar tongues which he included in his 1531 *Supplication,*
these articles form the table of contents of Barnes' entire theological writings. The 1531 *Supplication* expounded the sentences on faith, free-will, the church, the keys, councils, utra-

---

11. *Sentenciae ex doctoribus collectae* . . . (Wittenberg, 1530), passim. The
sentences became garbled in the 1572 edition of Barnes' works, and thus in
modern works, including H. E. Jacobs, *The Lutheran Movement in England*
(Philadelphia, 1890; revised ed. 1894), pp. 181 f.; Rupp, *Studies;* N. H. Fisher,
"The Contribution of Robert Barnes"; and Tjernagel, "Dr. Robert Barnes."
Rupp (p. 38 n.) has corrected Gairdner's error in *DNB* where the pseudonym is
given as "Antonius Amerius," a mistake originating in Strype, *Ecclesiastical
Memorials, I,* 356.

quism, human constitutions, and saints and images. In the 1534 *Supplication* he revised the arguments on faith and free-will; omitted discussion of the church, the keys, reading scripture, human constitutions, utraquism, and saints and images; and added a discussion of the right of priests to marry, comments on his dispute with the Church authorities in England, and an answer to More on the nature of the Church. These changes in the expositions between 1531 and 1534, together with other differences between the two *Supplications,* provide data by which to trace the ways in which Barnes' mind changed during the years that he labored and wrote as an English Protestant in exile.

Early in September 1531, Barnes became involved in an effort, which was to prove not only futile but frustrating, to lead Henry VIII and the Wittenberg theologians into friendly communication. On September 2 he obtained from Luther a letter on the "King's matter" in which the reformer denied the legitimacy of the dissolution of Henry's marriage to Catherine of Aragon, and counseled Henry to follow "the example of the patriarchs" who had many wives, rather than to "thrust his present spouse from her royal position." [12] That advice was theologically tenable for many sixteenth-century Catholics and Protestants alike, but it failed to take into account Henry's concern for the succession through a legitimate male heir. While Barnes probably would have relished a letter more to his royal master's liking, nobody at the time could anticipate that Henry would actually solve his dilemma between bigamy and divorce by following these paths seriatim.

Having obtained the letter, Barnes set out for London via Magdeburg and Lübeck, and was received by Henry in December.[13] The journey, of course, did not take so long. Barnes' campaign to justify himself at home necessitated a delay for printing in Antwerp at the press of Symon Cock in November 1531, *A supplicatyon made by Robert Barnes, doctoure in*

12. P. Smith, "Luther and Henry VIII," *English Historical Review, 25* (1910), 665 f., citing: *Luthers Briefwechsel,* ed. E. L. Enders, *9,* 80, 92, 105. But *WA* (*Br.*), *6,* 175 and 188, gives the date as September 3.

13. Smith, p. 666, citing: *Luthers Briefwechsel, 9,* 99; *LP, 5,* no. 593; and *Calendar of . . . State Papers . . . Spain, 1531–33,* no. 865. Smith skipped the stopover in Antwerp, but the itinerary was got right by Mozley, p. 201 n.

diuinite/ vnto the most excellent and redoubted prince kinge henrye the eyght (*STC* 1470; *Ned. Bibl.* 2372). The matter of the letter from Luther to Henry was but one of two reasons for the trip to England. Stephen Vaughan, reporting to Thomas Cromwell the publication of Barnes' *Supplicatyon,* judged it the Protestant book most appealing to the rank and file yet to appear in English "because he proves his learning by Scripture, the doctors, and the Pope's law." Vaughan thought Barnes would pay for the book with his life. To thwart its anticipated effect in England he strongly advised that Barnes be brought before the King to present his position so people would know he had been heard out and judged wrong. "Men's errors, in my poor judgment, should henceforth cease, if it would please the King to have this man examined before himself and the world, thus showing himself seriously to regard the truth of God's word." [14]

Barnes in 1531 began doing double duty. First he made himself a messenger between Wittenberg and London on a matter that certainly would command the King's attention; then he published his case for the Reformation and, at least for a brief spell, found himself the spokesman for Protestants before the King of England. Unless Henry acted out of character, he was far more interested in Barnes' news of the Wittenberg opinion of the validity of his marriage to Catharine than in what this tedious fellow had to say about the true church and the true faith. On December 21, 1531, Eustace Chapuys, ambassador of Emperor Charles V to the court of Henry VIII, reported to his lord that "An English friar of the Order of St. Augustine [whose description Barnes answers], who has long been with Luther and others, is come hither at the King's great solicitation." But Chapuys noticed Barnes only as involved in the divorce question. [15]

Thomas More, claiming that Barnes overstayed the safety guaranteed him as bearer of Luther's letter, intended to arrest and condemn him both as a relapsed heretic and as an apostate

---

14. *LP, 5,* no. 533, and cf. no. 532. Barnes' 1531 book, *STC* 1470, was described by *Ned. Bibl.,* no. 2372.
15. *LP, 5,* no. 593.

who had broken monastic vows. Both were true counts. Barnes was wary enough during his stay to shave his beard and don the clothes of a merchant (as both More and Chapuys remarked) and "also priuely to departe the realme" in January. More accused Barnes of violating the safe-conduct by raising money among "the congregacion" in England to pay for the printing of his book and for "his comming hither and going ouer agayne," and by commending to them the New Testament of Tyndale and English writings by Tyndale, Joye, and himself.[16]

One modern commentator contended that More had been kept ignorant of the invitation from Cromwell to Barnes to return to England, and that the journey was specifically in the interest of conveying Luther's opinion on the marriage question to Henry. This account had Barnes rushing to England, then hastily back to Wittenberg to obtain Luther's opinion, and making a quick trip to Hesse to persuade Duke Philip to influence Luther in favor of Henry's divorce. Luther's letter on that reckoning was dated September 5, 1531, and Philip's too-late letter to Luther September 22.[17] The criss-crossing of the channel by Barnes seems unnecessarily elaborate to explain the data at hand. Moreover, More's attempt to detain Barnes as a relapsed heretic sprang not from Barnes' reporting Luther's opinion of Henry's marriage, but from his presenting the views of his *Supplicatyon* to the circle of English Protestants from whom he solicited money and support. More apparently knew of the safe-conduct and interpreted it as expiring at Christmas 1531, but John Frith testified that he had read the document "which had but onely this one condition annexed vnto it, that if he came before the feast of Christmasse then next insueing, he should haue free libertie to departe at his pleasure. And this condition I know was fulfilled." [18] At any rate, Barnes was back on the Continent in January 1532, relieved of all responsibility to negotiate with the Wittenbergers for an opinion on Henry's business, for while Barnes was still in England

16. Frith, *Whole workes*, p. 155; More, *Workes*, p. 761.

17. Doernberg, *Henry VIII and Luther*, pp. 85 f.; evidence for this account was not cited, but a translation and summary of Luther's interesting letter was provided, pp. 86–91.

18. Frith, *Whole workes*, p. 156.

William Paget was sent to do Henry's business with Protestant princes; Paget appeared in Wittenberg in August 1532 on this mission.[19]

At least as early as 1531 Barnes was bent on obtaining preferment in the service of the King, to whom he was always remarkably loyal. Barnes' first venture into that field of work, joined with his effort to become spokesman for Protestantism before the King and others, had ended dismally when he departed from London in January 1532. Little that is definite or interesting is known of him during the ensuing year. He may have been in Hamburg with Aepinas on this occasion as he certainly was after a later return to the Continent from London.[20] During 1533 and part of 1534 he seems to have thought his vocation lay in professional theology. He visited again with Bugenhagen in Wittenberg, and it is not unlikely that this friend so counseled. On June 16, 1533, at Wittenberg Barnes participated in debates with Alesius at the granting of doctors' degrees in theology to Cruciger, Bullinger, and Aepinas. Four days later he matriculated as Antonius Anglus. At Wittenberg he prepared the second version of the *Supplication* and sent it for printing in November 1534 to Byddell in London: *A supplicacion vnto the most gracious prynce H. the .viii.* . . . . (*STC* 1471). Probably during this time he worked also on the *Lives of the Popes*.

BARNES' LATER CAREER

From August 1534 until January 1535 Barnes returned to London to negotiate with Henry on behalf of the cities of Hamburg and Lübeck. In March he consulted Melanchthon on the King's pressing business, returning to London late in May. In July 1535 he attained the status of royal chaplain and helped with Henry's ambivalent and vacillating negotiations with the Protestant princes of Germany.[21] In 1538 he aided the King by

19. Doernberg, p. 91; Smith, "Luther and Henry VIII," p. 666.
20. Rupp, p. 41; for Barnes' career as an ecclesiastical diplomat between 1534 and 1539, Rupp's account is reliable.
21. Foxe's summary of Barnes' life, *Whole workes,* *AAaiij^v, had Barnes continuing as "a faythfull preacher in this Citie of London all the time that shee [Anne Boleyn] remained Queene. And was well enterteyned and promoted." During these years he was very much in and out of London, and seems

baiting John Lambert as a sacramentarian. Henry thought his part in negotiating the royal marriage with Anne of Cleves not very helpful. Gardiner's dominance of ecclesiastical policy was signaled by the Six Articles, and for his stand against this policy Barnes was burned at Smithfield July 30, 1540.

While the parts that Barnes played in negotiating with German Protestants and in standing against the ecclesiastical reaction under Gardiner elucidate Henry's ecclesiastical and religious fickleness, they have little bearing on the efforts of the English Protestants prior to 1535. That he joined his fellow workers Frith and Tyndale in martyrdom only after these negotiations served to make him more memorable than they in Germany, and less so in England. Nevertheless, the rather stirring confession of faith that Barnes made at the stake led John Foxe to rank him among the most important of the martyrs of the English Reformation. In that testament Barnes denied yet once more that he had taught or preached anything contrary to scripture, or that he had given cause for insurrection. He portrayed his preaching as against the anabaptists "who say that . . . Christ took no flesh of the Virgin." He always had set forth God's glory, the King's obedience, "and the true and sincere religion of Christ." Luther always thought that the first and last of these three causes were incompatible with the second as long as the religiously inconstant and personally capricious Henry VIII sat on the throne. The personal tragedy of Barnes lies in the fact that he was as unwilling to admit in principle their incompatibility as he was unable to make them in fact compatible. Barnes professed at death his belief in the Trinity and Incarnation, Christ's death and passion as providing sufficient salvation to the world and the only satisfaction to the Father. No work of man other than Christ's passion earned justification before God, who commanded good works "to show and set forth our profession, not to deserve or merit" forgiveness. He believed the Church to be "a company of all them that do profess Christ." Whether saints prayed for the

---

to have thought himself never well promoted; his preaching in London is more certain during the days of Anne of Cleves as queen, for Barnes received £10 and a gown as one of three preachers left a small endowment in the will of Humphrey Monmouth of London; see Strype, *Ecclesiastical Memorials, I,* ii, pp. 368 ff.

souls of the living and dead only God knew. Barnes prayed for those who condemned him and enjoined prayers for the King's grace and for the infant prince. The King was to be obeyed; if he commands against God's law his subjects may not resist him. Four things he desired: that the spoils of the monasteries should go to relieve the poor, that the King should enforce reverence for matrimony, that abominable swearers should be punished, and that Henry would push to the end what he had begun in promoting Christ's religion according to scripture.[22]

Barnes' martyrdom settled forever Luther's opinion that it was impossible to negotiate theological and political matters with Henry VIII. The measures eventually taken by Henry and Edward VI to reform the Church in England were guided by Rhinelanders who stood with the reformed branch of continental Protestantism. They held little interest for German evangelicals. Thus Barnes was in many ways the last Englishman to command the attention of the Lutheran party. In England his martyrdom was only one of many more crucial events of the Tudor ecclesiastical reaction led by Gardiner, against which George Joye became a leading Protestant polemicist. In 1543 Joye defended Barnes against Gardiner's charges in *George Ioye confuteth Uvinchesters false Articles* (*STC* 14,826); Gardiner replied (1546) with *A declaration of such true articles as George Ioye hath gone about to confute as false* (*STC* 11,588) and in the same year Joye added to the controversy *The refutation of the byshop of Winchesters derke declaration of his false articles, once before confuted by George Ioye* (*STC* 14,827). Barnes left no such memorial as Tyndale did with the New Testament, nor as Frith did with what came to be the Anglican teaching on the Lord's Supper. Except for Foxe's publishing Barnes' works with those of Tyndale and Frith in 1572, and the accounts of Barnes in the *Acts and Monuments,* the man whom Luther called "Saint Robert" was not prominently remembered as a hero of the early English Reformation. Perhaps because of his reputation as a protégé

---

22. *AM,* 5, 434–36 reproduces the whole confession; it was also printed in *Whole workes,* *AAaiiij[r–v]. Already in 1540 a German translation had been printed in Augsburg, and probably another in Leipzig. In the same year the German translation was printed in Wittenberg with a preface by Luther.

of Luther his memory was not resurrected by English romantic historical scholarship in the nineteenth century as was that of Tyndale and, to a lesser degree, that of Frith.

Robert Barnes was "the one person who had known both Henry VIII and Martin Luther and who had yet considered that religious concord between them was not impossible."[23] Henry's opinion of Barnes has not been preserved. It would not be far wrong to suppose that the King regarded this theologian as tedious, ineffectual, religiously fanatical. But Luther understood Barnes better than Barnes understood himself. In him Luther saw a man of "exceptional humility," who had earnestly tried to plant the gospel in an England whose King uprooted every such planting. "He himself, Dr. Robert Barnes, told me often enough: *'Rex noster non curat religionum, sed est'* and so forth. But so great was his love for his King and country that he bore all this willingly; he always wished to help England." Such a love for king and country commanded Luther's entire admiration. Barnes' undoing was not this obedience; rather, Luther thought, "he was deceived by hope. Always he hoped that at long last his King would become a good man." It was a vain hope, because "whatever Harry wants that must be regarded as an article of faith both for life and death." Barnes failed to see that God "can make such masterly use of such devils and devil's companions [as Henry] towards our and all Christians' salvation and also to the punishment of themselves and of all who do not wish to know God; as He has always done through dreadful tyrants. . . . Likewise it is with our robber Harry."

Luther had no difficulty following his own formula of trusting God and obeying the prince. Barnes was miles apart from Luther, for he did not perceive the theological gulf in that formula between trust and obedience. For Barnes, to trust God meant to obey him; to obey the prince meant to trust him.

23. Doernberg, p. 123. Luther's preface is reproduced in English, pp. 124–26, from which subsequent quotations have been taken.

5. Barnes' Theology

HE theological thought of Robert Barnes between 1525 and 1535 underwent significant shifts. An original interest in repristinating the church came to be theologically grounded and qualified by the adoption of certain Lutheran positions. In turn, these ties to Luther's theology were slackened by Barnes' endeavor to work out a theology palatable to Henry VIII's ecclesiastical and royal policies, and by his increasing identification with the small circle of English Protestants then working on the Continent. Barnes wrote on a number of important subjects, such as ecclesiastical polity, justification, the keys of the church, free will, the sacraments, the authority and use of scripture, political theory, and priestly marriage. The development of his thought caused extreme alterations in his view of the King's rôle in ecclesiological matters and in his teaching on justification. His importance as a shaper of early English Protestant thought sprang, however, in the last analysis, not from his own creative efforts as a theologian but from his achievement of a certain synthesis of viewpoints originated by Luther and by Rhineland reformers.

Barnes' initial trouble with the church authorities in England involved no specifically Lutheran teachings, but turned on his vigorous, offensive attack, in the Christmas Eve sermon of 1525, on the worldliness of prelates. Between the time of that sermon and the ill-fated visit to England in 1531 and early 1532, Luther became his theological master. The full measure of his dependence upon Luther cannot, however, be perceived by examining his writings as collected by John Foxe and published by John Day in 1572. Major misinterpretations of

Barnes have sprung from recourse to this edition. To be sure, Foxe and Day faithfully reproduced six of the ten original chapters of the 1531 *Supplicatyon* and included the only slight revisions made in 1534 by Barnes in another chapter. But the 1572 folio reprinted only the 1534 version of Barnes' theologically and biographically crucial address to Henry, his discussion of the twenty-five articles alleged against the 1525 sermon, and his important essay on justification by faith.

Between 1531 and 1534 Barnes changed his mind radically on justification and on kingship. Therefore the overriding influence of Luther upon him in 1531, as well as Barnes' liberation from this strict adherence to Luther by 1534, may be discovered only by careful attention to sources.[1] Variations between the two *Supplications* were noted by sixteenth-century writers, but of course were not dealt with critically. Bishop Bonner's 1542 prohibition of Protestant books recognized two separate editions by the entry, "The booke of freer Barnes twyse prynted." [2] The "epitomizer" of some of Barnes' works who helped prepare the 1572 Foxe-Day edition and signed himself "T. G.," noted and in part quoted from "the first Edi-

---

1. *STC* 1470, *A supplicatyon made by Robert Barnes doctoure in diuinite vnto the most excellent and redoubted prince kinge henrye the eyght* . . . , is the edition of Symon Cock, Antwerp, 1531. Identical copies are at the British Museum [catalog no. C.53.h.25] and at Cambridge University Library [catalog no. SSS.47.13]. The 1534 edition is *STC* 1471, printed in London by J. Byddell: *A supplicacion vnto the most gracyous prince H. the .viii.* . . . . The 1534 version was reprinted *cum privilegio* by "H. Syngelton" [1550?] and is *STC* 1472: *The supplication of doctour Barnes vnto . . . kynge Henrye the eyght* . . . . The collection of Barnes' writings printed by Day in 1572 took the address, the twenty-five articles, and the essay on justification by faith from the 1534–1550[?] revision, and also the slightly revised discussion of free will; it did not identify the Answer to More, the Whole Disputation, and the article on marriage of priests as having appeared first in 1534; its Original of the Mass, Temporal Power, and Lawsuits discussions were excerpts from various writings by Barnes, apparently never published in English as such by him. Among writers on Barnes known to me, only W. D. J. Cargill Thompson has noted the differences in content between the 1531 and 1534 *Supplications,* and his findings corroborate mine; Cargill Thompson was chiefly interested in changes in Barnes' political thought; see his article, "The Sixteenth-Century Editions of *A Supplication unto King Henry the Eighth* by Robert Barnes, D.D.: A Footnote to the History of the Royal Supremacy," *Transactions of the Cambridge Bibliographical Society, 3* (1960), 133–42.

2. Bonner Register, fol. 39ᵛ, cited by *AM 5,* appendix X.

tion of his Englishe workes, whiche were first corruptlye
Printed beyonde the Seas." [3]

In 1531 Barnes supplicated Henry for redress of the grievance of his 1526 trial, setting forth eight articles of faith as
based upon scripture and tradition and therefore as claiming
the King's assent, and, at the end, daring Henry to put the
articles to a test: all who disagreed should write out their opinions on the basis of scripture, and if any three disagreements
coincided, let Barnes die! In 1534 Barnes changed his approach
to Henry entirely, recollecting in a complaining fashion numerous minor injustices of the 1526 trial, pleading his case at
length, revising the theological basis of two articles of belief,
omitting six of the original articles, adding an answer to the
eighth book of More's *The confutacyon of Tyndales answere*
. . . (1532; *STC* 18,079), and furnishing a new article on the
legitimacy of priestly marriage. Among many changes in tenor
and content, the most telling were Barnes' withdrawal from a
strict Lutheran stand on justification by faith alone, and his
shift from a Lutheran to a Rhenish or "proto-Calvinist" understanding of civil magistracy.

BISHOPS AND KING

The bishops who had condemned Barnes were castigated in
the earlier *Supplicatyon* for hypocrisy, ambition, pride, worldliness, and abominable living, but the chief accusation against
them was treason. The word of God, as Barnes saw it, would
have them obedient to the prince, unseat them from all positions of temporal power, and make them imitate apostolic
poverty. By 1534 he moderated all these accusations. He approved temporal power and wealth of the church provided
they had been come by honestly. The plea in 1531 for the
obedience of all men equally to the magistrate became in 1534
an argument that the common life ruled over by the King
should be modeled after scriptural precepts made available in
the common tongue. His accusation of forgery as the basis of
all claims to temporal power by the Church, and of treason as

3. *Whole workes*, pp. 358, 367. A "T.G." [Thomas Good] in 1626 published
some of Frith's writings under the title *Vox Piscis;* see below, ch. 8, n. 10.

its inevitable result, became an ad hominem rehearsal of specific ecclesiastical abuses in English history.

Barnes based his 1531 conception of absolute royal power in temporal affairs directly upon the will of God. The Crown signified that one person ruled throughout his life, and, more important, that there was no other power on earth superior to this one. Thus bishops were traitors to crowd in *underneath* the Crown and share a power which was essentially monarchical. Foreign ecclesiastical potentates were traitors to come in *above* the Crown and snatch its rightful power. Christ and Paul had submitted utterly to pagan princes, but those who claimed to be their vicars and successors would not submit to Christian princes. By the Pope's own law "the seat doth not make a priest, but the priest maketh the seat"; it was Henry's duty to unseat the traitors and put in their places men who were holy according to the word of God; thus the Church would have true bishops and priests. In deviating from scripture, the Church officials were the real heretics; therefore if temporal authorities must punish heretics, according to their law, it was they who should be punished.

The papists would say, Barnes predicted, that he qualified the liberties of the Church, but on his view its only true liberty was the word of God which Christ had left. Under the cloak of liberty the papists excluded from the Church men who were bought for it by Christ's blood. The Church in truth was the whole congregation of people. Were it exempt from the prince's sovereignty he should have no realm. On every score the Church authorities had acted against the prince and contrary to the scriptures; if they could prove Barnes guilty of one such action, he would gladly die. The Church fathers agreed with the scriptures (as did many of the Church's own laws) that the Church must submit to the temporal authority. As the prince was bound by God to rule over the realm given him, so bishops were bound to preach the word of God and to live under temporal authority. Temporal power of bishops robbed the princely vocation, and the prince who allowed that robbery was guilty of changing God's ordinances.

The nub of Barnes' 1531 argument was that in conscience

the prince was bound to recover the princely vocation as God-given, and this involved ridding the realm of so-called bishops who usurped royal authority. In closing his supplicatory epistle of 1531, Barnes placed squarely before Henry the choice either to consider Barnes a heretic and lose his realm to the bishops and his soul to the devil, or to judge the bishops to be heretics and save his realm by fulfilling his vocation under God. Barnes understood his direct appeal to the King to be an extreme measure forced by the bishops' blindness to truth. Barnes so appealed, he said, not for his own advancement, but to expose, in the King's name, the tyranny of the bishops for which the King must answer before God.

In 1534, however, Barnes found no great evil in episcopacy save as it was sworn to uphold the pretentious power of the Pope above that of the King. The internal usurpation of power by the bishops, upon which most of the earlier argument had turned, he forgot or put aside. Bishops made oaths of obedience to the Pope contradicting their oaths of obedience to the King. The King's plain duty was to demand full observance of fealty to himself. But the bishops perjured themselves with respect to their royal oaths when they took the papal oaths in conscience. From these papistical bishops Barnes would save his prince. For the Pope, not episcopacy, seemed now "the greatest mortall ennemy, that our Prince hath." [4] Throughout, the 1534 *Supplicacion* attempted to convince Henry that his authority in the realm could not be maintained unless in theory and practice universal papal power was rejected and its advocates expelled from places of influence—an argument as welcome to Henry late in 1534, when he had in principle repudiated papal authority in the English Church, as was the other argument unwelcome in 1531, when the King leaned heavily upon the bishops to support his impending divorce.

With less than complete honesty, Barnes put himself forward as having advocated royal independence from papal interference all along, for in fact he had pleaded for ecclesiastical reform, not specifically political reform, in the earlier book. This is not to say that, by stretching out his notion of the submission of the Church to the territorial prince, Barnes was

4. *Whole workes,* p. 198.

necessarily moving toward a precise understanding of ecclesiastical and political arrangements in England. Never did he
reckon that a worldly spiritualty might become as vital to the
Tudor throne as it had been to the papal cathedra. Never did
he glimpse the subtle solution by which reformers of the English church would plead the *consensus quinquasaeculorum* as
endorsing both the royal headship of the church and a magis-
terially potent spiritualty. Barnes rather moved from his earlier
position toward advocating a national church subservient to
its prince as the specific fulfillment of the New Testament pattern for church and state relations.

In 1531 Barnes saw the temporal and spiritual realms as
quite distinct politically, albeit ultimately united theologically
by the inscrutable will of God. In the temporal realm the king
was absolute and supreme; whether evil or good in his rule,
all must obey his will as from God, or, if they found the rule
personally intolerable, they might flee as Barnes himself had
done. But since the bishops had invaded and usurped the temporal realm, and the prince's duty was to hold that realm in-
violable under himself alone with his agents, the exercise of
this duty would effectually reform the church. In the spiritual
realm authority belonged to all, but, to avoid confusion, was
dedicated to chosen servants learned in the word of God to
which all authority was responsible. The spiritualty under the
scripture had no right to order temporal affairs, even for their
own institutional betterment.

Two kinds of violations of spiritual authority might, and
Barnes earlier taught in fact had, come about. First, open defiance of the word of God, such as condemning the vernacular
New Testament or teaching justification by works, were violations that must be repudiated steadfastly and openly so that
the word of God might be made to rule all spiritual matters.
All traditions against God's word and law must, in spiritual
affairs, be destroyed. Second, certain violations commanded indifferent matters as necessary to salvation under pain of deadly
sin, such as fastings, stipulation of religious apparel, and clerical celibacy; these must be withstood lest the faith of Christendom be damaged and the liberty of Christians abridged, for
these violations made binding precisely those things from which

the gospel set men free. On these points violent resistance was, however, inappropriate. Adiaphora commanded as necessary should be disavowed, not because such things were evil, but only because it was damnable to perform them as though necessary. Such things the Christian might obey for the sake of quietness and order, but in them he must set no confidence and to them he must impute no holiness. No more than any other Christian was the prince involved in these latter violations, save indirectly through his temporal sovereignty. Barnes recognized that in point of fact kings might forbid the vernacular scripture, the sacraments, preaching the word, etc., under temporal pains or even death. When that happened Christians were to pray to God and respectfully intercede unto the king's grace that the hindrance be removed; if he refused, they were to keep their Bible, observe its ordinances, and suffer the king's tyranny. They must not resist violently under pain of their own damnation, but must suffer punishments without compromise. "So that Christen men are bounde to obey in suffering the kinges tyranny, but not in consenting to his vnlawfull commaundement." [5]

Perhaps the most striking single change in the 1534 version of Barnes' *Supplicacion* was the elimination of the entire article "*That* mens constitutions, which are not grounded in Scripture, bynde not the conscience of man vnder the payne of deadly sinne." But the subject was not lost by that excision; new points of view were added to the initial address. The word of God became the single authority for matters temporal and spiritual. The king became the minister of God in both realms, under obligation indeed to run his kingdom and his church according to scripture, yet in the last analysis absolute. The duty of obedience to the king which Barnes originally taught as applicable only to temporal matters was extended in 1534 to all spiritual matters save one, so that the only choices open to the Christian were to obey or to flee; however, since the king stood under the authority of the word of God, scriptures must be retained even against the king's command, punishment suffered gladly for retaining them, and revenge reserved to God's judgment.[6]

5. *Whole workes,* p. 295.
6. Obviously, the conflation of Barnes' two points of view by his 1572

Both in tone and in content, the two *Supplications* diverged on matters of regal and episcopal authority. Barnes seriously revised his earlier political and ecclesiological views to accommodate direct royal sovereignty over the spiritual realm, but in so doing he retained and underscored the necessity of vernacular scripture as the rule of the spiritual life. Barnes shifted the details of his teaching as Henry's hold over the Church became evident. But, however he might surrender Lutheran political convictions, he would not compromise the biblicism he had espoused from the outset of his Protestant career.

WORKS AND FAITH

"That faith only justifies" was the first article of Barnes' 1530 *Sentenciae,* and his explication of that proposition was prominently displayed in both editions of the *Supplication.* To be sure, the reader of the 1534 edition came upon this essay only after attending to Barnes' long story of his controversy with his 1526 accusers, composed anew for this edition and entitled, "The hole disputation betwen the byshops and doctour Barnes." Nevertheless the shape of the treatise on justification remained the same in both editions, in spite of substantial and careful revisions. Barnes excised from near the beginning of the 1531 work a diatribe in which papists were held to be antichrists for paying some of the honor of redemption to human works instead of to Christ. This change marks the moderation of all Barnes' accusations in the revised book. He added paragraphs showing that the sermon on the mount was no new law but exposed the full meaning of the Old Testament law; although this argument recited Luther's slogan that Christ was no new Moses, Barnes accommodated the precepts of

editors produced irreconcilable contradictions. N. H. Fisher, "The Contribution of Robert Barnes," ch. 2, has held that Barnes sided politically against Stephen Gardiner in seeing temporal and spiritual realms as distinct from one another yet both under the demands of the word of God, thus repudiating the King's viceregency under God over matters both temporal and spiritual. On this view Barnes seemed to have acquiesced quietly in the royal headship over the church without sanctioning it theologically, and to have tried, with indifferent results, to merge continental and English views of ecclesiastical polity. Fisher's careful study of Barnes' politics, in the context of the conflicting views of his day, was based on the 1572 conflation; while it neatly summarized the Barnes of Foxe's and Day's editing, it overlooked the changes in Barnes' own thought.

the New Testament to the theological character of those of the Old. Here Barnes adopted the position that Tyndale worked out after the publication of his 1530 translation of the pentateuch.[7]

The most important difference between the two versions of Barnes' treatise on justification was the elimination in 1534 of an elaborate argument against the place accorded to good works by the Epistle of James. Barnes earlier flatly denied all instrumentality of works in the justification of sinners, openly repudiating the teaching of this Epistle, whose apostolicity he thought had always been doubted by ancient authorities, and claiming invincible scriptural proof that the Epistle was not from an apostle's hand. Abraham, according to the book of Genesis, had been justified by faith at least fourteen years before Isaac was born; Isaac was at least seven years old when Abraham demonstrated his willingness to offer his son, for the boy could then speak perfectly; thus Abraham's justification by faith preceded by at least twenty-one years the work to which James attributed his justification. Moreover, Paul's writings and the books of Maccabees and Hebrews all agreed that Abraham was justified by faith before the sacrifice episode. With respect to Rahab, Joshua 2 testified that she had spoken words of faith and demonstrated her trust in God's promises, and on the basis of that faith she performed the good work of receiving the messengers. Thus Barnes thought the Old Testament agreed with Hebrews 11 in assigning justification to faith, not works. The Epistle of James therefore was not apostolic, because it stood against plain scriptures and denied the gospel. This 1531 argument was neither more nor less than a detailed explication of points made by Luther in his preface to James.[8] Luther thought that James opposed Paul and the rest of scripture, for his portrayal of Abraham's justification denied Romans 4 and Genesis 15, and that James preached not Christ but general belief in God, pointing to the law and to works and being a lone voice against all other scripture.

All references to the non-apostolicity of James disappeared

7. See below, ch. 10.

8. *WA* (*Bibel*) 7, 384–87; tr. Bertram Lee Woolf, *Reformation Writings of Martin Luther* (2 vols. London, 1952–56), *2,* 306–308.

from Barnes' 1534 *Supplicacion,* and Augustine was cited as
having reconciled discrepancies between Paul and James without compromising the doctrine of justification by faith. Although the teaching of James was accommodated to that of
Paul in this revision, Barnes stressed a new connection between
faith and works: faith alone could justify a man before God,
but works as a necessary fruit of that justification made an outward declaration of justification before the world. Only faith
might receive Christ's promise; nevertheless good works would
have their reward when they sprang from faith. It will be seen
that Tyndale, who in adapting Luther's prefaces to the books
of the New Testament took gingerly any argument against the
apostolicity of the Epistle of James, during the last five years
of his life coupled justification by faith before God with justification by works before man. Precisely this modification of the
Wittenberg theology became the ground for a distinctive interpretation of Christianity by the early English Protestants.[9]

Regarding the doctrine of justification by faith, Barnes
shifted ground, but remained a Protestant if not a protégé of
Luther. From the beginning Barnes had grasped Luther's point
in its christocentric emphasis, but he missed the overriding theocentrism that motivated Luther in this teaching. Barnes resolved that no teaching should dishonor Christ, or, in the
phrase that he preferred, oppose the blood of Christ. A true
confession of Christ involved wholeheartedly granting that the
whole justice, redemption, wisdom, holiness, grace, and peace
of man before God inhered in Christ. All goodness in man was
of Christ, by Christ, and for Christ's sake. To withhold any
religious honor from Christ or to qualify Christ as sole reconciling agent between God and man seemed to Barnes sheer
blasphemy. Justification of sinners, Barnes contended, came
about only by imputation of Christ's righteousness to men and
women, who by nature lacked and could not attain such righteousness. As he was ever at pains to show, all good works
flowed from such justification. The material elements of justification by faith before God as held and taught by Luther were
always present in Barnes' argument, regardless of the 1534 in-

9. See L. J. Trinterud, "The Origins of Puritanism," *Church History, 20,* 1
(1951), 37–57.

terest in justification before the world. The Englishman's teaching lacked Luther's insistence upon the absolute dependence of sinful man upon a righteous yet merciful God, before whom man must learn to "take the second place." Precisely the heart of Luther's own religious quest, *um ein gnädigen Gott zu kriegen,* failed to inform Barnes' understanding of justification by faith. With Barnes the conception of faith remained tinted by its medieval denotation of *assensus* in contrast to Luther's radical denotation of *fiducia.*

Between 1531 and 1534 Barnes' theology exchanged its conception of autocratic magistracy for one of convenanted society, and traded its insistence on justification by faith alone for an acknowledgment of justification before the world by works. These shifts signify a momentous drift away from the religious theocentrism of the early Luther toward the socially and ecclesiastically concerned covenant theology represented by Bucer, later by Calvin, and perhaps most powerfully by the English Puritan tradition.

SACRAMENTS AND CHURCH

Still other important differences appear between the two versions of the *Supplication.* With only slight changes, Barnes reproduced in 1534 the twenty-five articles which the bishops had charged against him in 1526, and his argument that fallen man's free will can of its own strength do nothing but sin before God. The supplicatory address and the article of faith were substantially revised. The rest of the 1531 book was excised: the explication of the nature and constituency of the true church, the identification of the keys of the kingdom as the scriptures, the plea for the right of all Christians to read scriptures in the vernacular, the argument that human constitutions and ordinances are not binding on the conscience of man when they command him to sin, the utraquist plea, and the repudiation of the worship and veneration of saints and images. In place of these he composed anew a refutation of More's argument on the nature of the church, and an article claiming the right of priests who lacked the gift of chastity to marry.

All the above mentioned changes of content reveal that Barnes was departing from Luther not only with respect to justification, but also in his teaching on church and sacraments. Barnes removed from the 1534 tract the points of Reformation thought and action that were regarded in England as specifically Lutheran. In their place he argued ecclesiology against the official theological polemicist of the English Church. Setting forth of the right of priests to marry defended a practice already entered into by Thomas Cranmer, who before his sudden promotion to the archbishopric of Canterbury had married a niece of the German Protestant, Andreas Osiander. Hinging priestly marriage on the lack of the gift of chastity perhaps played upon the King's sympathy. But Henry was openly impatient with utraquism. English New Testaments were widely available at home in Tyndale's revised version and its pirated editions, and before many months the vernacular Bible would find royal approval. The general shifts in the emphasis of Barnes' writings thus fit into contemporary ecclesiastical and political affairs.

Regardless of his enrolling in 1531 as a theological disciple of Luther, and of his liberation by 1534 from that master, Barnes never laid aside the specific notions of church reform which he had espoused in the Christmas sermon of 1525. In both versions of the *Supplication* he promoted the principle that Christians ought not enter into lawsuits against one another, because to do so violated Paul's injunction to the Christians at Corinth. The point was of course not new with Barnes, for it had been pleaded during the previous generation by John Colet.[10] Yet by way of defending himself against the allegation that this part of his sermon constituted offense and heresy, Barnes took thought between 1531 and 1534. Earlier he had stood pat on scripture, asking sarcastically if it were not sufficient for a doctor of divinity to quote the Holy Ghost! Later he claimed that he had opposed only the practice of seeking vengeance at law, and had not objected to all lawsuits; of course he knew that magistracy was from God, for Paul himself had appealed his trial as a Roman citizen, showing that legal recourse was open to Christians. To prove that his sermon

10. I have described Colet's desire to repristinate the Church and distinguished it from the work of the reformers in an article, "John Colet and Reformation," *Anglican Theological Review*, 37 (1955), 167-77.

objected only to unjust and uncharitable suits, Barnes told a
maudlin tale of a poor widow in Cambridge whom he had tried
to protect against ecclesiastical greed. As in the case of justification, Barnes' theological convictions became pliable in the
space of three years, yet he never deserted the cause in support
of which he had been on record.

Barnes understood the true Church in terms of, and taught
that it drew its life from, the word of God. That Church alone
was unerring. The false church of the Popes, contrariwise, was
understood in terms of, and drew its life from, human institutions, ranks, orders, and hierarchies; it erred, and the keys it
held would not unlock heaven. These lines of thought guided
Barnes' ecclesiological teachings in the 1531 treatises entitled
"What the Church is: and who bee therof: and whereby men
may know her," and "What the keyes of the Church bee, and
to whom they were geuen." They also guided the 1534 reply
to More.[11] Against Luther's definition of the church in terms
of word and sacraments, Barnes first lodged the whole matter,
as the Lollards had, in the word of God, by which he meant the
scriptures; "where the word of God is truely and perfitely
preached without the damnable dreames of men, and where it
is well of the hearers receiued, & also where we see good
woorkes that doe openly agree with the doctrine of the Gospell,
these bee good and sure tokens whereby we may iudge, that
there bee some men of holy Church." [12]

Anticipating the Elizabethan theologian John Jewel, Barnes
found the keys of the kingdom to be the word of God; by
preaching or suppressing this word the Church bound or
loosed the souls of men. Priests like the apostles should be
servants, not masters, of the word and of the Church. The
Church, to be sure, contained good and bad, therefore in any
particular manifestation could err. But the inner character of
the Church was holiness given by God and tested according to
scripture, and the universal holy people could not err with regard to matters touching salvation so long as they followed the
word of God. "For the vniuersall church standeth in the elec-

11. *Whole workes,* pp. 242, 257.

12. Ibid., p. 249. In the 1534 answer to More, Barnes emphasized also the
orderly administration and reception of sacraments.

tion of all faythfull men, throughout the whole worlde, whose head & spouse is Christ Iesus." [13] Barnes was sure that reliable signs and tokens revealed certain men to be indeed of the true Church, but he did not expect every particular church to be conformed to all the signs and tokens of election. In a lively passage Barnes asserted "but whether they bee Iew or Greeke, kyng or subiect, carter or Cardinall, butcher or Byshop, tancardbearer or cannelraker, free or bounde, Frier or fidler, Monke or miller: if they beleeue in Christes word, & sticke fast to his blessed promises, and trust onely in the merites of his blessed bloud, they bee the holy Church of God, yea and the very true church afore God. . . . Boast, crake, blast, blesse, curse till your holy eyes start out of your head, it will not helpe you, for Christ chooseth his church, at his iudgement and not at yours." [14]

On free will's inability to avoid sin, Barnes argued the line laid down by Luther's 1525 *De servo arbitrio*. Man both rules and is ruled. If ruled by the spirit of God he rules well and produces good works. If ruled by free will without God he rules evilly and produces bad works. Therefore to be ruled by free will is to be enslaved to evil. Only by title, as it were, did Barnes touch upon the other side of Luther's doctrine which emphasized the marvelous liberty of being ruled by the spirit of God. Barnes wanted to show the folly of scholastic speculations— especially Scotist ones—about the inscrutable will of God, and in this interest he bypassed the understanding of vocation that Luther derived from the notion of the human will bound in heaven but free on earth.[15] The rather dull explication of the subject by Barnes in 1531 shows signs of hasty composition. The 1534 revisions only made the chapter less a diatribe against Fisher, then fallen into the bad graces of the King, and more an exhibition of Barnes' knowledge of the fathers and schoolmen.

From the character of the Church as a company of believers Barnes had earlier adduced the right of laymen to partake of

---

13. Ibid., p. 255.
14. Ibid., p. 244.
15. See G. Wingren, *Luther on Vocation* (Philadelphia, 1957), a translation into English by C. C. Rasmussen of *Luthers Lehre vom Beruf* (Munich, 1952).

the chalice. From the dependence of the Church on scripture as word of God he had argued the necessity of making the Old and New Testaments available in the vernacular. Saving his most bitter invective for the Church authorities—especially Stokesley, bishop of London since 1530, who banned and burned Tyndale's translation—Barnes had turned their opposition to vernacular scriptures into proof that they were antichrist. The 1531 utraquist plea had added nothing to the familiar run of Reformation arguments save a quaint title: "Alle maner of Chrysten men, bothe sprytualle and temporalle are bound whan they wylle be houslyd to reseue the sacrament in bothe kyndes vnder the payne of dedly synne." Under threat of eternal damnation Barnes had admonished Henry to honor God's word and Christ's blood by restoring the sacrament according to primitive use. Rejecting scholastic distinctions between veneration, honor, and worship, Barnes had damned the use of images and the invocation of saints as idolatry in reality if not in name, for in both instances regard due only to Christ was given to others. The revised *Supplication* of 1534 discarded the discussion of these three topics.

The comparison of Barnes' two *Supplications* may be completed by glancing at a piece composed anew for the 1534 edition, pleading the right—but not duty—of priests lacking the gift of chastity to marry. As early as 1529 a major Protestant writing on clerical marriage and on marriage as a spiritual estate had appeared in English when William Roy published his translation of Luther's 1523 *Das siebend capitel S. Pauli zu den Chorinthern*.[16] Since then the subject had been discussed in English publications by Erasmus, More, Tyndale, and others. The essay by Barnes was a peculiar mixture of almost whimpering pleas that Henry redress Barnes' grievances against the bishops, and masterful polemics on clerical marriage. Barnes, who always protested that he was not married, cast his argument against papal enforcement of clerical celibacy on a grand and systematic scale in this the ablest of his disputative works. The subject was tailor-made for him, combining matters of scripture, tradition, patristics, canon law, logic, reason,

16. See my article, "The Earliest Translations of Luther into English," for a description of this important contribution to English Protestantism.

common sense, and opportunity for slander. Celibacy for priests, enforced by pain of damnation, Barnes repudiated, found groundless in all the authorities save papal whim, ridiculed, and deplored. The Pope seemed to have made marriage, a divinely instituted and sanctified estate, into an evil thing; he drove priests who lacked the gift of chastity to sinful fornication; he fostered social ills which accompanied clerical whoremongering. Barnes seemed certain that in England not one priest in three was truly chaste. For all its literary vigor, theologically the treatise revealed nothing that Barnes had not displayed better elsewhere.

Scissors and Paste

As Barnes' first published writing was a Latin collection of sources, so was the last. Indeed all his writings borrowed heavily from written sources. Apparently after laboring at the project off and on for several years, he dedicated his *Lives of the Popes* to Luther in September 1535 and published it soon thereafter. Some bibliographies list a Basel edition as of 1535, but this printing came much later. The edition published by Clug in 1536, with preface by Luther, is probably original: *Vitae Romanorum Pontificum, quos Papas vocamus, diligenter & fideliter collectae per R. Barns (Deutscher Gesamtkatalog,* no. 11.7405). The book was an ambitious and pretentious undertaking, providing biographical sketches of some hundred and seventy-five pontifs between Peter and Alexander III (1159–1181), including some who are no longer regarded as having been true popes. The length of the reign of each was given in years, months, and days, but about most of them very scant information was provided. Sylvester, Leo III, Nicholas I and II, Alexander II, Gregory VII, Urban II, Paschal II, Calixtus II, Innocent II, Hadrian IV, and Alexander III received special attention, particularly for their negotiations with English kings. The entire work, however, was merely a catena of standard medieval and renaissance sources, to which Barnes brought the originality only of selection. Because it bore Luther's preface, the work enjoyed more reprintings than any other of Barnes' writings. Latin editions appeared in Basel in the 1550s and 1560s, Clug published a German translation in 1545, and in 1565 there appeared a Czech translation. John Bale brought the work forward with his *Acta Romanorum Pontificum,* and this was again extended by Johannes Lydius, minister at Frankfurt, in 1615.

The place of Barnes as a chief formulator of the earliest English-speaking Protestantism, however, owes little if anything to his *Lives of the Popes.* Luther judged that Barnes had been important for exhibiting substantial agreements between, on the one hand, the fathers of the Church, the doctors, and even the Pope's own law, and, on the other, the Reformation. That task, however, had been sketched out by a passage in a work written some years before Barnes joined the Protestant movement: "Many thynges myght be wryten of this boystous newe god [the Pope]: but who soeuer list to know his newe faith, his lyfe and his gouernaunce, let hym rede the canon lawe whiche he hath made/ and let hym compare it to the holy scrypture, and to the olde faythe of Christ: and it shall appere to him more clerly then the sonne, that he is a newe god and a newe faythe/ let ony man searche thoroughe out the cronycles, and hystoryes, and he shall fynde [it so]." [17] The task Barnes set for himself by his 1530 *Sentenciae* and carried out in the rest of his publications was to compare the papal religion with the scriptures, fathers, chronicles, and histories of the Church. Yet while he took it upon himself to prove articles of belief, derived from others, by appealing to scriptural and patristic authority, he made no original study of the Bible. In all the English writings he cited the New Testament in its 1526 and 1534 translations by Tyndale, only occasionally falling back upon the Latin of Erasmus or the Vulgate. His writings present no evidence to suggest that he employed the Greek New Testament after the manner of leading reformers and humanists. Old Testament citations, however, were made not from Tyndale's pentateuch and other recently Englished texts, but appear to be his own translations from Latin. Since the great majority of his scriptural appeals were to the New Testament, Tyndale must be reckoned as a leading source of his theology. Moreover, marginal notes by Tyndale, especially with reference

17. Joachim Vadianus (or von Watt) ?, tr. William Turner, *A worke entytled of ye olde god & the newe* . . . (1534; *STC* 25,127), Kij^v-[Kiij]^r.

to justification by faith, guided Barnes' treatment of theological topics.

Other writers among the early English Protestants focused their attention more upon scripture than did Barnes. His special methodology was to demonstrate patristic authority for certain Reformation propositions. In this respect he was at once original and epigonous. As far as English-speaking Christianity is concerned, Barnes was the first of a long line of spokesmen who discovered the right interpretation of scripture in the Church fathers, and he therefore may be called an originator of a theological method long prevalent, perhaps especially among Anglicans. But, like many a successor in this methodology, he did not gather the sense of patristic thought out of a broad acquaintance with the diffuse writings of the old Catholic authors. The majority of his articles employed patristic catenae which had been collected and arranged by other hands. Especially influential upon Barnes was the book *Unio Dissidentium,* published originally in Cologne December 10, 1522, over the pseudonym Hermannus Bodius.

Unio Dissidentium circulated in England before Barnes left Cambridge. While Barnes nowhere recorded his familiarity with it, the work appeared on the earliest lists of books proscribed in England. Not until 1548 did a part of the work appear in English, when William Hill of London printed a translation of the last article, which was some sentences out of Augustine's *De essentia divinitatis* pointing out that biblical, and especially prophetic, references to bodily parts and functions of God should be taken figuratively.[18] If, in spite of its availability, Barnes did not know the work in England, he had ample opportunity to come by it on the Continent, for it was printed in French and Latin versions ten times in Antwerp alone between 1527 and 1534.[19] Hermannus Bodius was the pseudonymous collector of the sentences in *Unio Dissidentium,* and the most interesting identification that has been made is of Martin Bucer.[20] Close examination reveals a double dependence by

18. *Certein Places gathered ovt of. S. Austeus Boke intituled de essentia diuinitatis . . . (STC* 919).

19. *Ned. Bibl.,* nos. 430, 2523–25, 4127, 4197, 4313–15, 0199.

20. W. G. Moore, *La Réforme Allemande et la Littérature Française* (Strassburg, 1930), pp. 157 ff. noted this identification by A. L. Herminjard and accepted

Barnes upon this book: first, for the very titles of most of the
1530 sentences and particularly for those which Barnes expounded at length in the 1531 *Supplicatyon,* and second, for the
specific patristic citations that buttressed these articles. Among
the sentences at least half of the propositions that Barnes advanced appeared as such in *Unio,* and great similarities appear
in most of the others. The patristic citations which Barnes employed in the essay on justification by faith were, with few exceptions, quoted in *Unio.* While this observation seems to rob
Barnes of the originality as a patristic scholar which Luther
attributed to him, it must be remembered that scholarship in
the sixteenth century frequently and without shame proceeded
in just this manner. If scholarly discredit is to be inferred in
this instance it must fall on Luther for his failure to know or
say that another than Barnes had done most of the historical
scholarship demonstrating agreements between Church fathers
and Reformation leaders.

The original contributions of Robert Barnes, then, are
limited. He presented directly to Henry VIII, not once but
twice, a major theological plea for reformation, in the manner
in which Calvin would submit the first edition of the *Institutes*
to Francis I. He placed that plea in the context of explicit statements, to be sure varying from one occasion to another, regarding the duty of Christian kings and people both as churchmen
and as members of the secular order. Since Henry was the kind
of prince who made personal, marital, religious, and other decisions in terms of their political contexts and consequences,
Barnes can be credited with making a more likely case for an
English reformation than most of his contemporaries.

Notwithstanding the disclaimer he entered when recounting
his 1526 trial, Barnes was learned in canon law and adept in
employing it. His use of historical chronicles was commonplace; Tyndale and to a lesser extent Frith similarly sharpened
their polemics by rehearsing episodes from the past, especially

it; *Ned. Bibl.* acknowledged this identification at 2523 and seemed more certain at 4197, but noted at 4313 that Bucer's recent biographers and bibliog-
raphers, H. Bornkamm and R. Stupperich, *Martin Bucers Bedeutung . . .*
(Gütersloh, 1952), made no mention of Bucer's possible authorship of this
work. The identification, if proved, would establish another direct link between an early English Protestant and a major Rhineland theologian.

those illustrating misbehavior of popes and usurpations of the power of English monarchs.

On the basis of his use of contemporary sources, Barnes as a theologian must be regarded as more polemical than constructive, more disputative than systematic. He was preoccupied by no special kind of theocentrism, as were Luther and Calvin. The ruling principle of his thought was, in the final analysis, that nothing must detract from the honor of Christ or from his exclusive agency in reconciling man to God. Always quicker to pick out what he took to be theological error than to articulate what he took to be theological truth, he in no sense occupied a front seat among sixteenth-century theologians. Others laid the foundations and fashioned the materials Barnes used.

By comparison with the contemporary Protestant writers among his countrymen Barnes suffers. The clarity and profundity of personal faith exhibited by Frith is nowhere manifest in what Barnes wrote. The single-mindedness that kept George Joye at work on liturgical scholarship failed to rivet Barnes' attention to any one religious or theological concern. Tyndale's mastery of language was given to Barnes only in fits and starts that produced a few purple passages. Yet the genius he displayed in his theological work between 1525 and 1535 made a unique example for those later Henrician, Edwardian, and Elizabethan reformers whose efforts eventually succeeded as markedly as Barnes' efforts failed: he thought and wrote about God and Church with one eye focused on the throne.

6. John Frith in Exile

FANCIED parallels between early Reformation activities in Germany and those in England have assigned to William Tyndale the significance of Luther, to George Joye the rôle of Andreas Karlstadt, and have made John Frith into the Melanchthon of the English Reformation.[1] Far from being the learned humanist and systematizer of doctrine that Melanchthon was, Frith displayed the finest mind, the most winsome wit, and the boldest spirit among the men who wrote theology in English between 1520 and 1535. From the literary perspective of C. S. Lewis, Frith "looms larger as a man than as an author, though he is not contemptible even in the second capacity." Though verbose he was keen and practical, though serious he did not lack humor.[2] Engaging Catholic theological writers of every variety—the highly trained Fisher, the tenacious More, and the tendentious John Rastell—Frith wove into a lovely theological tapestry various threads, including broad understanding of continental reformers, and sympathy for the viewpoints of the Lollards among his own countrymen. Withal he focused less on cardinal theological issues than did Barnes, less on scriptural authority than Tyndale, less on liturgy and worship than Joye. He centered his major original

1. E. Arber, ed., *George Joy. An Apology made by George Joy, to satisfy, if it may be, W. Tindale. 1535*, The English Scholar's Library, 13 (London, 1882), vi; the same assessment of Frith was made by Rupp, *Studies*, p. 10.

2. C. S. Lewis, *English Literature in the Sixteenth Century Excluding Drama*, The Oxford History of English Literature, 3 (Oxford, 1954), 196; Lewis incisively summarized the accomplishments of the early English Protestant writers and their foes in Book II, ch. I, "Drab Age Prose—Religious Controversy and Translation," noting the outstanding accomplishments of Tyndale as translator.

writings on the topical matters of purgatory and the sacraments. He crowded a fine education, a considerable literary output, three hazardous defiances of ecclesiastical authority in England, a long imprisonment, and a period of active leadership of the English Protestant underground into the thirty years that were given to him to live.

John Frith was born in 1503 in Westerham, Kent, but spent his childhood in Sevenoaks in the same shire, where his father Richard was an innkeeper. During Frith's childhood the county was a hotbed of late Lollard or "known men" activities. At Eton he learned Latin and probably Greek. He was at Queens' College, Cambridge, as a scholar 1523–24, and proceeded B.A. from King's College in 1525. Incorporated as B.A. at Oxford on December 7, 1525, he became a junior canon of Wolsey's new foundation, Cardinal College. According to one authority he never received ordination, since at that college only M.A.'s were clerics.[3] At Cambridge his tutor had been Stephen Gardiner, and probably he knew Tyndale there and the circle of men who met at "Little Germany." Foxe thought the acquaintance with Tyndale flourished in London after Frith had left Oxford, and that through Tyndale's instructions "he fyrst receaued into his hart the seede of the Gospell and sencere godlines."[4]

Certainly it was at Oxford, within the fortress of Catholic learning and orthodoxy, that Frith came into notice as an advocate of the Reformation. For the group of Cambridge men who staffed that college, Clark, Cox, Frith, and Taverner, together with followers such as Thomas Garrett, Anthony Dala-

---

3. R. E. Fulop, "John Frith (1503–1533) and His Relation to the Origin of the Reformation in England" (unpublished dissertation, New College, University of Edinburgh, 1956); this, the fullest modern work on Frith, gathers together a multitude of details and constructs a full biographical narrative—somewhat after the manner of Mozley's *William Tyndale*—but not all its theological judgments are reliable. A. C. Bickley's article in *DNB* is usually accurate. D. Alcock, *John Frith*, in the series "Six Heroic Men" (London, 1909) is popular hagiography. Rupp, pp. 199 f., furnishes scraps of information, and rightly assesses Frith as "the prodigy" of his circle. Most of Frith's writings were reprinted in *Whole workes* (1572), and in *The Works of the English Reformers: William Tyndale, and John Frith*, ed. T. Russell (3 vols. London, 1831).

4. *AM, 5,* 4; *Whole workes,* [GGiij]ᵛ.

ber, and probably also Sir Francis Bigod, lived to exert enormous influence on the English Reformation. Frith became an
outstanding Protestant writer. Garrett has been ranked "among
the earliest and most effective Lutheran propagandists in England." Bigod was a favorite in Wolsey's household and later,
from 1534 until his death in 1536, "appeared among the most
conspicuous agents of the English Reformation" before being
"appointed one of the commissioners for Yorkshire and York
City [to compile the] . . . survey of ecclesiastical incomes
upon which the Crown was to base its taxation of the Church." [5]
The spread of Lutheranism in this unlikely place was brought
to the attention of John Longland, bishop of Lincoln, late in
February 1528. At first it seemed that Garrett alone was involved, but then were "a marvilouse sorte of bookes founde
whiche were hydde undre the erth, and otherwise secretely
conveyede from place to place." The circle read not only Luther
and Melanchthon, but Hus, Oecolampadius, Wycliffe, Zwingli,
Bugenhagen, Brentius, Urbanus Rhegius, Bucer, Cellarius,
Francis Lambert of Avignon, and others; they had copies of
Unio Dissidentium and of *Oeconomica Christiana.*[6]

Upon learning of the abuse of his foundation, Wolsey had
the offenders accused of heresy. They were imprisoned in the
fish-cellar of the college for some months. Several died, including Clark, Sumner, and Bayly. Some abjured, such as Dalaber
and Garrett. Taverner was pardoned, and Frith made his way,
no earlier than September 1528, to the Continent. Perhaps
he was the "faithful companion" for whom Tyndale at this time
waited at Antwerp.[7] At any rate Frith fled without abjuring;
Wolsey had him released on condition that he not return to
Oxford. Frith is said to have been married in Amsterdam, where
he seems to have left his family when he finally and fatefully
returned to England. His exact itinerary on the Continent from
September 1528 until the spring of 1531 cannot be determined.
No data indicate that he visited Wittenberg. Certainly he spent

5. A. G. Dickens, *Lollards and Protestants in the Diocese of York 1509–1558*
(London, 1959), pp. 58, 69, 75, and passim.

6. Longland to Wolsey, March 3 [1528], printed in *AM, 5,* appendix VI.

7. See PS *1,* p. 37; S. L. Greenslade, *The Work of William Tindale* [*sic*]
(London, 1938), pp. 99, 119 n.; Fulop, "John Frith," held open the possiblity of
Frith's having met Tyndale at Marburg.

much time with Tyndale, and probably helped him translate Jonah and the pentateuch.[8] He engaged in literary activities in his own right, translating a tract by Luther and one by Patrick Hamilton, and setting forth his own disputation of purgatory against Fisher, More, and Rastell. Beyond that, he has been credited with composing Tyndale's famous reply to More's *Dialogue;* Frith's early death precluded his settling the question of the true authorship of the treatise, after George Joye stridently chided his more famous friend with the accusation that Frith wrote as well as supervised the printing of this 1531 diatribe.[9] Joye's attribution will be discussed later, but Frith does not need that credit to establish his reputation as a Protestant polemicist of great merit. That Frith and Tyndale were intimates and collaborators cannot be doubted, for Frith guided Tyndale to work mainly on translating instead of undertaking more extensive original writing.[10]

PATRICK'S "PLACES"

Assigning Frith a visit to Marburg after his flight from England rests mainly on the fact that he translated and published parts of the doctoral disputation that the young hero of the Scottish Reformation, Patrick Hamilton, wrote in Marburg under the tutelage of Francis Lambert of Avignon. Perhaps Frith attended the colloquy between Luther and Zwingli in Marburg in 1529 over the nature of the presence of Christ in the Lord's Supper, although Frith appears not to have matriculated at the Protestant university there.[11]

The translation of Hamilton's commonplace book on justifi-

8. See *Whole workes,* p. 115, where Frith linked himself with Tyndale as a translator.

9. Joye, *Apology,* ed. Arber, p. 33; the original, *STC* 14,820. Tyndale's biographers have acknowledged and answered only the latter half of the charge. Joye was explicit: "Frith wrote tindals answers to More for tindale/ and corrected them in the prynte/ and printed them to at Amelsterdam/ and whether he winked at T. opinion as one hauyng experience of Tindals complexion/ or was of the same opinion I cannot tel/ the man was ientle and quyet and wel lerned and better shuld have been yf he had liued."

10. *AM, 5,* 118. Henry Walter had Frith prematurely with Tyndale in 1526, resting on flimsy testimony of Spalatin and Cochlaeus; see PS *1,* pp. xxx f., esp. p. xxxi n.

11. See Fulop, p. 62.

cation by faith, while not necessarily indicating Frith's complete theological agreement with every point of the work, became a lasting contribution to English-speaking Christianity. The entire literary output of Frith makes only one fat volume of our sort, and *Patrick's Places,* probably first printed in 1529, was a slender tract. Yet after the rest of Frith's work fell into near oblivion, this tract enjoyed repeated discussion, reprinting, and praise through the centuries.

Hamilton returned from Marburg to his native Scotland, only to be condemned as a heretic and burnt February 29, 1528, just when Frith first fell under suspicion as a Lutheran sympathizer at Oxford. Hamilton, the scion of a Scottish noble family, had foregone auspicious opportunities for an ecclesiastical career because of strong Protestant convictions. John Knox, manager and historiographer of the Reformation in Scotland, named 1527 as the season when "it pleased God of his great mercy . . . to raise up his servant, MASTER PATRICK HAMILTON, at whom our History doth begin." [12] Within a year after Hamilton's martyrdom, Frith was turning into English this charter of Scottish Protestantism.

To the tract Frith added a terse preface, blessing God that "in these last days and perilous times" he "stirred up in all countries witnesses unto his Son, to testify the truth unto the unfaithful, to save at least some from the snares of Antichrist, which lead to perdition." He praised the martyred Patrick, noting that "God . . . hath reserved a little treatise" called "Patrick's Places: for it treateth exactly of certain common places, which known, ye have the pith of all divinity." Frith translated the treatise into English, Knox judged, "to the profit of my nation . . . that they may espy the deceitful paths of perdition, and return to the right way, which leadeth to life everlasting." [13] Frith's translation of the tract was published on the Continent in 1529; of this printing, a single quire is extant in the library of Emmanuel College, Cambridge. During the 1530s the piece was printed as *Dyuers frutful gatheringes of scrypture concernyng fayth a. workes* (*STC* 12,732–33).

---

12. Knox, *History of the Reformation in Scotland,* ed. W. C. Dickinson (2 vols. New York, 1949), *I,* 11.

13. "Patrick's Places," *AM, 4,* 563.

Probably the Redman edition is from 1534 and Copland's from the end of the following decade. Moreover, "Patrick's Places" soon earned a deserved popularity by being included in the 1535 Primer of John Gough, under a section headed "The nosegay or posee of lyght to lede and comfort al synner that walke in darknesse gadred out of the new testament." [14] In a 1539 list of books prohibited by the Church authorities in England appeared the entry "Spiritual Nosegay," perhaps referring to the "Places," but the book did not find its way into other such lists preserved to us, although these generally condemned Frith's works.

The early career of the work is of more than bibliographical interest, for the tract has been perhaps the most widely read of all early English Protestant writings save the Bible translations. It was popular again at the end of the sixteenth century as reprinted in Knox's *History of the Reformation in Scotland* and in Foxe's *Acts and Monuments*. Knox reproduced the treatise faithfully, omitting only whatever may have been the original title page, Frith's very brief preface to the Christian reader, and the identification of Frith as the translator. The "Places" appeared in the manuscript of Knox's book and in all printed editions since that of Vautrollier of 1586–87. Knox inserted the "Places" immediately after his account of the martyrdom of Hamilton, adding but one marginal note of significance at the section "Of Charitie." Hamilton had made love of neighbor a demand applicable equally to all regardless of the character of the neighbor. Apparently this was too radically Lutheran to suit Knox, who noted, "This is to be vnderstood of circumstance of worldly men and not of them of god for the nerer that men draw to God we are bound the more to loue them." [15]

Foxe far less faithfully inserted the "Places" into his martyrology. Hamilton found no place in the edition of 1563, but his story and his book, in Frith's translation with Frith's preface and with Frith identified as translator, were included in the

14. C. C. Butterworth, *The English Primers 1529–1545* (Philadelphia, 1953), pp. 127 f., 314.

15. Knox, [*The first (second and thirde) booke of the History of the Reformation of religioun within the realme of Scotland . . .*] (London, 1587; STC 15,071), p. 33.

1570 book and all subsequent versions. Foxe introduced (or reproduced) many changes. The format of the "Places" became that of an academic disputation. He noted propositions, premises, antitheta, conclusions, etc. not only in margins but in the text itself. A number of verbally minor changes bore theological significance. The prescription of faith as alone justifying before God was markedly qualified in the direction of emphasizing the necessity of works. Moreover Foxe's version subjoined to the work a set of "brief" interpretative notes, almost as extensive as the original tract. The final notes raised cautions "to be observed and avoided in the true understanding of the Law." Law and gospel were to be distinguished carefully in scripture. But the distinction was for the sake of a proper conjunction of the two in doctrinal matters. Preachers were warned that the injunctions of the law were to be set aside pastorally in the case of repentant sinners, and the tidings of the gospel were to be set aside in the case of unrepentant worldlings. Finally, "in public order of doctrine, let every discreet preacher put a difference between the broken heart of the mourning sinner, and the unrepentant worldling, and so conjoin both the law with the gospel, and the gospel with the law, that in throwing down the wicked, ever he spare the weak-hearted; and again, so spare the weak, that he do not encourage the ungodly." [16]

These neat dogmatic distinctions between law and gospel would popularly be ascribed to the Calvinistic theological tradition, not the Anglican. Yet the doctrinally dour Calvinist, Knox, remained true to the original emphasis upon faith-justification of Hamilton—and Frith—and the Anglican Foxe drew fine lines between the demands of the law and the demands of the gospel, finding law in the New Testament as well as in the Old. A similar shift in the theology of Barnes occurred between the 1531 and 1534 editions of his *Supplication,* and it will be seen that Tyndale in 1530 thus changed his theology. While the shift here described cannot be dated with accuracy nor attributed to Frith, it is interesting to note how drastically Foxe tempered the radical theology of the "Places." [17] In order to

16. *AM, 4,* 572–78.
17. I am unable to suggest from whose hand came the Foxean version of Hamilton's theses. It is somewhat mystifying that Hamilton's biographer cited

view the document in a form true to the original, the reader of more modern works must rely on the title and preface from Foxe and on the body of the work from Knox, or else Hamilton's argument and (presumably) Frith's theological conviction that "all that is in faith done pleaseth God" will read "he that hath faith is just and good"—a substantial variation.[18]

The theological import of Frith's translation of Hamilton lies not in the presentation of anything previously unsaid by Luther, but rather in the fact that here, much more succinctly and clearly than in Tyndale's early writings, the radical Protestant understanding of justification by faith was asserted in English. Indeed God gave a law, Hamilton held, but only to reveal man's evil and to drive him to faith. Faith was *fiducia* not *assensus,* and radical trust was the only availing stance of man *coram deo*. Gospel showed the remedy to the sin exposed by law; a word of grace supplanted a word of wrath; comfort and peace replaced unrest and despair. Law said to pay one's debt, gospel said Christ has paid one's debt. Faith, holding fast to the promise of God, was the opposite of sin, holding fast to one's own deeds and merits. Faith made a good tree, unfaith an evil tree, and each tree bore its proper fruit. To trust in one's works was to arrogate the place of Christ, while to trust in Christ was to find a merciful Lord who did all freely for man. Hamilton argued that understanding of justification by faith with inexorable logic, with urgency springing from personal involvement, and in language calculated to evangelize. When Frith published "Patrick's Places," he put into English a statement of the total dependence of man upon God for salvation, which for its consistency and clarity was rivaled, if then, only when Cranmer composed the Homily on Salvation.

Luther's "Antichrist"

While it is impossible to know which of Frith's two early translated works was published first, it is known that on July 12,

---

him from Foxe rather than from Knox; see Peter Lorimer, *Patrick Hamilton, Precursors of Knox, 1* (Edinburgh, 1857), 110–16, 128–31. Lorimer thought he had proved Hamilton's acquaintance with and dependence upon Tyndale's *Wicked Mammon*, but he did not notice that the latter tract was largely a translation from Luther; see ibid., pp. 95–97, 233–34.

18. Knox, *History of the Reformation, 2,* 223.

1529, he published, under the pseudonym Richard Brightwell, from the press of John Hoochstraten in Antwerp, an English rendition of Luther's *De Antichristo*.[19] The work's three distinct parts were clearly indicated by the title:

¶ *A pistle to | the Christen reader*
¶ *The Revelation of Antichrist.*
¶ *Antithesis/ wherein are compa|red to geder Christes actes | and oure holye father | the Popes* (STC 11,394).

Only the first section represents Frith's original work.[20] The "Revelation" is a stodgy but faithful translation, obviously from Luther's 1521 Latin rather than from any of the German translations, of the commentary on Daniel 8 concerning antichrist. "Antithesis" consists of seventy-eight contrasts between Christ and the Pope, heavily dependent upon *Passional Christi und Antichristi* (1521), a little tract comprising twenty-six woodcuts representing the deeds of Jesus contrasted with those of the Pope, made from designs by Hans Cranach, and brief contrasts of scriptural verses and statements drawn from the canon law. Frith's "Antithesis" elaborated the original German piece, which was frequently counterfeited in Germany. It is possible that Frith worked entirely from some expanded edition. Many of the biblical verses and canonical excerpts of "Antithesis" appeared in the 1521 German tract, said to have been by Luther but actually by Melanchthon, and originally printed by J. Grunenberg in Wittenberg.

Frith's publication was quickly recognized as Luther's when it arrived in England, for an early Henrician list of proscribed books entered "The revelation of antichrist of Luther." [21]

19. Luther, *Ad Librvm Eximii Magistri Nostri, Magistri Ambrosii Catharini, Defensoris Silvestri Prieratis Acerrimi, Responsio Martini Lutheri. Cum exposita uisione Danielis .viij. De Antichristo.* The text of the tract is found in *WA*, 7, 705–78; Frith translated the portions on pp. 722–72 and part of the last paragraph of p. 778. See my "The Earliest Translations of Luther into English." If Frith's pseudonym has significance, it has escaped me. A modern Luther translator Englished the piece again, as he thought for the first time; see Luther, *The Pope Confounded . . . ,* tr. H. Cole (London, 1836).

20. Fols. i–xii; despite the suspicion of Frith's modern editor, Thomas Russell; see *Works* (1831), *3,* 457. On Melanchthon's authorship of *Passional Christi,* see C. L. Manschreck, *Melanchthon* (New York, 1958), pp. 89–91.

21. Exeter Register (Voysey) fol. 62, in D. Wilkins, ed., *Concilia Magnae Britanniae et Hiberniae* (4 vols. London, 1737), *3,* 707.

There appears to have been only one printing of the work, in spite of the fact that it was equaled as a popular Protestant tract by only a few books of the period, such as Simon Fish's *A Supplicacyon for the Beggers* (*STC* 10,883), *Patrick's Places,* and a doggerel lampoon of Wolsey by William Roy and Jerome Barlowe. The work taught Luther's understanding of faith, not the compromised notion of double justification adopted by Tyndale, Barnes, and others in the early 1530s.

The heart of the book, Luther's exposition of Daniel 8, identified the fourth kingdom prophesied by Daniel with the temporal rulership of the popes who set themselves over the Germans by replacing faith with works and by distorting the true way of Christ into sects of religion. These sects were typified by monastic orders which produced a proud, self-regarding religion that despised the common life. The argument, as would be expected of Luther, was learned, intelligent, subtle, biblical, and above all theocentric. The popularly appealing "Antithesis" summarized the work on the note that Christ drew men to God by humble witness to the Father's mercy and love, while the one who claimed to be vicar of Christ fended men from God by haughty and prideful claims to be the dispenser of God's judgment upon earth. The summary attributed all initiative in true religion to God and saw the work of Christ as proper response to that initiative.

To these translated tracts Frith added a clever introductory epistle of his own. The potency of the forces of evil over man, he said, made urgent man's reconciliation with God. To believe Christ demanded not assent but trust. "It is not therfore sufficient to beleve that he is a sauiour and redemer: but that he is a sauiour and redemer vnto the/ and this canst thou not confesse/ excepte thou knowleg thy self to be a sinner/ for he that thinketh him silf no sinner/ neadith no sauiour and redemer. . . . Therefore knowlege thy silf a sinner *that* thou maist by iustifyed." [22] Against that justification worked devil, flesh, and world, embodied in the religion of the glory of man sponsored by Pope and official Church. Whatever persecuted the spirit was born of the flesh; the popes, cardinals, bishops, and their adherents persecuted the spirit; therefore the official Church

22. *A Pistle* . . . , iij^r.

was carnal antichrist. Frith cited Psalm 73, from which Leo X
had drawn the title of his bull excommunicating Luther, and
cleverly turned the argument against the papal Church by identifying it as the enemy of God.

It is impossible to know the precise nature of Frith's introduction to Protestant Christianity during the earlier days when
he was exposed to it in the circle of scholars at Cambridge and
Oxford. Nor is it certainly known to what place on the Continent he withdrew in 1528. But it is beyond question that his first
literary involvement with the Protestant movement drew on
German Protestant thought as it was coming to expression in
Wittenberg and Marburg. From Luther directly, and from
Francis Lambert via Patrick Hamilton, Frith made translations into English which thrust him into importance as a Protestant. On that foundation he then built his more original, although still dependent, theology, and then he launched his own
active leadership of the English Brethren for the last two years
of his life. For one reason or another, he engaged himself more
against English Catholic defenses of purgatory than with German theology, and he undertook to formulate an English sacramental theology drawn not from Luther, Lambert, or any other
Wittenberger or Marburger, but from Oecolampadius of Basel.

THE ABOLITION OF PURGATORY

By controverting English Catholic writers on the subject of
purgatory, Frith involved himself not only in a theological issue
salient to the Reformation but also in a stream of religious
libelli which sprang from Fisher's early anti-Lutheran books
and in 1529 began to flow profusely. During the previous year
Simon Fish, a gentleman of Gray's Inn, had written a lampoon
of purgatory which during 1529 achieved great popularity in
London. Fish minced no words in appealing to the monarch in
the name of justice and decency to bring the Church and its
hierarchy under discipline. The wealth and legal independence
of the spiritualty, he argued, fostered much social and personal
immorality, and to remedy the situation would only restore
Henry's royal prerogatives by subordinating to himself the
temporal interests of the Church. Fish pictured the doctrine of
purgatory and the penitential practices attendant upon it as the

means by which the spiritualty robbed the commonwealth. Many learned men, he asserted, held purgatory to be an unscriptural, false device manufactured by the hierarchy for its own gain. The pamphlet appeared after More had been licensed to read and commissioned to refute Protestant writings; before his advancement to the chancellorship of the realm on October 25, 1529, he had published a reply.[23]

More's reply sparked Frith to undertake a major work on purgatory, especially since More's defence of the doctrine was at odds with the earlier defence by Fisher in his *Assertionis Lutheranae confutatio* (1523). Frith asked a friend at home to send a copy of More's book, which he received along with others "vpon S. Thomas day before Christmasse, the yeare of our Sauiour a.M.ccccc.&xxx." The friend sent "one moe of Rastels makyng, wherin he goeth about to proue Purgatory, by naturall Philosophie." Frith "was meruelously desirous and tickled to see what reasons he brought for his probations." Frith resolved to dispute John Rastell's weak arguments because they impugned Christ's blood. He then read More. Rastell's work, *A New Boke of Purgatory* (*STC* 20,719), published October 10, 1530, was borrowed from More's, and much that More contended seemed to derive from Fisher. Therefore Frith "made . . . diligent enquire to come by my Lord of Rochesters booke which also writeth on the same matter," and reading and comparing these three writers convinced him that they brought "small probations & slender reasons," for purgatory, "considering also that they are the chiefest frendes, proctours and patrones therof, and that they had applied many reasons and Scriptures for their purpose (for lacke of matter) that rather made against them: yea and not that onely, but also that they dissented betwene them selues in their probations. . . . These thynges considered, it made mine hart yerne and fully to consent, that this their paynefull Purgatory was but a vayne imagination, and that it hath of long time but deceaued the people and milked them from their money." [24]

23. More, *The supplycacyon of soulys Made by syr Thomas More knyght councellour to our souerayn lorde the Kynge and chauncellour of hys Duchy of Lancaster. Agaynst the supplycacyon of beggars* (*STC* 18,092); in More, *Workes*, pp. 288–339. On Fish and his pamphlet, see below, ch. 10.

24. *Whole workes*, pp. 4 f.

The formulations of his adversaries made it easy for Frith
to divide his book into three parts, a philosophical treatment of
the subject contradicting Rastell, a scriptural debate against
More, and a briefer dispute with Fisher over patristic authorities. Fisher from 1530 onwards was on the shelf as far as theological polemics were concerned, and the argument in that
quarter went no farther than Frith's answer. After acceding to
the chancellorship, More was too busy to refute Frith's work
on purgatory, and forthcoming debates between these men
would turn upon the sacraments. But Rastell, barrister and
printer at London and brother-in-law of More, took up the
cudgels, wrote a reply to Frith while the latter was in the Tower,
read Frith's subsequent arguments on the subject, and was converted to his adversary's position. Such at least was the story
preserved by Foxe in the 1572 edition of Frith's works. Rastell
became impoverished later in life, and died in 1536, but left
a son, William, printer, judge, and stanch Catholic under Mary
Tudor.

Frith's big book on purgatory, *A disputacion of purgatorye
made by Iohan Frith which is deuided in to thre bokes* (*STC*
11,388), printed at Antwerp in mid-1531,[25] together with the
later and subsidiary reply to Rastell, furnish full details of his
thought on this and kindred matters, and reveal a polemicist
far more seriously concerned with the details of his subject than
was customary for his day. The personalities and foibles of his
enemies were passed over, save for an occasional thrust at rank
inconsistencies. His final appeal was always to scripture, to
stand against which constituted the unpardonable sin against
the Holy Ghost. Yet for Frith the very words of scripture themselves fell under test by the word of God conveyed by the gospel
of Christ in the whole Bible. Granting that knowledge of scripture waxed and waned from age to age, he attributed contemporary evils and abuses in the Church to its long seclusion from
the fount of the word of God. Appeal to scripture demanded
careful exercise of reason, but reason could accomplish nothing theologically or religiously of its own strength. The *Dis-*

25. *Ned. Bibl.* 3043 (*STC* 11,388) assigns the book to the press of Symon Cock
in Antwerp, 1531; this is the original edition. *Ned. Bibl.* 0526 (*STC* 11,387) is
the reprint.

putation of Purgatory abounded in scriptural citations, most of
them from the New Testament and remarkably many of these
from the Epistle to the Romans; Frith cited eighteen Old Testament and fourteen New Testament books.

Yet the proof-text method was not Frith's. He strongly preferred grammatical exegesis, although allegory was allowed
where indicated by the text. He used the Old Testament as
typologically christological, but more important than that was
the strong christocentrism that gave meaning to Old Testament texts. Strictly grammatical study of scripture seemed to
Frith arid and unproductive. The author knew Hebrew and
Greek well, and chided More for failing to refer to the Greek
text or even to the Latin translation of his friend Erasmus.
He relied upon patristic and medieval expositors only when
they agreed with scripture and when their expositions were controlled by the word of God within scripture, yet he interpreted
these historically in the light of the times, places, and interests
in which they wrote.

Frith found the purgatory taught by the Church nowhere in
scripture. Moreover, it negated his principle of man's universal
inability to make satisfactions to God. Purgatives of sin were
of two sorts only: the word of God received through faith,
and the spiritual cross of Christ borne through "aduersitie,
tribulation, worldly depression . . . [which] is called the
rodde or scourge of God wherewith he scourgeth euery sonne
that he receaueth." [26] Faithless clergy repudiated these genuine "purgatories" and invented another which contravened
the character of God, the uniqueness of Christ, the promises
of scripture, and the circumstance of man. Their invention
made God's justice into an attribute functioning independently
of the attributes of mercy and goodness, and answerable to
human standards of justice; these distortions attended every
portrayal of God as exacting human satisfaction for sin and
as demanding revenge instead of proffering redemption. Purgatory caused redemption to hinge on man's repentance rather
than God's free gift of grace. By emphasizing that point Rastell
"harpeth all of one string," and that one "out of tune." [27]

26. *Whole workes*, p. 5.
27. Ibid., p. 18.

The blood of Christ, to Frith's mind, wrought the only true satisfaction to God and the only Christian purgation of man. To seek another demeaned Christ. He would not have Christ's righteousness imputed to man, even though those chosen in Christ were *simul peccator ac iustus;* they were righteous because, being in Christ, God did not impute to them their sins. Moreover, the Catholic purgatory arrogated to Pope and clergy the proper work of God and his spirit—the distribution of the merits of Christ's passion. Thus manward as well as Godward the purgatory doctrine robbed Christ of his honor. By another arrogance the Pope measured and claimed the benefits of saints' merits, when in truth, as Frith saw it, they should have none if God entered into judgment against them. Purgatory was scripturally baseless. Worse than that it made God's promises in scripture into lies. Scripture held out Christ as mediator and advocate for sinners before God, but the Pope set up purgatory as another mediator and advocate. Where scripture made Christ the only door into the sheepfold and the only way to the Father, purgatory indicated another entry and another route. Christ invited the troubled to come to him for rest but the Church devised torments for the heavy laden. Scripture knew only one satisfaction for sin, the death of Christ, but purgatory's satisfactions rendered his death futile.

Frith thought that his opponents, especially More, by arguing for purgatory from Old Testament sacrifices, misunderstood their prefigurement of the one, true, efficacious, sufficient atonement of Christ. Thus the papal Church would make men into Jews, not Christians. Purgatory deluded the sinner into thinking himself capable of making satisfaction, and that very thought was itself the root of sin. The Pope might bind and loose under his own laws but not on behalf of God, for only God's word might truly bind and loose by being preached faithfully and received trustfully. Would the Pope loose souls from purgatory he should go there and preach the word of God— that, not dropping pennies into St. Dominic's box, would assist the souls of the departed. At any rate, they needed neither human nor ecclesiastical assistance, for they were committed to the grace and judgment of God alone.

The foregoing theological concerns gave substance to Frith's

writings on purgatory; he allowed their form to be determined
by the arguments of his opponents, first Rastell, then More and
Fisher, and Rastell again. Thus the works dealt with a number of theologically tangential matters: contemporary ecclesiastical claims and practices, scholastic defenses of purgatory, al-
legories of scriptural passages. Frith's patience in handling
these distractions shows that he always remembered that a
youthful bachelor of arts whose minor academic preferment
had been revoked for suspicion of heresy might not easily refute a centuries-old and religiously central dogma as defended
by the two leading humanistic scholars of England. Among his
opponents, to Rastell alone was he nearly equal in education
and status. Consciousness of being an upstart freighted his discussion with respect but burdened it with no intellectual timid-
ity. If More was foolish enough to plead for purgatory on the
basis of its having been believed and taught *semper ac ab
omnibus,* Frith was bold enough to reveal the folly by showing
from Augustine's *Enchiridion* that purgatory was no doctrine
of faith in the fifth-century Latin church. Tetzel's offensive
management of Archbishop Albrecht's indulgence sale, and
Luther's attack upon it, held no special fascination for Frith,
yet he did not avoid the subjects when his adversaries chose that
ground. Where More derived inferences of purgatorial doctrine from I Corinthians 3, Frith advanced a detailed exegesis
of the passage to show that even if purgatory were implied,
Paul applied it only to preachers; "therfore may the temporaltie be of good comfort, for I promise them that by this texte
they shall neuer haue hurt in this their [i.e. the clergy's] pain-
full Purgatory." [28]

The *Disputation of Purgatory* articulated Frith's full
thought on the topic and presented a well-reasoned understanding of Luther's conception of justification by grace alone
through faith. By the time the young Englishman came to answer Rastell's reply to this book, he was imprisoned in the
Tower of London awaiting events that would make him a martyr. Between the *Disputation* and the answer to Rastell there
intervened little, if any, more than two years. These were years
of crisis for the English Protestants, years during which two

28. Ibid., p. 44.

Protestant book-sellers in England and the Protestant preachers Bilney and Tewkesbury were arrested and executed; the setback to the Protestants came when they were deserted by the turncoat George Constantine.[29] During these same two years Robert Barnes shifted from a single-minded position on justification by faith to a compromised position of double justification. Precisely that shift was the question posed by Rastell's objection to Frith, a well-worn query in Reformation controversies but nevertheless a perplexing one for Rastell—how might evil deeds be restrained unless good works either avoided or shortened the soul's purgatorial pilgrimage?

Frith had dismissed the question as wrongheaded in the first book on purgatory. When he replied to Rastell in late 1532 or early 1533, the question commanded respect. A distinction must be drawn, he argued, between penitence as a work unavailing in justification, and true repentance which followed upon justification as a fruit of faith. Love of Christ brought hatred of sin. While works before justification were sinful, works after justification at once glorified God, sought the profit of the neighbor, and also gave evidence among men that justification had been accomplished. Good works "are a testimony to them that doth them by the which men may know *that* he is *the* very sonne of God, is that not auaylable?" [30] Frith specifically denied that this proof of justification played any part in man's justification before God, and he stopped short of Barnes' position, which, like Tyndale's, concluded that good works constituted a necessary justification before man. With Frith, good works availed to glorify the Christ whose redemption made them possible, not the man through whom they were wrought. In answering Rastell's question, Frith refused to dilute the finely stated, unqualified christological theocentrism that permeated his earlier work.

TYNDALE'S "ANSWER"

Frith remained on the Continent from September 1528 until about St. James' Day, July 25, 1532, except for a visit to Eng-

29. See Rupp, passim; the crisis was aptly summarized by Doernberg, *Henry VIII and Luther,* p. 98.
30. *Whole workes,* p. 76.

land during Lent in 1531.[31] While the occasions and events of
these journeys will demand later attention, it is to be noted
that the two translations, of Hamilton's *Places* and Luther's
De Antichristo, and the single original work on purgatory, are
the only extant writings generally conceded to have come from
Frith's hand while he was in exile. George Joye testified that
there was indeed another literary work by Frith, namely, Tyndale's *An answere vnto Sir T. Mores dialoge* (*STC* 24,437;
Ned. Bibl. 3988). Tyndale's biographers have acknowledged
that Frith saw this production through the press; Joye flatly
ascribed authorship to Frith, but since the ascription appeared
in a work full of accusations against Tyndale, it has not been
taken seriously. More to the point, the ascription's immediate
context was Joye's pique, not at Tyndale, but at Frith, for his
not having answered letters which Joye sent him in the Tower.
Joye complained that Frith "had . . . a longe tyme aftir in
the tower to haue wryten/ if he had sene his parte good:[.] " [32]
Were Joye's charge entirely reckless, why should it redound
to Frith's credit in this context? Tyndale's most competent
biographer noted Joye's statement, but did not deem it worth
consideration, since "Joye is not a careful writer," for Joye
had Frith seeing the *Answer to More* through the printing at
"Amelsterdam"; Mozley accepted the judgment of the bibliog-
raphers that the printing took place in Antwerp, but found
Joye reliable as to the date of Frith's presence in Holland.[33]
Even if the book, along with Frith's *Disputation of Purgatory,*
was printed by Symon Cock in Antwerp at the end of June 1531,
rather than in Amsterdam during the previous month as one
might conclude from Stephen Vaughan's letters of the times, the
larger rôle which Joye gave to Frith in preparing Tyndale's
Answer must be held open to some credibility.

The manner of citing the New Testament which runs through
the *Answer* points to Frith. Tyndale, in his undisputed writings
and translations, naturally preferred the readings of his own
1526—and later the 1534—New Testament. Frith was not so

31. "Acta et processus contra Johannem Fryth hereticum obstinatum et im-
penitentem," Stokesley Register, second series of folios, 71, printed in *AM, 5,*
appendix XXII.
32. *Apology,* ed. Arber, p. 32; the accusation, in the original edition, E.i.
33. Mozley, *William Tyndale,* pp. 200 f.

inclined, but remained content to argue from the Latin Bible provided the sense of the Greek was not thus impaired. Such is the case in the *Answer* where several of More's interpretations are debated on the basis of the Latin text. Frith was given to digesting long passages of the New Testament into pithy summaries, employing Tyndale's English as a source for key words but departing from that text wherever the sense of the passage might be conveyed by a word fitting the context of the argument. The *Answer* is replete with such summaries. There is lacking in this writing, to be sure, the deliberate substitution of different and clumsy English words for the terminology of the Tyndale New Testament which pervades a later tract, *The Souper of the Lorde* (*STC* 24,468–71), long ascribed to Tyndale, but actually written by Joye on the basis of Zwingli.[34] The manner of biblical quotations of the *Answer,* while not utterly foreign to that of Tyndale, is at many points characteristic of Frith.

On the other side of the argument, Frith commonly referred to the famous bishop of Hippo as "S. Austin" or "Austine" or "Austen," while Tyndale preferred the Latin form of the name. Here the *Answer* stands with Tyndale. Moreover, Frith certainly passed up opportunities to take credit or part credit for the work. Twice in the *Disputation of Purgatory,* while discussing whether the Church might err, he referred to the *Answer to More* as settling the point. The first instance noted that "William Tyndall hath declared aboundantly [on the subject] in a treatise which by Goddes grace you shall shortly haue," and the second referred readers "vnto a woorke that William Tyndal hath written agaynst M. More." [35]

Joye alleged specifically that Frith had written "the answers to More for tindale" without taking credit. A close examination of the work allows Joye to be taken quite literally. Frith was not the composer of the treatise replying to More's *Dialogue.* He wrote for Tyndale precisely the answers to More, particularly under the heading "The solutions and answeres vnto

---

34. See W. D. J. Cargill Thompson, "Who Wrote 'The Supper of the Lord'?," *Harvard Theological Review, 53* (1960), 77–91, and my "More Evidence that George Joye Wrote The Souper of the Lorde," ibid., *55* (1962), 63–66.
35. *Whole workes,* pp. 46, 56.

M. Mores [books]." The discussion on what the church is, the
explanations of Tyndale's choices of words in the New Testament, and the sections on ecclesiastical error, worship, ceremonies, and sacraments, may safely be ascribed to Tyndale—
with some dependence, for the account of the significance of
ceremonies, either upon Durandus as More thought, or, perhaps more likely, upon *Vom alten und neuen Gott, Glauben
und Lehre* (1521).[36] The portions specifically answering, point
for point, the four books of More's *Dialogue* were of a rather
different style, especially the answers to books three and four,
which cite a paragraph from More, then place an answer in
the next paragraph under the name of Tyndale. It is pre-
eminently in these sections that Frith's manner of citing the
New Testament appears, and the arguments follow the fashion of Frith's *Purgatory.* No detraction from the name and
reputation of Tyndale attends the conclusion that Frith, who
during 1530 and early 1531 was helping Tyndale translate
portions of the Old Testament, worked carefully through
More's *Dialogue* as he worked carefully through *Supplication
of Souls,* extracting paragraphs that bore heavily on theological issues at stake between More and the Protestants, writing
answers to one set of paragraphs for inclusion in the *Disputation of Purgatory* and answers to another set for inclusion in
Tyndale's *Answer to More.* Joye's accusation taken literally is
fully credible, and Frith may be assigned the rôles, with respect
to the *Answer to More,* of research assistant and supervisor of
printing.

The material in Tyndale's book which may be ascribed to
Frith, however, neither adds to nor detracts from the picture
of Frith as a theologian drawn from his books on purgatory.
It is notable that in the discussions of faith and works, which
fall mostly in the answer to the fourth book of More, the theological position of the *Answer* is that good works prior to faith-
justification are evil and that those performed on the basis of
faith have nothing to do with justification itself—a position

36. See More, *Confutation,* lxv, quoted in PS *3,* p. 73 n. See Judas Nazarei,
pseud. [Joachim Vadianus (or von Watt), supposed author], *Vom Alten und
Neuen Gott, Glauben und Lehre* (*1521*), ed. E. Kück, Flugschriften aus der
Reformationszeit, *12* (Halle, 1896); but more recent studies of Vadianus tend
to doubt Kück's ascription; cf. below, ch. 10, esp. n. 18.

precisely that of Frith rather than of Tyndale at this juncture.

By choosing purgatory as his chief theological interest of the first phase of polemical activity, Frith entered battle against the captains of English Catholicism's defensive war, Fisher and More. It was his notion that the whole edifice of Catholic religiosity and Catholic temporal wealth rested on this very doctrine. A false doctrine it indeed seemed, because it attributed the achievement of redemption to man's endeavors and the disbursement of grace to the Church's hierarchy. On both scores purgatory abrogated scripture. Primarily a theological offense, the falsity of the dogma and practice was provable by appeal to the Bible and to reason. Catholic religion, Frith reasoned, refused to take the second place after God. God provided redemption for the whole man in Christ: by means of the cross of Christ the body of man was purged, by means of the word of God the soul was purged. Thus by free grace salvation was given to faith. The Church displayed the consummate vanity of man when it elbowed into the transaction of redemption, imagining a human condition which God's grace could not redeem and inventing purgatory to make it redeemable by man and church. That a young upstart like Frith became the bane of More in subsequent years suggests that he had struck his blow near to the Achilles' heel of Catholicism. If there was another vulnerable spot, it was the dogma of transubstantiation, with its religiosity of the mass. Frith assailed just this spot during the months remaining for him to live. But to engage in that attack he forfeited the relative safety of his exile.

7. Frith's Theology

WHEN John Firth returned from the Continent to take active leadership of the persecuted Protestants in England, the necessary secrecy and deviousness of his work shrouded a brief phase of his career with a mystery unexplainable on extant data. He was in England during Lent in 1531 surveying the predicament of the Brethren. He then returned to the Continent in order to publish his book on purgatory and the reply to More's *Dialogue*. Barnes' trip to England late in 1531 had proved altogether abortive, and within a few months after Frith's return to Antwerp in early 1532, he determined again to go home, regardless of the consequences. From late July until October he moved about England building the courage of his oppressed fellow believers. Probably during these months he wrote a comment on the Protestant last will and testament of one William Tracy, sending a manuscript copy to Tyndale who saved it for eventual posthumous publication as *The testament of master Wylliam Tracie esquier, expounded both by W. Tindall and J. Frith* (*STC* 24,167; *Ned. Bibl.* 3997). Imprisonment from October 1532 until his execution in early July 1533 provided for Frith an unlikely opportunity for writing. He exploited it fully.

Writings from England by Frith, for the most part composed in the Tower of London, reveal the extent of his theological independence and intellectual brilliance. Books, pamphlets, and letters evidence a fertile mind ranging over subjects such as justification, ecclesiology, ethics, baptism, Lord's Supper, purgatory. From them a picture may be constructed of Frith as the most radically theocentric of all the early English

Protestants—theocentric in the decisions that he made as well as in the theology that he advanced. This chapter discusses that theocentrism of action and thought; the next chapter will investigate Frith's more direct contribution to the English Reformation as a theologian of the sacraments.

The End of Exile

The big book on purgatory and Tyndale's *Answer to More's Dialogue* seem to have been delayed in the printing by Frith's hasty reconnoitering trip to England during Lent in 1531. At that time Thomas Cromwell and his agent on the Continent, Stephen Vaughan, were anxious that English Protestants come home to present their cause before the King in order that a consistent and well-supported royal religious policy might be struck. To that end Barnes, conveniently important as a negotiator with Wittenberg on the royal divorce, was guaranteed safety during his journey to England late in 1531. Vaughan's letters to Cromwell reveal efforts at the same time to induce Tyndale to return. To what extent these entreaties led Frith to determine upon a trip home remains unknown; his summary arrest upon his arrival excludes any surmise that he might have been traveling under a safe-conduct from the Crown.

Distribution of Protestant books had become not only difficult but dangerous in England, owing to More's efforts to apprehend dealers and owners of such books and to end their spreading pestiferous heresies. That much is apparent from the vehement tone of the preface to More's *Confutation of Tyndale's Answer*, written in January 1532. More had persuaded George Constantine to defect from Protestant ranks and to inform on his erstwhile allies; later Constantine returned to his previous loyalty. At any rate More had new information on the book trade from Constantine. Frith's trip seems to have aimed at imploring Constantine to desist from informing More, and at finding agents to replace him. Specifically Frith attempted to enlist the assistance of the prior of Reading in the book trade.

Through his elaborate and strikingly accurate intelligence network, More learned of Frith's visit and ordered his arrest in March 1531 in Reading. As Foxe received and transmitted the story, Frith was arrested for a vagabond and put in stocks. After some time, being "almost pined with hunger," he asked to talk with the local schoolmaster, one Leonard Cox, who had studied at Cambridge. Frith bewailed his plight to Cox in Latin, winning Cox's sympathy and further attention. High converse ensued until they passed over into Greek; Frith recited from memory opening passages of the Iliad, moving Cox to seek and gain his release. More's orders frustrated, Frith escaped the country and returned to Antwerp to publish *Disputation of Purgatory* and the *Answer to More's Dialogue*.[1]

Frith left England about Easter 1531 and was in Antwerp through the summer. A year later he returned home to lead the Brethren, after several of their key men were burnt. No known writing from Frith is attributable with certainty to this year. Was he on the Continent for the whole of that time? At his trial he was charged with visiting England at Lent 1531 and with returning there in July 1532; he confirmed the allegations. What of the intervening months? Probably not accidentally, these times are markedly silent concerning the activities of Barnes, Tyndale, and Joye as well as of Frith. The silence was broken by Frith's last return to England, but continued some months longer with respect to the others. Perhaps the English Protestants were perplexed by the seemingly contradictory attitudes and actions of the authorities at home. Cromwell, through Vaughan, was sending entreaties under implicit royal approbation that these men should accept safe-conduct guarantees to return home and present their case openly to the King and his advisers. More, through Constantine and other informers, was efficiently tracking the same men's actions and writings, threatening apprehension abroad, death at home, and eradication of the movement for which they lived and worked. Barnes, holding the trump card of Wittenberg opinion on the divorce, accepted a safe-conduct but, by his own and Frith's accounts, was nevertheless threatened with burning by the re-

---

1. *AM,* 5, 5 f.; Mozley, *William Tyndale,* pp. 245 f., followed out Foxe's implications and had the incident occur on Frith's last return to England in 1532. But Fulop, "John Frith," placed it in 1531. Since More resigned as chancellor May 16, 1532, and by Frith's own testimony his trips to England were in Lent 1531 and again about July 25, 1532, Fulop's judgment is to be accepted.

lentless More; Frith had seen the guarantee extended to Barnes in early autumn 1531 for Barnes had showed it to him in Antwerp. Tyndale declined all such invitations.

From surmises and shreds of evidence the impression arises of men busily shifting their residence and dress to escape notice by the agents both of Cromwell and of More, yet communicating with one another, perhaps after mutual counsel deciding that Frith should go surreptitiously to Reading to enlist new leaders, then later on advising Barnes to use the safe-conduct to discover what he could about the real religious designs of the royal court; Tyndale, they may have determined, must hold fast to his project, which was succeeding despite all efforts to the contrary, and, indeed, must by its very nature succeed: spreading the knowledge of God's word among God's people.

Meanwhile, in England, More closed in on the influential leaders of the Brethren. Richard Bayfield, able importer and distributer of English Protestant books, was burnt late in 1531, following Bilney in death. About the same time Thomas Dusgate, who had placarded Reformation principles on English church doors, was burnt outside Exeter. In the spring of 1532, Hugh Latimer stood trial before the bishops in Convocation and was forced, in spite of an appeal from the bishops' court to the King, to recant his mildly Protestant opinions. In February 1532 James Bainham, lawyer and arch-Protestant, abjured, bore a fagot, and paid his fine, but in the next month he dramatically recanted the abjuration and was burnt at Smithfield April 30, 1532. Tyndale's former helper, William Roy, translator of Wittenberg and Rhineland religious tracts as well as lampooner of Wolsey, had been killed as a heretic in Portugal, according to More's usually reliable information.[2]

Then came the news that More had resigned his post as lord chancellor of the realm! The official defender of the Catholic Church in England, the assiduous executor of Protestants and other rebellious children of Mother Church, had at last fallen into the bad graces of the nominal defender of the faith who was having his way with his wives and with the recently submitted clergy and bishops. The new development provided new

2. The most reliable modern summary of the activities of these men is by Rupp, *Studies,* passim.

opportunities for the Protestants which must be intelligently and realistically explored, but the opportunities came just when no trusted leader was left in England to do the exploring. Of the two men who had made trips to England, Frith, not Barnes, had brought off his project. In spite of his recently having shouldered family responsibilities in Holland, the reconnoitering task fell to Frith. Perhaps after settling affairs for his family, and possibly after determining that the next Protestant attack must be aimed at the dogma and practice of the Catholic sacraments, Frith sailed for England in the summer of 1532, arriving about July 25. After some ten weeks he had discovered that the Protestants' opportunities under a royally dominated Church were no happier than they had been under a rigorously Catholic chancellor. He was hounded at every step. Worn by attempts to evade the authorities, he determined in early October 1532 to escape. But at Milton Shore, near Southend in Essex, ready to ship for Antwerp, Frith was arrested. During imprisonment in the Tower he did more writing and maintained contact with the Brethren who circulated and published the writings. The same contacts made it possible for one William Holt, a tailor, to play the rôle of agent provocateur by inducing Frith to lend him a manuscript which, in the hands of the authorities, gave grounds for firm accusations of the heresy of sacramentarianism, a teaching intolerable to the King.

TRIAL

On June 20, 1533, Frith stood trial before the bishops of London, Winchester, and Lincoln at St. Paul's; they condemned him and sentenced him to be burnt at Smithfield on July 4, 1533. Thus summarized, the story of Frith's trial is simple, direct, and credible.

John Foxe, however, came upon information by which to elaborate the narrative of Frith's examination, and he appended this hagiographical tale to the 1583 edition of *Acts and Monuments*. When Frith had been in the Tower some three months, a royal chaplain's Lenten sermon brought his case to the King's attention by complaining that sacramentarianism flourished because lax disciplines allowed a Tower prisoner to write in defense of that heresy. The chaplain, one Dr. Currein, was put up to pricking the monarch by Stephen Gardiner (to Foxe an archdaemon) and others. Henry ordered Cranmer and Cromwell to give Frith the choice to recant or be condemned. To avoid publicity, an examining commission held its investigation at Croydon. Cranmer "sent one of his gentlemen" and a porter named Perlebeane to escort Frith to Croydon. The constable of the Tower, one Fitzwilliam, felt himself well rid of his prisoner. While rowing from the Tower to Lambeth en route to Croydon, Cranmer's gentleman tried to persuade Frith to save his talents and learning for the future by moderating his view of the sacraments enough to allow Cromwell and Cranmer to exercise their favor toward him and to gain his liberation. Frith refused, predicting that his views, even though presently condemned, would win adoption as official doctrine of the realm within twenty years. Foxe's account here benefits from hindsight, for Frith's eucharistic teachings were paraphrased just twenty years later in the 1552 prayer book, especially its "Black Rubric" denying that Christ's body could be in more than one place at one time.

The trio landed at Lambeth for "some repast," Foxe's story continued, and set out on foot for Croydon. The gentleman drew Perlebeane into his plan to let Frith escape into the wood at Brixton Causeway toward his native Kent whence he might escape overseas. The custodians were to feign pursuit in the other direction, and would inform the bishops of their prisoner's escape only after he was safely distant. Perlebeane agreed. But at the appointed hilltop Frith refused to run, threatening to deliver himself to Croydon if his guards "lost" him. In his previous flight "beyond the sea, where I was a reader in the Greek tongue" he had steadfastly followed his vocation; now, as called by God, he must make his full scriptural and patristic testimony on the sacrament before the bishops. His would-be deliverers foiled, to Croydon he went.

At the examination Frith persuaded Dr. Heath to accept Augustine's authority on the eucharist (Foxe went on), and stirred Cranmer's interest in his position. The examiners feared defeat if they allowed an open disputation; thus Frith was given over to the bishops of London, Winchester, and Chichester in consistory at St. Paul's in London, and before them he subscribed his condemned views.[3]

Discounting as perhaps typographical the discrepancy in the list of bishops, Foxe's revised yarn is at once too intimately detailed to be dismissed and too neatly heroic to be taken entire. The conversations between Frith and his captors were recorded long after their purported occurrence and were palpably embroidered. Yet the kernel of the story of a proffered release, perhaps even with sanction from one or more of the bishops, rings true.

While awaiting execution at Newgate, Frith himself wrote on June 23, 1533, a brief but unadorned explanation of his trial and his refusal to recant. "The Articles wherfore Iohn Frith dyed," as Foxe entitled the writing, are more autobiographical than theological. Frith had been charged with heresy for denying the orthodox dogmas of purgatory and transubstantiation. Accounts of his trial by himself and by his judges agree that he did not insist upon his own understandings and conceptions of these controversial matters, but was stubbornly unwilling to acknowledge that the official teachings of the Church on these points must be believed under pain of eternal damnation. At stake in the trial was not only Frith's theology but also Frith's own soul. On the only specifically theological issue in the trial the accusers and the accused agreed, that the doctrines of purgatory and transubstantiation lodged in extra-scriptural, but not necessarily anti-scriptural, authority. Frith denied that the Church possessed spiritual authority to bind his soul to eternal perdition, asserting instead that he stood before God free to believe or disbelieve these specific dogmas.

By Frith's account he was examined on two articles only. Did he deny a purgatory for the purification of souls after this life? He claimed that the body was purged by Christ's cross and the soul by the word of God, and he knew of no other part of man needing purgation. Therefore he denied the Pope's purgatory.

3. *AM, 8,* 695–99. But *AM, 5,* 14, had not Chichester but Lincoln, as did the transcription of the official process against Frith from the Stokesley Register, *AM, 5,* appendix XXII. This dubious story was repeated as true by C. Anderson, *Annals of the English Bible* (2 vols. London, 1845), *1,* 370 ff.

But his own knowledge or ignorance of purgatory counted for
little, for he reckoned it no "necessary article of our faith, nec-
essarely to bee beleeued vnder payne of damnation, whether
there bee such a purgatory or not." So much for purgatory. Did
he think "that the Sacrament of the aulter was the body of
Christ"? Yes, as also was the body of Christian believers.
Frith answered further questions about the sacramental teachings of scripture and the fathers with his own considered opinions, insisting that neither his judgment nor that of the Church
might be required to be believed under pain of damnation. In
the contest of opinions Frith scored now and again, but less
effectively than he had in his writings from the Tower. Were
transubstantiation true, its belief must not be sanctioned by
eternal life and death.

How could he die for an article which he himself judged to
be adiaphora? "The cause of my death is thys," he wrote, "because I can not in conscience, abiure and sweare, that our Prelates opinion of the sacrament . . . is an vndoubted article of
the fayth, necessary to bee beleeued vnder payne of damnation." [4] He thought transubstantiation false, grounded neither
in scripture nor in approved fathers. Frith would not bind faithful Christians to admit any article of faith as necessary except
the creed; he would forbid the Church to compel belief in non-
scriptural doctrines. In fine, he dared not presume to enter
God's judgment by making, as the prelates did, a necessary
article of faith on the point of the sacrament. Should he do so
he would condemn the German and Swiss Christians or else
condemn the Catholic Christians. As catering to the prelates he
would not do the former; for the sake of his own conscience he
would not do the latter.

Frith's death-witness, then, was not to specific Protestant
doctrines. If martyrdom it was, it was martyrdom for the primary commitment of faith to a dependence for salvation upon
God's mercy as brought by Christ the "mid dealer" to man. The
Catholics abrogated true faith by proposing that the acceptance
or rejection of certain doctrines of *the* faith effected salvation
or damnation. Frith was concerned that God alone be God
even at the risk of his life. He did not pit his own private in-

4. *Whole workes,* pp. 170, 172.

terpretation of scripture, much less his own immediate access to God as believer, against the authority of the Church. He was constrained to deny the authority of the Church insofar as in fact it put both the prelates and conscientious believers in the position of usurping and arrogating to themselves the judgment of God. To the dogma of the official Church Frith could not assent because that assent was to him inherently blasphemous.

Were there any accuracy in the identification of Frith as the Melanchthon of the English Reformation, it would turn on Frith's employment of the doctrine of adiaphora in his conception of the sacraments. But by his death he testified eloquently that even the doctrine of adiaphora was, as a doctrine, indifferent.

LATER WRITINGS

After publishing his big book on purgatory, before writing on the sacraments from the Tower, and probably while in England in 1532 before the fateful October arrest, Frith composed a brief comment upon the last will and testament of William Tracy. When a manuscript copy was found among Tyndale's posthumous papers with a similar comment by Tyndale, they were published (1536?) together from the press of Hoochstraten in Antwerp.[5] The tract showed for the first time a theological breach between Frith and Tyndale—a fact which may explain why it was never published during Frith's or Tyndale's lifetime.

Tracy's testament had been judged heretical, after considerable discussion, on February 27, 1532, although the gentleman had died shortly after executing the will October 10, 1530. Archbishop Warham in 1532 directed Thomas Parker, vicar general of the bishop of Worcester, to exhume Tracy's body, and Parker, who with more zeal than judgment had the exhumed remains burnt at the stake, was sued by Tracy's son Richard and fined £300. The will itself seems to have been a popular tract among the Brethren not only for its having forbidden payments from the estate for masses for the decedent's

---

5. *STC* 24,167; *Ned. Bibl.* 3997. Frith's comment was reprinted in *Whole workes*, pp. 77–81, and dated 1531 by Foxe.

soul—parliament had limited the Church's exaction of mor-
tuaries the year before Tracy died—but also for its sharp
emphasis upon justification by faith in Christ as men's only
hope based upon scriptural promises.

Frith's comment on the testament addressed theological issues important to the early English Protestants. While it has
generally been thought that the only major disagreement among
them involved the sacramentarian views which Frith was to
expound from prison in 1532–33, this document shows that already in 1532 they disagreed on the question of an intermediate state of the soul between the time of death and the day of
general resurrection. Cryptically, and without naming names,
Frith noted that some persons argued from Paul's treatment
of death and resurrection in I Corinthians 15 that the soul was
mortal and that only in the general resurrection did there begin
a celestial life of the soul. That point seemed to be "more
suttelly gathered then either truly or charitably." [6] Apparently
Tracy's testament aroused arguments among the Brethren in
England about the implications of the Protestant renunciation
of purgatory—if souls of the dead were not in that nowhere,
where they might be? In 1534 the question became a topic
of violent public dispute between Tyndale and his erstwhile
friend Joye, an argument that will demand attention later
on.

Far more critical than that, Frith explicitly repudiated the
notion of double justification, and opposed Tyndale's conception
of the important though secondary rôle of works in the justification of sinners. Since Christ was the only "mid dealer" between
man and God, Frith denied the notion of the justification of
sinners before men by works, declaring, "before God we are
verely iustified by that roote of fayth, for he searcheth the
hart, and therefore this iust iudge doth inwardly iustifie or
condemne, geuing sentence according to fayth." So far Barnes
and Tyndale might have agreed, but they would go on to show
that works followed faith not only by inherent necessity but
for the sake of justification before men. Not so Frith: "men
must looke for the woorkes, for theyr sight cannot enter into
the hart, and therefore they first geue iudgement of woorkes,

6. *Whole workes,* p. 78.

and are many times deceaued vnder the cloke of hypocrisie." [7]
Justification before men was therefore a dubious matter, not
to be shown forth by good works which might easily deceive;
God alone determined, granted, and knew the justification of
sinners. So Frith stood with Luther as late as 1532, while his
cohorts abroad were moving toward Osiander and Bucer and
the Rhineland theologians on this critical point.

After being imprisoned in the Tower of London Frith busied
himself writing, in spite of formidable obstacles. In a work
composed during this period he complained that he was not allowed access to the books he needed, and could obtain pen,
ink, and paper "onely secretly, so that I am in continuall feare,
both of the Lefetenaunt and of my keeper, lest they should espy
any such thyng by me." He worked without the appropriate
materials in such snatches of time as could be found; "for when
soeuer I heare the keyes ryng at the doore, strayte all much
[must] be conueyed out of the way (and then if any notable
thyng had bene in my mynde) it was cleane lost." [8] When we
consider these difficulties alongside the fact that his imprisonment lasted only the eight months from mid-October 1532
until mid-June 1533, the amount and quality of Frith's literary
output are astonishing. In the 1831 edition of his works the
fruit of this period covers some two hundred and thirty pages,
slightly more than half disputing with More on the Lord's
Supper.

Although Foxe assigned dates to most of Frith's writings
from prison, they are difficult to set in their probable chronological order. On the surmise that Frith eventually found some
relief from the worst obstacles to his writing, it may be assumed
that the answer to Rastell on purgatory was composed first in
the autumn of 1532. Although Rastell's reply to Frith's 1531
book is preserved to us only in a manuscript fragment, Frith
stated that his adversary had shown him a copy of the book.
Apparently Frith discussed the subject of purgatory with Rastell in person, for the latter came to adopt Frith's position.
The conversion of the lawyer-printer, More's brother-in-law,
must have embarrassed English Catholics greatly. Since Frith

7. Ibid., pp. 79–81.
8. Ibid., p. 76.

dealt in his published reply only with certain rather minor points of logic and scriptural exegesis, the writing demands only brief mention. It was published as *An other boke against Rastel named the subsedye or bulwark to his fyrst boke/ made by Ihon Frithe presonner in the Tower* (*STC* 11,385). An anonymous hand added a brief preface noting that some persons recently rejoiced "that purgatorye was founde agayne. Because they read in a boke named the institution of a chrysten man this worde purgatory."[9] The reference, of course, is to the famous "Bishops' Book" of 1537. Frith's work was praised by the preface for its scriptural basis and for its having converted Rastell, and Frith's martyrdom was noted. The circumlocutory style reminds one of Joye, although one writer surmised that John Rogers, the compiler of Matthew's Bible which was printed in Antwerp in July 1537, composed the preface and saw the book through the printing.[10]

The other four books written in the Tower were:

(1) *The contentes of thys booke: a letter vnto the faythfull followers of Christes gospel. STC* 11,386: [n.pl., n.pr., 1540?].

(2) *A mirrour or glasse to know thyselfe. STC* 11,390: [n.pl., n.pr., 1533?].

(3) *A myrroure or lokynge glasse wherein you may beholde the Sacramente of baptisme described.* 1533. *STC* 11,391: *J. Daye,* [1548?].

(4) *A boke made by Iohn Frith prisoner in the tower of London/ answeringe vnto M. Mores lettur. STC* 11,381. Colophon: "⁋ Imprintid at Monster/ Anno. 1533 By me Conrade Willems," but *Ned. Bibl.* 3042 suggests Antwerp as the place.[11]

---

9. *An other boke against Rastell,* Aii^r; cf. *Whole workes,* p. 60. *STC* 11,385 dated the work 1533?, but *Ned. Bibl.* 0525 identified it as printed at Antwerp by Martin deKeyser ca. 1535. The reference to *The Institution of a Christian Man* proves that it was printed no earlier than 1537.

10. See Mozley, p. 179.

11. Fulop, pp. 115 ff., attempted to place these in a chronological order: he assigned *Know Thyself* to the first quarter of 1533, in spite of Foxe's assignment of 1532, on the ground that it replied to one of More's comments on predestination made in a letter of December 1532; but More had written on predestination elsewhere earlier; Fulop mistakenly asserted that Foxe was the first to print the piece in the 1572 *Whole workes. The Letter to the Faithful Followers* was assigned by Fulop to the same time, early 1533, but was also

Know Thyself was published abroad, possibly at Antwerp, probably very soon after Frith's death if not during his last days. With it was printed a much longer spiritual guide for the dying, under the title "A breffe instruccyon drawen out of holy scripture/ for to teache a person wyllingly to dye/ & not to scare death/ translated out of Frenche in to Englysh by a scolar of Parys. Which treatyse is in the Douche tonge all ready/ & printed with the preuilege of the Emperour. An. M.D. xxxiij." [12] Nothing suggests that Frith was involved in translating or printing this companion piece, except its inclusion, along with Frith's *Know Thyself* and his *Letter to the Faithful Followers* in the volume *Vox Piscis* of 1626 (*STC* 11,395).[13] This collection also included *The preparacion to the crosse, wyth the preparacion to deeth* (*STC* 11,392), often attributed to Richard Tracy, and a work called *The Treasure of Knowledge*, and it presented the translated *A breffe instruccyon* as a sequel to Frith's *Know Thyself*, as *STC* 11,386 had done.

The foregoing bibliographical tedium may serve to indicate how much confusion within a century surrounded the writings from prison by this popular Reformation martyr. Foxe's 1572 collection of Frith's works exercised judicous restraint in including only the five works from the Tower which can with certainty be attributed to Frith. Any greater product of eight months of writing under extreme impediments would be almost incredible. Frith was industrious enough to have written the answer to Rastell, the *Letter to the Faithful Followers, Know Thyself*, and *Mirror of Baptism*, in something like that order, meanwhile giving what time and attention he could to the long rebuttal of More on the sacrament of the altar. During these months he was also receiving and interviewing various of the Protestant party in London, including the treacherous Holt. He received at least two letters from Tyndale and wrote at least one to him about Joye. From Joye came the letter that Frith could not or would not answer. Notwithstanding his

---

wrongly said to have been first printed in 1572. Fulop took *Mirror of Baptism* to be Frith's last work.

12. *A mirrour or glasse to know thyselfe,* described by *Ned. Bibl.* 4230.

13. See below, p. 132.

apologies for the hasty and shoddy nature of the answer to
Rastell, four of these prison pieces reflect superb theological
and literary care. The rebuttal of More enjoyed three printings in England in 1546 and 1548, and it is possible that one
or more of the others was carefully preserved in manuscript
for printing later when Protestant presses flourished under
Edward VI.

THEOCENTRIC THEOLOGY

Everything that can be learned of Frith during his imprisonment indicates that from his arrest onward he was anticipating
only one outcome—execution. Late in the spring of 1533, Tyndale assured his friend that Frith's wife, who remained on the
Continent, was "well content with the will of God, and would
not for her sake, haue *the* glory of God hindred." [14] In the
Letter to the Faithful Followers, Frith assured his friends
that persecution was his proper lot: "I euer thought and yet
doe thinke, that to walke after Gods word, would cost me my
life at one tyme or an other"; should the King favor him with
intervention, "yet will I not thinke that I am escaped, but that
God hath onely differred it for a season to the intent that I
should woorke somewhat that he hath appointed me to do, and
so to vse me vnto his glory." All the faithful should "arme
them selues with the same supposition." [15]

Like many another person who has been imprisoned and
forced to face death for his beliefs, Frith deplored all coercion
of beliefs; this stand measures the farthest distance between
him and the successful European reformers. Within Christendom the advocates of freedom of conscience and the opponents
of enforced belief were all persecuted men. To these Frith belonged. Luther did not. Only by an inadmissible anachronism
might it be imagined that Frith favored a system of religious
toleration. He only knew the established religious order's im-
potence to coerce his faith. In that sense may properly be understood the accolade given to Frith as "the first and almost
the only martyr [under the Tudors] to the theory of tolera-

14. Tyndale to Frith, *Whole workes,* p. 454.
15. *Whole workes,* p. 82.

tion, to which neither Romanists nor Protestants, Anglicans nor Zwinglians, were yet ready to give ear." [16]

The tolerant mind shaped all of the Tower writings, even the polemic against More. Above all it commanded the tender sentiments of the *Letter to the Faithful Followers,* addressed to persons who, at jeopardy to life and goods, visited Frith and supplied his needs. As one of their prominent leaders and thinkers, Frith offered the Brethren hopeful encouragement in the face of apparent losses. God would send a Joseph to provide for them "an hundred fathers for one, an hundred mothers for one, an hundred houses for one, and that in thys life, as I haue proued by experience." But there were, nevertheless, tasks to be done, understandings to be gained, and converts to be made; if any brother scrupled over matters found in Frith's books they should write him and he would answer.[17]

Perhaps having seen Frith's gentle letter, and taking up the allusion to an expected Joseph, Tyndale wrote about January 1533 addressing Frith as "Dearly beloved brother Jacob." Tyndale advised silence on the subject of the presence of Christ's body in the Supper, for fear that divisions among Protestants on this score would wreak the same harm in England that had erupted on the Continent from the famous Marburg disagreement between Luther and Zwingli. He gave news of Melanchthon and Joye. Frith should beware of the vain persuasion that only by abjuring might he help the cause of the Protestants; so counseled Tyndale, who considered himself chief of the English Protestants and wrote obviously as the older man to the younger.[18]

Whether Frith answered Tyndale is unknown, but the Brethren in England certainly asked him to clarify points for them. *Know Thyself* was written at the request of a friend to whom Frith felt deeply obliged. A little treatise on the sacrament of the altar was composed in similar fashion, and shown to friends;

16. A. D. Innes, *England Under the Tudors* (10th ed., revised by J. M. Henderson, London, 1932), p. 143.

17. *Whole workes,* p. 82.

18. Mozley, pp. 248 ff. has reproduced the letter with spelling modernized and with Foxe's variants reconciled; Mozley's judgment that Frith followed Tyndale's advice in answering More (p. 251), accords with his admiration for Tyndale, but otherwise seems farfetched.

it fell into the hands of More who gruffly answered in a dull and tendentious letter.[19] Frith read More's refutation, according to his own testimony, on St. Stephen's Day, December 26, 1532, at the house of Gardiner, bishop of Winchester, and he determined to answer it completely even though his own first little memorandum on the subject had not been meant for publication. Little wonder that a prisoner so ready for conferences with plain people and debates with the mighty should fall into William Holt's trap!

While Frith's main theological interest during imprisonment turned to sacramentarianism, applied both to baptism and the Supper of the Lord, the *Letter to the Faithful Followers* and *Know Thyself* touched important matters. These writings dealt mainly with the nature and characteristics of the true congregation of believers in Christ. They clarify Frith's understanding of justification by faith and of the Christian life inaugurated by that justification.

Trinterud has asserted that Tyndale and Frith shared a commitment to an anti-scholastic Augustinianism learned by them from the Rhineland reformers and leading to a conception of justification as placing the believer and God in a contractual relationship that obligated God to bestow rewards for the performance of the divine law.[20] Tyndale indeed adumbrated such a proto-Puritan conception of Christianity, thereby casting aside some of his earlier doctrinal borrowings from Luther, as will be seen. While Frith undeniably appreciated Augustine and deprecated Duns Scotus and Thomas Aquinas, and while Frith was intimately acquainted with certain aspects of the thought of the Rhineland theologians, especially Oecolampadius, he did not conceive of justification as initiating a contractual relationship between the believer and God.

A favorite polemical thrust of Catholics against all early Protestants was that their teaching on justification by faith inevitably committed them to antinomianism. More and his brother-in-law Rastell made such thrusts at Frith. But what

19. More, *A letter of syr Tho. More knyght impugnynge the erronyouse wrytyng of Johñ Fryth agaynst the blessed sacrament of the aultare* (London, W. Rastell, 1533; *STC* 18,090), written December 7, 1532, from Chelsea; reprinted in More, *Correspondence,* pp. 439–64.

20. Trinterud, "The Origins of Puritanism," pp. 38–44.

Trinterud aptly called the "law-covenant-contract" conception, employed as a defence against the charge of antinomianism by Rhinelanders and Tyndale, was not the only way to answer the accusation. It was not Luther's way nor that of the Wittenbergers taken as a whole. Nor was it Frith's. Frith indeed thought justification the free gift of God, initiated by God, involving the remission and non-imputation of sin for the sake of Christ's righteousness; that conception did not involve Frith in (mature) Luther's and Melanchthon's notion of direct imputation of Christ's righteousness to the justified sinner. For Frith "where fayth is present no sinne can be imputed, but this faith is not in thy power, for it is the gift of God." [21] As an inward grace of which baptism was the outward sign, faith only manifested a prior election that was both free and inscrutable; no man might know of another man's election or reprobation, and only by the presence of faith within himself, which produced a will to fulfill God's law, might he have an indication of his own election.[22] That election made nonsense of rationalizations about free will, for where free will was exercised apart from the gift of justification it was wretched and bound to sin, but where the will was bound by God to the love of righteousness and the welfare of the neighbor, there was a genuinely liberated will. Since justification by grace through faith was to Frith in all its aspects, including its initiation and sustenance of a sanctified life, the absolutely free and undeserved gift of God, the deeds of the transformed will which loved to fulfill the law of God put God under no obligation. What was wrought by a justified man was God's working, not that man's, though it was the man's will that was made to pursue good works. Thus everything a Christian man saw himself as possessing— life, health, wealth, abilities, knowledge, faith, wisdom, etc.— he should know to be gifts placed in his stewardship for the sake of his neighbor.

Hence More's desire that the Protestants cease to spread the scripture in the vernacular struck Frith as not negotiable; "it

21. *Whole workes*, p. 86.
22. Ibid., pp. 92 f.; Frith was acquainted with the Anabaptist position on the necessity of a manifest faith prior to baptism, but he trusted that "the English (vnto whom I wryte this [*Mirror of Baptism*]) haue no such opinions."

is not possible for vs whiche haue receiued the knowledge of
gods word, but that we must cry and cal to other, that they
leaue the perillous pathes of their owne foolish phantasies."
Unless a means be found to accomplish "a reasonable reformation" and to instruct "the poore commons" in the word of God,
"I neither will nor can cease to speake, for the worde of God
boyleth in my body, like a feruent fire, and will needes haue an
issue and breaketh out, when occasion is geuen." If More would
arrange to make the vernacular scripture available to all,
Frith and his brother Tyndale would promise to stop writing.[23]

While each man must exercise for the neighbor's welfare the
special talents given him, in principle every Christian man
standing in the light of God's word was given the care of the
souls of his fellows, Frith taught. By failing so to act and live,
the established Church and its functionaries stood condemned
for theft and murder of neighbor. This very harsh judgment
upon those commissioned to be agents of Christ, Frith exhorted,
should cause no great alarm, for even among the twelve apostles
chosen by Jesus was one who betrayed him. The official Church
had been infected for centuries by its desire for wealth and
possessions, but it would never be without a remnant of faithful men and women. Occasionally these latter must and would
stand in defiance of their ecclesiastical officials.

Frith's entire conception of the church and of the activity
in which he himself was engaged sprang directly from the conviction that God chose to himself persons to receive in faith
the unearned benediction of justifying grace. As that gift initiated with God so all that it accomplished in the life of the
recipient redounded to God's glory, however patently it might
achieve the benefit of the neighbor. The neighbor's thanks, if
any, belonged rightly to God, not to the immediate worker of
his welfare. The neighbor's enmity and hate, as in the case
of the wrath of the ecclesiastical authorities, was to be endured
patiently even to death. This radically theocentric theology and
religion determined the character of Frith's soteriology, ecclesiology, and ethics, and it also fashioned and permeated the
teaching on the sacrament which came to be his most direct
legacy to English Protestantism.

23. Ibid., p. 115.

8. Frith's Sacramental Thought

RITH'S sacramental theology has been traced out by various modern writers and attributed to diverse and disparate sources. Mozley had Tyndale furnishing the form of it and Zwingli supplying its substance. Rupp regarded Frith as England's Melanchthon, and left as an open question the influence of Oecolampadius upon him. Porter thought Frith in his sacramental views a slavish follower of Barnes, in turn a mere imitator of Luther. Jacobs portrayed Barnes as a follower of Luther on this point, and Tyndale too, until Frith, the thorough Zwinglian, persuaded Tyndale to give up his Lutheran convictions. Anticipating Dugmore's hypothesis that English reformers made fresh studies of the Church fathers, Fulop absolved Frith's sacramental theology from dependence upon any of his contemporaries and made him a renovator of Ratramnus, finding a kindred spirit in Bucer. Long before all this confusion began, a man who owed much to Frith's thought about sacraments, Thomas Cranmer, accurately took Frith at his own word: he was heavily dependent upon Oecolampadius.[1]

Rejecting the scholastic distinction between form and mat-

1. Mozley, *William Tyndale*, p. 251; Rupp, *Studies*, p. 10; H. C. Porter, *Reformation and Reaction in Tudor Cambridge* (Cambridge, 1958), p. 65; Jacobs, *Lutheran Movement in England*, p. 38; C. W. Dugmore, *The Mass and the English Reformers* (London, 1958), vii, 85 f. and passim; Fulop, "John Frith," p. 71; Cranmer to Hawkins, June 17, 1533, *LP*, *6*, no. 661, quoted in Anderson, *Annals*, *1*, 375. These contradictory statements exemplify the futility of discussing sixteenth century (or later) sacramental theories in terms of such misleading labels as "Zwinglian," "Lutheran," etc.; since the Marburg Colloquy Protestant tempers have been hot on the subject, and the labels have become pejorative.

ter, Frith based his sacramental theory upon three elements as requisite to every sacrament: the sign, the signification, and the trust of the believer in the divine promise of grace. The current notion of sacramental grace as achieved *ex opere operato,* Frith thought, falsely stressed the palpable, outward sign to the depreciation of the other two elements. Frith, with Luther, understood grace not in the scholastic manner as a metaphysical substance to be infused by sacraments into the soul of the recipient, but as the efficacious favor of God toward creation. Thus understood, grace was incapable of simple and automatic conveyance by sacramental matter of bread, wine, water, oil, etc. Whether expressed sacramentally or otherwise, grace was the benevolent attitude of God, neither to be managed by religious rites nor made to inhere in sacred objects. For Frith, grace preceded and enabled all expressions of it, verbal or sacramental. Where it was taught that the action guaranteed and the object conveyed grace, there sacraments became idols. Grace as divine benevolence originated faith as a specific gift of that benevolence, and only where faith had been given and received might effective signs of grace be rightly employed.

BAPTISM

Baptism of infants, as Frith understood it, accorded with this notion of grace and faith, since by God's promise infants were accounted members of the congregation of faithful believers. Had Frith emphasized faith as a possession of the believer and made sacramental expression dependent upon that faith, consistency would demand an antipaedobaptist stand; but he emphasized faith as a gift of the giver, either to individuals or to the whole congregation. Therefore God's favor toward the congregation might be appropriated by or imputed to any individual who did not actively resist. God was originator and worker of the sacraments. They, like all concerns of true Christian religion, depended upon God. Frith thought the favor that God bore toward his people indeed capable of being expressed by finite objects. Like Luther, he never questioned the objective reality of God's favorable attitude. But he thought that the Church had objectified the atti-

tude itself by tying it to certain specified objects and by guar-
anteeing its conveyance through the recitation of formulae
over those objects, thus making the objective reality contingent
upon the subjective act of the Church's authorized representatives. An equal and opposite danger hinged the favor of God
to man's faith, conceived as a possession of the believer, making the reality contingent upon the subjective act of the individual Christian. As Frith viewed the teachings of his times,
the official Catholic Church perpetrated the first error, and
the Anabaptists courted the second.

Equally as explicit as Frith's denunciations of two opposite
wrong conceptions of the relation between faith and sacramental signs was his affirmation that each sacrament's particular signification properly related signs and faith. The signification of baptism was the plunging of the candidate into water
as an enactment of his death and Christ's death, and the bringing of the baptized person out of the water as an enactment
of his and Christ's rising again. Thus in baptism the old man
died and the new man came alive. The sacrament of the altar
bore a double signification. The body and blood of Christ,
broken and shed once for all on Calvary for the weal of the
world, found signification in the bread and wine broken,
poured, and received as food and drink. The same bread and
wine also signified the true congregation of Christ (known
only to him) living in the world as men and women gathered
from all the nations and united into one true body, just as
bread was composed of wheat gathered from many fields and
as wine combined the fruit of many vines. These significations,
Frith taught, revealed and guarded the true character of the
sacraments. Although baptism as an external rite was administered once only to an individual, its signification taught
that Christian life was a continual baptism or an oft-repeated
death and resurrection. So the sacrament of the Supper taught
that the career of the Church was a continual experience of
being gathered together as a body of believers, feeding upon
and united with the very life of its Lord.

These significations controlled the right use of sacramental
signs, saving them from the idolatry of being assigned super-
natural virtues and powers; the sign must subserve its signifi-

cation. The significations also directed the attention of faithful persons to the promise and favor of God, teaching them to know themselves as utterly dependent upon that promise and favor. As the instructor of faith, the signification also controlled the rites attendant upon the signs. Yet the reality articulated by the signification, and thus expressed by the sign, was appropriable only by faith; a thousand baptisms without faith were as unavailing as a goose's ducking itself under water.[2]

To see the sign as working by itself a transfer of grace struck Frith as palpably erroneous. But he thought that an equally destructive tendency of his times was a radical misunderstanding of ceremonies. In this latter connection Frith applied the notion of things indifferent—adiaphora—more specifically and precisely than in any other aspect of his theology. He did not follow Melanchthon in distinguishing between certain points of Christian doctrine and practice as essential and others as non-essential, but leaned to the young Luther's notion of adiaphora. Ceremonies in themselves were neither good nor bad, neither useful nor harmful, and therefore they were things truly indifferent but not unimportant. Unlike Zwingli, Frith did not see the signs of sacraments as indifferent. They were quite necessary, albeit under the control of their significations, but whatever ceremonies attached themselves to the signs in the performance of sacraments were

---

2. Frith emphasized the distinction between sign and signification, and (to More's great offense) likened any person seeking to draw virtue from the bread and wine themselves "vnto a fond fellow, which when he is very drye, and an honest man shew him an alepole and tell him that there is good ale inough, would goe and sucke the alepole, trusting to get drinke out of it, and so to quenche his thyrste. . . . for the alepole . . . shall not ease him, but rather make him more drie," *Whole workes*, p. 113. Barnes had played with the same simile but missed the point when he complained that good ale or wine would not always be found "where there hangyth out a grene sygne," *A Supplicatyon* (1531), lix'; cf. *Whole workes*, p. 244. Even earlier than that, in 1528, Tyndale had pointed out that hearing masses without faith was as futile as "to beholde a bushe at a tauerne dore, if thou knewest not thereby that there were wine within to be solde," *Whole workes*, p. 143. See More, *Workes*, p. 1138. *Oxford English Dictionary* (Oxford, 1888) credited Frith with original use of the word "alepole," but Tyndale had employed it in his 1530 Prologue to Exodus: "And hee that goeth aboute to purchase grace with ceremonies: doth but sucke the ale pole to quench his thyrst," *Whole workes*, p. 10. None of his cohorts employed the arresting simile with such pungency as did Frith. If the figure was borrowed from a continental writer, the source has eluded me.

indifferent. In certain instances ceremonies might be extremely valuable and expedient, and in others extremely obstructive.

Frith's rule regarding ceremonies was to avoid offending the weaker brother. The consciences of four kinds of men must be considered in making any decision about ceremonies. Young and immature believers needed ceremonies to teach and lead them toward a more perfect understanding; as milk enabled the infant later to eat meat, ceremonies teaching the nature of a sacrament's signification prepared the young to employ the sacrament without regard to ceremonies. Secondly, persons of flickering faith needed ceremonies to sustain their faith; they must not be offended by the impugning of ceremonies. A third kind of men were mature Christians whose full knowledge of the right relation of sign and ceremony to faith and grace needed no ceremonies; these would nevertheless tolerate them for the sake of the young and the weak. Lastly, there were obstinate, self-willed, stiff-necked men who put their trust and confidence in ceremonies and the petty paraphernalia of religion, men who insisted that external actions controlled internal realities; these must be opposed and resisted until corrected or condemned, for as idolaters they put secondary things in first place, refusing to take the second place *coram deo*. For them baptism was impossible without "holy water, candle, creame, oyle, salt, godfather, or godmothers, or any other, popatrie." Ceremonies were their *sine qua non* of sacramental grace, and to use ceremonies in their way would subvert the whole of Christian faith and religion.

Frith deemed necessary only the elements of sacraments provided by dominical institution. All other externals were indifferent, to be employed or not employed with reference to their value to the four kinds of men. Frith would not abolish the indifferent externals, but would teach that they commanded no confidence. So to teach was the duty of "the Seniours [elders] and ministers of the congregations." Only if "people cleaue to sore to them" ought a convenient time be found for their abrogation. Frith found a *locus classicus* for changing ceremonies in the early Church's rejection of the Jewish Sabbath and adoption of the Christian Sunday. Some such day helped the weak, not the strong. The Sabbath might have served as well as Sunday for the Church, save that men put confidence in it when it was really a thing indifferent.[3]

LORD'S SUPPER

Frith drew the main lines of his sacramental thought in a treatise on baptism written during imprisonment in the Tower. In spite of its brevity, this lucid work was a masterpiece of constructive theology. *Mirror of Baptism* served no polemical purpose and entered no particular controversy. With an economy rarely exhibited by English Reformation writings, it set forth a general theory of sacraments summarized above, and spelled out a detailed conception of baptism in the context of neatly defined understandings of justification by faith and of the church.

Frith intended to draw up a companion piece on the sacrament of the altar. Before he could do so, one of the Brethren persuaded him to state his eucharistic theology. Applying the notion of adiaphora both to ceremonies and to theories of the mode of Christ's presence in the sacrament, Frith concluded that transubstantiation was no necessary article of belief. From scriptural evidences and official creeds he showed that Christ's body as alluded to in the institution narrative was a natural body incapable of occupying two places at once. Rationally, linguistically, and theologically he saw the crucial text of the institution to mean that bread and wine were significations of, not identifications with, body and blood. Finally, he recommended how the sacrament might be received in accordance with Christ's institution of it.

When his friend urged him to write out the whole discussion, Frith composed a treatise which he thought was "like to purchase me most cruell death" in spite of wishing not to have it published. This writing fell into the hands of More, who answered with the long letter that Frith saw in print at Gardiner's house late in 1532. Unable to obtain the book other than in a mutilated copy, Frith set about to answer More in detail. The product was a sacramental treatise far more prolix than the one on baptism, more polemical than constructive, yet cogent, and professing reliance upon and preference for Oeco-

3. *Whole workes*, pp. 95 f.

lampadius of Basel over all other continental theologians who had written on this subject.

The treatise is easily summarized since Frith gathered his crucial points into a few paragraphs.[4] The prelates denied that bread remained in the sacrament after it became the natural body and blood of Christ. Frith contended that this was no article of the Christian creed and therefore could not be enforced. He preferred to stand with Paul in the conviction that bread remained, and argued that assertion both from nature and from the old doctors of the Church. The prelates said Christ's flesh was present to the teeth of the recipient of the sacrament, and therefore the wicked recipient ate the true body. Frith found no such teaching in the creed and did not believe it, asserting instead that a natural body could be in only one place at a time, and Christ's body, being in heaven, could not be on one altar, much less a thousand. By scripture, doctors, and reason Frith demonstrated that the wicked received the sacrament but not Christ's body, while the faithful partook of the body in faith while eating the same natural food. Failing the spiritual eating, the wicked ate bread alone but to their own damnation. The prelates demanded that the sacrament be worshiped. Frith allowed its receipt in reverence for that which it signified, and would honor it with a regard equal to that for the scripture, but contended that to worship or reverence the bread and wine for themselves, or for what they were alleged to have become, was idolatry pure and simple.

But thus to summarize the argument is to lose all the theological juice and be left with a rind. The Supper of the Lord was like a feast welcoming a dear friend on his return after a long journey. Enemies might eat the food but could not join the feast. Friends "more eate his welcome home then the meate." Only the food profited the enemy, but since the feast was more than the food they participated under a hindrance and to their damnation. Or again, "it is not his presence in the bread that can saue me, but his presence in my hart through faith in his bloud, which hath washed out my sinnes and pacified *the* fathers wrath toward me." Or yet again, "the

4. Ibid., pp. 164–67.

Masse doth but onely represent hys passion. And so doth the
Sacrament represent his body. And yet though the Masse doth
but represent his crucifying, we may truly say he is crucified,
euen so though the Sacrament do but signifie or represent his
body, yet may we truly say that it is his body." The argument
sparkled with simplicity and good wit that diminished neither
its profundity nor seriousness. The prelates, and even more
emphatically More, adverted again and again to the inerrancy
of the Church. Frith cleverly saw this as "the grounde of all
their doctrine. But the truth of this article is nowe sufficiently
knowen. For if Queene Katherine be kyng Henries wife, then
they do erre, and if she be not, then they have erred." [5] If
More could not concede a "touché" to that, he was the lesser
man for it.

But regardless of the tone of the treatise, its content was
as simple as Frith's summary. Spiritual eating was availing and
reasonable. Carnal eating was unreasonable, against the best
church tradition, and availed nothing. Characteristically Frith
saw the whole sacrament theocentrically, and its application
christocentrically. Though the body of Christ remained in
heaven it might be eaten spiritually on earth by faith, so steadfast was God to his promise. Abraham, and Adam before him, to
say nothing of the Israelites under Moses, ate the true manna of
heaven which was the body of Christ, but they ate spiritually
by faith. Any theory of carnal eating must exclude them.

Frith pleaded not for the authority but only for the authenticity of his view. He would allow belief in transubstantiation as a thing indifferent, but he would not allow it as a necessary article to be believed under pain of damnation. Although
in itself adiaphora, transubstantiation had led to a number of
damnable idolatries, especially that of worshiping the con-
secrated host itself. Frith earnestly wrote against the doctrine,
not to disprove it but only to strip away the idolatries. Perhaps
the matter of the book may at once be summarized and its
form illustrated by quoting the prayer which Frith recommended for use before receiving the sacrament:

Blessed be thou most deare & mercyfull father whiche
of thy tender fauour and benignity (notwithstanding our

5. The four quotations, in order, are from *Whole workes*, pp. 161, 108, 128, 126.

greuous enormities committed agaynst thee,) vouch-
sauedst to sende thyne owne and onely deare sonne, to
suffer most vyle death for our redemption. Blessed be
thou Christ Iesu our Lord and Sauiour, whiche of thyne
aboundaunt pitie consideryng our miserable estate, willingly tookest vppon thee to haue thy most innocent body
broken and bloud shed, to purge vs and wash vs which
are laden with iniquitie. And to certifie vs thereof, hast
left vs not onely thy word which may instructe our hartes,
but also a visible token, to certifie euen our outward
senses of this great benefite, that we should not doubt,
but that the body and fruite of thy passion are ours
(through faith) as surely as the bread, whiche by our
senses we know that we haue with in vs. Blessed be also
that spirite of veritie whiche is sent from God our father
through our Sauiour Christ Iesu, to lighten our darke
ignoraunce, & leade vs through fayth into the knowledge
of hym whiche is all veritie. Strength we beseech thee our
frayle nature and increase our fayth: that we may prayse
God our most mercyfull father and Christ hys sonne our
Sauiour and redemer. Amen.[6]

Modern interpreters have noted similarities between Frith's
sacramental views and those of several of his contemporaries,
and have inferred his direct dependence upon them. The evidence reveals Frith's familiarity with his contemporaries on
the subject of sacraments as well as on less volatile topics.
Throughout his writings appears evidence of knowledge of
leading schoolmen, particularly Thomas, Duns Scotus, and
William of Ockham. He knew something of Hus and Wycliffe,
and maintained fruitful theological contact with the Lollards
in England. On the sacraments in particular he knew the
thought of Luther and Zwingli, probably in terms of their
conflict at Marburg, but he took leading themes of sacramental theory from neither of these. By his own assertion, the
defence of his eucharistic theology by reference to the fathers
of the Church, and especially to Augustine, was drawn directly from the work of Oecolampadius. More, in his letter,
accused Frith of having cited only "certaine new felowes: as

6. Ibid., p. 157.

Dominic. [sic] S. Thomas, Occam, and such other whiche haue made the Pope a God." Frith claimed to be completely in line with Augustine and with "all the old fathers, as Oecolampadius hath well declared in his booke, *Quid veteres senserint de Sacramento eucharistiæ*. And some of their sayinges I shall alledge anone." [7]

The patristic quotations by which Frith buttressed his explanation of the eucharist consist of hardly more than a rearrangement and abbreviation of Oecolampadius' work, not only the 1530 book named, but also the famous *De genuina verborum domini, Hoc est corpus meum, iuxta vetustissimos authores, expositione liber* (1525). The order of Frith's argument followed, of course, that of More's letter which it rebutted rather than Oecolampadius' exposition, at least up to the point where it made an explicitly patristic appeal. The heart of the book not only culled the Basler's catena of the fathers, but reproduced much of his exposition. That the burden of Frith's interpretation of the Supper is owed to this source and neither to Luther nor Zwingli, nor even to Frith, is plain throughout the book.

Barnes was already known as a strict Lutheran on the question of the presence of the Lord in the Supper. Tyndale urged Frith not to write on the subject, knowing that Frith was not in agreement with Barnes. Perhaps Tyndale's letter led Frith to accentuate his negatives by insisting that theories of the mode of Christ's presence were adiaphora over which honest men might disagree. But the position on which Frith stood against More was distinctly Oecolampadian; implicitly it denied every alternative position. The body of Christ was in heaven and not in two places at once (against Luther and all ubiquitarians); it was received spiritually not carnally (against all scholastics); the sign did appropriately convey the thing signified (against Zwingli); the thing signified was present to faith more clearly in the sacrament than in the scripture (against the rationalists).

Frith had no interest in utraquism as required by scripture, as did Tyndale and Joye along with Barnes and Luther and

7. Ibid., p. 126. Oecolampadius, *Dialogus quo patrum sententiam de coena domini bona fide explanat* (Basel, 1530).

Zwingli. More had said that Frith drived his argument from Wycliffe, Oecolampadius, Tyndale, and Zwingli. Frith denied dependence on any but Oecolampadius.[8] His literary dependence on Oecolampadius was, moreover, as heavy as his theological dependence—so much so that it is hard to imagine that Frith wrote the disputation against More without access to the specific book of Oecolampadius which he cited, or at least to notes. Yet Frith's work was no mere translation of Oecolampadius. The Englishman seems to have had no assistance from this quarter in bringing in the testimonies of Prosper, Druthmarius, and Bartram (Ratramnus), but these authorities did not dominate the argument as did the fathers whose writings Oecolampadius had carefully pondered and excerpted. Insofar as Frith was the English progenitor of the doctrine of the eucharist adopted by Cranmer, and by him made the official teaching of the Church of England, Canterbury, aware or unaware, borrowed from Basel.

INFLUENCE

Among Henrician Protestants who were killed for their beliefs, Frith stands with the most famous. For a full century after he was burnt at Smithfield his life and his death, his faith and his writings were portrayed alternately as exemplifications of true religion and as satanic incarnations. His fame among Protestants and infamy among Catholics are to be explained by several reasons, none of which is alone adequate or paramount. Among the martyrs of the English Reformation Frith was the first literary figure to burn at the stake in England. He was acknowledged by his enemies and praised by his friends for his learning, especially in the classical languages. Henry's religious advisers seem to have set higher premium on the enlistment of Frith than even Tyndale himself in the defence of the established religion. Frith was not a permanent refugee like Tyndale, but a bold young man willing to return to England to give active, day-by-day leadership to the oppressed adherents to the Protestant cause. Even from prison he was able to guide and inspire this group at a time of severe trial.

8. *Whole workes*, pp. 116–18, 126.

Frith must be ranked as strategically the most effective of England's first generation of Protestant polemicists, for his books attacked the most valued and the most vulnerable fortresses of the Catholic religion in England. He was prominently identified with the work of translating scriptures into English, even though in this rôle he was but an understudy of Tyndale and less prominent than Roy or Joye. He translated writings of Luther, and Englished the handbook of Protestant faith by the originator of the Scottish Reformation, Hamilton. More important than all this, however, Frith was the English writer to undercut the current theory and practice of purgatory, by which the Church controlled the popular religious imagination, mulcted the privileged, and determined the careers of the dead and the hopes of the living. The dogma of the intermediate state of souls and its religious reception was not, of course, expunged by Frith's writings, but its chief English defenses in the works of Fisher and More were badly shaken, and their helper Rastell was won over.

Frith went on, even against the advice of Tyndale, to attack the mass. To portray sacramental grace as issuing from God's favor to the believer's faith, rather than from the empowered priesthood to the sacramental stuff, undermined the whole religious system by which Latin Christianity had extended its influence over the common and public life of western Europe. Without an *ex opere operato* sacrament of baptism the whole ideal of Christendom as a social unity, entered by being engrafted into a uniform religion, would inevitably erode. If the visible Chruch was not identifiable with God's elect, the weapon of excommunication would lose its power to produce conformity in religion, society, and politics. If the power to transmute bread and wine into the veritable food and drink of salvation were stripped from the Church, it must forfeit the power of the interdict and of the ban which held the temporal sword in bondage to the spiritual. To be sure, Frith wrote about no such social and political consequences. Yet, should the viewpoint of his sacramental theology prevail, these pre-eminent powers of the Church would no longer be supportable. The mass was keystone, as purgatory was cornerstone, in the great edifice of Catholic religion that housed the imagination of western civilization for a millennium. Five years after Frith deserted his career in the most ecclesiastical college of Oxford, the Church had branded and burnt him as the destroyer of purgatory and the mass. Neither Catholics nor Protestants soon forgot him.

The Church authorities at the time of his execution heightened their lament over his obstinacy because they regarded him for his learning. His answer to More's letter on the mass lived on to command a respect that warranted swift denunciation. Shortly after Frith's burning on July 4, 1533, there was written, and in the following year published, *A letter of a yonge gentylman named mayster Germen Gardynare, wryten to a frend of his, wherin men may se the demeanour & heresy of Iohñ Fryth late burned/ & also the dyspycyon & reasonynge uppon the same, had betwene the same mayster Germen and hym* (STC 11,594). The author claimed intimate knowledge of Frith's theology and its condemnation, and yearned to discredit the man as well as his position. Little is known about Gardynare beyond what may be learned from this letter, which William Rastell printed. If not a nephew of the bishop of Winchester, Stephen Gardiner, Germen was surely his intimate and probably a member of his household. To a close acquaintance, who had studied at Frith's college at Cambridge, Gardynare briefly rehearsed Frith's career since his dismissal from Cardinal College at Oxford until his death, and then at great length recounted Gardynare's vain visits to the Tower to persuade Frith to abjure his opinion of the mass. Gardynare knew Frith's doings well, and relayed information accurately. He knew of letters from Tyndale and Joye that reached Frith, and chided Frith for sharing Joye's views on the somnolence of the souls of the dead until judgment day. He noted Frith's disregard of Tyndale's advice not to write regarding the mass, and praised the lords temporal and spiritual for the kindness by which they encouraged Frith to abjure. He narrated in detail Bishop Gardiner's attempts to enlighten Frith by calling the latter to visit in his house during the last days of 1532, and predicted that Gardiner would write on the mass. Acknowledging Frith's learning, especially in classical tongues, this ardent Catholic thought the prisoner vaingloriously obstinate, intellectually dishonest, tragically misled. Several conversations about patristic opinion on the presence of Christ in the Supper were recounted in such a way as to display the author's wit, learning, and devotion, and to deprecate Frith's. These discussions had turned mostly on the old fathers, particularly Chrysostom and Augustine. At points Gardynare represented Frith as virtually admitting and repenting his errors, but on the next visit the demonic spirit again would possess him and prompt him to balk over a flimsy scruple of conscience. Other persons whom the bishops sent or Gardynare took to set Frith onto orthodox paths of belief could not avail. Finally the prisoner sought his own glory by being burnt at the stake, having succumbed to the flattery of Tyndale, Joye, and the Brethren.

This letter corroborates interesting data about Frith's last days, and reveals the Catholic party's need to discredit both his teaching and his reputation. By 1536 another attempt was made to smear Frith's name and fame, when there was published at St. Alban's, by J. Hertford for R. Stevenage, a lengthy tome by one John Gwynneth, entitled *The confutacyon of the fyrst parte of Frythes boke, with a dysputacyon before whether it be possyble for any heretike to know that hym selfe is one or not. And also an other/ whether it be wors to denye directely more or less of the fayth* (STC 12,557). Gwynneth, who flourished during the reign of Mary Tudor, was a Catholic divine and musician, educated at Oxford on a scholarship inspired by the hope that he would write against heretics. He held livings in Wales 1534–43, in London and Bedfordshire 1543–56, and died before the accession of Elizabeth I. He wrote one musical work, a providential interpretation of the accession of Mary, and four books against Frith. Three of the latter were printed long after Frith's death, during the last brief blush of England's official Catholicism. The earlier work, however, was prompted by Gwynneth's acquaintance with men who praised Frith for learning, gentleness, and patience, and, worse than that, who questioned the justice of his execution.

Gwynneth imagined a tendentious dialogue between Catho-

licus and Hereticus, the latter a straw man who for the first
half of the book consistently lost every point against the absolute singleness, authority, and truth of the official Church's
dogma. Only when the battle was going against him was he
allowed to defend Frith's doctrine of the mass, especially the
point that transubstantiation was not an article of faith to be
believed under pain of eternal damnation. Gwynneth avoided
all the subtleties of Frith's controversy with More over the
eucharistic opinions of the fathers as well as all matters of
his biblical exegesis. Thus the *Confutation* only reasserted the
necessity of believing the Church's dogma on the ground that
the Church's dogma was necessary to be believed. The writing
is of no theological and of little literary interest, but it indicates Frith's standing as the most subtle, learned, fascinating,
and admired of the Protestant martyrs before 1536.

That Gwynneth was able some twenty years later to continue—"repeat" is more accurate—his argument against Frith
testifies perhaps as much to the pettiness of Gwynneth's mind
as to the persistence of Frith's popularity. Complaining that
the earlier book was hastily issued while the author was ill,
Gwynneth said he would have dropped the work except that
Frith's view of the sacrament was widely believed at the time
of Queen Mary's accession, and therefore he must revise his
earlier treatise into three volumes. In 1554 Thomas Berthelet's press published Gwynneth's *A declaration of the state
wherein all heretikes dooe leade their lives* (*STC* 12,558)
and *A manifeste detection of the falshed of J. Friths boke*
(*STC* 12,559), and in 1557 Thomas Powell printed *A playne
demonstration of J. Frithes lack of witte and learnynge* (*STC*
12,560).

During late Henrician days Frith came to be lauded by
English Protestants, particularly in William Turner's *The
Huntyng and fynding of the Romishe fox* (1543; *STC* 24,-
353) and *The Rescuynge of the Romishe fox* (1545; *STC*
24,355). Under Edward he was acknowledged as a martyr
of the faith, and later in the century John Foxe nominated
him as second only to Tyndale among the great founders of
English Protestantism. Early in the seventeenth century the

Jesuit Robert Parsons castigated Foxe's work and derided Foxe's admiration for Frith.[9] Parsons was, of course, refuted; Matthew Sutcliffe in 1606 published *The subuersion of R. Parsons his worke entituled, A treatise of 3 conversions (STC 23,469)*, and Frith's place among the heroes of English Protestantism was reaffirmed.

Appreciations and depreciations of Frith during the century after his death reflected, of course, the shifting religious policy of the last four Tudors and the first two Stuarts. Shortly after the accession of Charles I he again enjoyed brief popularity as a Protestant "in the formost ranke for comfortable exhortation & soundnesse of doctrine . . . [who] did not light his candle at the lampe of *Mr. Caluin* . . . nor of great *Luther.*" Some theologian with a sense of humor and good timing claimed to have found miraculously in the Cambridge market a fish whose belly when cut open disgorged printed copies of tracts by Frith and others. These he published in 1626 under the title *Vox Piscis (STC* 11,395). Deriding the "more elaborate and artificiall composures" of religion in his own time, the editor claimed his discovery to have occurred just at the time that Charles' ecclesiastical policies and Laud's manner of executing them had become plain. Since the Laudian Church reminded him of Wolseyan Catholicism, the writings of a martyr under the latter seemed appropriate to oppose the former. Of the works included in the published book, only *Know Thyself* and the *Letter to the Faithful Followers* are certainly from Frith's hand. But Frith's ardent spirit was invoked to sanction the whole collection: he combined "the rare learning of a Doctor, the noble resolution of a Confessor, the admirable constancie of a Martyr, and the diuine spirit of a Prophet"; therefore "God by speciall prouidence hath thus in a sort reuiued him an age after his death . . . so that like another *Ionas* hee now speakes to thee out of the belly of the Fish." [10] In this strange manner Frith's advocacy of English Protestantism echoed long after his death.

9. R. Parsons, *A Treatise of Three Conversions of England (STC* 19,416), pt. 1, ch. 12, para. 24, and pt. 3, ch. 11, para. 1–18. Cf. J. F. Mozley, *John Foxe and His Book* (London, 1940), pp. 176–80.

10. *Vox Piscis: or, the Book-fish* . . . (1626; *STC* 11,395), in order, pp. 30, 29, 34 f.

The high regard in which many Church officials of his own time held Frith may be accounted for by recalling that among his contemporaries at Cambridge were four men who were to become archbishops, Cranmer, Heath, Parker, and May, and a number of future bishops including Latimer, Ridley, Shaxton, Bale, and Day; some of these men chiefly compiled and wrote the English Prayer Books of 1549 and 1552. His Cambridge teacher, Gardiner, spared nothing to obtain the younger man's abjuration and thus save his life. More, who excelled in vituperating the Protestants, railed at Frith's youth and presumption but withheld the personal castigation that he loosed on Tyndale, Barnes, Joye, Roy, and others.

Frith's statement of the manner of Christ's spiritual presence in the Supper came to be embodied in the English Prayer Books of 1552 and 1662, especially in the last rubric of Holy Communion. For that fact and for the striking similarity of Cranmer's mature eucharistic views with those of Frith, Foxe took for granted that the young theologian directly influenced the archbishop. Foxe himself thought that no man had written of the Supper "more learnedly and pithily" than Frith, and therefore felt himself excused from rehearsing the content of Frith's answer to More's letter by the fact that Cranmer had made Frith's view fully known in England. Although Cranmer acknowledged no such debt, Foxe asserted that the archbishop's apology against Gardiner gathered its most important and reliable arguments from Frith. Foxe thought himself familiar enough with this part of Cranmer's work to "doubt much whether the archbishop ever gave any more credit unto any author of that doctrine, than unto . . . Frith." [11]

11. AM, 5, 9. Strype, Memorials of . . . Thomas Cranmer (Oxford, 1840), I, 370, objected to this notion, granting that although Cranmer "might peruse Frith . . . yet he was too well versed in the ecclesiastical writers, that he needed to go a borrowing to the reading of any others, for sentences and allegations out of them." That estimate of Cranmer's independent knowledge of the Church fathers has been reinforced and extended to the other English reformers by Dugmore. With the assistance of Dr. P. N. Brooks, then of Cambridge University, I discovered that Cranmer's commonplace books usually cited the fathers verbatim from Reformation manuals such as Oecolampadius' De Genuina Verborum . . . ; cf. Brooks, "Thomas Cranmer's Doctrine of the Sacraments" (unpublished dissertation, Cambridge University, 1960). If Cranmer was not steeped in Frith he was steeped in Frith's major source, Oeco-

FRITH'S ORIGINALITY

Despite his admitted borrowings in sacramental theology from Oecolampadius, Frith as a theologian cannot be counted the slavish disciple of any continental reformer. His thought reveals a theocentric organizing principle, and his theocentrism was highly christological; at this point there is a striking kinship with the younger Luther. On such matters as justification, predestination, election, church, and vocation, this christological theocentrism produced understandings which, although reminiscent of Luther, found independent expression in Frith's work. Frith rejected Luther's notion of the imputation of righteousness in favor of a conception of the nonimputation of sin to the faithful believer in Christ; thus his doctrine of justification was as theocentric as, but not identical with, that of Luther.

On the matter of vocation Frith agreed with Luther that the Christian was given work to do in the world as his vocation under God, and that no particular work was intrinsically more godly than any other. But Luther's doctrine of vocation was grounded in an understanding of society as calling forth each man into his *Stand,* and that *Beruf* was to be taken as *vox dei.* Men were not to seek vocation other than the one in which they found themselves, save for the monks who must desert their false *Stand* because it pretended to be holier than other walks and led inevitably to idolatry. Frith based his idea of vocation upon no particular sociology but simply upon the notion of stewardship. Whatever physical attributes and human abilities a man found himself to possess were to be understood as God's gift to be employed for the succor of the neighbor. Frith did not want to eliminate monasticism as an order of society and as a walk of life; he wanted monks to accept the vocation of constant service to the needy for which their institution truly existed. He wished to summon the monks, and especially the friars, to this abdicated and forgotten task. He claimed to have "compiled an whole booke . . . [as] a rule

---

lampadius. Thus, insofar as Cranmer influenced the Anglican doctrine of the eucharist, its definitive lineaments find their origin among Reformation writers in the thought of the Basler.

of more perfection vnto oure religious, then any that they haue vsed this hundreth yeare." But it was not, as he hoped, appointed by God that he should "finishe it, and set it forthe." [12]

On the sacrament of the altar it has been seen that Frith was heavily indebted to Oecolampadius, but his understanding of the signification of sacraments was also indebted to Zwingli, and it was possible for Joye, in rebutting More's reply to Frith, to remain generally consistent with Frith's argument by translating and paraphrasing Zwingli.

Frith was less the protégé of Tyndale than Mozley has portrayed him to be, just as he was less the original interpreter of the fathers than Foxe thought. Certainly his attitude toward Tyndale was one of thorough appreciation for the older man's work in translating the New Testament and pentateuch into English, and one of common dedication to the reformation of the English Church. Yet Frith was thoroughly independent in translating texts of scripture in his own way for citation in his writings; only in the early translation of Patrick's *Places* did he follow closely Tyndale's New Testament. Their intimate relationship did not produce in Frith full confidence in Tyndale's theological judgments. Germen Gardynare's otherwise factual report indicates that Frith agreed with Joye against Tyndale in their controversy over the state of souls in the interim between death and the general resurrection, although personal regard for Tyndale seems to have restrained Frith from openly declaring himself with Joye on this matter.

In his appeal to the Church fathers Frith was no "proto-Anglican." His writings show no concern for the *consensus quinquasaeculorum* by reference to which most leaders of English church reform looked to scripture as the highest religious authority while making room for caesaropapism as a dominant feature of ecclesiology. Frith was not interested in writing about royal headship of the church, but he clearly did not allow royal headship as a leading theological idea. Had he and his early teacher Gardiner debated their central theological convictions, Gardiner's placement of ecclesiastical author-

12. *Whole workes*, p. 89.

ity in the king would have evoked hot disagreement from Frith. His notion of adiaphora set him against elevating what he took to be historically conditioned aspects of Christian belief and practice to the level of doctrine to be believed under pain of damnation.

Not to be dismissed lightly is the relationship between Frith's concern to distinguish essential beliefs from non-essential doctrinal opinion—a distinction he made to turn on a rigorous theocentrism—and his contact with the late Lollard emphasis upon conscientious adherence to biblical doctrine alone. Surely Frith was much affected by the Brethren. That they should not be leaderless he was willing to face personal danger and abbreviation of life and career. His most personal and fervent writings were books addressed specifically to them. But he did not only represent them, just as his relation to Lollardy was not only to symbolize the movement. Rather, Frith's vocation was to rally the English Protestants around a simple, direct, conscientiously-held theology in which God alone would be God, Christ alone would be redeemer, and man would always take the second place. With that as the aim and motivation of a career too busy to suffer distraction and too brief to cultivate petulance, there is little wonder that Frith won encomiums from many generations as an advocate of pure, evangelical Christianity.

9. Tyndale as Luther's Protégé, 1524-1529

VER since Thomas More became official defender of the Catholic religion, English opinion unanimously has acclaimed William Tyndale the chief spokesman of original English Protestantism. He translated the entire New Testament and large portions of the Old; he was expositor of a normative biblical religion; he pamphleteered against an entrenched Catholic hierarchy; although not always obeyed, he directed the activities of English Protestant exiles on the Continent; he was the elusive grand prize of heretic hunts arranged by More and his predecessors and successors. Tyndale indeed occupied the leading position among the early English Protestants, and has virtually pre-empted the attention of interpreters of that movement from John Foxe to the present. The modern remark of Henry Guppy reflects the high esteem in which he has been held by these interpreters: "No voice of scandal has ever been raised against William Tindale. There are no black spots in his life, which it has been necessary for his biographers to whitewash. . . . [T]he more the life of Tindale is examined the more he is found to be deserving of the love and veneration of his countrymen." [1]

Tyndale (as he seems to have preferred to spell the surname in earlier life, or Tindale, in the usage he adopted on the Continent) sought to be and became, above all else, a translator of holy scripture into English. As such, his influence upon English language, letters, and religion is hard to exaggerate. With good reason he has been hailed as "the man who

1. Henry Guppy, "William Tindale: scholar and martyr . . . ," *Bulletin of the John Rylands Library*, 20 (1936), 267.

more than Shakespeare even or Bunyan, has moulded and
enriched our language," for indeed until the appearance of a
welter of twentieth-century translations of scriptures it was
very largely in Tyndale's words that the English-speaking
world read its Bible.[2]

Considered as a theologian, however, Tyndale must be
regarded at once as less persistent than Luther, less consistent
than Frith, and less insistent than Barnes. For Tyndale
adopted first one and then another theme as the clue to scripture's meaning and therefore as the heart of Christian faith.
By the end of his career, personal morality seemed to him
the key to theology and the basis of Christianity. Should his
work be taken as the achievement of unity between moralism
and theology, then he achieved that unity by cutting his conception of God to fit his overriding concern for right living.
Put another way, Tyndale's religious-intellectual pilgrimage
pursued two directions at once; starting always from justification by faith, he sought both a thorough reformation of the
Christian religion and a simple rule of righteous deeds capable of earning divine rewards. If, as must be affirmed in a
certain sense, he was the founder of English Puritanism,[3] he
was also the inventor of the device by which English-speaking
Protestantism avoided being rigorously theological.

THE TRANSLATOR

The career of Tyndale has been recounted frequently by
modern writers. Of his biographers, Mozley most carefully
chased down fugitive data and wove them into a continuous
narrative, filling lacunae by ingenious surmises, but tending to
slight Tyndale's intellectual and theological development.
Tyndale's originality at conflating borrowed theological
themes hardly shows independence from formative continental
theologians. His great facility as a translator hardly argues
freedom from enormous debt to Luther's German Bible;
everywhere Tyndale imitated Luther's pungency of verbiage

2. J. R. Coates, "Tyndale's Influence on English Literature," *Tyndale Com-
memoration Volume,* ed. R. Mercer Wilson (London, 1939), p. 244, quoting *The
Times Literary Supplement,* review of S. L. Greenslade, *The Work of William
Tindale* (London, 1938).

3. Trinterud, "The Origins of Puritanism," p. 55 and passim.

and uncanny capacity for protraying biblical passages with contemporaneous religious vigor and vividness. His penchant for banal polemics, which Mozley either lamented or excused, was recognized by C. S. Lewis' judgment that Tyndale's scurrility matched More's, "except that hard words sound less unlovely from the hunted than from the hunter." [4]

The early years of his life, adequately narrated by Mozley, are of little importance for a theological estimate of Tyndale. Born about 1494 in Gloucestershire, he proceeded B.A. at Oxford July 4, 1512, and M.A. July 2, 1515. Not before 1516, probably in 1519, he went to Cambridge and made the acquaintance of men interested in the new theology issuing from Wittenberg, among them those who later would become his co-workers in Germany and the Low Countries. As priest he became a tutor at the manor of Little Sodbury during 1522–23, and probably at this time undertook to translate Erasmus' *Enchiridion of a Christian Knight* (*STC* 10,479–88) into English. Through the good offices of a wealthy and generous London merchant, Humphrey Monmouth, Tyndale sought a place in the household of the bishop of London to translate the New Testament into the common tongue. Failing utterly to captivate Tunstall's interest in or patronage for this project, a disillusioned Tyndale set his face against the official Church's enmity toward a vernacular Bible, and turned toward Germany in the spring of 1524. On May 27, 1524, he matriculated at the University of Wittenberg.[5]

Perhaps Tyndale and his new-found assistant, William Roy, former friar of Greenwich, practiced by translating Bugenhagen's 1525 *A compendious letter . . . sent to . . . Englande* from Latin. They stayed at Wittenberg during the

4. Mozley, *William Tyndale,* passim; Lewis, *English Literature in the Sixteenth Century,* p. 191.

5. Mozley, p. 53, recalled his discovery that *"Guillelmus Daltici ex Anglia"* in the Wittenberg register meant *"Daltin,"* a transposition of the syllables of the name *"Tindal."* Mozley "had taken for granted that the Wittenberg registers had been thoroughly searched by the investigators of a hundred years ago." More than a decade earlier, Preserved Smith had made the same discovery, had had it verified by Prof. F. A. Weissenborn, archivist at Halle, and had reported the discovery in much the same way that Mozley later did; see Smith, "Englishmen at Wittenberg in the Sixteenth Century," *English Historical Review, 36* (1921), 422, citing: *Album Academiae Vitebergensis, I,* 121.

crucial period when Luther was marking off his religious movement from various social and intellectual impulses of the time,
such as Erasmian humanism and the revolt of the peasants. In
August 1525 Tyndale and Roy moved to Cologne for the
abortive first attempt to publish their New Testament in English at the press of Peter Quentel, who printed late in 1525
the pages of Matthew's gospel. Pursued by Catholic authorities, Tyndale and Roy fled to Worms where in March 1526
the first printed English New Testament was produced (*STC*
2824). Shortly thereafter Roy went to Strassburg and undertook his own work as a writer and translator of religious
tracts. Tyndale remained at Worms, printing late in 1526
A compendious introduccion vnto the pistle to the Romayns
(*STC* 24,438), and undertaking the study of Hebrew preparatory to translating the Old Testament. It is probable that
he visited Marburg, perhaps during 1527, but if it was there
that he renewed his acquaintance with Frith, the visit must be
dated 1528 to allow for Frith's arrival.

Many have noted that Tyndale's career as a Bible translator followed closely that of Luther. With surprising rapidity
he produced the English New Testament, then turned immediately to the Old. But whereas Luther's German pentateuch
was ready the year after the New Testament, Tyndale's English pentateuch waited four years. In the meantime other interests came to the fore. *The parable of the wicked mammon*
(*STC* 24,454) and *The obedience of a christen man* (*STC*
24,446) were printed in 1528 at Antwerp, the former on May
28 and the latter on October 2. Learning Hebrew, searching
for the right man to help translate the Old Testament, or
wavering conviction that he was the man to carry out this
work, might singly or together account for Tyndale's delay.
Early in 1529 he sailed from Antwerp to Hamburg, suffering
shipwreck which cost him his books and effects. At Hamburg
he found the right partner in Miles Coverdale, and the translation of the pentateuch proceeded—perhaps with the advice
of Bugenhagen who was busily establishing the Reformation
in that city. From early 1530 until his death in the autumn
of 1536, Tyndale made Antwerp his home base and the headquarters of English Protestants in exile. Tyndale published

several expository writings and his 1534 New Testament revision in Antwerp during these years.

Apart from his direct translations of the Bible, which include the entire New Testament, the pentateuch, Jonah, and
probably Joshua, Judges, and Chronicles, all of which found
their way into Matthew's Bible in 1537, Tyndale's writings
fall into several classes. Extremely important as revealing his
theological development were the many prefaces, prologues,
and introductions to portions of the Bible. Expository works,
on the parable of wicked mammon, on the sermon on the
mount, and on I John, were theologically more important
than the specifically polemical books, *Obedience* (1528), *The
Practice of Prelates* (1530), and the *Answer to More's Dialogue* (1531). A little book on the origin and nature of the
sacraments and some miscellaneous minor pieces complete the
list of his writings. The Bible translations and introductions
were modeled after Luther's writings of this character. Expositions owed much to Luther. While Tyndale determined
the form of all his libelli, he employed literary sources freely,
and in the book against More relied upon Frith as a research
assistant. As a literary corpus, Tyndale's life work was quite
considerable. The nearest approach to a critical edition of his
works, the Parker Society edition prepared by Henry Walter
and published 1848–50, runs to three moderate volumes; that
edition included only samples of the Bible translations, and
excluded several miscellaneous works.[6] In Foxe's 1572 folio
edition, Tyndale's writings were set at the beginning and occupied four hundred and fifty-six pages without the Bible
translations and the miscellany.

THE NEW TESTAMENT

In spite of an occasional excursus into ecclesiastical polemics,
Tyndale's great achievement was in translating the scriptures.
All the notes to the reader that he attached to printed portions
of the Bible show him sensitive to the gravity and difficulty of
the task. Living in the first blush of enthusiasm over the availability of Erasmus' Greek text for the entire New Testament,

---

6. Included, however, as Tyndale's was George Joye's *The Souper of the
Lorde,* PS *1,* pp. 216–68.

he thought of the gospel writers and epistlers as unanimous recorders and definers of the Christian message. Erasmus' translation of the New Testament into Latin either refreshed or shocked ears attuned to the Vulgate, leaving no doubt that many distinctive colorations of medieval Christianity could be traced to the pigments of Jerome's legalistic Latin, and Tyndale belonged to a generation that produced a veritable guild of Bible translators striving for vernacular expressions of original Christianity. While familiarity need not imply dependence, it must be noted that Tyndale knew the translating work of many of his contemporaries. The particular religiosity which Luther caused to permeate his German New Testament of 1522 and Old Testament of 1523 became a model for Tyndale, as it did for most translators after him. He knew also the accomplishment of the Zürich scholars Zwingli, Pellican, Juda, and others who were publishing their German Bible between 1524 and 1530, as well as Jacques Lefèvre's French translation made from the Vulgate between 1523 and 1534. But Tyndale made it unmistakably clear that he did not rely upon the familiar Wycliffite English gospels. Apologizing for the "rudeness of the work" in the note subjoined to the 1526 complete New Testament, he declared that he "had no man to counterfeit [copy]" in any language. Nor was he "helped with English of any that had interpreted the same or such like thing in the scripture beforetime." Modestly he recalled the obstacles that impeded the work, asking that the product be counted "as a thing not having his full shape, but as it were born before his time, even as a thing begun rather than finished." [7]

Many translating problems were solved for Tyndale and many English words were suggested to him by Luther's German and by Erasmus' Latin. Nevertheless Tyndale the translator resembled the proverbial cow grazing several pastures but giving her own milk. His wide and (for his day) accurate knowledge of Greek and Hebrew is indisputable, but his New Testament was neither a mere English rendition of Luther's

7. "Epistle to the Reader . . . 1526," PS *1*, p. 390. The best discussion of Tyndale's use of other Bibles is by B. F. Westcott, *A General View of the History of the English Bible* (New York, 1905), ch. III, section 1.

German nor a direct and completely independent rendering of the Greek text into English.

Tyndale as a translator sought precise, common English words able to convey the Christian message "to the plowman at his plowbeam and to the weaver at his loom," as Erasmus' *Paraclesis* had put it. Yet the Christian message that Tyndale found in the New Testament struck him as stark, exciting, rediscovered good news for every man *coram deo,* as tidings traduced by the dogmas, traditions, and cultic practices of Catholicism. For that reason, among others, he set little store by his own first translation. Much remained to be done. Words and phrases perhaps "added superfluously" must be "put out." Whatever had been "overseen through negligence" must be made up. Dark places needed illuminating. Passages called for "more proper English." The work lacked "a table to expound the words which are not commonly used, and [to] shew how the scripture useth many words which are otherwise understood of the common people, and to help with a declaration where one tongue taketh not another." The remaining task was "to seethe it better, and to make it more apt for the weak stomachs." [8]

Repeatedly Tyndale, and on his behalf Frith, proffered the 1526 New Testament to the revising, emending, improving endeavors of anybody who would undertake them, stipulating only the Greek text as court of last appeal. Tyndale made this proposal both by soliciting the assistance of learned men and by daring the ecclesiastical and civil authorities of England to let the word of God go abroad in the common tongue. During his lifetime only one man accepted the offer, but the improvements made by Joye in 1534 evoked Tyndale's chagrin and intemperate denunciations; only after being offended by Joye's effort did he publish his own revision in November 1534. Similar chagrin had met specific attacks made by More on several of Tyndale's choices of words—the clumsy "seniour" for *presbyteros* (which by 1531 Tyndale was willing to replace with "elder" but not with More's preferred "priest"), for *ekklēsia* the common term "congregation" rather than "church," for *agapē* "love" rather than the religiously familiar

8. PS *1,* pp. 390 f.

"charity," for *charis* "favour" instead of "grace," for *metanoia* "repentance" rather than "penance," and so on. Increasingly, Tyndale's modesty about the character of his work and his desire for criticism diminished. His estimate of the finality of his early work hardened as years passed. When the promised revision finally came it was, on the whole, quite minor, and Tyndale implicitly forbade others to improve it.

Resistance to More's attacks on certain words was for Tyndale philological and literary but above all theological. So seems to have been his reluctance both to accept Joye's revision and to proceed with his own. During the mid-1520s Tyndale was sure that the New Testament proclaimed graceful, free, unmerited, benign promises of God to mankind, just as he was sure that the Old Testament described another and preparatory work of God, an *opus alienum* before an *opus proprium* (as Luther put it). Tyndale took directly from Luther's preface to the 1522 German New Testament these words of his 1525 Prologue:

> ¶ The olde testament is a boke, where in is wrytten the lawe and commandments of god/ and the dedes of them which fulfil them/ and of them also which fulfill them nott.
>
> ¶ The newe testament is a boke, where in are conteyned the promyses of god/ and the dedes of them which beleue them or beleue them nott.[9]

In fact this Prologue depended so heavily upon Luther for its verbiage that More justly regarded the 1525-26 English New Testament as a translation of Luther's heresies and errors into English. Not only the preface led to that conclusion; the format of the 1525 fragment was that of Luther's 1522 testament, and the lengthy marginal glosses more often than not said what Luther's glosses said.

Prefaces to individual books, which Tyndale added to the 1534 revision, reinforce the notion of Tyndale's dependence upon Luther, for hardly a thought expressed in these pieces is

---

9. *Cologne Fragment*, Aijᵛ; cf. PS *1*, p. 8; the words "and commandments" were omitted in the Parker Society edition, which added punctuation to the second paragraph cited.

not to be found in the German's prefaces. That dependence is seen most clearly, however, in the Prologue of the 1525 Cologne Fragment, its notes, and the theological character of the translation. Although Tyndale's hand is everywhere to be found in its formation, especially in its regard for faith as empowering the believer to love God and to do God's will, nevertheless Luther generated the substance of Tyndale's conception of the book which he was translating. To the law of the Old Testament was assigned the single theological use of driving a sinner either to his appetites for gratification or to Christ for succor; in no sense was it a charter of human activities set forth as pleasing to God and capable of men's achievement. "Eua*ngelio*n (that we cal the gospel) is a greke worde/ & signyfyth good/ mery/ glad and ioyfull tydings/ that maketh a mannes hert glad/ and maketh hym synge/ daunce and leepe for ioye." [10] Tyndale understood the testament as a free legacy and bequest of a benevolent donor. Only by faith—*fiducia* not *assensus*—might that legacy be received. Human deeds of righteousness, with moral virtues, "all are nothi*n*ge in the sight of god." [11]

If the Prologue left any doubt that Tyndale had allied himself with what was popularly known as the new Lutheran heresy, it was dispelled late in 1526 when Tyndale published a periphrastic translation of Luther's *Introduction to Romans,* hailing the epistle as the purest and principal statement of the Christian gospel. The 1526 New Testament itself taught that the gospel was explicit in the epistles and that the stories and sayings of the gospels were to be interpreted by that gospel. Occasion will arise later to enter a caveat against the judgment that everything Tyndale "wrote was directly or indirectly devoted to the same purpose: to circulate the 'gospel'— not, on his view, to be identified with the Gospels—either by comment or translation." [12] Of the Tyndale of the mid-1520s the judgment is true enough, for the gospel was identified as

10. *Cologne Fragment,* Aij^v; cf. PS *I,* p. 8, where punctuation varies enough to alter the sense of the passage.

11. *Cologne Fragment,* B^v; PS *I,* p. 14. See also L. J. Trinterud, "A Reappraisal of William Tyndale's Debt to Martin Luther," *Church History, 31,* 1 (1962), 24–45.

12. Lewis, *English Literature in the Sixteenth Century,* p. 182.

good news heralded in the promises of God which Paul in Romans contrasted with the impossibility and vanity of works-righteousness. If a theological difference of importance is to be drawn between Luther and Tyndale as of 1525–26, it is that Tyndale tended to mistrust Luther's very careful distinction between law and gospel, preferring to portray justification by faith as enabling man to do good. The tendency was to grow by leaps and bounds—translating the pentateuch made for a leap, and the writings after 1532 found him bounding into a validation of works-righteousness of sanctification.

To assess the amount of Tyndale verbiage, if any, rendered directly from Luther into English seems futile because Tyndale's governing genius was for finding the simple, direct, powerful way of putting the Christian message into English, and his general conception of that message was, as far as the period 1524–29 is concerned, made in Wittenberg. Thomas More understood better than many later writers that the 1526 English New Testament was, from the Catholic standpoint, wrongly called "the new Testament" but was really "Tyndals Testamente or Luthers Testament. For so hadde Tyndall after Luthers counsayl corrupted and chaunged it from the good and wholesome doctrine of Christ to the deuelishe heresyes of their own, that it was cleane a contrarye thyng." [13]

PROTESTANT POLEMICS

The early polemical writings exhibit clearly Tyndale's dependence upon Luther. Bishop Westcott wrote: "The extent to which Tindale silently incorporated free or even verbal translations of passages from Luther's works in his own has escaped the notice of his editors. To define it accurately would be a work of very great labour, but the result, as exhibiting the points of contact and divergence in the opinions of the two great reformers, would be a most instructive passage in the doctrinal history of the time." A generation later, Rupp noted that nobody had taken Westcott's hint; various modern scholars have agreed that Tyndale's 1528 *Wicked Mammon* in-

13. More, *Dialogue, 3,* 8, *Workes,* p. 220.

corporated a whole sermon by Luther and that the remainder of the work owed its character and content to Luther.[14]

During the Reformation period, *Mammon* and Tyndale's other 1528 writing, *The Obedience of a Christian Man,* became by far the most popular of all his treatises; before Foxe published the first collection of Tyndale's works in 1572, each of these writings had had no less than eight separate printings. Just as *Mammon* taught Luther's understanding of justification by faith alone and defended it against the common charge of antinomianism that arose after the peasants' revolt of 1525, *Obedience* explicated Luther's social ethic, which emphasized the rôle of the state in the divine economy, and defended this doctrine against the common accusation that it engendered revolutions. In both instances, but more explicitly in the political treatise, Tyndale made detailed applications of Luther's fundamental positions to the situation in England.

Mammon was originally published by Hoochstraten in Antwerp, using his pseudonym, "Hans Luft, Malborowe," on May 8, 1528. The address to the reader was headed, "William Tyndale, otherwise called Hitchins"; there should be no mistake as to the author, for Tyndale wished to separate his effort from the name and reputation of his erstwhile fellow worker Roy, who had recently put forth a piece of verse lampooning Wolsey. Tyndale scorned and denounced that dialogue, *Rede me and be nott wrothe For I say no thynge but trothe* (*STC* 21,427), calling Roy untrustworthy and foolhardy. It was not the last occasion on which Tyndale would renounce a friend and assistant, for Joye would be dealt with similarly in 1534. Tyndale's primary interest in this instance was to set himself on a level of literature high above that of

14. Westcott, p. 146; Rupp, *Studies,* pp. 49, 51; Jacobs, *Lutheran Movement,* pp. 30–32; Mozley, *William Tyndale,* p. 127, reckoned one-sixth of the whole treatise to be a direct translation of Luther's 1522 sermon on the Ninth Sunday after Trinity (*WA, 10,* 3, pp. 283–92). Trinterud, "A Reappraisal," noted the persistence in these tracts of Tyndale's dissent from Luther's overwhelming emphasis upon faith-righteousness; but as yet Tyndale had not discovered the covenant theme—the theme on which he later put such emphasis as to break clearly away from Luther.

vilifying rhymes: "It becometh not then the Lord's servant
to use railing rhymes, but God's word; which is the right
weapon to slay sin, vice, and all iniquity"—a standard Tyndale compromised two years later when, in *Practice of Prelates,* he stooped to vilification if not to versification.[15]

In Germany the Reformation was linked with the recent
revolt of peasants against temporal and ecclesiastical authority; *Mammon* took pains to assert that the Protestant movement was religiously revolutionary but socially stable. Therefore the work bore its author's name, but Tyndale concealed
the fact that the theme and much of the phraseology originated with Luther. Tyndale undoubtedly knew that John
Fisher had charged Luther and all Protestants with antinomianism in his sermon at the book-burning service in February 1526. Fisher depicted the doctrine of justification by
faith as inevitably developing anarchism of the kind displayed
by Münzer's followers in the Münster revolt of 1525. It is
not too much to mark down *Mammon* and *Obedience* as
answers to Fisher's accusation, for in making it he represented
a powerful body of conservative, upper-class opinion in all
Europe. Tyndale's May treatise showed how purely religious
a teaching justification by faith was, and the companion piece
that followed in October pointed out that the Protestant teaching urged not revolution, but invoked divine sanction on the
status quo of social-political life.

Given their polemical purpose, Tyndale's 1528 tracts might
be expected to slight the religious distinction between faith
and works which formed the core of Luther's early theology.
They aimed to demonstrate as compatible the unavailing
character of works before God and the inevitability of works
as the fruit of faith. The recurrent theme of *Mammon* was
that false faith eschewed works and reveled in licentiousness,
while true faith sought to perform good works more assiduously than the Catholic religious scheme of merits which put
a ceiling on works necessary to justification. Rightly considered, the Protestant would outwork the Catholic, for the
former knew an absolute demand to seek the neighbor's welfare and received divine empowerment sufficient to the task,

15. PS *I,* p. 41.

while the Catholic had to obey only the precepts for his justification, and thought of good deeds as springing from his own limited energy. Underneath all that, however, lay the conviction that only faith, in the sense of confidence not of credence, availed the imputation of Christ's righteousness to man; the goodness evaporated from good works when man traded upon them to depict himself as meriting God's decree of righteousness. Here Tyndale agreed with Luther's single-minded notion of justification. He stressed good works without according them any function in justifying sinners. His underscoring of works as faith's fruit implies no distance between Tyndale's theological conviction and that of his then master. Luther had composed his sermon on the parable of the wicked mammon long before the peasants' uprising, while Tyndale's translation and elaboration of the sermon answered Fisher's accusation that justification by faith made for personal licentiousness and social chaos. Tyndale had not yet departed from Luther on the doctrine of justification.

Tyndale withheld vituperation of Fisher from *Mammon,* saving that for *Obedience.* Fisher was almost studied in his misunderstanding and misrepresentation of Luther in the 1526 sermon—a fact that may be explained by the public, popular, and commissioned character of the sermon, but that can hardly be excused in so competent a theologian. In *Obedience,* twice as long as *Mammon,* Tyndale's polemical venom flowed freely, leaving no doubt that he regarded Fisher as the chief defender of Catholicism in England. The surmise that Tyndale knew of Fisher's 1526 sermon is borne out by the substance of *Mammon* and *Obedience,* but in the latter he took Fisher to task for errors and blunders, as he thought, in the 1521 sermon against Luther. He called Fisher a "school-doctor" who was "past all shame" in making "us believe in a bull" (a feeble pun on papal decrees and Aaron's calf), a man afflicted with "malicious blindness" who "playeth bo-peep with the scripture" and juggles citations from the fathers, an ignorant idolater who took the Pope for his god and mistook the heretic Origen for a faithful doctor;—"God stop his blasphemous mouth!" for he was "both abominable and shameless, yea, and stark mad with pure malice, and so adased in the brains with spite" that he knew not truth from falsehood.[16] Harsh words, indeed, to modern ears, but in their day more culpable for impertinence as from a priest to a bishop than for personal calumny as from man to man. Amidst such invectives Tyndale subtly answered a dozen of Fisher's main points against Luther. Despite the fact that Tyndale wrote against the phrases of the 1521 sermon, *Obedience* and *Mammon* controverted the substance of Fisher's 1526 sermon: works-righteousness and the alleged anarchism of Protestants. Some recent arrival from England, perhaps Frith, apparently told Tyndale in detail of Fisher's accusation.

Tyndale undertook in *Obedience* to set out a Protestant view of the orders of society—"the obedience of children, servants, wives and subjects [which] four orders are of God's making, and the rules thereof are God's word." Beyond being a sufficient guide to Christian living, the treatise claimed to contain "all obedience that is of God." [17] Duties of children, wives, husbands, parents, servants, masters, subjects, kings, princes, rulers, landlords, judges, and officers covered the subject of civil authority; the proper place of the spiritualty was minutely described. The assertion of each person's right to vernacular scripture, the only guide to true obedience, pervaded the entire argument. The Popes' claim to divine prerogatives engendered a false obedience to the Church which in fact meant blatant disobedience to God's rules for the orders of society. Far from demanding obedience to itself, the Church should inculcate knowledge of the scripture and a faith that would inculcate the desire and ability to live by the scripture. Thus detailed prescriptions for the affairs of society compromised no whit the doctrine of justification by faith. Tyndale erected *Obedience* squarely upon the foundation of *Mammon,* to which the reader of the former was referred: "Of prayer and good deeds, and of the order of love, or charity, I have abundantly written in my book of the Justifying of Faith." [18] The main contention against Fisher, in fact, was that faith must precede love.

16. PS *I*, pp. 189, 209, 213, 214, 220, 221.
17. PS *I*, pp. 331, 163.
18. PS *I*, p. 296; Tyndale admitted, for whatever reason, no debt to Luther.

Obedience, moreover, was as much in line with Luther as *Mammon.* Two kingdoms, earthly and heavenly, claimed the Christian's allegiance. In the latter, only faith availed; in the former, either faith or fear might produce an orderly society. Tyndale, following Luther, thought magistracy a direct divine agency:

> God hath made the king in every realm [on earth] judge over all, and over him there is no judge. He that judgeth the king judgeth God; and he that layeth hands on the king layeth hand on God; and he that resisteth the king resisteth God, and damneth God's law and ordinance. If the subjects sin, they must be brought to the king's judgment. If the king sin, he must be reserved unto the judgment, wrath, and vengeance of God. As it is to resist the king, so is it to resist his officer, which is set, or sent, to execute the king's commandment.[19]

But in the heavenly kingdom the names of king, subject, master, servant, were nothing, for "In Christ no man ruleth as a king his subjects, or a master his servants; but serveth. . . . We be here all servants unto Christ." [20]

Christians were to obey magistrates as occupants of the room of God, yet when they commanded evil they must be disobeyed and their punishment for disobedience suffered; there was no ground for rebellion against authority, however tyrannical. It was here that Tyndale introduced a thought of his own into the otherwise Lutheran conception of civil authority, and yet sensed no need to reconcile an inherent contradiction. That the king should place himself at the service of his neighbor even when the latter was his subject was a typical Lutheran hope for the Christian vocation of the prince. But Tyndale made the king responsible to the law of God in his governing; he was "not to rule after his own imagination." [21] This dissent from Luther was faint, as it were a slip of the pen, and in 1528 Tyndale made little of it. Yet it would crescendo and reverberate in Tyndale's mind over

19. PS *1,* p. 177.
20. PS *1,* p. 334.
21. Idem.

the next eight years, until the law of God became the tonic chord of his theological composition. With that exception, *Obedience* rigorously allowed only one theological use of divine law: it was to be taught to men that they might perceive their duty to God and their betters, so that "when thou hast meeked them and feared them with the law, [thou canst] teach them the testament and promises which God hath made unto us in Christ." [22]

Again in agreement with Luther, Tyndale perceived a law written into the universe to restrain evil and to promote social order, so that "law" had a broadly applicable *usus civilis*. On the theological side, however, law was the revealer of man's inability to do good, the mirror of rectitude in which man faced the evil within him preparatory to placing confidence before God not in his own capacities but in God's promises. Theologically, the law could do nothing but teach man to take the second place. Having done that, a man's faith would produce in him a love for the good ends which the law sought, but "the children of faith are under no law . . . and . . . need . . . no law to compel them." [23] On this basis, with the one incidental exception mentioned above, Tyndale's treatise on the obedience of Christians within and to the established orders of society qualified in no way the single-minded emphasis upon faith expressed in *Mammon*.

Tyndale's trenchant attack upon the existing Church in England arose from the notion, also derived from Luther, that the church was no specific order of society as were magistracy, marriage, and the market place. Only by robbing both the law of God and the promises of God, only by usurping both the magistracy of the prince and the obedience of the subject, had the hierarchy established itself in England and in Europe; the robber and usurper was falsely anointed— literally "antichrist." The Pope and his minions established their own canon law alongside and against the law of the land, demanding that kings be their hangmen. In so doing the church robbed subjects of proper rule by civil magistrates who were appointed by God to preserve order in society. Be-

22. PS *I*, p. 156.
23. PS *I*, p. 297.

yond that the Catholic Church demanded adherence to false ceremonies—religious artifices falsely invested with power to accomplish salvation. These ceremonies covered and hid the true salvation freely offered in God's word. Little wonder, then, that Church officials in England ordered and presided over the burning of God's word in Tyndale's translation. The hierarchy usurped not only the place of the king but also the role of God, nullifying God's promises and setting in their stead ineffectual idolatries.

In ecclesiology, theology, and politics Tyndale's 1528 treatises echoed Luther just as clearly as the 1525–26 New Testament translation and introductions had done. At the end of this first phase of the theological career of the English reformer-translator, the rediscovered gospel found on each page of the New Testament was the center of all his thinking. This is not to say that Tyndale was simply epigonous. Certainly he gave original expression in English to the theocentric theology that Luther articulated in Latin and German. Yet in Luther's own sense of the term, Tyndale had not become a theologian, "For a man becomes a theologian by living, by dying, and by being damned, not by understanding, reading or speculating." [24] It was for a different theology from the one that he read, understood, and translated in the period 1524–29 that Tyndale would become a theologian.

24. *WA, 5,* p. 163, lines 28 f.: "Vivendo, immo moriendo et damnando fit theologus, non intelligendo, legendo aut speculando."

10. Tyndale's Rediscovery of the Law
1530-1532

ETWEEN 1528 and 1530 Tyndale himself free from preoccupation with the New Testament and with the theology of Luther by undertaking to translate the Old Testament. In 1530 he published English renditions of the first five books of Moses. He had learned Hebrew, and had overcome discouraging obstacles. By shipwreck he had lost his personal possessions, notes, books, and paraphernalia. It had been necessary to move from Antwerp to Hamburg and back again.

God's gospel as the central theme of the New Testament had previously been the hub of Tyndale's thought; now God's law as the central theme of the pentateuch established itself as a second focus in his thought. The shape of his theology became elliptical. Alongside the benign promises of a gracious God willing to restore undeserving man to favor, Tyndale set the moral code demanded by a stern God whose pleasure was evoked by man's efforts to live out divine prescriptions for goodness. This is not to say that Tyndale left off teaching a righteousness based on faith and adopted one based on works. Faith remained for him prerequisite to righteousness much as a gift is prerequisite to gratitude. His conception not of the gift but of the gratitude changed. Adherence to the moral law of the Old Testament replaced free striving after the welfare of the neighbor as a pattern of a life justified by faith. In a still later phase of his thought, Tyndale would interpret gospel in terms of law; in 1530 law and gospel became twin pillars of the edifice of salvation. Without gospel, law still merely condemned. Once gospel was received in faith it engendered the desire and capacity to fulfill the moral regimen of law. Thus faith remained primary even as law became equally necessary. Law was no longer God's *opus alienum* paradoxically hiding and presaging gospel as *opus proprium* of manifest promises. In 1530 Tyndale understood law as a strange work only in its function as preparation for gospel. Gospel, although primary, became only half of God's *opus proprium,* and law—now not feared but loved—became the other, if latter, half. Thus Tyndale introduced into his theology a second theological use of law, and thereby renounced his discipleship to Luther.

The writings that announced Tyndale's bifocal theology of gospel and law were the translations of and prologues to the first five books of the Old Testament, the general preface to the pentateuch, and the polemical *Practice of Prelates.* These works represent his whole literary output for the years 1529–30. By the end of 1531 this new position had been consolidated by the *Answer to More's Dialogue,* an exposition of I John, a translation of Jonah, and a subtle but telling revision of the preface to the 1525 New Testament, now separately printed as *A pathway to the holy scripture* (*STC* 24,-462). After these there ensued a strangely silent period before the announcement of his third and final theological position.

THE PENTATEUCH

Tyndale never defaulted his early vocation to translate scripture into English. He was always more the translator than the theologian, and his theology shifted as his primary work concentrated upon first one portion of scripture and then another. Law dominated his thinking, appropriately enough for a translator, when he made his English version of the great Hebrew legal writings.[1] But in 1530 Tyndale applied the

---

1. Trinterud, "The Origins of Puritanism," p. 40, noted that "the development of Tyndale's theological outlook has not been traced in any useful manner, and it is not possible from what is known of his life to discover all the Continental influences which he took up." While external influences are indeed hard to trace, his own career can be made to account for much of the development of his thought, as this chapter and the next attempt to show. In this connection I am indebted to researches carried out under my direction by J. R. Copeland,

theological term "law" only to the moral injunctions of the Old Testament, not to the ethical and religious precepts of the New which he later embraced as law.

Tyndale's English pentateuch of 1530 was printed, apparently in Antwerp at the press of John Hoochstraten, as five separate booklets (*STC* 2350). Only Genesis carried a colophon, dating the printing January 17, 1530, and the dating was not old style for 1531, for the book was proscribed in English lists of mid-1530 as well as of 1531 and 1532. It is possible that the first and last books of the pentateuch were printed first—Genesis since it was prefixed by "Aprologe shewinge the vse of the scripture," Deuteronomy because it was Tyndale's favorite—and that Exodus, Leviticus, and Numbers came somewhat later. The work of translating occupied Tyndale for a long time; apparently he prepared the final draft with the assistance of Coverdale in the house of Miss Margaret von Emersen in Hamburg between Easter and December 1529, as the 1570 edition of Foxe's martyrology reported.[2]

Tyndale used the prologue to recount his difficulties in translating the New Testament as well as to complain against the opposition it had met among English church leaders; he also retracted the previous offer that any might revise his work. He submitted "this boke and all other that I haue other made or translated, or shall in tyme to come . . . unto all them that submytte them selves vnto the worde of god." Tyndale now counted himself a member of a circle of Englishmen who served the word of God, meaning not the personal *logos tou theou* but the very words of scripture. Only such men should judge his work, and they only by reference to the original biblical tongues. They might disallow and burn it if

Jr., and reported in "The Place of the Five Books of Moses in the Career of William Tyndale Translator and Reformer" (May 14, 1960; typescript in my possession).

Tyndale's prologue and prefaces to the books of Moses are in PS *1*, pp. 392–446, but the prologue to Genesis is given as revised in 1534, not as first published in 1530. The 1530 pentateuch was reprinted with introduction, collations, and notes as *William Tyndale's Five Books of Moses, Called the Pentateuch* . . . , ed. J. I. Mombert (New York, 1884).

2. See Mozley, *William Tyndale*, pp. 145 ff.

they found it wanting, provided they publish "of their awne translatinge a nother that is more correcte."[3] The dare involved little risk. Stanch Catholics opposed a vernacular Bible, and Protestants in England could not command the scholarship necessary to produce another translation. Tyndale was taunting More, whose *Dialogue* of mid-1529 chided Tyndale over his choice of words in translating the New Testament. Tyndale then brushed aside discussion with More as futile. In 1525 Luther had likened Erasmus to a donkey who brayed scripture but understood none of it; now More was marked among the "ydle disputers, and braulers aboute vayne wordes, ever gnawenge vppon the bitter barcke with out and never attayninge unto the swete pith with in." Tyndale wrote only for those who sought to suck out the inner meaning.

What was the inner meaning? No longer were promises of God the kernel of scripture. Now one must look first to the law for the true way of living, then to the promises for the true way of hoping. The books of law contained useful examples, "firste of comforte, how god purgeth all them that submitte them selves to walke in his wayes, in the purgatorye of tribulatyon, delyveringe them yet at the latter ende, and never soferinge any of them to perysh, that cleave faste to his promyses." There were also examples "written to feare the flesh that we synne not."[4]

Tyndale was translating the pentateuch in 1530 as Luther had done in 1523, but it was determining Tyndale's thought in a way that never occurred to Luther. Theologically, Luther saw in Moses a ministry of sin and an office of death that ceased when Christ came to free men from religious bondage to the law. With Tyndale, Moses was now a proto-Christ; a few years later he would see Christ as a second Moses.[5] So

---

3. *Five Books,* p. 6.
4. Ibid., pp. 7, 9, 10.
5. Tyndale warned in the prologue to Exodus, *Five Books,* p. 162, against making "Moses a figure of Christ with Rochestre," choosing to hold up Moses as "an ensample vnto all princes and to all that are in authorite, how to rule vnto goddes pleasure and vnto their neyghbours profette." Nor was Aaron a "figure of christ vntill he come vnto his sacrifisinge, but an ensample vnto all preachers of goddes worde." Tyndale was objecting to Fisher's typological exegesis on exegetical grounds, not to a prefigurement of Christ by Moses and Aaron on theological grounds. In the theological, not typological, sense of

the whole pentateuch seemed a guide to good living for Christians. To be sure, he deemed its ceremonial rules, so prominent in Leviticus, no longer binding, but while these constituted a law from whose bondage Christ delivered men, the moral law of the Old Testament remained to guide men's lives thus delivered. Therefore Tyndale judged Deuteronomy the best book of the five, because the *gesta dei* it rehearsed filled people's hearts with love for the moral law and led them to obey it. Deuteronomy promised penalties for disobedience that likewise produced obedience to the law.

The Old Testament was deficient only in that it could not produce sufficient motivation to obey the law. That was the role of the New, which when "preached and beleued, the sprete entreth the hart and quyckeneth it, and geueth her lyfe and iustifieth her. The sprete also maketh the lawe a lyuely thing . . . in the herte, so that a man bringeth forth good workes of his awne acord without compulsion of the lawe." [6] Although the right way to obey was found in the gospel, that which must be obeyed was found in the law. True believers, to be sure, still sinned, but they sinned by the body and its members, not by the heart enlivened to the law. For the heart's love, God forgave the members' transgressions, and the souls of the dead, which lived free of the conflicting desires of the body, might do no sin. [7]

The theology of Tyndale's prologues to the pentateuch sharply underscored the theme of law as distinct from, but corollary to, gospel. They hint only faintly at his construing God's covenanting with man as so involved with both gospel and law that God came into man's debt when the law was obeyed. But law had become prominently the stuff of divine-human encounter. Without faith which trusted God's promises—now, for the first time in Tyndale's thought, promises referred to the future life—man was incapable of obeying the law. The gospel elicited a life centered on trusting prom-

---

"proto-Christ," the quotation establishes my point; Moses, like the good ruler, is the anointed of God. In 1530 Tyndale was still of two minds about Christ as lawgiver, but the matter became clear to him soon thereafter.

6. *Five Books,* p. 167.
7. Ibid., pp. 292 f.

ises rather than expecting rewards for works, and the gospel still inaugurated the appropriation of Christian salvation. But the path of salvation was the way of Moses. It is not difficult to see how Tyndale might, with one step forward from this position, make God's fulfillment of his promises contingent upon man's fulfillment of God's law, without thinking that he had compromised the doctrine of justification by faith, for neither the promises might be believed and yearned for nor the law loved and lived without faith. That step forward (or backward as the case may be) Tyndale later took.

The actual translation of the 1530 pentateuch confirms these assertions, made on the basis of the prologues, about Tyndale's theology. The force with which the translation struck the reader with the divine decrees was more important to the translator than his text. Tyndale's inclination to choose several English terms to render a standard term in the original is illustrated repeatedly. He did not shrink from periphrasis whenever the moral could thereby be conveyed. The Hebrew verb *yadah,* used to express sexual intercourse, itself quite apt and direct, was made "know" twice, but he usually preferred "lay with" and even resorted to "do our lust." Here Tyndale veered from all his possible sources. He solved the problem of at least one corrupt text, Genesis 4:7a, by conflating several versions rather than choosing one, in order to produce a meaning found in none: "Wotest thou not yf thou dost well thou shalt receave it? But & yf thou dost evell, by & by thy synne lyeth open in the dore." [8] So the translation bespoke the theological concerns of the translator. As will be seen, the 1534 revisions of Genesis reflect Tyndale's final theological convictions.

POLITICS AND PRELATES

The most slanderous of all Tyndale's writings was the vituperative 1530 libellus, *The practyse of Prelates.* ¶ *Whether the Kinges grace maye be separated from hys quene/ because she was his brothers wyfe (STC* 24,465). For it he earned Henry's lasting enmity. It is also the most miscellaneous of Tyndale's works. Only about one-third of its rambling length

8. Copeland, pp. 30 f.

was topical, in rejoicing over the fact that Wolsey had fallen on evil days and in offering unsolicited advice about the royal divorce. These internal evidences demand assigning the tract to the last weeks of 1530 or the early months of 1531.

For the most part the book was a pejorative rehearsal of the history of the Church, drawn from Platina's *Lives of the Popes,* interlarded with matter borrowed from *Vom Alten und Neuen Gott,* and from the kind of contrasts between Christ and his self-styled vicar on earth that Frith had put into English the previous year. Portraying the early Church and its leaders as consumed with a pure religious zeal, Tyndale saw troubles begin with the appointment of deacons to handle money. As these men had grasped the episcopal office, the Church had sought temporal power at the cost of its spiritual purity: "they that had the plough by the tail looked back, the plough went awry; faith waxed feeble and fainty; love waxed cold; the scripture waxed dark; Christ was no more seen. He was in the mount with Moses; and therefore the bishops would have a god upon the earth whom they might see." [9] Thus the papacy arose to hold the Church in idolatry for centuries. Tyndale chose his illustrations of papal arrogations of regal prerogatives ad hominem mostly from English history. He pictured the present reign in England as having fallen under the evil influences of "Thomas Wolfsee . . . this wily wolf . . . and raging sea." [10]

As an estimate of Church history, *Practice of Prelates* falls in the class of tracts written under the spell of the renaissance humanists' view of the past. A pure, golden age of following the *philosophia christi* prevailed until distorted—for Erasmus by the monks, for Tyndale by the prelates. The crying need of the time was to perceive error and to revert to the past by re-establishing the pure Church of earliest times. The song

9. PS *2,* p. 257. The manner in which Tyndale used and abused history in his polemic against Henry and English Catholicism has been noted by Rainer Pineas, "William Tyndale's Use of History as a Weapon of Religious Controversy," *Harvard Theological Review,* 55 (1962), 121–41; only with respect to England can it be held that Tyndale "was the first to use history as a weapon of religious controversy" (p. 121); Pineas noted several English sources that Tyndale used or might have used.

10. PS *2,* p. 307.

had earlier been sung in England, and in purer tones, by John
Colet. Tyndale, not quite at home with humanism, uttered
a ditty. He was less strained when he discussed the political
and ecclesiastical machinations of his own times, explaining
how Wolsey repeatedly led Henry VIII down the garden path
in negotiations with the King of France and the Emperor. As
if that were not affront enough to a proud monarch, Tyndale
gratuitously entered the debate over Henry's marital affairs,
noting the political intrigue by which the marriage with Catherine had been made canonically allowable, but judging against
the dissolution of the bond on a literalistic interpretation of
the pentateuch. Following reports current at the time, Tyndale cast Wolsey in the rôle of instigator of the divorce.

Since the canonical and theological issues at stake in the
King's matter turned on interpretations of the Mosaic law, it
is understandable that Tyndale, fresh from his studies and
translations of these passages, should have firm opinions. He
proposed that the King should "search the laws of God" to
discover "whether it [the divorce] be lawful or not; foras-
much as he himself is baptized to keep the laws of God, and
hath proposed them and hath sworn them." The King was
obliged to come to his own conclusions as to what course of
action scripture dictated, quite apart from counsels of divines
and from canonists' decisions. His conclusion he should write
out, print in English, and pursue without regard to the stance
of "the emperor, or of his lords, or of his commons and subjects: for God hath promised to keep them that keep his
laws." Here occurred Tyndale's first mention of the notion
that the covenant between God and man in terms of law was
a bipartite agreement, equally binding upon God and man.
Casually Tyndale elaborated his advice to Henry into a
general principle: "If we care to keep his laws, he will care
for the keeping of us, for the truth of his promises." As to
the King, should the law of God prohibit the divorce, the
ruler must fear God, not man, and follow God's law. If the
marriage to Catherine was truly made before God it could
not be broken by any man, not even the Pope. Tyndale set
out rules for understanding the laws of God. There were ceremonial laws that ceased with Christ's self-offering, there were

laws to punish evil-doers which were binding only upon the
Jews, and there were laws pertaining to faith and love which
were binding forever upon all. "For whosoever is of God, the
same consenteth unto this [natural] law, and unto all that
followeth thereof naturally." These laws, essentially the decalogue, summarized all duties to God and neighbor.[11] As to
the divorce itself, Tyndale reported having searched the
scripture and consulted with learned men; he found no sanction for putting aside Catherine, but he did not foreclose every
possibility that the King might interpret the laws of God so
as to dissolve the marriage.

Most important of all its many themes, *Practice of Prelates*
prophesied doom for the realm because for so long it had
been manipulated by Wolsey along the crooked path of canon
law, ecclesiastical politics, and political intrigue. Tyndale
lodged hope for the country's social stability and political
order in publication of the scriptures in English, so that
every man might have before him the law of God and live by
it. Otherwise chaos, conspiracy, and rebellion were inevitable.
Either the scripture was forbidden out of ignorance, or its
prohibition sprang from hatred of the law of God. The former
circumstance demanded immediate repentance to avoid destruction, but was in principle forgivable; the latter involved
the sin against the Holy Ghost, and conjured for the realm
a fate too bleak to behold. In either case, Tyndale had told
them so! His *Obedience*, as he looked back upon it, had fore-
warned the land. Now the prelates had brought England to
the brink of rebellion, he thought, and no obedience might be
found to maintain law and order. Should social violence and
political disobedience arise, the prelates, and the King who
suffered them to rule him, stood to blame. The law of God,
specifically that of the Old Testament as summarized in the
New, was the only true rule for the body politic, as Tyndale
now saw it. Establish a biblically defined theocracy, or perish!
was his warning to Henry. Tudor pride and Tudor might
would soon find a neat way between the horns of this dilemma
by forging into a unity the will of God, the policies of bishops,
and the King's own desire.

11. PS *2*, pp. 323 f.

By the end of 1530 the second focus of Tyndale's theology, the law of God, became the point around which his interpretation of the disturbing affairs of his own time revolved, as well as his understanding of church history. The other focus of the ellipse was still clearly defined and central to matters specifically religious. But the currents of Tyndale's thought were eddying around the law more than around the gospel. Only proleptically and with reference to a specific occasion in the affairs of his King and countrymen did the focus of gospel find explications as something dependent upon that of law. If the figure of the ellipse may be extended to carry the narrative, Tyndale in late 1530 was gradually relaxing the polarity between the two foci; the ellipsoid becomes elongated. Law is assigned an essential, if not yet independent, theological function.

LAW IN THE NEW TESTAMENT

Tyndale's literary output during 1531 exceeded that of any other year in his career. The year also brought circumstances that thrust the reformer into clandestine negotiations with agents of the King of England. It demanded of the English Protestants on the Continent strategic decisions of such consequence that their entire endeavor might either find royal sponsorship at home, or be wiped out and forgotten. Theologically Tyndale was consolidating and explicating the theme of law that entered his thought during the Old Testament translating activity of 1530. He translated *The prophete Jonas with an introduccion before teachinge to vnderstonde him,* published by Martin deKeyser in Antwerp in May (*STC* 2788). The prologue, considerably longer than the book of Jonah itself, was the first actual composition of Tyndale to be published in this busy year, although at the end of February there had come from deKeyser's press an old tract, probably edited by Tyndale, called *The praier a. complaynte of the ploweman unto Christe* (*STC* 20,036). The long *Answer to More's Dialogue,* 'which Frith saw through the press and some portions of which Frith probably composed, came out in July, but was known in manuscript to the authorities in England earlier in the year. In September there followed *The*

exposition of the fyrste epistle of seynt Jhon (*STC* 24,443),
whose preface testifies that it was preceded by Tyndale's subtle but radical revision of the 1525 New Testament introduction, now published separately as *A pathway to the holy
scripture.*

Nowhere in all this literature was the new-found significance of law as God's proper way of dealing with man given
clearer expression by Tyndale than in the prologue to Jonah.
Recalling the single understanding of all scripture as gospel
which Tyndale had taught in his 1525 preface to the New
Testament, this passage shows how drastically he had to revise the earlier guide for the sake of consistency.

> The scripture containeth three things in it: first, the
> law, to condemn all flesh; secondarily, the gospel, that
> is to say, promises of mercy for all that repent and ac-
> knowledge their sins at the preaching of the law, and
> consent in their hearts that the law is good, and submit
> themselves to be scholars to learn to keep the law, and
> to learn to believe the mercy that is promised them; and
> thirdly, the stories and lives of those scholars, both what
> chances fortuned them, and also by what means their
> schoolmaster taught them and made them perfect, and
> how he tried the true from the false.[12]

Now the schoolmaster not only brings man to Christ, he rules
the lives of his pupils. The law is now no outward thing, but
the regulation inscribed in the heart to be kept "naturally
without compulsion" because of love toward the God whose
law it is and because of love toward the neighbor for whose
sake it regulates action. Tyndale now taught that "the fulfilling of the law is a fast faith in Christ's blood, coupled with
our profession, and submitting ourselves to do better." That
fulfilling could earn no forgiveness for past sins, but it was to
be learned from scripture that God deals kindly with those
of his elect who "learn to walk in the ways of his laws, and
to keep them of love." Tyndale had discovered a way to make
of God's law and of God's promises two keys to unlock the
scripture. Neither key worked until one abandoned the idea of

12. PS *I*, p. 449.

human deserts before God. The grace of justification showed the spiritual character of law and the promises; it set a man on a path of performing divinely commanded acts and of receiving, undeserved, the rewards of a loving heavenly father.[13]

The fact that Tyndale skipped over the chronicles and prophets to make Jonah his next Old Testament translation after the pentateuch seems only partly accounted for by the convenient brevity of the book. To be sure, in 1530 Joye had published an English Psalter from Bucer's Latin, but more important scriptures than Jonah were still wanting in English. The prologue only hints at reasons for choosing the book. Tyndale allegorized and moralized on the narrative: it taught in a figure the resurrection of Christ which Christians must constantly ponder; it exhorted fidelity to the task of preaching God's word to Englishmen as well as to Ninevites. Tyndale seems to have seen himself, as New Testament translator, in the lineage of Gildas and Wycliffe who of old had preached repentance in England. Now once again the message of God's word was set loose, and by past example one must expect terrible times to befall the country unless it harkened to the call to amend its way. It seems that Tyndale offered himself as a more willing messenger than Jonah had been, but he patently identified himself with that figure as having been charged to sound the judgment of God over the idolatrous English religion. He presented the story of Jonah as an urgent parable of his own times and career.

Tyndale sought to have his countrymen read the Bible as an immediately applicable rule of God for their present lives. The large place accorded to the law in the prologues to the pentateuch and to Jonah in fact contradicted the thoroughly evangelical note of the 1525 prologue to the New Testament. With almost incredible deftness Tyndale took the earlier document, itself in the main a translation of Luther, and by a few strokes of the pen entirely changed its theology. The *Pathway* left the sympathetic reader convinced that God's law, over and above its value as convicting the conscience of human sin and helplessness, was everywhere eminently worth striving to fulfill, and that true faith enabled a man to

13. PS *1*, pp. 450 f.

obey that law. A dozen or so new sentences wrought the doctrinal upheaval, forcing retraction of only a few old sentences.
The law still ministered death, and the gospel, life. Justification was still by Christ's blood. But by that justification, and
in that gospel-ministered life, "we receive love unto the law,
and power to fulfil it, and grow therein daily." Where the
prologue in 1525 had law requiring an unattainable "love
from the bottom of the heart," *Pathway* defined that love as
an attainable means of fulfilling the law. Men of right faith
"have delectation in the law (notwithstanding that they cannot fulfil it [as they would,] for their weakness); and they
abhor whatsoever the law forbiddeth, though they cannot
[always] avoid it"—the words in brackets were added in the
1531 *Pathway*.[14]

In the 1525 prologue Tyndale had declared: "Rightewesnes
is divers/ Blynde reason ymageneth many-maner of rightewes-
nesses. As the iuste ministracion of all manner of lawes/ and
the observinge of them/ and morall vertues w[h]erein phi-
losophers put there felicitie and blessednes/ which all are
nothinge in the sight of god."
But *Pathway* read:

> Rightwisnes is dyuers/ for blind reason imagyneth
> many maners of rightwisnesses. There is the rightwisnes
> of works (as I sayd before) whan the hert is away &
> is nat felte how the lawe is spūall [i.e. spiritual] & can
> nat be fulfylled/ but from the bothom of the herte. As
> the iust ministracyon of all maner of lawes/ & the ob-
> seruing of them/ for a worldly purpose & for our owne
> profyte & nat of loue vnto our neyboure without/ all other
> respecte & morall vertues/ wherin philosophers put their
> felicite & blessednes/ which all ar nothynge in the sight
> of god in respecte of the lyfe to come.[15]

The promises of God found in the prophets, psalms, and
pentateuch had in 1525 been understood to foretell or preach
Christ, but in *Pathway* this preaching was specifically identi-

14. PS *I*, pp. 11 ff.
15. *Cologne Fragment*, B^v; *A pathway into the holy scripture* (*STC* 24,463),
[Biij]^v–[Biv]^r.

fied as "the Gospel or glad tidings." No reward in heaven or earth was allowed by the prologue "for our deeds"; *Pathway* qualified that phrase by inserting after "for" the words "the deserving and merits of," going on to comment that "we know that good deeds are rewarded, both in this life and in the life to come." And a few paragraphs afterwards, the later book identified heaven as "the reward of well doing" even while warning that good deeds must not be motivated by the hope of heaven! The deeds thus rewarded might be done only by lives "created anew by the Spirit and doctrine of Christ, [which lives] wax perfecter alway, with working according to the doctrine, and not with blind works of our own imagining."

Tyndale felt called upon to elaborate his new understanding of the worth of good works under the law, and appended to the prologue one-third its original heft before publishing it as *Pathway*. A Christian's deeds served three functions. Good deeds "certify us that we are heirs of everlasting life, and that the Spirit of God, which is the earnest thereof, is in us." With good deeds the Christian tamed his flesh and slew the remnants of sin within himself, thus walking a path of increasing perfection. Good works discharged duties toward the neighbor, whose relief also strengthened the reliever—thus acts of enlightened self-interest "draw all men unto the honouring and praising of God." Knowing and obeying the law, the Christian whom Tyndale envisioned nevertheless gave thanks to God alone for the gift of the law and of the capacities to know and obey it. This particular understanding of the law became for Tyndale the key that unlocked the meaning of the entire scripture—Old Testament and New. Tyndale taught it to the humble laity of England, but the proud ecclesiastics would not learn it; they "cannot come in" who "corrupt the true understanding of [Moses'] law"![16]

Tyndale by a few emendations turned the very Lutheran prologue to the 1525 New Testament into an explanation of scripture that without exaggeration can be called the *magna carta* of English Puritanism. Two original commitments, and two alone, remained: justification was by faith, not works, and

16. PS *I*, pp. 19–24, 28.

scripture was the priceless possession of the Christian. Otherwise, the entire flow of the argument was turned from a specifically religious to a specifically moral end, so neatly did
Tyndale subsume religion under morality. The Christian life
centered not in the spiritual humility of taking the second
place in the presence of a merciful God. Rather, the Christian
life consisted in adhering to a moral system that looked to
the Bible for a sufficient guide to all ethical decisions; the true
Christian society was a commonwealth of saints living singly
and together according to scripture.

Probably it was this shift that led Barnes to develop the
notion of double justification that permeated the 1534 version
of his *Supplication*. In a much less marked way, Frith drew
away from the doctrine of the imputation of the righteousness
of Christ directly to the account of the forgiven sinner, and
warmed to the doctrine of God's willingness for Christ's sake
not to hold the forgiven one's sin against him. With Frith
the shift was slight indeed. Frith did not follow Tyndale's
moralism, which became patent just when Frith went to England to guide the destinies of the Brethren. At about the same
time, as shall be seen, and over closely related issues, Joye
parted company with Tyndale.

SOURCE OF TYNDALE'S LEGALISM

Tyndale's *Answer to More's Dialogue*, printed in mid-1531,
has been discussed in connection with Frith's part in writing
and publishing the book. The legal and moral considerations
that were occupying Tyndale's attention manifested themselves in the portions that may be ascribed confidently to Tyndale. The law of God served in this debate as the cornerstone
of the Christian life, and became the norm by which the Christian differentiated between "the laws of man, which are right
and which tyranny." True Christian men were seen as at once
sinners and not sinners. In the attitude of their hearts toward
the law, in their repentance for past evil, and in their yearning for the promises of God they were no sinners, but, as
finite and frail-bodied creatures whose deeds were imperfect,
they were sinners. The Pope, Tyndale asserted, played the

antichrist precisely because he erected his own law in place of God's law, especially in regard to ceremonial laws, which in Tyndale's view had been nullified by Christ. With Tyndale, like Frith, only the signification, not the ceremony itself, counted, for ceremonies, like sacraments, were given solely for the preaching of Christ.

This emphasis upon ceremonial laws points to a literary source of Tyndale's legalism. A particular discussion of mass vestments in the *Answer,* readily spotted by More in his *Confutation,* was borrowed, as More thought, from "a good frerys boke called *Rationale diuinorum."* [17] It seems more likely that Tyndale took the argument from *Vom Alten und Neuen Gott.* Certainly that presumably Swiss writing had been a major source for the historical portions and citations of canon law in the 1530 *Practice of Prelates,* as it was for Tyndale's oft-quoted similitude between the papal church and an ivy-tree being choked by the vine. The book upon which Tyndale drew has been attributed to Joachim Vadianus, or von Watt, who reformed the church in his native St. Gall in Switzerland along the lines followed by Zwingli in Zürich. He was born December 28, 1484, and lived until 1551. An education and brief career as teacher at the University of Vienna put him in touch with Luther by correspondence and equipped him for a friendship with Erasmus. As a reformer he owed much to the humanists, but he stanchly opposed Anabaptists by drawing upon the whole scripture, not only the New Testament, as the rule for Christian living. Prominent as chief magistrate of St. Gall in 1526 and as moderator of the 1528 disputation at Bern over the course of the Swiss Reformation, he founded a school of biblical studies which long guided the Reformation in his city. From a Latin edition of a writing dated 1522 and frequently attributed to Vadianus, the English translation, *A Worke entytled of ye olde god & the newe,* (*STC* 25,127), was made by William Turner and printed in 1534 by John Byddell in London, under the auspices of William Marshall. Foxe attributed the work to Coverdale, but its

17. PS *3,* pp. 6, 32, and passim, esp. pp. 73 ff.; More, *Confutation,* lxv, cited p. 73 n.

original author was possibly the Swiss reformer, and the attribution of the translation to Turner seems reliable.[18] Turner knew the circle of early English Protestants at Cambridge, and became prominent in their movement after 1534.

The dependence of Tyndale upon this work, either in Latin or in one of many German editions, is evident in many places in the *Answer to More's Dialogue,* especially in the historical portions and the discussion of ceremonies. The original concluded with twenty instructions in the religion of the old (true) God and old (true) faith; among these it taught that the Bible was sole authority for doctrine, discipline, and worship, that justification was by faith understood as assent to the Bible as word of God, and that the obligation to provide pure religion fell first to princes and bishops but on their default to the commonalty. There was no explicit theological emphasis upon law, although scripture was held to be the rule of daily living for all Christians.

The decisive turn of Tyndale's theology toward the law is not, then, to be attributed entirely to Vadianus—if indeed *Vom Alten und Neuen Gott* be his. The same theme was of crucial importance in the thought of the Rhineland theologians, such as Oecolampadius, Bucer, Bullinger, etc., and the presumed literary dependence of Tyndale upon one Swiss theological book makes it easier to surmise that he also learned from others.

In September 1531 Tyndale published a major expository work explaining in detail the meaning of I John. Like all his specifically biblical writings, this exposition, printed by de Keyser in Antwerp, probably owes a literary debt to Luther.[19] Modern writers in the field mark it down as one of the least valuable of Tyndale's compositions, for it reiterated the author's favorite complaints against the Church of the day, and otherwise adhered closely to the text of the epistle. What concerned Tyndale in this book, and distracted him once again from the task of translating the Bible into English, was the

18. See Judas Nazarei, *Vom alten und neuen Gott,* ed. Kück, which identified the Latin translation from which the English was taken as by Hermann Tulich, 1522; cf. Butterworth, *English Primers,* pp. 59, 116 n., and below, p. 254 n.

19. A point noticed among writers on Tyndale only by Rupp, *Studies,* p. 51.

fact that in spite of the availability of the New Testament, and now also of the pentateuch, in the common tongue, the official Church still regarded him as a heretic and the users of his translations as subversives. At the beginning of his reforming career the gospel seemed to be shouted unmistakably from every page of the New Testament, and especially from the epistles of Paul. Yet the Church and the realm mistook it. It had not been so in Wittenberg, nor in much of Germany nor in most of Switzerland, where the scripture became literally *sui ipsius interpris*. But in England the light of scripture was still hidden under the hierarchy's oppressive bushel.

Tyndale was driven to the conclusion that some new key to the scripture was necessary. He had furnished maps explaining the Christian life there portrayed, but these had not enticed many to begin the journey to biblical religion. Now he undertook to weld into one book the expository and the polemical approaches, exposing the true key to scriptural faith and explaining why the official Church hid that key. The key consisted in a personal knowledge of the law of God as summarized by Christ in the sermon on the mount (now Christ is indeed a new Moses), and in knowing the promises of God's mercy made by Christ, namely that God will deal kindly and lovingly with those who love his law and believe in Christ. The profession of baptism operated through consenting "unto the law that it is righteous and good," through loving the law in the heart, through submitting to the law "to rule and square all thy deeds thereby," through believing that Christ accomplished forgiveness of those sins of which every man was guilty prior to the moment of his faith, through placing one's hope for forgiveness of future sin in Christ rather than in his own merits.[20] Without using the term, Tyndale now taught a twin justification, by faith before God and by works before men. With outward deeds one could and must satisfy the law of God in the eyes of men, including oneself, and that satisfaction certified that the man was indeed justified; but outward deeds were worthless with reference to God, for before him only his free forgiveness could cover a man's guilt.

20. PS *2*, p. 136.

All this, as Tyndale saw it, scripture taught plainly. But until the lesson was learned, until a person's own inner being was caught up in the law and the gospel, he could not understand why his works, important as they were, should be reckoned worthless before God. All were baptized, but the papal Church failed to teach the content and operation of the profession of baptism, thereby withholding the key to understanding scripture. The hierarchy were blinded by their doctrines, glosses, and ceremonies, able to see only the outward manifestation of Christianity and not the inner signification. Only by his expounding scripture, Tyndale was persuaded, might scripture be made to take hold in England.

The same Tyndale who six years earlier poured all his energies into making the Bible available in English, by 1531 was explaining that to have the scripture in the common tongue was not enough:

> as it is not enough that the father and the mother have both begotten the child and brought it into this world, except they care for it and bring it up, till it can help itself; even so it is not enough to have translated, though it were the whole scripture into the vulgar and common tongue, except we also brought again the light to understand it by, and expel that dark cloud which the hypocrites have spread over the face of the scripture, to blind the right sense and true meaning thereof.

For that reason, Tyndale said, he had written the introduction to Romans and *Pathway,* and now put forth the present exposition.[21] He no longer deemed scripture a self-evident, joyous expression of the overflowing mercy of God in accepting the unrighteous as his own. To construe the Bible correctly one must be schooled and personally involved in the intricacies of the negotiations between man and God that it taught.

In this exposition, for the first time the steadfastness of God came to be interpreted by Tyndale explicitly as that of a reliable negotiator of agreements who bound himself to the terms of a contract. Covenant came to mean appointment. Indeed, God was the promiser of the appointment, and a gener-

21. PS *2,* p. 144.

ous one, for he alone could assist man in the human plight. The appointment was made in Christ's blood and was signified by the sacramental representation of Christ's blood. Surely the man who put his faith in this God was bound by the appointment. But God, too, was bound; he "hath bound himself to give us whatsoever we ask in his name . . . and that he will be a father unto us, and save us both in this life and in the life to come . . . and that our unperfect deeds shall be taken in worth." Tyndale described the agreement, with reference to God's part in it, as "this indented obligation"; God was the master and man the apprentice, but the obligation bound the one as it bound the other.[22] The apprentice, totally undeserving when taken into the master's service, by his work put the master under stipulated obligations. The reward for the apprentice was to walk in the master's ways; the man of faith found himself by grace keeping the laws of God. Here was a certain means by which a man might know whether he was in a state of grace. The righteous man kept God's laws, and in keeping them brought forth works of increasing perfection which, through a rugged ascent, would match the full perfection of the works of Christ by which merits were earned for mankind.

Not only I John seemed to Tyndale to teach this system of morality; he attributed it in detail also to Paul. As a man might know that he was righteous by his performance of the laws of God, so he was to know that sin consisted simply in the transgression of these laws. They were not ceremonial laws, but laws of duty to God and to neighbor summarized by Jesus in the sermon on the mount: "For love is lord over all laws, and the thing that Christ commanded above all others." [23]

The middle period of Tyndale's theological development, inaugurated by the translation and explanation of the first five books of the Old Testament, erected the law of God into a theological principle quite as important as the promise of God. Tyndale left this middle period, terminated by the exposition of I John, persuaded that the gospel consisted pre-

22. PS *2*, p. 166.
23. PS *2*, in order, pp. 172, 151, 170 f., 188.

cisely in the set of conditions and bargains that made it possible for man to live according to the law of God. No longer were there two foci of gospel and law in an elliptical theology. Now there was a theology as concerned for law, as "nomocentric," as Frith's thought was first and last theocentric. Gospel, or good news, remained the right designation for the Christian message as Tyndale taught it, for it heralded to man the possibility and the condition of his living by the law of God. But law provided the content and the meaning of that message.

THE SILENT YEARS

Tyndale's theological development from 1525 through September 1531 carried him from a conception of the gospel as liberating man from moralism and legalism, to a moralistic and legalistic understanding of Christianity as the divine capacitation of man to fulfill the ethical injunctions of the Old and New Testaments. In 1534 Tyndale reluctantly published a revised English New Testament with new prefaces to the various books, and a corrected edition of the English Genesis with revised prologue. Although the composition of several other works can be traced to 1533, and perhaps even to late 1532, the only other publication attributable to the last five years of his life is the English translation of Erasmus' *Enchiridion* printed by de Worde in 1533, itself not conclusively identified as Tyndale's work. Most modern commentators have ascribed also to Tyndale the 1533 tract by Joye, *The Souper of the Lorde*. From September 1531, when the exposition of I John was printed, until the 1534 Bible revisions, Tyndale, strangely enough, published no theological writing.

One can only resort to contemporary letters and recollections to guess at the reasons why he stopped. The crucial decisions occurred early in 1531. On March 25, Stephen Vaughan reported from Antwerp to Thomas Cromwell that he had obtained a rough copy of Tyndale's reply to More's *Dialogue,* and that the author was delaying publication until he might determine the King's probable reaction to the work. Vaughan had been informed that Tyndale was composing an epistle to the King; he was reluctant to condemn the *Answer to More,* for he thought it a gentle book. If Henry, too, liked it, Tyndale might be persuaded to return home under a safe-conduct, but, however that might be, Tyndale "will make no more works after this."

Vaughan's letter and incidents surrounding it pose crucial questions for the interpretation of Tyndale's life and work. The reported prediction can be construed as according with the facts of Tyndale's career; he subsequently made for publication during his lifetime no really new works. Acknowledging the difficulty of accounting for Tyndale's life during the silent year 1532, and accepting as probable several uncertain ascriptions to him during the years 1533–34, Mozley surmised that many details of Vaughan's reports were based on inaccurate, second-hand information. On this reading, Vaughan obtained his reports from an English refugee in Antwerp, possibly Joye (in Mozley's estimate, a man usually misinformed and inaccurate). Mozley disputed Vaughan's report that Tyndale was composing a letter to Henry, on the ground that the *Answer to More* appeared in 1531 without any such letter; the plan to delay printing the book seemed to Mozley wholly out of character; the promise to write no more books appeared preposterous and imaginary even though More referred to the *Answer* as Tyndale's "last booke." [24]

On April 18, 1531, Vaughan wrote again to Cromwell, sending a manuscript copy of one-fourth to one-third of Tyndale's *Answer to More,* asking to know the King's opinion of it, and reporting that he had interviewed Tyndale near Antwerp. Since at this time Vaughan had become unsure of his own standing with the King and indeed also with Cromwell, it is difficult to think that he would have reported in detail his interview with Tyndale, including a nearly verbatim record of what Tyndale had said, without carefully ascertaining the reliability of such startling reports as he had conveyed in the earlier letter, and without correcting any misinformation which might have reached the court through his letters. Yet in April he confirmed to Cromwell the data furnished on March 18. Furthermore, the printing of Tyndale's *Answer*

24. More, *Workes,* p. 505, where "last" need not mean most recent; Mozley, p. 192 n. For Vaughan's letter and related correspondence see Mozley, pp. 191 ff.

to More was overseen by Frith while Frith's *Disputation of Purgatory* was in the press, and it is unlikely that Tyndale's book was printed before July. While Frith perhaps worked at this project less rapidly than Tyndale might have done, one must wonder that the younger man was made responsible for supervising the printing of Tyndale's book in Antwerp where Tyndale was residing. Nor could Frith's 1531 trip to England have been the cause of the long delay, for by his own testimony he was at home during Lent, a season which fell in 1531 between February 22 and April 9. By mid-March Vaughan knew enough of the book to characterize it as gentle—by our standards hardly an apt description, although it was indeed more moderate than *Practice of Prelates*.

The temptation arises to make surmises opposing those of Mozley. Reports from home of the circulation of Latimer's open letter of December 1, 1530, to Henry, pleading for an authorization of the English Bible, must have encouraged Tyndale.[25] Frith was, early in 1531, reconnoitering in England, and enlisting new Protestant book-sellers there. Wolsey, symbol of worldliness in the English Church and of ecclesiastical dominance of the Throne, had fallen. Might not Tyndale gladly have delayed printing his *Answer to More,* and even have stopped all his writing, if the vernacular Bible were to be put forth with royal approval? That, after all, had been the single goal of his career. Might he not have sensed an opportunity to return to England commissioned to produce an English Bible and thus enabled powerfully to influence the course of church policy? If so, his willingness to bargain everything short of life and conscience seems credible.

Although one surmise may excel another, no surmise, however feasible, can become concrete evidence. The fact of the matter is that, whereas before September 1531 Tyndale pursued a very busy career of translating, writing, and publishing, interrupted briefly, and only, by known personal dangers and necessary studies, after that date he became strikingly reluctant about publishing. That fact, however related to the stated ground of Vaughan's prediction, accords with it.

The proposal to Tyndale by Vaughan, that he should go to

25. See Chester, *Hugh Latimer,* pp. 61–65.

England under safe-conduct guaranteed by the King, has been depicted by Mozley as a snare that Tyndale cleverly avoided. But the matter of a safe journey home had been on Tyndale's mind before the overture of the spring of 1531. In the prologue to the book of Numbers (1530), he had employed a series of illustrations in the first person to show how God's gifts came to those who strove, though not as rewards for the striving. One of the most poignant of these posed a hypothetical situation in which "the king's grace should promise me to defend me in mine own realm, yet the way thither is through the sea, wherein I might haply suffer no little trouble." Were he to accomplish the voyage and live in peace at home it would be thought that his trouble received its reward, but the happy state he "would not proudly ascribe unto the merits of my pains taken by the way, but unto the goodness, mercifulness, and constant truth of the king's grace whose gift it is, and to whom the praise and thanks thereof belongeth of duty and right." [26] There is no reason to doubt that Tyndale knew the King was reported to have looked with pleasure upon his *Obedience*, even though the book was proscribed from general reading in England. *Practice of Prelates* made the opposite impression on His Royal Highness, but Cromwell persuaded Henry to withhold any denunciation in hopes of winning Tyndale to the royal side in the impending battle with the hierarchy; Henry, of course, accepted no compromise of his autocracy in determining religious policy. In March 1531 Vaughan was seeking Tyndale in Antwerp to persuade him to come home; in May he met his man face to face and made his offer as compellingly as he might. Vaughan reported Tyndale's reply in direct discourse:

> What gracious words are these! I assure you . . . if it would stand with the king's most gracious pleasure to grant only a bare text of the scripture to be put forth among his people, like as is put forth among the subjects of the emperor in these parts, and of other Christian princes, be it of the translation of what person soever shall please his majesty, I shall immediately make faith-

26. PS *1*, p. 434.

ful promise never to write more, nor abide two days in
these parts after the same; but immediately to repair
into his realm, and there most humbly submit myself
at the feet of his royal majesty, offering my body to suffer
what pain or torture, yea, what death his grace will, so
this be obtained. And till that time, I will abide the
asperity of all chances, whatsoever shall come, and en-
dure my life in as many pains as it is able to bear and
suffer. And as concerning my reconciliation, his grace
may be assured that, whatsoever I have said or written
in all my life against the honour of God's word, and so
proved, the same shall I before his majesty and all the
world utterly renounce and forsake, and with most humble and meek mind embrace the truth, abhorring all error,
sooner at the most gracious and benign request of his
royal majesty, of whose wisdom, prudence, and learning
I hear so great praise and commendation, than of any
other creature living. But if those things which I have
written be true, and stand with God's word, why should
his majesty, having so excellent gift of knowledge in the
scriptures, move me to do anything against my conscience? [27]

After discounting its hyperbole as from a respectful subject
to a mighty monarch, Tyndale's proposal remains clear and
characteristic. For the currency of scripture in the common
tongue he would bargain away anything save conscience as
to the primacy of scripture. Henry's intended moves were
unpredictable at this as at every other time. Should he publish
the English Bible, Tyndale would surrender. Should he choose
Tyndale as translator of that Bible, Tyndale would accept.
All this Vaughan reported, and there is no good reason to
doubt the fidelity of his account. Regarding the *Answer to
More*, it was then too late for Tyndale to promise to keep
the book from publication, for Frith had the copy and would
print it soon; nevertheless Tyndale would hold off if pos-

27. Vaughan to Henry VIII, May 20, 1531, cited by Mozley, p. 198; cf. also
pp. 141 ff., 170 ff., 187 ff. In describing Cromwell's plan to enlist Tyndale, Mozley commented, p. 172, "To us who know our William, the project will not
appear very hopeful: but Cromwell did not know him."

sible. It was Vaughan's second interview with Tyndale. A month earlier Tyndale had refused a safe-conduct, fearing that the clergy would persuade the King to break his promise, on the ground that a pledge made to a heretic might with impunity be disregarded. Knowing that Frith had visited England and returned to the Continent prior to Vaughan's April meeting with Tyndale, it seems fair to suppose that information about the sate of religion in the realm led Tyndale to venture the slim hope that his condition might be met by the King, even that he might be the translator of a royally commissioned English Bible. For such fortune he had yearned since the early 1520s. The hope was swiftly dashed when, late in June, Vaughan returned to England, leaving off all negotiations with Tyndale. No answer to Tyndale's proposal could mean only a negative answer. The *Answer to More* was given the green light, and Frith had it published in high summer 1531. Before that the translation of Jonah was printed, as Vaughan reported on June 19 without naming the translator. *Pathway* and the commentary on I John would follow by September. In the autumn Vaughan again attempted to lure Frith and Barnes to England under safe-conducts. Barnes accepted, and verified Tyndale's guess as to the uncertainty of the guarantee. Frith bided his time until he heard from Barnes and learned of the bad fortunes of the Brethren in late 1531 and early 1532; in July he went home for good, under conditions of very unsafe-conduct. Vaughan busily defended the rectitude of his earlier dealings with Tyndale, but no longer worked to have him join Henry's cause. From the standpoint of the court, Frith from this time onward became the prize catch, not Tyndale who demanded the bait of a vernacular Bible.

There is evidence that the circle of English Protestant writers on the Continent relaxed its personal ties in late 1531 and 1532, leaving Tyndale on his own—a stark contrast to the previous succession of close co-workers and assistants. Roy, who had helped with the 1525–26 New Testament project, had from 1527 onward gone his own way under sharp disdain from Tyndale; he died in 1531. Coverdale, helper on the pentateuch in Hamburg, drops from our sight at the end of 1530 until late 1534, and no data indicate his having been associated with Tyndale during these years. In mid-1532, Frith, closest to Tyndale of all these men, returned to England. While Tyndale wrote affectionately to him, Frith flatly rejected Tyndale's advice not to enter controversy over the Supper of the Lord, and stood against Tyndale, with Joye, in the controversy over the state of departed souls. About the same time Joye became persona non grata with Tyndale; their animosity was to erupt in 1534–35 so violently that each publicly vented his enmity toward the other—Tyndale first, it must be noted. Barnes always referred to Tyndale with admiration for the New Testament translation, but their known personal contacts were few indeed after late 1531. Only Barnes among this group became interested, and he only half way, in Tyndale's theological preoccupation with law as contract between God and man. From 1532 onward Tyndale worked alone, both theologically and professionally. As to whether he was lonely in his final theological stand or in his late professional activity, and whether there was a causal connection between such loneliness and the new direction which his theology took, the extant testimony is mute.

Tyndale's career as translator, reformer, and theologian withstood several severe wrenches during the years 1531–32. His friends and erstwhile associates pursued independent courses. His chief opportunity to secure a legitimate English Bible suddenly rose and as suddenly vanished. For months and even years he stopped publishing. When the silent years ended, Tyndale had revised his theology radically around the controlling notion of covenant, understood as a moralistic contract between God and man.

11. Tyndale's Theology of Contract

LTHOUGH any continuous narrative of Tyndale's career from 1532 until its end in 1536 builds on supposition after supposition, his theology, newly organized around the idea of covenant as a bipartite, divine-human contract binding upon both parties, shouts itself from every writing attributable to the period. Two posthumously published tracts, traceable to 1533 or late 1532, one on the sacraments and the other a comment on the will of William Tracy, emphasize his conception of the relation between God and man as an "indented agreement," a conception first expressed in the commentary on I John. The notion also marked his exposition of the sermon on the mount, written perhaps as early as 1533 but of uncertain date of publication. Revised Bible translations published in 1534 and 1535 reveal the centrality of this covenant-contract idea in Tyndale's mature thought.

The theological tissue connecting the final phase of Tyndale's thought with the middle period came from the Old Testament. He revised the 1530 Genesis, and reissued the entire pentateuch in 1534 (*STC* 2351), with a slightly emended preface to Genesis, and a new prologue to the whole. Apparently only the separate Genesis translation in the 1530 edition had sold out, for the revision of the book with its new introductions was bound with remaining copies of the other four 1530 pentateuchal translations and sold as new sets. Since Genesis carried in 1530 a preface and a prologue guiding the reader into the scripture, the revision presented an opportunity to set the whole biblical message in the context of contractual theology.

LAW AND CONTRACT

The prologue was given a new title and skillfully emended. Whereas the reader of the 1530 pentateuch had been advised to seek in scripture first the law of God, then the promises of God, and then examples of God's dealing with obedient and disobedient men, the 1534 book counseled one to seek "chiefly and above all, the covenants made between God and us; that is to say, the law and commandments . . . ; and then the mercy promised unto all them that submit themselves unto the law." Every scriptural promise "include[s] a covenant: that is, God bindeth himself to fulfil that mercy unto thee only if thou wilt endeavour thyself to keep his laws." Never before had the "indented obligation" as binding God been so baldly put by Tyndale.

This new contractual theology demanded a new contractual politics; rulers were portrayed as "the governors and ministers of the law that God hath ordained to rule us by, concerning our outward conversation of one with another." If they did not so rule, Christian men must "tarry patiently" in the assurance that God would act to "reap tyrants off the face of the earth, as soon as their sins are ripe." Both the theology of the law and the politics of rule under that law were to be learned from the Bible, whose stories showed how God would deal with every episode of history. "As it went with their kings and rulers, so shall it go with ours. . . . As there was among them but a few true-hearted to God, so shall it be among us. . . . All mercy that is shewed there is a promise unto thee, if thou turn to God. And all vengeance and wrath shewed there is threatened to thee, if thou be stubborn and resist." [1] No New England federal theologian of the late seventeenth century, but the man who first fashioned the language of Bible-reading, English-speaking Christianity, wrote these words! The few changes of the 1530 Genesis translation itself that Tyndale made in 1534 were theologically fateful. His translating style characteristically employed various English terms to render the same word as it occurred repeatedly in the original; quite contrary to that tendency, the 1534 Genesis

---

1. PS *1*, pp. 403–05, where the revisions were noted in modern spelling; cf. also *Five Books*, pp. 8 n. through 10 n. and passim.

rendered *berith* as "covenant," discarding the 1530 alternates "appointment," "bond," and "testament." Although the Hebrew verbs in Genesis distinguish between "cutting," "establishing," and "giving" covenants, Tyndale leveled all these to "making" covenants.[2] Slight in themselves, these emendations demonstrate the central place which the covenant notion had come to occupy in Tyndale's thought.

This understanding of covenant as contract between God and man, binding eternally upon both, exhibits at once Tyndale's repudiation of Luther's theology and his discovery of a lodestar by which to set his own theological course. Yet major writings of this period exhibit an unmistakable literary dependence upon Luther's work. Extant data display abundantly the theological breach and the literary debt, but they are mute as to Tyndale's motives.

Tyndale composed and printed the exposition on the sermon on the mount perhaps as early as 1533: *An exposicion vppon the v.vi.vii. chapters of Mathew* (*STC* 24,439–40; *Ned. Bibl.* 3839). The earliest known notice of the book appeared in Joye's *Apology* of February 27, 1535, a notice that took into account the ambivalence of the book's relation to Luther: "for all his [Tyndale's] holy protestacions/ yet herd I neuer sobre & wyse man so prayse his owne workis as I herde him praise his exposicion of the v.vj. and .vij. ca. Mat. in so myche that myne eares glowed for shame to here him/ and yet was it Luther that made it/ T. onely but translating and powldering yt here and there with his own fantasies." Modern students of Tyndale have been puzzled by the ambivalence. Mozley found Joye "guilty of a flagrant untruth . . . [for] although Tyndale certainly used Luther's exposition, and draws from it a number of thoughts and a few sentences, yet the treatment is almost entirely his own." On the other side, Rupp appreciated Joye's having "left us an apt description of Tyndale's use of Luther . . . . 'Powldering' is a good word for Tyndale's habit of adding phrases and references to give his translation an English setting." [3]

2. Here again I am in debt to Copeland's researches; see above, p. 155 n.
3. Joye, *Apology*, ed. Arber, p. 42. Cf. 1535 ed., F3ᵛ–F4ʳ; Mozley, *William Tyndale*, pp. 283, 241 f.; Rupp, *Studies*, pp. 50 f.; the ambivalent dependence was commented on by Trinterud, "A Reappraisal," pp. 37–39.

Tyndale conceived the sermon on the mount as the epitome of God's laws and promises, cast in explicitly contractual terms. Thus Tyndale "puritanized" as well as "powldered" Luther's insistence upon the single theological use of law as driving man in guilt to Christ. Tyndale superimposed upon that idea a second use of law as the model of life lived in faith. Indeed to cleave to law apart from faith meant to sin unforgivably, but to trust in justification by faith and then to transgress the law of love was forgivable. Faith knew the law to be impossible of fulfillment by human strength, but faith also generated strength sufficient to obey the law, for faith loved the law instead of fearing it. Therefore for Tyndale "the law in her right understanding is the key, or at the least way the first and principal key, to open the door of the scripture." Or, more explicitly, "all the good promises which are made us throughout all the scripture . . . are all made us on this condition and covenant on our party, that we henceforth love the law of God, to walk therein, and to do it, and fashion our lives thereafter . . . because there is no promise made him, but to them only that promise to keep the law." [4] Tyndale interpreted the entire sermon as three summary chapters of the law of Christ and, as such, the very center of the biblical message. Since Christ's law had restored the pure law of Moses which the Pharisees had corrupted, Tyndale advertised his book as restoring the pure law of Christ which the papists had corrupted. Thus the author called his prologue to the commentary "very necessarie, contaynynge the whole somme of the couenaunt made betwene God and vs, vppon which we be baptised to kepe it." This book became one of the most popular of Tyndale's writings, and was reprinted several times during the reign of Edward VI.

From the Edwardian period come extant copies of Tyndale's *A briefe declaration of the sacraments* (*STC* 24,445), which in the 1572 edition of Tyndale's works was headed "A frutefull and godly treatise expressing the right institution and vsage of the Sacramentes of Baptisme, and the Sacrament of the body and bloud of our Sauiour Iesu Christ. Compiled by William Tyndall." The mode of this work is typological

4. PS *2*, pp. 3, 6.

exegesis of the Old Testament. Its style is clumsy. Its thesis is that sacraments are only the signs of covenants between God and man, in themselves unimportant, but to the faithful they become "seals of his [God's] obligations, wherewith he hath bound himself," serving "to keep the promises and covenants better in mind, and to make them the more deep sink into our hearts, and to be more earnestly regarded." [5] Tyndale argued that theories explaining the mode of Christ's presence in the Supper were not theologically adiaphora, as Frith had thought, but they were really inconsequential save as they became the devil's devices to stir up brawling between men of faith. He treated neither baptism nor eucharist with Frith's systematic care and profundity, but he amply proclaimed his contractual theology. Tyndale's comment upon the will of William Tracy, found among his papers after his death, and published along with Frith's comment, also emphasized the covenant between God and man as the only means of their encounter and as binding each party to the contract.

New Testament and Contract

By far the most important literary achievement of Tyndale during the final period of his activity was his revising and printing in November 1534, with new introductions, the English New Testament (*STC* 2826). The Worms octavo edition of 1526, although banned in England, had enjoyed wide circulation there and frequent reprinting on the Continent. Evidence furnished by contemporaries, particularly Joye, indicates that the Antwerp printer Endhoven published an edition as early as October 1526, another about 1530, and yet another in early 1534, before Joye was asked to supervise and to arrange for Tyndale to check the revision which the Endhoven press put out in August 1534 (*STC* 2825). No Antwerp edition prior to that edited by Joye seems to be extant.[6]

Tyndale's long promised revision seemed to Antwerp

5. PS *I*, p. 362.
6. Joye, *Apology*, passim; Mozley, pp. 347 ff. and passim; *STC* 2823-25; C. C. Butterworth, *The Literary Lineage of the King James Bible 1340-1611*

printers and to Joye long overdue. Many errors had crept
into the copy since 1526, errors which "so corrupted the boke
that the simple reder might ofte tymes be taryed and steek."
When these mutilated editions sold out, the Dutch printers
asked Tyndale to give them his revision early in 1534, but the
translator "prolonged and differed [i.e. deferred] so necessary a thing and so iust desyers of many men." Finally the
printers persuaded Joye to correct the copy for the August
1534 edition. Joye despaired of Tyndale's completing his
own revision, now long delayed, especially since Tyndale
then had no helper. That was Joye's story. As Tyndale told
it, Joye covetously seized the task before Tyndale had sufficient opportunity to complete his revision.[7] Be that as it may,
the changes that Tyndale made in the November 1534 text
were many but incidental; in the following year he put out
another revision with some further improvements. Joye's involvement in the matter reminds us that Tyndale worked
alone in the last phase of his career, and Joye's testimony to
Tyndale's indecisiveness and hesitancy about changing his
1526 work stands firm. The November 1534 revision was
certainly accelerated by the appearance of the August edition.

Marginal notes, prefaces, and the prologues to many individual books set the theological context in which Tyndale
wished his 1534 New Testament to be read and understood;
the clue to the scripture was its statement of covenants and
promises. "Fayth now in God the father thorow oure Lorde
Iesus Christ, according to the covenauntes and apoyntment
made betwene God and vs, is oure salvacion," Tyndale declared in the new edition's preface. "Wherfore I have ever
noted the covenauntes in the mergentes, and also the promises.
Moreover where thou findest a promyse and no covenaunt
expressed there with, there must thou vnderstonde a covenaunt.
For all the promyses of the mercie and grace . . . are made

(Philadelphia, 1941), 56–93. *Ned. Bibl.,* 0170–0176, lists seven possible printings
at Antwerp between 1526 and the appearance of Joye's revision in August
1534, and frequent issues of English New Testaments between 1534 and the
appearance of "Matthew's Bible" in 1537.

7. Joye, *Apology,* p. 20; "Willyam Tindale, yet once more to the christen
reader," *1534 NT.*

vpon the condicion that we kepe the lawe." [8] With great care, the translator, by inserting the word "covenaunt" or "promise" in the margins, drew the reader to passages that described divine demands involving rewards and punishments in this life. So he treated the beatitudes, many dominical injunctions recorded in the fourth gospel, and various sayings attributed to Jesus by the synoptic gospels.

Since Tyndale's 1526 New Testament lacked glosses, these 1534 marginal notes can be compared only with the fragmentary 1525 edition of Matthew 1–22, and the sharpest theological contrasts arise from this comparison. The 1525 margins, while explaining some terms thought to be difficult for the reader to understand, in the main comprised an almost continuous theological treatise on justification by faith as young Luther had understood it. The 1525 edition explained the narrative of Jesus' baptism in Matthew 3 thus: "All Rightwesnes/ ys fulfilled when we forsake all oure awne rightwesnes/ that god only maye be counted he which is rightwes/ & maketh [the] righ[t]wes/ rightwes/ throw feith. This doeth Ihon in that he putteth from hym hys awne rightwesnes/ & wold be wesshed of Christ and made rightwes. This also doeth Christ/ in that he taketh nott rightwesnes & honour on hym: but suffreth hym silfe to be baptised & killed/ for baptim is none other thinge then deeth." By 1534 all that was discarded for the statement, "All ryghteousnes: that is to do all the ordynauncesof God for soche purposeas godordayned them for." Consistently the 1534 book eliminated the 1525 comments on human undeserving and inserted notes on covenants as binding agreements between God as first party and good or bad men as the second party.

Tyndale reiterated the same theme throughout the notes to the 1534 version. Jesus' saying in Mark 4 that to those who have more shall be given, etc., was labeled "A couenaunt to them that loue the worde of God to wynne other with worde and dede: and another to them that love it not, that it shalbe their destruccion." Paul's discussion of the law in Romans 2 evoked these comments: "Dedes are an outeward righteousnes before the worlde and testifie what a man is withinne: but

8. *1534 NT*, p. 5.

iustifie not the hert before god: ner certifye the conscience
that the foresynnes are forgeuen"; "The deseruinge of Christ
is promysed to be the rewarde of oure good dedes: which
rewarde yet oure dedes deserue not." Paul's axiom that all
things work together for good to them that love God prompted
Tyndale to note that "God choseth of his awne goodnes and
mercye: calleth thorow the gospell: iustifieth thorow faith
and glorifieth thorow good workes." The opening verses of
I Peter were pointed to as truly apostolic testimony that
"fyrst setteth forth the treasure of mercye which god hath
bounde him selfe to geue vs for christes sake and then ouredutie
what we arebounde to do agayne yf we wilbe partakers of the
mercie." The stress on works in James drew almost continuous
glosses, of which the following on the second chapter is ex-
emplary: "To worke offeare and compulsion is bondage: but
to loue is libertie and the fullfillinge of the lawe before god,
and maketh aman mercifull to worke of his awne accorde And
to the mercifull hath God boundehim selfeto shew mercie
And contrary vnto the vnmercifull hethreatneth iudgement
withoute mercie. . . . God hathpromysed all mercie to the
mercifull only." Tyndale's preface to the New Testament of
1534 made the most trenchant statement of contractual theology that he ever wrote, gathering the themes of these marginal notes, binding them into a discourse starkly different
from the 1525 New Testament preface, and developing contractual law into a theological cornerstone. The revisions of
the text itself only faintly reflect this theological base, for it
seems that Tyndale made a studied effort to let the 1526 translation stand wherever the wording was not patently clumsy,
faulty, or misleading—a procedure indicating his growing concern for the text of scripture in the original tongues and for
the word and letter of the translation he and Roy first
wrought. However, the theological context set by the marginal notes, and most pointedly by the preface, continued for
many years to provide the matrix in which Englishmen understood the New Testament. Bibliographical descriptions of
twenty-five separate printings of the Tyndale New Testament
from 1535 until 1552 show that only ten lacked copious re-
productions of the marginal notes of 1534; four of the ten

were scholarly editions in English and Latin, and a fifth was printed in Zürich. The preface was omitted from only seven of these twenty-five, among them the four English-Latin and the Zürich editions. Similarly the 1534 prologues to the various books accompanied most of the New Testaments which came into the hands of English readers throughout this very crucial period.[9]

Text, preface, notes, and prologues of 1534 show Tyndale seriously and theologically pondering the circumstance that, while God's covenant could be read—under some strictures, to be sure—by Englishmen, the official custodians of the Christian religion condemned the book, many who read it forsook its faith, and, in the words of the prologue to Genesis, "As there was among them but a few true-hearted to God, so shall it be among us." No longer was Tyndale proffering a lamp to light the realm, but a two-edged sword to excise sin from the few who accepted it and to cut off hope of salvation for those who rejected it. The word of God, understood as this scripture, was nothing more nor less than the contract of God's offer of hope and happiness to men. Whoever faithfully accepted the offer confided in the merits of Christ, not in his own good deeds, yet the contract made his deeds the condition, if not the earning, of his reward. The terms of the covenant bound God on his part to bestow blessings upon the righteous, just as they bound the faithful to be righteous. God was under obligation not to the goodness of man but to the steadfastness of the divine character. He must execute the promised mercies in this life and bestow bliss in the life to come upon those who remained righteous in faith. To be sure, he chastened them to help them keep down the desires of the flesh and to make them improve with every renewal of their faith.

Then there were those who refused the contract, and in 1534 Tyndale had an explanation to cover them. Since a sovereign God made the offer, all fell under its provisions, whether they entered the agreement or not. Rejection subjected a man to the judgments which the covenant described. Daily in this life such sort would be made worse and worse,

9. See Francis Fry, *A Bibliographical Description of the Editions of the New Testament* (London, 1878).

and their hearts would grow ever harder in their resistance to God's spirit, until finally they would be cast away in the life to come. A third kind of man was provided for in the same covenant, who, having once favored the word of God, later found himself unwilling or unable to check the sinful desires that beset him. Protesting his faith, but failing to follow God's laws, this person would receive in present life scourges of a sharpness that increased daily. Nothing here might turn out well, for God "shall vysit him with pouertie, with sycknesses and deseases, and shall plage him with plage vpon plage, eche more lothsome, terryble and fearfull then other, tyll he be at vtter defyaunce with his fleshe." [10] On no point was scripture more certain, in Tyndale's opinion, than in specifying such punishments for the false believers who walked not in the Lord's law. Such a sword was let loose by the Bible in the common tongue, that the faithful doers of the word would be rewarded in this life and the life to come, the unfaithful might here seem to prosper but were doomed to perdition, and those of little or feigned faith would be punished both here and hereafter.

The contract theology of Tyndale's 1534 New Testament preface conceived of the creation and fall as well as the restoration of man in terms of his attitude and action with respect to the law of God. To have loved the law and to have kept it without compulsion described the original, innocent state of mankind. Desire to obey God remained a natural circumstance of fallen man. After man had disobeyed, God's law served to reveal the disobedience. Law seemed man's enemy but was really his friend. Thus the distinction in Tyndale's thought between God's strange work and God's proper work was not the distinction between law and gospel as such, but simply between law as enemy and law as friend. Ineluctably this theology hinged on the attitude and motivation of man. Certainly, for Tyndale, God had accomplished a transaction, for no man could on his own merits escape the enmity of the law, before which he always stood guilty. But what God accomplished in that transaction happened really in the heart of man. Restored man was enabled to love the law and to want to obey it from

10. *1534 NT*, pp. 7-8.

the bottom of his heart. Indeed, if truly restored, he fully
obeyed. Restoration was earned by Christ for all, but remained
conditional upon each man's steadfastness in obeying not only
the old law (enemy) but also the new law (friend).

Tyndale construed the whole action of God toward mankind legalistically. The whole Bible comprised the whole law
of God, embodying and telling that whole action to the world.
To be without the Bible therefore was to be in the course of
eternal punishment. To have the Bible, and to love it as law
and to do what it prescribed, was to be in the course of eternal rewards. The chief predicament of man was for Tyndale what it had been for Augustine and the Middle Ages, a
specifically and explicitly moral predicament. To teach the
good, and to enable man to do it, religion needed the merit of
Christ and the power to transform men's hearts. But the object
of religion was morality. Here Tyndale was actually far
closer to the Catholic humanists of England, such as Colet
or Fisher or Gardiner or even More, than he was to Luther.
In Wittenberg the predicament of man was seen as religious:
get that straight, and morality would take care of itself.
Luther could counsel his associates to sin bravely. Tyndale's
adherents must bravely avoid sin.

Tyndale regarded the New Testament issued in November
1534 as a right rendering of the word of God. Of course it
was not verbally inerrant, for he himself would make a few
theologically inconsequential revisions in his final edition of
1535 (*STC* 2830). But unless a man should appeal directly
to the Greek text, Tyndale would tolerate no changes by another hand. If his readers found typographical errors and
printer's faults, they should refer to the New Testament books
already printed and thereby arrive at the true English rendering! The oft-repeated offer of his early career, inviting men
to improve his work rather than criticize it, he withdrew. A
reflection against Joye was certainly involved in this shift,
but there was more than that. Under the covenant-contract
theology that Tyndale had espoused, the Bible's very text took
on a sacred character. Faults might occur in the text, but might
be corrected only by men learned in the original tongues.

Because of his change of theology between 1530 and 1534,

Tyndale found heart to make only unsubstantial revisions in the work he and Roy had given the world in 1526. There were, to be sure, many changes, but most of them were for the sake of clarifying the English meaning, eliminating awkward phrases, or sometimes standardizing the translation. Some changes indeed enshrined the contract theology in the text. In Hebrews 13-D (Tyndale divided chapters into sections, not verses) the 1526 version had prayed that men would be made "parfet in all workes, to do his will, andbrynge to passe, that whatsoever ye do, maye be accepted in his sight, by the meanes of Iesus Christ," emphasizing the freedom of the Christian man to offer his deeds to God through the mediation of the Savior. The passage in 1534 prayed that God would "make you parfect in all good workes, to do his will, workynge in you that which is pleasaunt in his sight thorow Iesus christ"; the paths of righteousness were assumed to be well marked. Again in I Timothy 6-C, the 1526 text had emphasized the strain in Paul's ethics that considered the religious influence of the actions of Christians: "kepe the commaundement with outspott, so that noman fyndefaute wyth the, vntyll theaperynge" of the Lord. But in 1534 the injunction was specifically aimed at Christians' perfection in the sight of God: "kepe the commaundement, and be with out spotte and vnrebukeable, vntyll the apperynge of oure lorde." Philippians 4-A in 1526 urged that Christians "socontinue beloved in the lorde," but in 1534 exhorted "so continue in the lorde ye beloved"; the latter was syntactically clearer, but also more inescapably moralistic.

These examples show that theological considerations were not absent from Tyndale's 1534 textual changes. Yet his growing regard for the text commanded restraint. Thus he canceled the early pledge to make a full revision, as well as the invitation for others to improve upon his work. In 1534 Tyndale served the vocation of having *his* Bible, especially the New Testament and the pentateuch which was so necessary to its understanding, sent abroad as the pure word of God, the belief in which brought life, disbelief death, and fainthearted belief misery. "The generall covenaunt," he declared in the 1534 preface, "wherin all other are comprehended and included, is this. If we meke oure selves to god, to kepe all his lawes, after the ensample of Christ: then God hath bounde him selfe vnto vs to kepe and make good all the mercies promysed in Christ, thorowout all the scripture." [11]

The theological context in which "testament" means "contract," binding equally upon God as party of the first part and man as party of the second part, remained that in which the English Bible was read long after other translators and revisers superseded Tyndale's own work. Just a year before Tyndale's death, Coverdale printed the first complete Bible in English (*STC* 2063). Tyndale's prefaces and notes were not there, but his translation of much of the Old Testament, and all of the New, exerted enormous influence upon Coverdale's readings of the text and renderings into English. Coverdale's own preface, moreover, adopted Tyndale's covenant theology, and introduced the Bible as the book by which to govern one's life and by which to work for the promised rewards that God bestowed—for Christ's sake, to be sure—on the just. It was a book to be neglected or disobeyed at the peril of one's soul. "The New Testament or Gospell, is a manyfest and cleare testymony," Coverdale echoed Tyndale, "of Christ how God perfourmeth his ooth and promes made in the olde Testament, how the New is declared and included in the Olde, and the Olde fulfylled and verifyed in the New." [12]

The whole Bible of John Rogers, issued in 1537 over the pseudonym Thomas Matthew (*STC* 2066), followed Tyndale's translation far more faithfully than Coverdale had done. This book borrowed many of Tyndale's 1534 marginal notes, as well as many from the French translation by Jacques Lefèvre of the same year. It was hailed by Cranmer as the translation that he liked "better than any other translation heretofore made." [13] Henry VIII was prevailed upon to license it for circulation in England; when Tyndale was only eleven

11. Ibid., p. 4.

12. *Biblia the Bible that is the holy scrypture* (*STC* 2063), [*vi]^v; cf. *The Holy Scriptures, Faithfully and truly translated by Miles Coverdale . . . Reprinted . . . for Samuel Bagster* (London, 1838).

13. Cranmer to Cromwell, August 4, 1537, cited in Westcott, *History of the English Bible*, p. 69.

months dead, his ripest translation and his marginal notes—
his text of much of God's word and his theological context
in which God's word was God's law—received the imprimatur
of the supreme head of the Church of England.

Neither Tyndale's text nor context lost influence when
Rogers' and Coverdale's Bibles were superseded by the Great
Bible of 1540–41. As far as text is concerned, Tyndale's
work has remained a base upon which translators into English
have built, even as recently as the American Revised Standard
Version of 1946–57, with few exceptions (Rheims and Douay,
of course, and the modern translations of Rieu, Moffatt, and
the New English Bible New Testament of 1961). Context
for the Great Bible, in the edition sponsored by Cranmer, was
set by a prologue to the reader, in which the Archbishop
quoted at length John Chrysostom and Gregory Nazianzen on
the value of vernacular scripture, and adopted the leading
lines of Tyndale's view that the Testaments were to be
understood as the rules of God for Christian living. Tyndale
might have written these sentences by Cranmer:

> In the scryptures be the fatte pastures of the soule,
> therin is no venymouse meate, no vnholsome thynge,
> they be the very dayntie and pure fedynge. He that is
> ignoraunte, shall fynde there what he sholde learne. He
> that is a peruerse synner, shall there fynde his damnatyon
> to make hym to tremble for feare. He that laboureth to
> serue God shall fynde ther his glorye, & the promissions of
> eternall lyfe, exhortyng him more diligently to laboure.
> Herin maye prynces learne howe to gouerne their sub-
> iectes: Subiectes obediece [sic], loue and dreade to theyr
> prynces. Husbandes, howe they shulde behaue them vnto
> their wyfes: howe to educate theyr children and seru-
> auntes. And contrary the wyfes, chyldren, and seruauntes
> maye knowe there dutye to theyr husbandes, parentes and
> masters. Here maye all maner of persons, men, wemen,
> yonge, olde, learned, vnlerned, ryche, poore, prestes,
> laymen, Lordes, Ladyes, offycers, tenauntes, and meane
> men, virgyns, wyfes wedowes, lawers, marchauntes, arti-
> fycers, husbande men, and almaner of persons of what

estate or condityon soeuer they be, maye in thys booke learne all thynges what they ought to beleue, what they ought to do, & what they shulde not do, aswell concerning almyghtyeGod as also concernynge them selues and all other.[14]

Tyndale should not have agreed with Cranmer that the King's authorization was sufficient grounds for accepting the scripture in England. Tyndale should have argued that every Christian's obedience, specified in the Bible as God's rule for the governing of, and for living in, his universe, bound Henry and all his subjects whether he was called head of the Church or not. Royal headship of the Church came to be the basis upon which Anglicans built an ecclesiology, and indeed a theology. Tyndale built only upon the Bible as the book of the obedience of a Christian man, king or commoner.

TYNDALE'S ORIGINALITY

Tyndale furnished prologues to the individual books of the New Testament for the first time in 1534, and they had many reprintings for a generation to come. Like his exposition of the sermon on the mount, these prefaces depended literarily upon Luther, but theologically they were Tyndale's own. Modern scholars have disagreed on the matter of Tyndale's debt to Luther, some making much of Tyndale's interjections of original paragraphs into the Luther prefaces, others noting that the substance of each introduction to a New Testament book was borrowed from Luther no matter how Tyndale may have expanded or contracted the original. Rupp has pointed out that, all things considered, "there are, on careful examination, hardly any points where disagreement between Tyndale and Luther can be found, even in the matter of James"; that judgment allowed "for the fact that Tyndale was definitely working towards an edition which might be authorized for England," but it proposed that Tyndale thought "private theological meaning was out of place" in his 1534 edition.[15]

14. Cranmer, "The prologe to the reader," *The Byble in Englyshe* . . . (*STC* 2070), *ij^{r-v}; facsimile of prologue reprinted in H. R. Willoughby, *The First Authorized English Bible and the Cranmer Preface* (Chicago, 1942), at end.
15. Rupp, 50 n.

There remains a gulf between Tyndale's introductions and Luther's, a gulf that is theological but not literary. For Luther, a book was apostolic if it preached Christ clearly, regardless of authorship; for Tyndale, a book was apostolic if it was included in the canon, regardless of the clarity with which it preached Christ. All the suspicions that Luther brought trenchantly against James and Jude, and even against Hebrews, Tyndale acknowledged as legitimate, but discarded as irrelevant. For Tyndale, books were in the New Testament because they recorded God's bargain with creation. Tyndale realized that Luther never intended his criterion of apostolicity to be applied to forming a new canon, and Tyndale saw no use in emphasizing it. Tyndale placed emphasis upon Luther's positive statements about the instructive character of the lesser books. Tyndale's prologues were not independent of the great German reformer at any major point, yet they consistently viewed the Bible as the words of a reliable, legislating God, rather than as the preaching of the glorious and totally undeserved mercy of a God who acted *sub contrario*, unexpectedly. He took the critical and literary pulp of Luther's introductions but not Luther's heady theological wine.

Not only in the New Testament prefaces, but in the exposition of the sermon on the mount, Tyndale borrowed words and sentences and paragraphs from Luther, even while articulating a different theology. As a translator, Tyndale worked mainly to render the words of biblical writers in English; otherwise, save for his probable part in making available in English Erasmus' *Enchiridion* and Bugenhagen's letter, Tyndale translated no contemporary but Luther. As the leading biblical theologian of his generation, Luther was naturally the chief literary source of Tyndale throughout his career. Nevertheless, Tyndale veered constantly away from Luther's radical religious theocentrism and theological christocentrism. No doubt, Tyndale's theological learning increased during the process, through reading Melanchthon, Bugenhagen, Zwingli, Oecolampadius, possibly Vadianus, and probably Bucer, Lefèvre, Aepinas, and Capito, to say nothing of Frith.

Literary faithfulness to Luther persisted while Tyndale built a theology inimical to Luther by virtue of its eminently

moral and legal concerns. The religious pilgrimage toward
that theology cannot be fully accounted for by Tyndale's occasional reliance upon and reference to Rhineland theologians.
The stages of his journey were marked by the barriers that
impeded the progress of his English Bible. At the outset Tyndale, with Luther, conceived of Christianity as a bald proclamation of undeserved divine mercy toward man, and Tyndale
expected this proclamation to be received joyfully in his 1525–
26 New Testament. When that did not come about, he set
forth the pentateuch, and by reference to the legalism of those
books explained why his New Testament translation had
failed. Thus the Old Testament became a guidepost to true
Christianity along with the New. In the final stage of his
thought, Tyndale sought to explain why Church reforms
initiated by Henry still proscribed his biblical translations.
He found that explanation by interpreting both the Old Testament and the New Testament as the hard law of God, as the
two-edged sword referred to above, and as the contract between God and all men.

The word of God, conceived as scripture (although to Luther the phrase meant more than that), made its own way
into the life and faith of Saxons. Not so in England. At the
beginning of his career Tyndale put the New Testament—
the word of God—into clear, readable English, but events
proved the English Bible incapable of being *sui ipsius interpris*.
Therefore Tyndale undertook to be its interpreter, and chose
as his clue and rule the concept of God's law. Englishmen
were not informed that Tyndale had, as he thought, improved
upon the Wittenberg theology. But they, who on the whole
were unmoved by the New Testament presented as gospel,
warmed to it as the divine code for human living. Tyndale
fashioned the spectacles through which generations of Englishmen read their Bibles. One lens, of theological legalism, made
the New Testament look like the Old. The other lens, of
religious moralism, made the Bible everyman's book of pru-
dential ethics.

Although the revisions of Tyndale's final New Testament
of 1535 were on the whole incidental, the excision of his 1534
pejoration of Joye deserves mention. That Tyndale thought

it appropriate in 1534 to append the vehement attack on Joye's revision and person hardly coheres with his regard for the Bible as a sacred book. The note reveals that Tyndale was deeply offended that anybody, especially an erstwhile assistant, should seize his earlier offer to improve the first translation. The note was self-aggrandizing. Tyndale portrayed himself as the accomplished translator and Joye as the neophyte, himself as the humble, injured party and Joye as the reckless imposter. The facts of the case, as related by Tyndale, remain confused: Tyndale had almost finished his labor when Joye secretly undertook the revision, yet Joye's book was published in great number "yer myne beganne"; Tyndale first forgave Joye his imposition, yet he did not see a copy of Joye's revision until the printing of his own revision was nearly finished; Joye had played "boo pepe" by signing some but not all of his books, yet Tyndale had done the same earlier in his career; Joye was dishonest in not calling the book his own translation as well as in using Tyndale's translation as the basis for revision; Joye was wrong to render the same Greek word by different English words, yet that was Tyndale's hallmark as a translator; in righteous indignation Tyndale was fully convinced that Joye had not played fair, yet he humbly submitted the question to the judgment of his readers. If Joye's 1535 *Apology,* as often remarked, hit below the belt, it must be admitted that Tyndale made the first foul blow. If for no other reason than the elimination from its pages of the vituperations against Joye, the 1535 New Testament was an improvement over that of November 1534.

Soon after publication of the 1535 revision Tyndale fell into the snares of the imperial authorities. An English acquaintance in Antwerp sprung the trap as Tyndale took him out to dinner. Imprisonment at the castle of Vilvorde near Antwerp terminated, in spite of efforts of friends and countrymen, in condemnation and execution. Early in October 1536, probably on the sixth day, in the town of Vilvorde, Tyndale was tied to the stake, strangled, and burnt. The labor to which and for which he gave his life would receive within a year official endorsement from the King (and in his name from the Church) who had exiled Tyndale from his homeland and had condemned as heretical his translations and his writings.

Tyndale first, among English writers, gave literary expression to the major theological themes of law, covenant, works, and rewards upon which the Puritan tradition within English-speaking Christianity built. Among interpreters of the beginnings of the English Reformation, Trinterud has noted this important fact, but without distinguishing theological disagreements between Tyndale and Frith. To be sure, the rendition of English Christianity commenced by Tyndale was echoed and proliferated by younger men among his contemporaries, such as "John Bale, John Hooper, John Bradford, and their associates." Indeed, "Their ideas . . . remained as a permanent leaven in English thought and life because they were authentic expressions of the English spirit and heritage." These ideas had arisen among continental reformers in the Rhineland such as Zwingli, Bucer, Oecolampadius, Vadianus, and others with whom Tyndale and his associates were familiar. Evidence is lacking, however, to indicate that Tyndale borrowed his notion of God's relation to man as a bipartite contract. Moreover, even if borrowed, it became attractive and amenable to Tyndale through the development of his own career and work and was fully assimilated into a thoroughly English articulation. If, for example, Tyndale was familiar with Oecolampadius' *In Jesiam* (1525) early in his career, its acceptance of the "covenant idea as an organizing principle of theology" left no traceable mark upon the mind of the Englishman, and only as he worked his way through the problem of theologizing upon both testaments did the theme become for him "*the* organizing principle for an understanding of the Scriptures." Granting the accuracy of Trinterud's basic insights, it has nevertheless been "possible from what is known of his [Tyndale's] life to discover" the development of his theology and many of the influences which continental thinkers exerted upon it.[16]

The clue to Tyndale's life is his burning determination to make his version of the scriptures available to his countrymen. His endeavors toward that end furnish also the clue to

16. Trinterud, "The Origins of Puritanism," pp. 38, 41, 43.

the development of his theology. From the beginning to the
end of his reforming career, Luther, not any of the Rhinelanders, looms as the Protestant writer upon whom Tyndale
constantly leaned. The 1525 prologue to the New Testament,
Tyndale's earliest extant composition, was made in Wittenberg. So, literarily, were the 1534 prologues to the books of
the New Tstament, which, among the works that can be dated
accurately, were his last theological compositions. Yet everything that he published directed the reader to the scripture,
first to the New Testament alone as gospel, then to the Old
Testament as law with two theological uses, and finally to the
whole Bible conceived as the divine-human contract.

If Tyndale surpassed many of his fellow writers in style and
facility of expression, his was still the prose of what Lewis
called "the drab age." He saved his most discriminating intellectual powers and his masterful command of the English
tongue for the translations of scripture. With the model of
Luther's German Bible in mind, Tyndale chose the religious
vocabulary for all modern English-speaking people. "Our
Bible is substantially Tyndale corrected and improved" by
emendations borrowed from the Geneva Bible, the Rheims
translation, and by the Authorized Version's originalities.[17]
Influences upon Tyndale include also his associates Roy, Joye,
Coverdale, and Frith; the other Wittenbergers whom he
knew, such as Melanchthon, Bugenhagen, and even Spalatin;
the editor of his Greek text, Erasmus, whose *Paraclesis* and
Paraphrases of Matthew he publicly endorsed; the enemy
More, who, in spite of Tyndale's polemics, scored points which
found their way into the revised New Testament; Hebraists
such as Pellican, Reuchlin, and Pagninus; and many another
humanist, linguist, translator, and theologian. Yet the enduring prose of the Bible translations, like the legalism of the
later theological writings, arose out of Tyndale's own very
considerable genius. Credit for both the translation and the
theology remains Tyndale's.

The jubilant tidings of the New Testament recently re-
covered by Luther seized Tyndale's life, thought, and work

17. Lewis, *English Literature in the Sixteenth Century,* p. 214; cf. Westcott,
pp. 212 ff., 245 ff., 255ff.

when he launched into translating the gospels and epistles. A religion of traditional rites and ceremonies designed to make men presentable to God crumbled before the floods of mercy exhibited by a God who received the unpresentable in forgiveness. That message leaped up before Tyndale's eyes from every chapter of the clear Greek text, clamoring for expression in English. The amenability of Hebrew and Greek to English translation struck Tyndale; religious Latin, after centuries of scholastic neatness and liturgical legalism, seemed difficult or impossible to render accurately into English. However linguistically accurate, Tyndale's opinion was both religious and theological. The Greek and Hebrew texts bypassed the ecclesiasticism of the Vulgate, stating a message that was clear and fresh and joyous. Nobody else had described the discovery as compellingly as Luther, and it was natural that Tyndale looked to Luther's descriptions as a model. If Tyndale's earliest theological writings were theocentric and christocentric, it was because the New Testament as Luther had described it was that kind of book.

Turning in the natural course of things to the pentateuch, Tyndale found a different message, to be superimposed without contradiction upon the central message of the New Testament. The God who with fatherly forgiveness welcomed home wayward sons, also with legalistic righteousness ruled his household. Justification by faith in Christ remained the only solvent of sin, but the justice of God perceived by Moses set the forgiven sinner into a path of unswerving obedience. Like Barnes after him, Tyndale reconciled the double movements of gospel and law into a two-pronged justification—before God through faith and before man through good works. That theological insight arose in the timely context of Catholic accusations that all Protestants were antinomians. Tyndale's scriptural theology became quite nomistic. He made the law of Moses binding, save in its ceremonial dimension, on the brethren of Christ. Lawlessness, not true religion, as Tyndale, like Luther, saw it, prompted the German peasants to try to break their shackles; contrariwise the Bible demanded obedience to the rulers of earthly kingdoms and obedience to the ruler of the heavenly. These two obediences Luther al-

ways kept distinct in his thought and teaching. Tyndale conjoined them and gave to his newfound theology its corollary
politics. Still, the established Church was wrong, for it placed
men under a ceremonial code that Christ had abrogated. By
1530, Tyndale was convinced by study of the pentateuch that
the practice of the Catholic prelates was but pharisaism redi-
vivus, and that the true law of God enjoined both by Moses
and Christ bound kings as it bound subjects.

Yet the campaign to spread scriptural truth and justice over
England met heavy opposition. The crucial blow to the program as well as to the theology that undergirded it was less
the opposition of the prelates than the callousness of the King.
The blow fell in 1531, a year that opened with the preferment
of crypto-Protestants by Henry, and closed with the martyrdom of chief lieutenants in the struggle for a vernacular Bible.
It opened with the King's seeking various theologians' opinions about his marriage; it closed with his defiance of the
biblical injunctions against divorce. Tyndale then conceived
of scripture as the only right charter of human society and
life, a charter which men might evade only to their eternal
peril. Such a charter needed and found its highest sanction
from a God so invested in his covenant with mankind as to
be under its conditions. If men disobeyed the Bible they would
be damned. The mercy of God was limited by the bargain into
which God had entered.

Tyndale's friends and associates on the Continent went
their own ways when Tyndale went his new way: Joye to his
translating labors, Frith to disputations over the sacraments,
Roy to his death, Barnes to negotiations with the Germans on
behalf of Henry, Coverdale to brief oblivion. The English
Protestant writers fell at odds with one another over the
issue that since 1529 had divided the continental Protestants,
the presence of Christ in the Supper of the Lord. Thus the
indomitable More was provided ammunition for his most telling shots at his opponents: they agreed only on the relative
unimportance of their disagreements, thereby degrading the
mass itself and impugning the blood of Christ in which they
claimed to have been washed. Frith in 1532 ingeniously defended the sacramentarianism of Oecolampadius, rejecting

Tyndale's advice to let the matter lie, stirring up the enmity of Barnes who stood with the Wittenbergers, and providing Joye and opportunity to expand and publish his Zwinglian tract, *The Souper of the Lorde,* which Tyndale wanted to suppress. Finally Tyndale himself treated the subject, but not for publication until after his death. When Joye advanced his theory on the resurrection, which was to guide his 1534 revision of the New Testament, he greatly offended Tyndale. On this issue Frith stood with Joye.

In these circumstances Tyndale retreated more and more to the absolute authority of the scripture, not only as describing the way of life that God enjoined on the faithful, but as stating the principles and practices that would receive divine rewards. The covenant-contract theology crystallized in Tyndale's mind. The Old Testament and the New Testament comprised one covenant, and a covenant was understood as a contract. God had revealed what men may do and may not do. God had furnished personal strength to do and not to do according to his rules. God had bound himself to reward man's obedience, to punish man's disobedience, and to indicate in this life whether a given man stood within or without the covenant.

Tyndale gave to Puritanism its first English theological expression. He founded the theology upon which seventeenth- and eighteenth-century English-speaking Calvinists built Bible commonwealths in Cromwell's England and in the New England of the Mathers. Quite unequivocally Tyndale made prosperity or poverty on earth the visible tokens of men's consignment to heaven or hell. Theology became handmaid to morality. Appropriately enough, the theology of morality demanded explication more in the realm of politics than ecclesiology. For the former, princes must obey scripture to deserve obedience from subjects. As for the latter, the Bible, purged of ceremonial laws and prescriptions, allowed no debate over the rightness or wrongness of specifically churchly affairs, for the Church was purely instrumental to righteous living according to the rule of God.

Henry VIII in 1537 licensed a Bible that was largely Tyndale's translation, but Henry by then had found a rule contradictory to Tyndale's for interpreting the word of God: royal authority over religion. For a century and a half to come—that is, until the Toleration Act of William and Mary —Englishmen argued and fought the issue, whether the Bible authorized kings or kings authorized Bibles.

12. The Practical Piety of George Joye

URING the first decade of English Protestant literary activity, Tyndale, Barnes, and Frith sought to turn the religious progress of the realm into Protestant ways. At best, partial and temporary success crowned their efforts, for Henry VIII defended the faith, and that shrewd monarch always decided what faith was to be defended. Intellectual efforts by Protestant exiles found practical execution at home in the dangerous and costly activities of a network of preachers and teachers, believers and learners, booksellers and readers who valued the new liberty of the Christian man above churchly preferment, personal and familial security, and life itself. While their religious opinions were formed by the publications of Tyndale, Frith, and Barnes, their religious practice fell most profundly under the influence of George Joye. In 1530 Joye published the first Protestant English psalter. In the late medieval and early Reformation period, domestic piety focused on little prayerbooks known as primers; Joye compiled the first printed English primer with such skill that it set the standard for these books for at least a decade and a half, and its influence continued throughout the first Reformation generation. Theologically always the debtor, Joye earned credit as a shaper of English Protestant religiosity.

Born about 1490 at Renhold near Bedford, Joye (Jay, Gee, Geach) was educated at Christ's College, Cambridge, proceeding B.A. 1513 and M.A. 1517. Having been ordained by the bishop of Lincoln in 1515, he became a fellow of Peterhouse from 1517 until 1528, when the preferment was revoked on account of his Lutheran leanings. Even before the investigation that led to dismissal and exile, Joye had fallen under suspicion for owning Protestant books, but Stephen Gardiner had defended him and others of his circle. No evidence connects Joye with the first vociferous act of the Cambridge Protestants when Barnes preached his inflammatory sermon on Christmas Eve, 1525, but probably in the aftermath of this trouble, early in 1526, Joye's rooms were searched for forbidden books and he then enjoyed Gardiner's protection.[1]

Certainly the authorities thought of Joye as a prominent member of "Little Germany" in Cambridge, for, in the first concerted effort to discipline that group, he was apprehended along with Thomas Bilney of Trinity Hall and Thomas Arthur of St. John's. On Saturday, November 23, 1527, the university's vice-chancellor received letters from Wolsey commanding the apprehension of Protestants and demanding that Joye and the others appear at Westminster the next Wednesday for examination and correction of their errors. On Monday the master of Peterhouse summoned Joye from the country to show him the letters bearing the Cardinal's seal and sign. "I gote me horse when it snewed, and was colde," Joye later recounted the incident, "and came to Londen and so to Westmynster," but he arrived later than the designated time of nine o'clock to find that Bilney and Arthur already were being examined. Joye "was not ouer hastye to thruste in amonge them, for there was a shrewd mayney of bishpos [sic] besides the Cardinal with other of theyr faction." Frightened and wishing to escape, "I went to my diner & taried walkyng in the cyte." Well he might have wavered. Bilney's and Arthur's examination continued intermittently through December 7, the august examiners and judges being Wolsey, the archbishop of Canterbury William Warham, and bishops

1. Joye, *The refutation of the byshop of Winchesters derke declaration* . . . (London, 1546; *STC* 14,827), lxxxi^r–lxxxiii^v; the story was recounted in the Tunstall Register, printed in *AM, 4,* 754. J. A. Muller, *Stephen Gardiner and the Tudor Reaction* (London, 1926), p. 18, suggested the improbable date of 1521 for the event. My dating has been substantiated by an excellent book on Joye that appeared too late for consideration in preparing this chapter, C. C. Butterworth and A. G. Chester, *George Joye 1495?–1553* . . . (Philadelphia, 1962), p. 30.

Tunstall of London, Fisher of Rochester, Nicholas West of Ely, John Veysey of Exeter, John Longland of Lincoln, John Clerk of Bath and Wells, Henry Standish of St. Asaph's, and John Kite of Carlisle.[2]

Joye never came to trial. The examination of Bilney and Arthur continued through a Friday. On Saturday Joye went to Sir William Gascoigne, a former master whose intimate knowledge of the affair convinced Joye that he had begun the trouble. Appointed to present Joye before Wolsey was one Doctor Capon, whom Joye was to meet in "the chamber of prese*n*s." Never having heard of such a room and being ashamed to expose his ignorance by asking directions, Joye followed his nose to a kitchen, retreated, and, finally directed to the proper room, waited almost an hour for Capon. Now and then a bishop emerged from the examination room. There seemed to be a dozen of them. Joye feared for his life. Gascoigne notified him that Wolsey would not see him, but that he was to appear before the bishop of Lincoln whose suffragan had accused him. At the bishop's place, Joye was told to return the next day at six in the morning. He did so, and waited until eight o'clock when the bishop directed him to remain while all the bishops went to Greenwich to wait upon the Cardinal and King. Joye's request for a statement of the charges against him did not avail. Reporting to Gascoigne once again, he discovered that he was accused of reading the heretical Origen and of sharing the views of Bilney and Arthur.

At Longland's palace another long wait ensued. Joye requested permission to go to his lodging and return on the morrow; asked where he lodged, he lied. Recalling that as a Cambridge scholar he was under the jurisdiction of the vice-chancellor and "the great God the Cardinal," and that Wolsey, as Gascoigne reported, had not sent for him, Joye determined not to report again to Longland. He rode away next morning toward the sea to go abroad and live in a "strange lande amo*n*ge rude & boisterous people, with whose maners I

2. The process against Bilney and Arthur, from the Tunstall Register, was printed in *AM, 4,* appendix.

can not wel agre." By the end of 1527 or very early in 1528 he was on the Continent.[3]

PRIMERS AND TRANSLATIONS

During the eight years of his early reforming career Joye remained in touch with the activities of the English Protestants, who for most of the period centered in Antwerp. From 1529 through 1531, he compiled and composed devotional books, defended himself against his accusers, and began translating portions of the Old Testament. As for Tyndale, 1532 was a quiet year for Joye. From 1533 through 1535 he was busy again, and by the end of 1535 had published through Antwerp and London presses no fewer than fourteen books.

Joye's first public literary endeavor consisted of compiling, and in part translating, the first Protestant devotional manual to be published in English. No copy of this "first printed English Primer" has been preserved to us, but from subsequent revisions and contemporaneous accounts its contents have been reconstructed.[4] Possibly it bore the title by which Foxe recalled it later in the century, "Mattens and Euensong, vij. Psalmes, and other heauenly Psalmes, with the commendations, in Englishe." Whatever its name, we may assume that it closely resembled Joye's second primer, which was discovered to be extant when in 1949 a copy offered for sale in London was bought by the British Museum. Bearing the deceptive imprint of "Francis Foxe, Argentine," this work (*Ned. Bibl.* 4246) was really published by Martin deKeyser in Antwerp in 1530 under the title: "¶ Ortulus anime. The garden of the soule: or the englisshe primers (the which a certaine printer lately corrupted/ & made false to the grete sclaunder of thauthor & greter desayte [i.e. deceit] of as many as boughte and red them) newe corrected and augmented."

During the years 1529–43 when the Protestant movement falteringly made its way upon the English religious scene, a large number of primers appeared, first from abroad, and after 1534 from London presses. Only in 1545 did Henry

---

3. Joye told his story in *The letters whyche Iohan Ashwell . . . sente . . .* (Antwerp, 1531; *STC* 844), [Cviii]ʳ–Diiiʳ.

4. Butterworth, *English Primers*, pp. 11–17, 21–24, and passim.

VIII authorize an official primer for use by his subjects; it embodied the Catholic devotion he yearned to spread during the last years of his reign. Joye's early work became the standard and model for almost every known edition before 1545, excepting an English primer published at Rouen in 1536. The religious character of Joye's work was incalculably important to English Protestantism.

Joye first set forth a calendar of saints' days and holy days, interspersed with comments designed to protestantize the popular regard for saints, feasts, and fasts. He warned that relics put those who venerated them in jeopardy of punishment for idolatry. He read his times as ominous because false prophets preached a false message and unwittingly invoked God's harsh judgment. Joye interspersed a synopsis of the passion of Jesus, as told by the four evangelists, with moralistic interpretative comments. This synopsis was a translation of an earlier Latin harmony of the passion narrative, but it borrowed phraseology from Tyndale's 1526 New Testament and hinted that the Catholic hierarchy acted like the Jewish religious officials who crucified Christ. Next followed a brief guide to the religious rearing of children, providing the decalogue, Lord's Prayer, and Hail Mary in English. Butterworth noted that the text of the Lord's Prayer that Joye published in the 1530 *Hortulus* "After going through many subsequent modifications . . . ultimately formed the basis of the wording adopted by the Church of England in its Book of Common Prayer." The primer's brief catechism owed much to Luther, noting that "it is the faithe and truste only in owre hartes that maketh other [i.e. either] god or ydole." [5] Users of the *Hortulus* found a long form for confessing to God their sins. There followed prayers from the Old Testament, selected from continental Protestant devotional manuals. Daily offices of devotion from Matins to Compline, "not altogether like those of Sarum use," were provided, including "the text of thirty-nine different Psalms," scriptural lessons, "hymns that Joye devised in crude English verse . . . translated from Latin, perhaps from a Lutheran source," and New Testament canticles altered from the Tyndale text. Joye

5. Ibid., pp. 32, 36.

omitted familiar "elaborate prayers and devotions addressed to the Virgin under poetic names." The volume concluded with psalms and commendations, and a motto from Isaiah 59: "Lo, the lorde is yet alyue, whose power is not so minisshed but he maie vs yet saue, nether are his eares so stopped but he will vs yet heare." [6]

Joye's *Hortulus* for the most part confronted its readers with familiar biblical passages for instruction and meditation, arranged for use by simple folk. By careful selection of introductory materials and by excision of devotional formulae offensive to the Protestant point of view, Joye attempted to reform popular religion in England. His efforts of 1529 and 1530 commanded the attention of the Church authorities, who condemned both these books as well as subsequent derivative primers. More railed at the faults of Joye's primers.

In every age Christians have centered personal and family, as well as monastic, devotion upon passages from the Old Testament psalms and prophets; Joye next translated into English just these books. Very early in 1530, probably before the *Hortulus* of that year was printed, he had Englished the entire psalter, working not from Hebrew or the Vulgate but from a Latin version that Bucer of Strassburg had made in September 1529. Like the *Hortulus*, Joye's first psalter (*STC* 2370; *Ned. Bibl.* 2476) claimed to have been printed by Francis Foxe in Argentine [i.e. Strassburg], but was from deKeyser's press in Antwerp. This inscription, and the obvious fact that Joye knew Bucer's Latin psalter very soon after it was printed, have caused Joye's early activities to be assigned to Strassburg. All his early works were printed in Antwerp at the very press which Tyndale and Frith were employing at the time. If Joye was in any way a disciple of Bucer during his early work on the Continent, he soon shifted, for he translated, and published in 1533 after considerable delay, a work of Zwingli's, and in August 1534 he took trouble to make a new English psalter (*STC* 2372) from a Latin version by Zwingli. The earlier psalter was reprinted, in 1534 or 1535, by Thomas Godfray (*STC* 2371), and again in 1541 by

6. Ibid., pp. 24, 37, 39, 43, 44, 46.

Edward Whitchurch (*STC* 2374); Butterworth aptly called it a "free-handed translation." [7] It lodged itself in various English primers of the 1530s, and stamped its verbiage on the minds and souls of Protestants who prayed by these books, thus extending its influence more deeply and more broadly than its intrinsic literary value merited. Joye's second English psalter exerted similar influence, for no fewer than thirty-eight individual psalms from this version were quoted directly in Robert Redman's *Prayers of the Bible,* printed early in 1535.[8]

Since Tyndale's translating proceeded from the New Testament of 1526 to the pentateuch of 1530 to the historical books of the Old Testament, Joye moved from the psalms to the prophets to other wisdom literature. On May 10, 1531, deKeyser printed his translation of Isaiah (*STC* 2777; *Ned. Bibl.* 2482), and three years later another Antwerp press published his English Jeremiah and Lamentations (*STC* 2778; *Ned. Bibl.* 2484). Somewhat later Joye Englished also Proverbs and Ecclesiastes, printed in London by Thomas Godfray (*STC* 2752). Unlike Tyndale, however, Joye refrained from specifying certain parts and themes of scripture as keys that unlocked the whole. He always held that the common reader should feed his soul on scriptural and devotional materials with minimal assistance from translator or editor. To be sure, the 1530 psalter, his first biblical translation, carried a brief preface headed "Johan Aleph greteth the Englishe nacion," imploring the reader to thank God for the vernacular psalms and warning him not to judge the translation by the Vulgate but to leave criticism to persons learned in Hebrew. Each psalm bore a little introduction, apparently of Bucer's making, simply stating the meaning of the psalm and guiding the reader to ponder its message in the twin context of biblical history and present times. These comments reveal nothing of Joye's own interpretation of scripture. He spoke truth, partly as a jibe against the introductions and

7. Ibid., p. 19.
8. Ibid., p. 81; the pervasive influence of Joye's translation upon the Authorized Version of the psalms is exhibited pp. 293 ff.

marginal notes that Tyndale put into his 1534 New Testament, when he declared, "I wolde the scripture were so puerly and plyanly translated that it neded nether note/ glose nor scholia/ so that the reder might once swimme without a corke." [9] Joye always followed that principle.

A brief prologue to Isaiah in Joye's translation noted the importance of the book to Jesus and the evangelists, and likened Isaiah's world to present times as marked by destruction, captivity, and the worship of idols. True godliness, Joye anticipated, would expose the hypocrisy that taught vice to be virtue, fables to be God's word, and idols to be God; at the right time God was restoring his prophet to speak in plain English. The reader needed only a pure heart, not glosses, to receive the prophet's message. The slogan, a favorite device of Joye, exhorted, "Burne nomore goddis worde: but mende it where it is not truly translated." The preface to Jeremiah (1534), although longer, followed the same lines. Joye showed how the prophet warned against turning from Christ to idols. He labeled traditions, laws, and papal decrees the "poysoned pittis of our owne invention" against which Jeremiah preached to the English. Only the lazy would fail to understand the message because, like the old Israel in Babylon, the Church was in captivity.

Joye's 1534 revision of Tyndale's 1526 New Testament, like the original, carried neither prologue, preface, nor marginal notes other than references; it occupies a minor place in Joye's literary career. His contribution to the English Bible involved the Old Testament, from which he translated the Psalter twice, Isaiah, Jeremiah, Lamentations, Proverbs, and Ecclesiastes—no minor achievement for labors of less than eight years. Plain, readable English was his goal. Although his warnings against judging his translations by the Vulgate may sound pompous to modern ears, they signify no more than Joye's desire to reach common folk in their personal devotions and meditations with a simple, self-explanatory Bible. Scripture always appeared to Joye to be its own interpreter, calling on the reader only for a pure heart and an open mind.

9. *Apology*, ed. Arber, p. 23; cf. 1535 ed., [C7]ʳ.

THEOLOGY

In the first of his two major periods of writing, both spent on the Continent, Joye produced, in addition to primers and portions of the Bible, four major writings. A self-defence, similar to those made by Barnes in 1531 and 1534, was published by deKeyser June 10, 1531, entitled *The letters whyche Iohan Ashwell Priour of Newnham Abbey besydes Bedforde, sente secretly to the Byshope of Lyncolne, in the yeare of our Lord M.C.xxvii. Where in the sayde pryour accuseth George Ioye that tyme beyng felow of Peter college in Cambrydge, of fower opinyons: wyth the answer of the sayde George vnto the same opynyons* (STC 844–46; cf. *Ned. Bibl.* 3281). Unlike Barnes, Joye escaped the theological cul-de-sac of defending and explicating his opinions of subjects on which he was accused of heresy; he attacked the errors in his accuser's allegations.

When Frith debated More on the sacrament of the altar, Joye's interest in worship drew him into the fray. He published, on April 5, 1533, the most important and influential discursive writing of his career, *The Souper of the Lorde* (STC 24,468). Although modern scholars have asserted what Foxe doubted, that this book was by Tyndale, it may now confidently be ascribed to Joye.[10] More dignified the book with a lengthy reply which Joye rebutted with *The Subuersion of Moris false foundacion* (STC 14,829; *Ned. Bibl.* 3282). Joye loved false identifications of printers and places for his books, inventing "Nornburg, Niclas twonson" for *Souper,* and "Jacob Aurik of Emdon" for *Subuersion.* In September 1535 he pub-

---

10. J. F. Mozley, *Coverdale and His Bibles* (London, 1953), p. 342, thought "the evidence is decisive for Tyndale," citing his contributions to *Notes and Queries,* November 21, 1942, and July 31, 1943; harboring distinct animus against Joye, Mozley judged *Souper* "too able for Joye" and thought the style not his. External evidences pointing clearly to Joye's authorship, buttressed by consideration of Joye's and Tyndale's political theories, have been recited by Cargill Thompson in "Who Wrote 'The Supper of the Lord'?" I think the controversy decided conclusively for Joye, first, by the identification of most of the contents of the work as originally from the pen of Zwingli, and, second, by consideration of abundant internal evidence; see my "More Evidence that George Joye Wrote The Souper of the Lorde."

lished through Byddell in London *A Compendious Sum of the very Christian Religion* (*STC* 14,821), a translation of *Summa totivs sacrae scripturae, Bibliorum veteris & noui testamenti* (*Ned. Bibl.* 1970: Antwerp, 1533).[11]

Joye exhibited his own miscellaneous theological convictions only in the *Ashwell Letters*. The prior of Newnham in Joye's home region of Bedfordshire had complained to Bishop Longland of the "Lutronus opinio*ns*" that Joye had popularized thereabouts, but Ashwell feared that he, by reporting Joye's deviationism, would lose favor in his own bailiwick! He accused Joye of having contended that simple priests had powers of binding and loosing equal to those of bishops or popes, that faith was sufficient without works, that every priest might have a wife or a concubine, that laymen might hear confessions, that the scriptures damned the worship of images. Moreover, according to the prior, Joye had spread "many lewde opinions amo*n*g the people" which offended some and delighted others. Joye replied by spelling out his views on binding and loosing, justification by faith, priestly marriage, confessing to laymen, pilgrimages, and the worship of images.

As Peter's confession at Caesarea Philippi spoke for all the apostles, Joye argued, so to them all were the keys given as the power of preaching the gospel to all men. Prohibiting vernacular scriptures closed the kingdom and violated the injunction to open it by preaching. Preaching the law bound men in sin, while preaching the gospel loosed "the captiue co*n*scyence in to the quiet lyberte of the spirit." Popes, bishops, and clergy would not stoop to preaching the Bible's twofold message of convicting law and saving gospel because they thought it a mean and lowly office. True apostles and their true successors knew no lordship in spiritual affairs; the real power of the keys was exercised by simple preachers more than by popes and bishops. Scripture called priests, bishops; scripture's bishops preached. Salvation extended as the word of God spread abroad; therefore in opposing vernacular scriptures the official church opposed salvation. Here were no fresh theological insights, yet Joye stated the gist of Reforma-

---

11. Mozley, *Coverdale*, p. 340; *Ned. Bibl.* noted that this is not the *Sum of the Holy Scripture* which Simon Fish translated.

tion doctrine with a theological terseness quite incommensurate with his literary diffuseness.

Faith without works sufficed to justify man before God, but works as necessary fruits of faith justified man before fellowmen; so Joye in 1531 endorsed the notion of double justification. Joye wrote or borrowed this moving description of faith:

> faith is an infallible & vndouted certaintye in our hartes, wherby we beleue and truste in the inuysible God. . . . Fayth is that same constante and fast persuasion in our hartes assured vs by the holy gost, certifyeng vs of the goodnes of God and of his promises towarde vs, by the which persuasion we beleue verely hys wordes and ar assured in our hartes (the holy gost testifyeng it in vs) that he is oure God, our father, to vs an almyghty helper and delyuerer, and that we are receyued in to hys fauour by the deth and merites of hys sonne Iesus Christ our sauyour, vpon the whych belyefe and assured persuasion we loue hym so ernestly agayne that we cease not (the occasyon and tyme offred) to fulfyll his pleasures in doyng the worker [i.e. works] of loue or charite to our neighbours.[12]

Joye repudiated priestly concubinage and contended that priests lacking the gift of chastity ought to marry, on scriptural authority. Since sexuality as the gift of God at creation was not changeable by man, a priest (or other person) erred when he strove against its urges for the sake of a feigned purity; the right path was to marry. To share in this order of society, Joye thought, would increase priests' effectiveness as teachers and preachers. The Church claimed matrimony to be a sacrament, but inconsistently thought that it nullified the grace of ordination. Joye claimed never to have advocated confessing to laymen, although he thought a good case might be made from scriptural injunctions. Quiet consciences, being made by faith, were better known by laymen than by most clergy. Only in case of an unfaithful clergy should lay con-

---

12. *The letters whyche Iohan Ashwell . . . sente . . . (STC* 844), Bii^v; other brief citations above are from this little tract.

fession be allowed. Yet if every sin must be told to the ear of a priest, a quiet conscience might never be attained, for many sins escaped memory. He thought pilgrimages and worshiping images were idolatrous despite scholastic distinctions between veneration and worship.

Joye wrote with literary infelicity against the clumsy accusations in Ashwell's letters, but he thought clearly and made his points compellingly. Perhaps the very colloquial and unpolished style, cloaking a sure Protestant conviction, added to the charm that earned his little book three printings.

Five editions met a persistent demand for Joye's treatise on the Lord's Supper, first printed in 1533 against More in defense of Frith. Joye vehemently attacked the mass, the very heart of established Catholic religious practice in England. As late as 1548, on the eve of official approval of a common liturgy for the Church of England, his work was reprinted with the commendation of the radical Protestant divine Robert Crowley. Joye originally devised a simple explanation of the Supper, but from Tyndale's correspondence with Frith, it is known that Joye was restrained from printing the book until Frith's controversy with More became public. The original treatise was simply a digest and translation of Zwingli's 1526 treatise *On the Lord's Supper,* summarizing Zwingli's paraphrase of John 6: 26–59 and his view of the institution, use, significance, and theology of the sacrament. After reading More's reply to Frith's book on the Supper, Joye added a refutation of More and some patristic citations. The book's origin explains its elaborate title; it was on "The Souper of the Lorde," but in order that the reader might "be the better prepared and suerlyer enstructed," the Johannine passage was explained. Then "incidently M. Moris letter agenst Iohan Frythe is confuted"—so incidently that the confutation took only a dozen paragraphs. The tract nowhere deviated from Zwingli's conception of the Supper as a physical, and therefore only an indirect, representation of a spiritual reality, with the significance of the meal arising from the participants' inwardly realizing the spiritual presence of Christ. In the formula of consecration from the institution narrative, *est* meant *significat,* for Christ made no crafty, invisible miracles of a magical character, but appealed to the senses in order that God might be glorified by the inner man.

Joye specifically recommended a service of spiritual communion that he thought should be established in England to commemorate truly Jesus' last supper with his disciples. This service, he urged, should be authorized by secular princes in their rôle as "the very pastors and head rulers of their congregations" for observance "once or twice in the week." The ideal service, "restored to the pure use, as the apostles used it in their time," concentrated upon the reading and exposition of portions of scripture. At the outset I Corinthians 11 is expounded, and a sermon made on Christ's death as sufficient sacrifice "to purge all the sins of the world." A psalm or prayer of thanksgiving is said or sung in the vernacular. Bread and wine are "set before them, in the face of the church, upon the table of the Lord, purely and honestly laid," and the meaning of these signs is explained. Participants are "lovingly to draw near unto this table of the Lord, and that not only bodily," but spiritually as well. The minister comes down from the pulpit and with the other ministers approaches the table. John 6 is read. Prayer and praise follow, and a minister reads I Corinthians 11. Articles of belief are openly rehearsed in the vernacular. Each person confesses "his sins secretly unto God." True and active faith and love are exhorted, and all kneel to say "secretly with all their devotion their *Paternoster* in English" after the example of the curate. The minister eats bread and drinks wine "in the sight of the people, hearing him with a loud voice, with godly gravity, and after a christian religious reverence, rehearsing distinctly the words of the Lord's supper in their mother tongue"; all eat and drink as other ministers distribute bread and wine while the chief minister reads "the communication that Christ had with his disciples after his supper, beginning at the washing of their feet." All kneel to give high thanks to God. "This done, let every man commend and give themselves whole to God, and depart." [13]

Joye interspersed his model service with frequent exhortations and scripture readings; otherwise he emphasized the cen-

13. "The Souper of the Lorde," PS *3*, pp. 264–67.

tral elements of a Protestant communion service and gave
them a strictly Zwinglian interpretation. Such of his elements
as the Creed and Lord's Prayer in the vernacular became
standard for Church of England eucharistic liturgy, as did
also the drawing near to the Lord's table by the communicants.
As probably the first printed description in English of a communion service, Joye's recommendation influenced specific liturgical reforms under Edward VI, and its stress upon recollection of the last supper remained in all official English prayer
books.

After resigning the office of lord chancellor, More wrote,
and published in 1534 from William Rastell's London press,
¶ *The answere to the fyrst parte of the poysened booke, whych
a namelesse heretyke hath named the souper of the lorde*
(*STC* 18,077). Now free from duties at court, More no
longer wrote after hours, but his *Answere* was nevertheless as
loose-jointed, diffuse, repetitious, verbose, and overly long as
his previous religious polemics. More knew well that Joye
"longe hadde in hande and redy lyenge by hym, his boke
agaynst the sacrament," and that *Souper,* if Joye's, was a
version recently lengthened "by a pyece that he hath patched
in agaynst me." More seems to have been convinced that he
was dealing with Joye in this argument, but, as always, preferred to engage his several enemies en masse.[14]

Joye's book hardly deserved a disputant of More's stature.
In the *Answere,* More followed his own unclever policy of
citing Joye's book *in extenso.* Probably he drew to *Souper*
notice it otherwise would not have received. Joye seized the
occasion to publish, in 1534, a reply called *The Subuersion of
Moris false foundacion: where vpon he sweteth to set faste
and shoue vnder his shameles shoris, to vnderproppe the popis
chirche.* More's strongest point, aside from repeated assertions of the inerrancy of the official Church's doctrine,
was that the Protestants and their English representatives
such as Barnes and Frith and Joye disagreed on the manner
of Christ's presence in the sacrament. As earlier he had scored
disagreements among continental Protestants against Frith,

14. *Answere* (*STC* 18,077), [Aaviij]ʳ; cf. *Workes,* p. 1037.

now he lodged those between English Protestants against Joye, whose reply was theologically insignificant.

JOYE AND TYNDALE

If the Supper was the first major bone of contention among English Protestants, Joye soon picked another with Tyndale over the state of departed souls: did resurrection of the dead with their bodies await the last trumpet's call, or were the souls of the faithful departed already living a resurrected life? —"a doctrinal controversy which had slumbered in Christendom since the days of Pope John XXII," [15] but which touched on late medieval Christianity's preoccupation with purgatory. Tyndale hotly contested Joye's changing his term "resurrection" in the New Testament to terms designed to convey the notion of life beyond death. Tyndale made his complaint in a second foreword to his November 1534 New Testament. Aside from reckoning Joye a scoundrel for revising another's translation, Tyndale counted him a heretic for believing that the souls of the dead received celestial embodiment without waiting for their mortal flesh to be revivified at the general resurrection. Thus, thought Tyndale, Joye repudiated resurrection of the flesh, and, worse yet, sent "secret lettres" to England that led many of the Brethren to "vtterly denye the resurreccion of the flesshe and bodye, affirminge that the soule when she is departed, is the spirituall bodye of the resurreccion, and other resurreccion shall there none be." Moreover, Tyndale said that Frith, while in prison, wrote that Joye should be restrained from such teachings. Tyndale's version of the story told only his side of the matter, for, in fact, Frith agreed with Joye on this particular point and probably converted more Brethren to it than Joye. Tyndale had "talked with some of them . . . so doted in that folye, that it were as good perswade a post, as to plucke that madnes oute of their braynes." [16]

Joye ably defended himself with ¶ *An Apologye made by George Ioye to satisfye (if it maye be) w. Tindale: to pourge*

15. Rupp, *Studies,* p. 50.
16. *1534 NT,* p. 16.

and defende himself ageinst so many sclaunderouse lyes fayned
vpon him in Tindals vncharitable and vnsober Pystle so well
worthy to be prefixed for the Reader to induce him into the
vnderstanding of hys new Testament diligently corrected and
printed in the yeare of oure lorde. M.CCCC. and xxxiiij. in
November (*STC* 14,820). Always ready with the slogan,
Joye now chose two: "¶ I knowe and beleue that the bodyes
of euery dead man/ shall ryse agayne at domes daye" and,
from Psalm 120, "Lorde/ delyuer me from lyinge lyppes/
and from a deceatfull tongue. Amen." Friends had arbitrated
the controversy with Tyndale; Joye should leave his New
Testament revision to the judgment of the reader, Tyndale
should recall his epistle, and the two men should sign a joint
preface to Tyndale's next (November) New Testament,
showing their accord. Instead, Tyndale published the epistle
with his Testament, prompting Joye to answer and clear his
name.

Out of Tyndale's own works and out of scripture, Joye made
a good case for his viewpoint on the resurrection. Bucer, Pellican, Melanchthon, Zwingli, and others were cited as on Joye's
side. Actually, Joye took his position directly from Zwingli,
whose *On the Lord's Supper,* which Joye had digested and
translated, commented that "in Scripture words like 'resur-
rect' and 'resurrection' are used not only of the general resurrection of the dead but of the life of the soul after this present
age." [17]

Joye's keen eye for Tyndale's several theological inconsistencies also perceived aspects of the great translator's per-
sonality which, although brushed aside by biographers, find
support from primary evidence. Tyndale had both welcomed
others' corrections and promised his own revisions in the
1525–26 New Testament; by 1534 he regarded not only scripture but his own translation of it as sacrosanct, for, what he
earlier conceived as human testimony to divine mercy, he
later took to be a contract binding God as well as man. The
promised revision by Tyndale not having appeared, Joye only

17. G. W. Bromiley, tr., *Zwingli and Bullinger,* Library of Christian Classics,
24 (Philadelphia, 1953), p. 202.

sought to eradicate inaccuracies in printing and to clarify some points of confusion. He had been prevailed upon by Antwerp printers to supervise a revision. With respect to the New Testament project, Joye justly accused Tyndale of having "slept" from 1526 to 1534. Joye had decided not to append his name to what was really Tyndale's work, lest he be guilty of the very vainglory of which Tyndale accused him. On hearsay Tyndale dubbed Joye a heretic. Joye reserved the knowledge of his own conscience to God as sole judge. Tyndale's epistle, as Joye perceived, feigned humility and charity while actually castigating a former friend. Joye cut close to the bone with the prayer, "God forbyd that T. shulde so thinke of hymself/ that he hathe so exquysitly/ (ye and that at firste) translated the testament that yt cannot be mended." [18]

Joye had copies of his letters to a man in England concerning the state of departed souls; in them he had not denied resurrection of the flesh, and their circulation among the Brethren was none of his doing. He had replied to Frith's inquiry about such letters, but had received no answer. Two of Joye's letters in the case are preserved. He wrote to Latimer on April 28, 1533, deploring controversy over the resurrection, and asking Latimer to read the "secret" letter on the subject. Of the same date was a letter to "Brother William," the extant copy of which is signed "John Coke"; Butterworth has shown the high probability, against Mozley's judgment to the contrary, that the second was from Joye to the William Hill mentioned as messenger in the letter to Latimer. Joye stood against Luther and the Anabaptists as well as against Tyndale on the question of the state of the departed, and, as far as he knew at the time, against Frith also. While Latimer's reply to Joye, if any, is not known, sermons from about this time indicate that he, like Frith in his last days, stood with Joye. Regardless of these alignments, the letters show that Joye turned every stone to avoid controversy among the Brethren, that he stuck to his own opinion, and that he pleaded, against Tyndale's new doctrine, that a variety

18. *Apology,* ed. Arber, pp. 21, 29 and passim.

of scriptural interpretations was necessary and desirable.[19]

Joye with literal accuracy credited Frith with having composed "tindals answers to More for tindale." Although Tyndale praised his own exposition of the sermon on the mount, Joye knew it was the product of Tyndale's "translating and powldering" Luther. Joye perceived how "sore yt gnaweth his herte to be correcked and warned of me/ but a fole and vnlerned as he bothe reputeth me and telleth yt me to my face." Tyndale seemed "afrayd lest any man wolde steale awaye frome him the glorye and name of his translacion," whereas Joye yearned for a day when other men would edit all the early translations into versions of the full English Bible. Joye suggested some revisions of Tyndale's work that Tyndale in fact adopted in his own last version. Ironically, Joye prayed for reconciliation with Tyndale so that their souls after death "might liue with crist in heuen vntyl our bodyes aftir that sleape in the duste be awakened with the trompet of god/ and resumed of our soulis to ryse and come forth togither into that gloriouse lyfe." Joye hoped that Tyndale would overcome the notion that the Holy Ghost spoke only in his own translation.[20] Joye wrote in the bitterness of personal controversy with a former friend, and confessed it; modern commentators have roundly blamed him for it. Joye pointed out that Tyndale had written in the same bitterness, and had struck the first blow; Tyndale's biographers have absolved him. In fact, Joye was not without fault. Neither was Tyndale.

The controversy over the state of departed souls surpassed in theological importance the personal issue of Joye's revision of Tyndale's New Testament. Prior to its publication in August 1534, More had written disparagingly of the disagreements among the English Protestants. In *The answere to the . . . poysened booke*, More reckoned Tyndale "the captayne of our Englyshe heretyques," and credited him with the reputation of wit and learning before he fell into heresy. "Fryth was lo a proper yonge man and a to warde, tyll he fell vnto

19. *LP, 6,* no. 402; Butterworth, pp. 25 ff.; Chester, *Hugh Latimer,* pp. 94 f.; cf. Mozley, *William Tyndale,* pp. 268 ff.

20. *Apology,* ed. Arber, pp. 33, 42, 43, 44, 49.

these folyes." Barnes and Joye, however, according to More, were thought even by the Brethren to be men of "wyttes so wasted" and of "lernyng waxen so slender, that the bretherhed hath lytle lyste to reade them." Their books were numerous but contradictory. They disagreed radically on the interpretation of the Lord's Supper and on purgatory. Some had the souls of the departed "slepyng tyll domys daye," while others were "sendyng all strayt to heuyn"; putting out the fire of purgatory seemed to More to imply eventual elimination of hell.[21] Both Tyndale and Joye actually showed great concern for unity among English Protestants, but, for Joye, that meant unity in spirit with a variety of thought and opinion, whereas, for Tyndale, it meant uniformity of opinion and agreement on one authoritative English New Testament.

The note in the November 1534 New Testament derogating Joye, and Joye's answer in the *Apology* of February 1535, mark the eruption but not the beginning of dissension. An earlier act by Joye had already touched off Tyndale's ire. Tyndale wrote to Frith about May 1533 that "George Joy at Candlemas [February 2] printed . . . two leaves of Genesis in a great form, and sent one copy to the King, and another to the new Queen, with a letter to N., to deliver them." To this act Tyndale traced rumors in England that a new Bible was about to appear, and upon it he blamed the intensification of heretic hunting in Antwerp.[22] Thus early Joye looked to shape official policy on religion in England.

After Tyndale's imprisonment in May 1535, Joye sought to end his own exile just when Barnes was enlisting in the royal service as a negotiator of religious matters. For on June 4, 1535, Edward Fox wrote to Cromwell that Joye was lodging with him in Calais. Fox pledged that Joye would speak and write no more against the prevailing notion of the sacrament; he found him "conformable in all points as a Christian man should be," and promised to intervene with the King in Joye's favor. Regardless of the opportunities that lay ahead of Joye at home, the rift with Tyndale served to brand

21. More, *Answere*, Bb[v], [Bbii][r-v], ccxxxii[r]; cf. *Workes*, pp. 1037 f., 1120.
22. Tyndale to Frith, May 9 [?], 1533, *LP, 6*, no. 458; cf. *AM, 5,* 132, and Mozley, *William Tyndale*, pp. 257 ff.

him as a treacherous fellow. At the end of July one Thomas Theobald wrote to Cranmer reporting that Henry Phillips, who arrested Tyndale, was commissioned to take Barnes and Joye also, noting that it was said in England and in Antwerp "that Joye was of counsel with him [Phillips] in taking Tyndale, but he [Phillips] said he had never seen Joye to his knowledge," much less worked with him. Theobald wrote "because Joye is greatly blamed and a[bu]sed among merchants and others who were his friends, falsely and wrongfully." [23] While correspondence of the time indicates that Joye lost favor with the Protestants after the arrest of Tyndale, it shows as clearly that Joye ranked with Tyndale and Barnes as a major leader of English Protestantism.

Apparently in the latter half of 1535 Joye went back to England. In September he published from the London press of Byddell his translation, *A compendyouse somme*. Although he may have worked on some of the primers that appeared in the late 1530s, no publication bearing Joye's name is extant from this period. He was in England for five years, but his activities have left no trace. About 1540 he again fled England to escape punishment under the reactionary policy of Henry which forbade priestly marriage.

For the rest of Henry's reign Joye remained on the Continent, with Antwerp as headquarters for his printing. In the period 1541–46 no fewer than ten books by Joye were printed. Two pleaded the cause of the rightness of priestly marriage. In August 1541 works appeared from the press of the widow Endhoven on this subject. Over the pseudonym James Sawtry was published *The defence of the mariage of priestes* (*STC* 21,804) as from the press of "Jan Troost in Auryk." *A very godly defense, defending the mariage of preistes* (*STC* 17,-798), by Melanchthon, purported to be translated out of Latin into English by Lewis Beuchame and to be published by Ubryght Hoff, Lipse; "Beuchame" was Joye.

Earlier in 1541 came Joye's anonymous book, *A frutefull treatis of baptyme and the Lordis souper* (*STC* 24,217),

23. Edward Fox to Cromwell, June 4, 1535, *LP, 8,* no. 823; Thomas Tebolde to Cranmer, July 31, 1535, ibid., no. 1151, printed in Mozley, pp. 304 f.

from the same Antwerp press, but attributed to one Grunning. March 1543 saw published Joye's translation of *The rekening and declaration of the faith of H. Zwingly* (*STC* 26,138), supposedly from "Zurik" but really from Endhoven's press in Antwerp. There were other translations: *The exposicion of Daniel the prophete,* "Emprinted at Geneue, 1545" (*STC* 14,823) and drawn from writings by Melanchthon, Oecolampadius, and others, a book twice reprinted in London in 1550; and *The coniectures of the ende of the worlde* by Andreas Osiander, published in May 1548 with a preface by Joye (*STC* 18,877). There were three polemical tracts against the established religion, the first from February 1543, called *Our sauiour Iesus Christ hath not ouercharged his chirche with many ceremonies* (*STC* 14,556), published anonymously by the Endhoven widow but ascribed to "Zurik." June of that year brought forth a little book "gathered by George Ioye" called *The unite and Scisme of the olde Chirche* (*STC* 14,-830). There was printed in 1544 over Joye's initials *A present consolacion for the sufferers of persecucion for ryghtwysenes* (*STC* 14,828).

In 1543 Joye took up the cause of the late Barnes, defending him against, and commenting upon, the twelve articles alleged by Gardiner under which Barnes was condemned and burnt as a heretic, in *George Ioye confuteth, Uvinchesters false Articles* (*STC* 14,826), to which Gardiner replied. Joye called his 1546 rebuttal *The refutation of the byshop of Winchesters derke declaration of his false articles* (*STC* 14,827). The last extant writing by Joye attacked books by John Foxe, *De non plectendis adulteris* (1548; *STC* 11,235; reissued 1549 as *De lapsis in ecclesiam recipiendis consultatio*). Joye replied in *A contrarye* (*to a certayne manis*) *consultacion: That adulterers ought to be punyshed wyth deathe* (*STC* 14,822). Joye's later literary production is remarkable mainly for its size, and throws light on Joye's earlier thought and action only by virtue of some autobiographical paragraphs. The second burst of publishing activity ended by 1550 as suddenly as it had begun in 1541. During the reign of Edward VI, Joye was back in England, and on March 21, 1552, he was instituted into the living of Ashwell, Hertfordshire. He died in 1553.[24]

Joye's second sojourn on the Continent during the last seven or eight years of the reign of Henry VIII coincided with the exile of Coverdale, but there is no evidence that the two collaborated. His enduring legacy to English Protestantism were the primers and the Old Testament translations, rather than the later polemical books and translations. In spite of the regard in which Joye was held by his contemporaries among Reformation leaders, most modern writers have been bent upon magnifying Tyndale, often by minifying his associates. Joye's accusations against Tyndale have been written off as the fulminations of a near crank against an always patient and godly man. He possessed a reckless pen and, on the whole, a minor intelligence, but even Joye was capable of telling the truth. He knew Tyndale and Tyndale's affairs intimately, and he occupied a high position among the early English Protestants. The only really false note in his *Apology* is that of his astonishment that Tyndale should attack a person as viciously as he did Joye; knowing Tyndale's capacity for ill temper as well as he said he did, Joye might have expected the outburst. Yet even this point Joye adequately explained as Tyndale's breach of an agreement into which he and Joye had entered lest English Protestants should be offended by their enmity.

Joye was indeed "one of the most ardent of the first generation of English reformers" but to count him "one of the strangest and most cantankerous" of that group is more modish than deserved.[25] Mozley found Joye at best a poor third behind Tyndale and Coverdale as a translator, a defective scholar, vain and egotistic, not meritless for his Old Testament translations, "a man . . . [of] no heroic quali-

---

24. Mozley, *Coverdale,* pp. 43 f.; pp. 340 ff. identified and described ten of Joye's writings, especially the anonymous and pseudonymous ones. John Bale, *Illvstrivm Maioris Britanniae Scriptorvm . . .* (1548; *STC* 1295), 239ʳ–240ʳ, listed twenty-one books by Joye, of which all have been identified save one, a translation of Erasmus; it is possible that Bale mistook Joye for Roy as translator of Erasmus' *Paraclesis* (*STC* 10,493, *An Exhortation to the diligent studye of scripture,* Antwerp, 1529).

25. Chester, p. 94.

ties" who, nevertheless, "schooled himself to undergo two long and bitter exiles for the sake of his religion" (no heroism there?). Mozley thought that "we need not refuse Bale's description of him as *fidelis et robustus veritatis assertor,* a stout and faithful champion of the truth." Mozley discounted Joye's enduring gifts to the English Bible save for his having originated such phrases as "saving health" and "backslide." [26] Foxe, however, who had tasted the poison of Joye's pen, reckoned his two books against Gardiner such satisfactory answers to the articles lodged against Barnes that there was no need for Foxe to discuss the topic beyond referring his readers to Joye's books. In listing Protestant leaders whose teachings the papists misrepresented, Foxe named Joye alongside Luther, Tyndale, Frith, Lambert, Barnes, and Roy. The data with which Foxe worked showed Joye as a very prominent and important early Protestant. When More examined George Constantine for information about the Protestants abroad he named Tyndale and Joye as ring leaders. When Henry VIII issued a proclamation in 1546 abolishing certain English books, he gave blanket condemnation to the works of Frith, Tyndale, Wycliffe, Joye, Roy, and others. [27]

Like him or not, the man translated into acceptable and influential English much of the Old Testament: Psalms, Proverbs, Ecclesiastes, Song of Solomon, Isaiah, Jeremiah, and Lamentations; all these he was the first to put into modern English, and maybe also Job. He neither knew nor claimed to know Hebrew well, working usually from some Reformation Latin version. Both Rogers and Coverdale incorporated parts of his work into their complete Bibles, although Joye was not a major source of either editor. He worked on those parts of scripture to which Tyndale's efforts did not extend. But his chief interest was to provide English Protestants with usable books of devotion. On that ground he recommended the prophetic and wisdom literature which he translated, and to that purpose he compiled the first Protestant devotional

26. Mozley, pp. 59, 53 f. Butterworth and Chester, in *George Joye,* estimated Joye's character and achievements generously without refuting common criticisms.

27. *AM, 4,* 671; *5,* 433, 565, 568.

manuals in English. Theologically clever but not profound, polemically strident but effective, Joye left a legacy that enriched the piety and shaped the worship of English Christians. He eluded martyrdom under Henry VIII, unlike Tyndale, Frith, and Barnes. So did Cranmer, Latimer, and Ridley, but they became martyrs under Mary Tudor. Joye died an apparently natural death, in an age when to do so was, for leaders of English religion, unheroic.

13. Protestant Translators and Propagandists

FEW men of rather more zeal than ability, apprentices who never became journeymen, enlisted in the early English Protestant literary endeavor led by Barnes, Frith, Tyndale, and Joye. Often they helped, occasionally they hindered, the cause. The monuments to their labors are slim tracts embodying translations of continental Protestant writings and original compositions ridiculing the established religion. The total character of the movement, however, will be understood only when their writings have been examined, and the Catholic reaction will be misunderstood unless it is seen that the Church tended to estimate all Protestant writers by the measure of the lowliest of them.

WILLIAM ROY AND JEROME BARLOWE

The most famous member of the outer circle of early English Protestant writers, and the one whose ability is most difficult to assess, was William Roy or Roye. A student at Cambridge probably during the heyday of "Little Germany," Roy became an observant friar of the Franciscan order at Greenwich. Humphrey Monmouth, who sponsored Tyndale's first labors at translating the New Testament, helped Roy go to Germany to work with Tyndale. Nearly a year after Tyndale matriculated at Wittenberg, on June 10, 1525, there was entered in the register of the University the name *Guilhelmus Roy ex landino*.[1] Roy acknowledged that he took the

1. *Album Academiae Vitebergensis, I,* 125, cited by Smith, "Englishmen at Wittenberg in the Sixteenth Century," p. 422.

minor part in producing the 1525–26 English translation of the New Testament, but he remained proud of his association with "the good ma*n* which did it translate." [2]

While Tyndale was waiting for a companion to help him make the translation and compare texts, possibly hoping that Frith or Coverdale would join him, Roy offered assistance. Later, Tyndale estimated Roy's character as that of "a man somewhat crafty, when he cometh unto new acquaintance, and before he be thorough known, and namely [i.e. especially] when all is spent." What Tyndale expected of a helper, Roy did not provide. "As long as he had no money, somewhat I could rule him; but as soon as he had gotten him money, he became like himself again." The helper's work was utilized, his person barely tolerated. As soon as the project terminated, Tyndale "bade him farewell for our two lives, and (as men say) a day longer." Tyndale recalled the association with bitterness and calumny.

Not content with breaking personal relations with Roy, about May 1527 Tyndale warned Jerome Barlowe to have nothing to do with him. Later on, Tyndale smarted when he was taken to be the author or endorser of a scurrilous poem attacking Wolsey which Roy and Barlowe produced in 1528 under the title *Rede me and be nott wrothe For I saye no thynge but trothe* (*STC* 21,427). Tyndale apparently thought the satirical verse damaged prospects for official reception of his New Testament at home. Taking the stance of injured superiority that he later assumed toward Joye, Tyndale announced that Roy, "whose tongue is able not only to make fools stark mad, but also to deceive the wisest, that is, at the first sight and acquaintance . . . set him [Barlowe] a-work to make rhymes, while he himself translated a dialogue out of Latin into English." From Tyndale's perspective, Roy had both tricked Barlowe and betrayed Tyndale. It unbecame

2. Luther, *An exposition in to the seventh chaptre of the first pistle to the Corinthinans,* tr. William Roy (Antwerp, 1529; *STC* 10,493), Cij*ʳ*; cf. my "The Earliest Translations of Luther into English." In the preface to his translation of a tract popular in Strassburg, Roy spoke of "William Hitchyns, vnto whome I was (after the grace geven me of the lorde) as healpe felowe, and parte taker of his laboures." See *William Roye's Dialogue between a Christian Father and his Stubborn Son,* ed. A. Wolf (Vienna, 1874), p. 37.

"the Lord's servant to use railing rhymes" offensive to many
readers: "Let it not offend thee, that some walk inordinately;
let not the wickedness of Judas cause thee to despise the
doctrine of his fellows. No man ought to think that Stephen
was a false preacher, because that Nicholas, which was chosen
fellow with him to minister unto the widows, fell after into
great heresies."[3] Tyndale feared guilt by association with
Roy because Church authorities in England, on the basis of
reports from Cochlaeus and other informers, identified Roy
as one of two Englishmen who translated the New Testament
in Germany; in some reports Roy's name preceded Tyndale's.
Modern writers' relegation of Roy to an insignificant rôle
in the work hardly accords with the vehemence of Tyndale's
assertion of their complete breach. Tyndale's denunciations
neither say nor imply that Roy helped him little or badly.

Roy was a popularizer. His and Barlowe's book of rhymes
goaded Wolsey and other Church officials to energetic efforts
toward eradicating it, efforts similar to those directed against
the New Testament in its earliest years and against Simon
Fish's *Supplication for the Beggars*. The book bore on its
title page a caricatured coat of arms for Wolsey, picturing
him as a butcher of true religion,

> The mastif Curre bred in Ypswitch towne
> Gnawynge with his teth a kynges crowne.

For page after page—through dialogue between the author
and the personified treatise, through a mocking lament over
the demise of the mass, and through dialogue between two
servants of a priest—the poem described ecclesiastical and
social ills in a way calculated to embitter common people
against prelates and priests. It asserted the supremacy of
scripture, but otherwise posed no theological issue. Protesting
corruption of the gospel by ecclesiastical power, the authors
proposed eliminating that power, but suggested no ecclesiological reconstruction. The personal attack on Wolsey which
dominated the first half of the poem was crude but effective. Its

---

3. Tyndale, Wicked Mammon, PS *1*, pp. 37–42. *Rede me* (*STC* 21,427) was
published anonymously by J. Schott in Strassburg, and was reprinted in 1546
in London (*STC* 21,428).

complaint against Church-bred injustices toward common folk was seldom clever.

While the concern of the hierarchy to eradicate the little book indicates its effectiveness, Tyndale justly thought the book was theologically peripheral. The authors understood something of Luther's own religious pilgrimage, for they adroitly had a character search in vain for a single element of monastic religiosity that would pass muster before the evangel of Christ. The writers knew something of Reformation leaders, and wove into their story the names of Bucer, Capito, Cellarius, and other Strassburg Protestant leaders, as well as those of Lefèvre, Eck, Emser, Murner, Erasmus, Cochlaeus, Bugenhagen, Luther, and others. In a jestful account of the attacks upon and defenses of the mass, one disputant asked,

> Medled nott Erasmus/ in this matter
> Which so craftely can flatter/
> With cloked dissimulacion?

To which his friend replied,

> He was busy to make will fre/
> A thynge nott possible to be/
> After wyse clarckis estimacion.
> Wherfore he intermitted lytle/
> As concernynge the massis tytle/
> With eny maner assercion.
> He feareth greatly some men saye/
> Yf masse shulde vtterly decaye/
> Least he shulde lose his pension.
> Notwithstondynge he hath in his hedde/
> Soche an opinion of the god of bredde/
> That he wolde lever [i.e. rather] dye a marter.[4]

The book sought popularity, not profundity.

Roy as Translator

At the end of August 1527 Roy published another popular book attacking the sacraments and furnishing guides for the

4. *Rede me*, [bvij]ᵛ; cf. *Rede me*, ed. Arber, English Reprints (London, 1871; Westminster, 1895), p. 42.

religious training of youth. *A Brefe Dialoge/ bitwene a Christen father and his stobborne Sonne* was a translation of a little work "late turned out of douche into latten" and widely used in Strassburg. The original seems to have eluded identification. Impressed by the influence of the dialogue on daily life in that city, Roy dedicated his translation to its civic leaders and citizens. In a preface he claimed to "have allredy partly translated, certayne bokes of the olde testament, the whiche, with the healpe of God, yerr longe shalbe brought to lyght." If help arrived, light never dawned, for there has been found neither trace nor notice of such translations. Tyndale, upon reading the preface, thought his former assistant had promised more than he could deliver. Roy stated that while waiting to publish these translations he wished "to make some smale treatous" on the Old Testament's "profunde misteries and greate iudgementes."

A Brefe Dialoge presented a highly spiritualistic interpretation of New Testament religion, after the fashion of Zwingli and his exaggerators. All external acts were seen as remote from the inward and purely spiritual truth of religion. Scripture ordained neither singing nor reading in church, for these contradicted the rule that "God wylbe honored and worshipped in the sprete only." Recitation of the Lord's Prayer under dominical injunction was refuted, the purpose of the prayer being seen as only to declare "of what mynde and herte we ought to be when we praye." Each phrase of the paternoster was shown to invoke a spiritually meditative attitude in which vocal words should be discarded. Indeed "all thynges that the outwarde churche hitherto hath brought vp, and kepte, are vayne and of none effecte." Temporal rulers were to be obeyed to the letter, for God granted their authority. Religion bore no corollary authority and observance. Roy's translation advocated Zwingli's (later Joye's) teaching on the state of departed souls: "Though christen menne shlepe in the lorde. [*sic*] yett dye they not, for the soule departynge out of this wretched boddy entreth immediatly into grett ioye and rest, so remaynynge vntill that oure lorde shall awake it agayne." [5] Also Zwinglian with regard to the Lord's Supper,

5. The foregoing citations are from *William Roye's Dialogue between a Christian Father and his Stubborn Son,* in order, pp. 35, 42, 81, 42 f., 52.

the book gave a radically spiritual interpretation of the other sacraments. In England it was proscribed both under its own name and by the title "Roye against the seven sacraments." Calling the book an attack on all the sacraments was appropriate enough, for it repudiated every sacramentalist assumption that materiality might manifest spiritual reality. It attempted to destroy the *ex opere operato* explanation of the sacramental process, it denounced auricular confession, and it extolled matrimony as a simple order of creation. It specifically reconstructed baptism and the Lord's Supper as services of spiritual virtue by means of recollection stimulated by outward tokens. It implicitly repudiated the other sacraments; only ordination, confirmation, and extreme unction escaped specific attack.

A Brefe Dialoge first stated in English the viewpoint of the Reformation radicals. The position won few adherents before its ecclesiology was adopted by separatists after 1580, although sacramental spiritualism found advocates among some more radical English Protestants in the reign of Edward VI. In 1550 the book was reprinted without Roy's preface, under the title *The true beliefe in Christ and his sacramentes* (*STC* 14,576).

Roy's writings and translations reveal an eclectic theological interest. Two years after publishing *A Brefe Dialoge,* he issued, in a single volume, translations of writings by Erasmus and Luther, neither of which endorsed the spiritualist theme. Erasmus' *Paraclesis,* with the English title ¶ *An exhortation to the diligent studye of scripture* (*STC* 10,493), stood at the beginning, but Roy devoted the lion's share of the little volume to his translation of Luther's *Das siebend Capitel S. Pauli zu den Chorinthern* (1523) arguing that marriage was a godly estate for persons lacking the gift of chastity. Roy omitted Luther's brief prefaces in order to spare his volume the embarrassment of bearing the name and brand of the arch-heretic. He headed Luther's commentary ¶ *An exposition in to the seventh chaptre of the first pistle to the Corinthians.* Hoochstraten printed the book in Antwerp, under the misleading imprint "¶ At Malborow in the londe of Hesse. . . . By my [*sic*] Hans Luft," on June 20, 1529, three weeks before Frith's translation of Luther's *De Antichristo* came out.

Thus Roy first published an English translation of a complete treatise by Luther. But if he wished to purvey Wittenberg theology as though it were produced by Erasmus, he failed, for the two portions were judged independently by Church authorities in England. Luther's piece earned condemnation, and had but one printing, while Erasmus' exhortation in Roy's translation was reprinted twice by Robert Wyer about 1540 (*STC* 10,494), and was prefixed to editions of the English New Testament in 1536, 1549, 1550, and 1552.[6]

Erasmus' endorsement of vernacular scriptures had embarrassed English church leaders long before Roy's translation was published. Worse yet, Roy now invoked Erasmus to advocate Tyndale's New Testament. The treatise argued that all might comprehend the *philosophia christi* (Roy translated the term, "teaching," "doctrine," "scripture") if only the gospels and epistles should go abroad in the common tongue. "I wold to god/" Roy had Erasmus pray, "*the* plowma*n* wold singe a texte of the scripture at his plowbeme/ And that the wever at his lowme/ with this wold drive away the tediousnes of tyme." Cleverly pressing home Erasmus' declaration, "The first poynte of Christianite is to knowe what Christ hath taught," Roy diligently cited all scriptural passages in the volume from the 1525–26 New Testament.[7]

Luther's argument for marriage as an order of creation typified the great reformer's view of sexuality. Married life was a Christian vocation for layman and cleric alike, unless one possessed the rare gift of lifelong chastity. To Henry VIII that was a disagreeable view, for it abandoned clerical celibacy and enforced monogamous fidelity. But Cranmer, like Luther, had already acted on the conviction, and it eventually became a cardinal teaching in the Church of England.

ROY AS EDITOR

Another work probably to be ascribed to Roy was a miscellaneous book combining doggerel verse, dialogue, protests

6. Cf. Fry, *A Bibliographical Description*, nos. 10–12, 23, 27, 29, 34. The Henry E. Huntington Library (catalog nos. 24,482 and 62,017) holds two quite distinct, yet apparently contemporaneous (1540) copies of *An exhoration* from Wyer's press, both of which include a translation of Erasmus' *Paraphrases on Matthew*.

7. Erasmus, *An exhortation* (*STC* 10,493), [*vi]^r, Aij^r.

against temporal power of the clergy, and pleas for vernacular scripture. Its reference to Tyndale by name virtually eliminates him as author or editor. After his 1528 denunciation of "railing rhymes," he could hardly have composed them in 1529! Its style points either to Roy or to Barlowe. In a letter to the King in 1533 recanting heresies and begging forgiveness for errors, Barlowe confessed to "have made certayne bookes, and have suffred theym to be emprynted," naming "the Treatyse of the Buryall of the Masse" (*Rede me*), "a Dyaloge betwene the Gentyllman and Husbandman," and two other tracts which seem not to have been preserved.[8] The second book in the list is without doubt *A proper dyaloge/ betwene a Gentillman and a husbandman/ eche complaynynge to other their miserable calamite/ through the ambicion of the clergye*.[9] Printed by Hoochstraten in Antwerp, 1530, as though from Hans Luft in Marburg, this book is a collection of miscellaneous pieces which were condemned separately by the authorities: an "A.B.C. to the spiritualte" in doggerel verse; a versified note to the reader; a dialogue between a gentleman and a plowman, in the midst of which were rehearsed a prose treatise "made aboute the tyme of kynge Rycharde the seconde" complaining against the secular authority of the church, and an argument quoting Cyprian on

8. The letter was reprinted in T. Wright, ed., *Three Chapters of Letters Relating to the Suppression of Monasteries* (London, 1843), pp. 6 f. Rupp, pp. 52 f. and passim, confidently ascribed *Rede me* and the *Proper Dyaloge* now being considered to Barlowe, leaving as "Roye's sole indisputable claim to fame" (p. 55) the translating of the *Dialogue between a Christian Father and his Stubborn Son;* Rupp exhibited a marked animus against Roy, contending that his martyrdom was attested by "only a bit of gossip," p. 199. Rupp attributed to Barlowe *A dyaloge descrybyng the orygynal ground of these Lutheran faccyons (STC 1461)*, composed after recantation at the suggestion of More or Stokesley, p. 60. Rupp rightly distinguished between this Barlowe and the William Barlow who in 1535 aided Barnes and complained to Cromwell against the suppression of vernacular scriptures in the diocese of St. David's; cf. Wright, pp. 77–80.

9. Reproduced in facsimile with an introduction by F. Fry (London, 1863), from which the subsequent quotations are drawn. The edition is *STC* 6813, the same as *Ned. Bibl.* 2775, attributed to Hoochstraten in Antwerp, 1530?; but *Ned. Bibl.* 4215 (not in *STC*) is thought to be the original edition, possibly as early as 1529. *A proper dyaloge* was reprinted in the Arber editions of *Rede me* cited above, n. 4; for Arber's judgment on style cited below, see *Rede me,* ed. Arber, p. 127.

the same subject; a summary of all the foregoing in verse dialogue; and a prose piece, introduced as more than a hundred
years old, entitled "A compendious olde treatyse/ shewynge/
howe that we ought to haue the scripture in Englysshe."

The rhymes by which the editor connected his miscellany
fell, in Arber's phrase, far short of "the grasp, virility, and
strength" of *Rede me,* suggesting that the talents of one of
the collaborators was missing from the work. The association
of Roy and Barlowe seems impervious to all attempts at
disentanglement. The fact that Roy published his 1529 translations of Erasmus and Luther from the press of Hoochstraten in Antwerp, which Tyndale and his friends were then
employing, suggests that Tyndale's temper may have cooled
somewhat since he had vowed lifelong separation from Roy
in 1528. It seems probable that it took the slim genius of
both Barlowe and Roy, as well as Wolsey's prominence as
an object of satire, to produce the strong invective of *Rede
me.* Wolsey had fallen when the present dialogue was written,
for it commented upon the November 1529 meeting of parliament. The author of these rhymes was left with the less
tractable and hackneyed subject of clerical riches in general.
If only one of the partners of *Rede me* worked on this dialogue it may have been Roy, who, wishing restoration to membership in the circle of English Protestants in Antwerp,
showed that verse might be adopted to the Protestants' program.

A Proper Dyaloge, whether edited by Roy or Barlowe, was
printed either very late in 1529 or in 1530, just when Henry
VIII first showed clear signs of bringing about, for whatever
motive, some reformation of the Church of England. Nobody
yet knew, save possibly himself, that Henry would occupy
the English ecclesiastical authority previously exercised by
the Pope. But Wolsey, symbol of worldliness and of papal
manipulation of kings and emperors, was bereft of power,
and the time seemed ripe to sound a popular protest, not
against the man, but against all the things for which he stood.
The book also aimed at consolidating Protestant and Lollard
viewpoints into a demand for ecclesiastical reform and for
scripture in the common tongue.

Regardless of the insipidity of its rhymes, *A Proper Dya-loge* was timely. Two old Lollard tracts were updated and made to speak for the Protestant movement, and a specifically Protestant attack on the established Church borrowed the classical Lollard protest against the exercise of secular power by the clergy—a neat complement to Frith's translation of *Revelation of Antichrist* and to Tyndale's *Practice of Prelates*! Those sophisticated treatises might not reach the commonalty as might the "A.B.C. to the spiritualte," designed as it was to teach rudiments of literacy via Protestant-Lollard indoctrination. The device merits quoting (in modern spelling):

Awake ye ghostly [i.e. spiritual] persons, awake, awake
Both priest, pope, bishop and Cardinal.
Consider wisely what ways that ye take
Dangerously being like to have a fall.
Everywhere the mischief of you all
Far and near breaketh out very fast;
God will needs be revenged at the last.
How long have ye the world captived
In sore bondage of men's traditions?
Kings and Emperors ye have deprived
Lewdly usurping their chief possessions.
Much misery ye make in all regions.
Now your frauds, almost at the latter cast [i.e. stroke]
Of God sore to be revenged at the last.
Poor people to oppress, ye have no shame,
Quaking for fear of your double tyranny.
Rightful justice ye have put out of frame
Seeking the lust of your god, the belly.
Therefore I dare you boldly certify.
Very little though ye be thereof aghast
Yet God will be revenged at the last.

The dialogue proper showed that the complaints lodged by Fish's *Supplication for the Beggars* were no novelties but at least several generations old, and proved that the growing demand for vernacular scriptures was no newfangled heresy. The gentleman and the plowman conveyed their message by piecing together knowledge of clerical abuses in controlling secular life largely by threats of purgatorial suffering. The plowman recited parts of an old Lollard tract complaining that churchly wealth and dominion violated the Old Testament law and the new law of Christ. The "Compendious Old Treatise" stood apart from the dialogue; its rhyming introduction presented it as a century-old tract relevant to the day, because "oure prelatz & theyr adherentes . . . so furiously barke ageynst *the* worde of God/ *and* specially the new testame*n*t translatyd & set forthe by Master Willia*m* Tyndale/ which they falsely pretende to be sore corrupte." The editor dated this treatise about A.D. 1400, but it recounted the demise of Richard Fleming, bishop of Lincoln, who died in 1431. The book found its way to England along the well-worn secret routes of merchants and Brethren. Although it escaped censure by the King's proclamation of June 22, 1530, bishop Tunstall's book-hunters knew of it that year. Accusations against Protestants and Lollards were turned back on the hierarchy: not the reading but the suppressing of English scriptures was novel; allegations against Tyndale's New Testament actually convicted the clergy who forbade it; it was the spirit of antichrist that denounced the true gospel as antichrist.

His contemporaries on both sides of the ecclesiastical argument of the early sixteenth century reserved a high place for Roy. Largely because of his connection with the 1525–26 New Testament project, Roy stood near the top of every list of chief English heretics to be hunted out on the Continent during the remainder of that decade. Roy's writings were regarded during the pro-papal reaction under Mary Tudor as subversive enough to earn him a place among proscribed authors; so Mary's father had judged in 1546. After publishing *A Proper Dyaloge,* he drops from sight except for reports of his martyrdom in Portugal in 1531, an event of which Foxe was convinced "by divers notes of old registers and otherwise," and one which More confirmed. Foxe thought the reasons for his being burnt "may be easily judged by the testimonies which he left here in England."[10]

10. *AM, 4,* 696; More, *Workes,* p. 342.

Roy wholly dedicated such meager talents as he possessed to the Protestant movement. He did not always do what Tyndale wanted done, but evidence mounts that nobody did just that. He did not live through the years of perplexity over Protestant strategy, of hopes for royal favor that never came, of theological disagreements within the ranks, of great demand at home for the vernacular Bible. He lived only to face, and be faced down by, the first great concerted action against his cause. Before papal or imperial agents caught and killed him, he had helped Tyndale translate the New Testament; he had made the first English translation of a whole treatise by Luther; in a manner that endured for a generation he had invoked words of Erasmus on behalf of the vernacular New Testament; he had spread the Protestant repudiation of purgatory and written against churchly assumption of political power; to more effect than anybody else except Frith, he had merged late Lollardy with Protestantism. Regardless of the extent to which Barlowe aided and abetted him, the record of Roy's six- or seven-year reforming career is, if not unspotted, enviable.

Simon Fish, Propagandist

The Protestant threat to England's comfortably entrenched Catholicism seeped slowly but steadily into the ranks of scholarship during the first half of the 1520s. After the vernacular New Testament became available, Protestantism bid for popular espousal at home, and enlisted a considerable secret constituency outside the universities. From this particular danger the realm was guarded by the antiquated Oxford Constitutions, designed to prohibit circulation of manuscript copies of biblical books among lower-class Lollards. Printed Testaments soon circulated conveniently, appealed to the educated, and brought profit to traders, prompting Church authorities to weave a finer weir by which to catch these books and their users. A prominent early vendor of Testaments was Simon Fish, gentleman of Gray's Inn, Oxford graduate and amateur actor, who crowned a fortuitous and brief career in the Protestant movement by writing the most influential of all early English Protestant tracts, and by translating perhaps the most

comprehensive summary of Protestant teaching to appear in
English during our period. Despite his education and social
status, Fish's life is known only for these achievements. Discrepancies between contemporaneous accounts make any detailed reconstruction of Fish's career difficult.

Fish moved to London about 1525, and by late 1526 had
established himself as a major dealer in copies of Tyndale's
Testament. Through contacts with one Richard Herman or
Hermond, an English merchant abroad, Fish received these
books in appreciable numbers, for he sold them to others by
the fives, tens, twenties, and thirties for distribution and re-
sale. He was a bold man. At Christmas 1526 a play was to
be produced in London, composed in the early years of the
century by one Master John Roo, dealing ungently with
the person of Wolsey. When no other dared play the mocking
part, Fish volunteered for the rôle, incurred the Cardinal's
wrath, fled to the Continent, and associated himself with
Tyndale at Worms. He appeared again in London about
Christmas 1527, possibly to look into New Testament sales,
but returned to the Continent and remained there until after
the middle of 1529, when he went back to London for the year
or eighteen months that elapsed before he died of the plague.[11]

In late 1528 or early 1529 Fish published, in Antwerp, the
most inflammatory and probably most widely read libellus of
the early years of the English Reformation, *A Supplicacyon
for the Beggers* (*STC* 10,883; *Ned. Bibl.* 3032: "Antwerpen,
Joannes Grapheus? 1528"). At the time, Protestant writings
in English numbered only six: the manuscript letter of Bugenhagen to the English, Tyndale's translation of Luther's introduction to Romans, Tyndale's *Wicked Mammon* and *Obedi-*

---

11. Fish's biography in *AM, 4,* 656–67 and passim has no certain chronology;
with each successive edition Foxe became less sure of his dates. Fish's involvement in the sale of Testaments was told by one Robert Necton before Wolsey
about May 1528, and was preserved in Foxian MSS. cited in *AM, 4,* 763; cf.
Mozley, *William Tyndale,* pp. 349 f. These and other testimonies were sifted
by E. Arber, ed., [*Simon Fish . . .*] *A Supplication for the Beggars,* English
Scholar's Library (London, 1878), introduction. Certain chronological problems
can be avoided by having Fish selling Bibles and acting in the play during the
same season, particularly the clumsy matter of two returns to England before
the final one. Arber's dating, which seems judicious on the whole, placed
Fish's death in 1530.

ence, and the poem *Rede me* and *A Brefe Dialoge* from the hand of Roy. Nothing since the New Testament had appealed so strongly to the popular imagination as did Fish's brilliant propaganda. Swiftly commanding the attention of commoners, the broadside was also pondered by the royal prince himself, and not with full disfavor.

The piece was addressed "To THE KING OVRE *souereygne lorde,*" and it lamented the plight of his subjects. The "wofull mysery" of "lepres, and other sore people, nedy, impotent, blinde, lame, and sike," Fish argued, received no relief in spite of well-disposed, generous almsgivers, because there had "yn the tymes of youre noble predecessours passed, craftily crept ynto this your realme" the minions of Satan, "Bisshoppes, Abbottes, Priours, Deacons, Archedeacons, Suffraganes, Prestes, Monkes, Chanons, Freres, Pardoners and Somners" who "haue gotten ynto theyre hondes more then the therd part of all youre Realme." Citing statistics like a modern advertisement, all to his advantage, Fish reckoned that the Church each year garnered unconscionable amounts of money from household taxes, fees for services, pence for friars, levies for masses and dirges, etc., etc. Four hundred years ago, he argued, these wolves calling themselves shepherds had owned nothing. Would Henry restore the liberty and prosperity achieved by his noble predecessors? Then he must realize that no mighty kingdom ever before suffered such draining of its economic life-blood. Fish would show that the amount of English wealth siphoned off by ecclesiastical scoundrels was well over half the gross national product, yet they were only one person in four hundred among Henry's loyal but pitiable subjects. With wealth the spiritualty exempted itself from royal obedience, incited rebellion by threat of interdict, and usurped royal powers. They dirtied an otherwise moral people by a professed celibacy that actually enlisted an army of whores. They spread diseases and drew wives from husbands, but they stood immune to punishment. Emulating them, thieves and beggars multiplied in the land. Statutes, parliament, and royal suzerainty to the contrary notwithstanding, they flourished. Fish taunted, "Are they not stronger in your owne parliament house then your silfe?"

They used popular belief in a nonexistent purgatory to further their own well-being. They did nothing to imitate the Christ they professed. Fearing exposure of their consummate evil, "they will not let the newe testament go a-brode yn your moder tong."

If Henry studied the book seriously, his confidence in Wolsey must have waned, the notion of assuming headship over the Church of England probably crossed his mind, and better use of monastic lands suggested itself. For Fish knew his monarch, and played on Henry's jealousies and ambitions as well as on his sense of justice and pity; Fish rehearsed the great days of an earlier England as recoverable—all in the name of "the good christen . . . sore, impotent, miserable people, your bedemen." Fish promised the very flowering culture for which Henry yearned and strove, if only the prelatical brigands were expelled:

> Then shall . . . the nombre of our . . . baudes, hores, theues, and idell people, decreace. Then shall these great yerely exaccions cease. Then shall not youre swerde, power, crowne, dignite, and obedience of your people, be translated from you. Then shall you haue full odedience [sic] of your people. Then shall the idell people be set to worke. Then shall matrimony be moche better kept. Then shal the generation of your people be encreased. Then shall your comons encrease in richesse. Then shall the gospell be preached. Then shall none begge oure almesse from vs. Then shal we haue ynough, and more then shall suffice vs. . . . Then shall we daily pray to god for your most noble estate long to endure.[12]

That the book reached Henry's hand is beyond doubt, although various accounts of the episode were told only long afterwards. Anne Boleyn received a copy which her brother read and recommended that she show to the King. Henry kept it several days, and liked it well enough to guarantee

12. Fish, *A Supplicacyon for the Beggers,* in *Four Supplications 1529–1533 A.D.,* ed. F. J. Furnivall, Early English Text Society, Extra Series 13 (London, 1871), pp. 1–2, 8, 11, 14–15; cf. *A Supplication,* ed. Arber, pp. 3, 8, 11, 13. Fish's tract was also reprinted in P. Dearmer, ed., *Religious Pamphlets* (London, 1898).

safety in his realm for its author. Later Fish himself had an interview (possibly two) with Henry, and expressed his fear of More's wrath in spite of the King's warranty. Henry explicitly directed More to keep hands off Fish's person. By then, of course, Wolsey's might had waned and the layman More, author not only of the *Dialogue* but of a direct retort to Fish, kept the great seal. At least two years after Fish was dead, More looked back on the event coolly, noting what "good zele had . . . Symon Fishe whan he made the supplicacio*n* of beggers. But God gaue hym suche grace afterwarde, *tha*t he was sory for that good zeale, & repented hymselfe and came into the church agayne, and forsoke and forsware all the whole hill of those heresyes." [13] Other evidence shows that Fish came into the King's good graces, which from More's standpoint at the time might mean "into the church," but More's word alone suggests that Fish changed his mind. With the *Dialogue* and *The Supplycacyon of Soulys* against Fish, More emerged as front line defender of English Catholicism, and a modern biographer noted that "Of all the heretical pamphlets, he [More] had most to dread that of Simon Fish." [14] When Henry first seized authority over the Church as Fish recommended, Wolsey lost his office, and before the King had done, steadfast More had lost his head.

Although *A Supplicacyon for the Beggers* abetted the English Protestants' cause like nothing since the translation of the New Testament, there is little to warrant classifying the book as a Protestant tract save that it condemned blatant abuses of late medieval Catholicism in its English dress. An attack on purgatory and a commendation of vernacular scriptures, both cursory, fairly exhausted its theological content. Fish's interests were economic, social, and political. The Church entered the picture only as it touched upon these spheres, which it did with heavy hand. The book's tangential relation to the Lutheran Protestantism then fostered by Tyndale and his English associates is demonstrated by the fact that the ink was hardly dry on Fish's tract before it was published in German by the controversial spiritualist reformer Sebastian

13. *Workes,* p. 881.
14. Mozley, p. 220; R. W. Chambers, *Thomas More* (New York, 1935), p. 258.

Franck, whom Luther called "the devil's mouth." That translation appeared as *Klagbrieff oder supplication der armen dürfftigen in Engenlandt, an den König gestellat, widder die reychen geystlichen bettler,* in 1529, when Franck was joining forces with Kaspar Schwenkfeld at Strassburg. Franck appended his own preface, turning the tract to the support of revolution in the name of religious reform, a junction that Tyndale repudiated in his *Obedience.* Nevertheless Tyndale, who castigated the "railing rhymes" by which Roy and Barlowe derided Wolsey, commended such a radical tract as Fish's was and as Franck took it to be. Fish's book appealed to Tyndale by drawing More's fire and the official Church's wrath.[15] The *Supplication* appeared in a 1530 Latin translation as *Supplicatorius Libellus pauperum, et egentium nomine, Henricho VIII.* The English original was printed again in 1546, with *A supplication of the poore Commons (STC 10,-884),* probably by Henry Brinkelow ("Roderyck Mors"), and subsequently in all recensions of John Foxe's martyrology.

FISH'S TRANSLATION OF "SUM OF SCRIPTURE"

In sharp contrast to the *Supplication for the Beggars* was Fish's only other known publication, a translation of the most complete compend of Protestant theology to appear in English during the time of the early Henrician exiles: *The summe of the holye scripture/ and ordinarye of the Christen teachyng/ the true Christen faithe/ by the which we be all iustified. And of the vertue of baptesme/ after the teaching of the Gospell and of the Apostles/ with an informacyon howe all estates shulde lyve/ accordynge to the Gospell (STC 3036; Ned. Bibl. 3912)*; Hoochstraten, in Antwerp, seems to have made the book. Very shortly it was reprinted, again apparently on the Continent. As soon as it was safe to publish such books in England, Robert Redman made two editions (1535?), and others followed in 1547, 1548, and about 1550 *(STC 3036a–3041).*

While the contents of the work are of primary concern, its origin and transmission pose troublesome questions. There is no reason to doubt early reports that Fish translated *Sum*

15. Tyndale, Practice of Prelates (1530), PS *2*, p. 335.

of the Scripture from a Dutch book entitled *Summa der god-liker scriftvren Oft een duytsche theologie* which had appeared perhaps as early as 1523 (*Ned. Bibl.* 3910; cf. *Ned. Bibl.* 3911, 1968–70 and passim), probably the first literary work of Henricus Bomelius, priest, who in 1539 wrote *Bellum Trajectinum*. Fish made his own emendations, but they were not important enough to suggest that he worked from some version other than the Dutch one. But what lies behind the Dutch work? Sections came from Luther, especially *Von weltlicher Oberkeit,* and parts from Oecolampadius' *Das Testament Jesu Christi,* although the latter were omitted from at least one Dutch edition and from Fish's English. Van Toorenenbergen, with others, identified the original piece as the compend of Christian teachings which Francis Lambert of Avignon had written to be presented to the Emperor Charles V, and Benrath traced it to a summation of the *Theologia Germanica*. But there was printed in Basel in 1523 ¶ *La Summe de lescripture saincte/ et lordinaire des Chrestiens enseignant la vraye foy Chrestienne: par laquelle no' sommes tous iustifiez. Et de la vertu du baptesme/ selon la doctrine de Leuangile/ et des Apostres. Auec une information comment tous estatz doibuent viure selon Leuangile.* Weiss argues convincingly that this was, in fact, the original edition of the work that flourished in Latin, German, Italian, and Dutch translations, and that Fish turned from the Dutch into English. Weiss speculated that its original author was William Farel, Reformation leader in Geneva who was first assisted, and then supplanted, by Calvin.[16]

There can be no doubt of the dependence upon Luther by *Sum of the Scripture,* but that dependence was highly selec-

---

16. J. J. van Toorenenbergen, ed., *Het oudste nederlandsche verboden Boek. 1523. Oeconomica christiana Summa der godliker Schrifturen,* Monumenta Reformationis Belgicae, *1* (Leiden, 1882), introduction; on Bomelius see *Nieuw Nederlandsch Biografisch Woordenboek,* ed. P. C. Molhuysen and P. J. Blok (10 vols. Leiden, 1911–37), *1,* 397–98; another view was advanced by K. Benrath, ed., *Die Summa der Heiligen Schrift. Ein Zeugniss aus dem Zeitalter der Reformation für die Rechtfertigung aus dem Glauben* (Leipzig, 1880); the solution to the problems of origin and transmission seems to have been made by N. Weiss, "Le Premier Traité Protestant en Langue Française . . . ," *Société de l'Histoire du Protestantisme Français Bulletin 68* [5th ser., *16*] (1919), 63–79, esp. 70 n, 78.

tive. Material chosen was characterized by marked preference for the Swiss' rather than Luther's position on sacraments, on other ecclesiological matters, and on certain political matters. At the time of the book's translation into English, a sharp cleavage between Lutheran (or evangelical) and Rhineland (or reformed) Protestantism was everywhere evident. Disagreement arose at the Marburg Colloquy of 1529 only over the manner of Christ's presence in the Supper, but this fact should not conceal fundamental divergences between the Wittenbergers and the Rhenish theologians. Broadly speaking, specifically theological concerns characterized evangelical Christianity, while reformed Christianity made morality the major test and manifestation of religion. As between those alternatives, English-speaking Christianity, as often remarked, inclined toward the reformed rather than toward the evangelical tradition. *Sum of the Scripture* reminds us once again that the English preference was thoroughly established long before the alternatives achieved their second-generation expression in the writings of Calvin on the reformed side and of the Lutheran scholastics on the evangelical side. The preference was in part circumstantial, in that the earliest Protestant tracts in English already attempted to defend the Reformation against charges of antinomianism and social-political radicalism; thus Tyndale's 1528 writings, *Mammon* and *Obedience,* placed a high premium on morality. Yet Tyndale maintained his early commitment to Luther's position regarding justification by faith, after he had translated the pentateuch, only by revising his theology on the rule of morality during the last five years of his life. Whereas Barnes began writing in 1530 and 1531 with a clear preference for the theological (Lutheran) or even dogmatic (Melanchthonian) mode, his 1534 *Supplicacion* marked his capitulation to the view that morality was the chief end of religion. In 1529, Frith was a neophyte translator of Luther just contemplating his theological attacks on purgatory and the mass, and he, alone among English Protestant writers of the decade 1525–35, remained specifically theological until the end of his career. When *Sum of the Scripture* appeared in English, Roy strongly preferred the morally oriented Protestantism of Strassburg in spite of the fact that he translated Luther's exegetical defense of clerical marriage. Joye at the time was already more concerned for the practice than the theory of Christianity.

Sum of the Scripture, then, early and influentially turned the face of English Protestantism away from Wittenberg toward Geneva and Strassburg, and toward the reformed religion then rapidly winning over Lutheranism in the Low Countries through the efforts of Cornelius von Hoen, Hinne Rhode, and others. Whether Fish himself, or another English Protestant, chose this book for translating and printing in English, is not known, but it is hardly likely that he and the circle of friends with whom he worked were ignorant of the employment of the original *Sum* on the Continent to place Netherlands Protestantism in the reformed rather than in the Lutheran camp.[17]

Sum of the Scripture stated no contractual theology such as found expression in Tyndale's last writings. The book insisted upon justification by faith as tenaciously as Luther, but it taught that justification was verified by the moral life of the believer. The book was divided into thirty-one succinct chapters falling into six major parts. Significantly, the first subject was not faith, not Christ, not God, but baptism; this eminently practical book on Christian living began just where Christian living itself began. Baptism was the basis of Christian salvation, the outward mark, the sign and the token of inward faith. He who stuck to the outward sign faltered, for the inward reality of faith received the saving grace of God. Faith consisted in a willingness to disregard one's own virtue totally and to cling to God's promise of salvation to those who trusted in him. God offered the gift of faith to all mankind but gave it only to those who believed in Christ, which was to say, who trusted in God alone and thought him the rewarder of those who seek him. If the inner part of baptism was faith, the inevitable result of faith was charity from which proceeded good works. Faith produced a love of God that issued in the desire to please God, therefore the faithful man lived obediently to the will of God. In no sense could good works produce hope, and hope, faith, for the faithful

17. Weiss, pp. 76 f.

person began by knowing that his works counted for nothing before God. Even so there were two kinds of people: men of true faith who knew that God was righteous and merciful even if he damned them, and men of pretended faith who thought God was indebted to them for their good works. Proper good works followed the example and commandments of Christ, knowing the vanity and emptiness of ceremonial observances which the Church falsely taught to be saving works.

After discussing baptism, faith, and works, *Sum* rehearsed religious teachings in terms of the true aim of the Christian life, namely, security in God, not the fear of death but a yearning for the future state of blessedness beyond death. The book worked systematically through the falsely "religious" vocations that the established Church taught to be the way of Christ. Monks, nuns, canonesses, and all such cloistered persons stood in a tradition that originally sprang from a true faith in God and a sincere desire to imitate Christ, but when the Church attached virtue to these estates they became idolatries from which Christian parents must guard their children. The state of man and wife, living together for the religious uprearing of their children and for the welfare and benefit of their neighbors, was the highest calling of man. Such involvement in the common life demanded that a specific Christian obedience be spelled out. Parents should teach and govern their children according to the precepts of the gospel, just as common citizens or householders should live after the teachings of the gospel. So should rich people pattern their lives after the injunctions provided for them in the scripture. Here *Sum* interjected a rather literal translation of Luther on the two regiments (*Von weltlicher Oberkeit,* 1523).[18] Secular power, the book thus taught, sprang from God as necessary to restrain sin, while spiritual government, working by the spirit of God, placed people under Christ's lordship in his kingdom. In both kingdoms the Christian lived, never redeemed by law, yet upholding the civil law as from God. Instructions were laid out

18. Luther, *WA, 11,* 247, line 21–*11,* 255, line 36, was rendered with only occasional omissions. Subsequent portions reveal direct but not literal dependence on this and other Luther treatises.

for governors, judges, bailiffs, taxpayers, soldiers, servants, and widows.

The secular prince's demand upon Christians for the payment of taxes and for participation in war received special treatment. The prince was to be obeyed by Christians and the Christian prince was to govern under heavy responsibility to God. No right of revolt was allowed. Regarding war, *Sum* struck a generally pacifist stand. It accused doctors and theologians of wrongly pleading for war by Christians on the basis of exceptional evangelical passages and of canon law. The gospel knew neither war nor any soldiering; it was evil for Christians to fight Christians, and true Christians should not fight at all, since the teaching of Christ forbade all war. Nevertheless, defensive war was condoned as the exercise of the love of order, and the sin of war might be used Christianly under these circumstances.

Sum had nothing to say about the Supper of the Lord. Probably Fish worked from the Dutch edition that had excised Oecolampadius' eucharistic passage from the original treatise, and certainly the English Protestant writers were still keeping up the appearance of unanimity on all matters by virtue of the fact that none commented on this one. Any amateur theologian familiar with continental currents of eucharistic thought might ascertain that *Sum* promoted a general view of sacraments which, applied to the Supper, would emphasize the purely spiritual character of the things signified by bread and wine. But heresy hunters found in the book no impugning of the mass. Not that they did not try. When the bishops issued their declaration of May 24, 1530, banning heretical English books and listing the heresies to be found in each, they damned *Sum of the Scripture* for no less than ninety-two propositions against the established teaching of the Church. By comparison, Tyndale's *Mammon* and *Obedience* scored thirty-one and thirty respectively; Luther's *Revelation of Antichrist* (translated by "Brightwell" [Frith]) and *Exposition of I Corinthians 7* (translated by Roy), forty-nine and forty-eight; Fish's *Supplication for the Beggars,* only one. *Sum* was proscribed by the royal proclamation of June 22, 1530, and by the list recorded in Bishop Tunstall's register for the same

year. It was found in 1531 among the possessions of the Protestants Richard Bayfield and Walter Kiry, was banned by
Bishop Stokesley that December, and was officially condemned
by the provincial synod of 1532.[19]

The great significance of the book lay, of course, in a
teachable and learnable summary of Christian faith and life
to which the early English Protestants were amenable. In
translating *Sum of the Scripture,* as much as in writing *Supplication for the Beggars,* the lawyer Simon Fish displayed
his interest in morality and his skill in propagandizing the
Protestant cause.

The literary remains of Roy and Fish, then, include no
original works of theological significance. Their libelli voiced
popular protests against the worldliness, the secular power,
and the earthly riches of the Catholic Church in England and
of Wolsey, its chief functionary before 1529. The leading
English Protestant exiles recognized these writings as peripheral to their movement, but, after assessing the effect of
Roy's and Barlowe's *Rede me* and Fish's *Supplication for the
Beggars,* they received Roy and Fish into their alliance against
the common enemy. Roy promoted Rhineland religion, specifically that of Strassburg, and translated Luther's tract
against clerical celibacy as well as Erasmus' *Paraclesis.* Fish's
more enduring literary work, the translation of a reformed
compend, furnished English readers with a manual of practical Protestant religion and morality, while Roy's other major
translating project gave the English Protestants their earliest
book from the spiritualist "left wing" of the Reformation.
These theologically various works of propaganda disclose a
single element of unity in that each made direct appeal to the
Protestants' readiest followers at home, the remaining Lollards.

19. Wilkins, *Concilia, 3,* 728–33, 739; *AM 4,* 684 f. and *5,* 38; *LP, 5,* appendix
18, p. 768. The number of heresies was reported with slight variations by
Chester, *Hugh Latimer,* p. 59.

14. Progress at Home: Books and Men

RITINGS and translations by Tyndale, Barnes, Frith, Joye, Fish, and Roy comprise the earliest English expressions of Protestantism. They reflect the increasingly specific, and therefore increasingly diverse, theological and religious understandings held by their authors. This variety was influenced by continental Protestant thinkers, but it also appealed to a wide assortment of Protestants at home. The activists of the movement remained in England, circulating proscribed books, advocating vernacular scripture, enlisting the services of printers and merchants, infiltrating the hierarchy, and, as opportunity arose, pleading their cause before the monarch. Booksellers, preachers, individuals willing to assist accused heretics to flee, and above all the large company of Brethren who studied scriptures and fashioned plain lives on biblical precepts—these mostly anonymous men and women filled the roll of honor of the early Protestant movement in England. The faint imprints left by most of them between 1520 and 1535 furnish few clues by which to trace their theological development. Some seem to have found in Protestantism a viability missing from late Lollardy, and these walked happily the theological path marked out by the English Protestant writers. These writers not infrequently painted their theology in colors attractive to the people for whom they wrote, and thus the hues of Wycliffe tinted the English Reformation. Other persons, impatient of the slow workings of officialdom toward reform, seem to have come into the Protestant movement by way of yearning, with humanists in the tradition of Colet, for a purified Church. Still others harbored sympathies

252

for the Protestants, but, exalting the royal prerogative, wished to guide religion toward a Protestant position while still obeying their king save only in cases of strained consciences. These men, of the breed of Latimer and Cranmer and Ridley, have become the oft-sung heroes of the English Reformation. All owed and most acknowledged a heavy debt to the English Protestant writers of 1520–35.

TRANSLATORS AND PRINTERS

From the numbers of those eager to hurry Reformation upon England more rapidly than Henry VIII would allow arose several men to make lasting, if minor, literary contributions to English Protestantism. As translators rather than authors, these men wanted to print in England a variety of Protestant books, and before the end of 1534 they succeeded. Prominent among them were William Turner and William Marshall; there were others, such as John Gau, Richard Taverner, Richard Tracy, and Miles Coverdale. As theological followers, not leaders, they translated and printed books chosen to emphasize the moralistic theme that Tyndale and others established after Frith's death in 1533.

Turner studied at Cambridge after the circle of Lutherans dispersed; he became an intimate of Ridley and Latimer. Proceeding B.A. in 1529–30, Turner was fellow of Pembroke from 1530, and was ordained in 1536. He went into exile during the years 1540–46 when Gardiner dominated Henry's religious policy, lived at Cologne, Bonn, and Basel, became a doctor of medicine in Italy, and returned to England in 1547 to be physician and chaplain to Somerset. He received preferment to the deanship of Wells in 1551, suffered exile again under Mary Tudor, returned once more to England as a radical Protestant under Elizabeth I, pioneered the study of botany in England, and died in 1568. Of this fascinating and varied career only his translation of Protestant books during the 1530s demands our attention. Turner's earliest and most significant Protestant translation, printed June 15, 1534, by John Byddell in London, under sponsorship of William Marshall with money supplied by Thomas Cromwell, was *A worke entytled of the olde god & the newe/ of the olde faythe & the newe, of the*

olde doctryne and the *newe/ or orygynall begynnynge of Idol-
atrye (STC* 25,127). Anonymously published, the book was a
translation from Hartmannus Dulichius' Latin version of *Vom
alten und neuen Gott* (1521).[1] The book had influenced Tyndale and Barnes in Latin or German editions; whole passages,
especially on the history of papal dealings with kings and emperors, were lifted for *Practice of Prelates* and for both versions of Barnes' *Supplication.* Behind the German edition stood,
however, the ubiquitous theology of Luther, whose notable
treatises of 1520, especially the Sermon on Good Works and
the Address to the German Nobility, were echoed time and
again. Yet the work bore rather the stamp of biblical humanism
than of Wittenberg theocentrism, since its paradigm for the
true Church emerging in the Reformation was the pure Church
of earliest days, and since it discerned in the Bible a standard
for everything from ecclesiology to ethics. The anti-ceremonial-
ism of the spiritualist wing of the Reformation permeated the
book. No really new notes were sounded, then, when Turner's
work appeared, but it enriched melodies already sung by Tyndale, Fish, Roy, and Joye with theological harmonies from the
Rhineland.

Another Protestant sympathizer who began to flourish under
Thomas Cromwell's prominence at court was William Marshall. Licensed as a printer in 1534, and in 1535 enlisted as a
confidential agent of Cromwell, Marshall printed and revised
Joye's primers. Cromwell financed his publishing activities
through personal loans, and his choice of books to translate and print appears to have been guided as much by

1. Identification of Turner as translator is highly probable but not beyond
question; cf. Butterworth, *English Primers,* p. 66, and *British Museum Catalogue of Printed Books, 1881–1900* (58 vols. Ann Arbor, 1946), *57,* 26. Mozley,
Coverdale, p. 345, called the work "a translation from Dulichius by William
Marshall," citing *LP, 7,* no. 423, where Marshall asked Cromwell for money to
print the book but made no claim to have translated it; he did claim the
translation of Marsilius' *Defensor pacis* and a work by Erasmus. "Dulichius"
was Hermann Tulich. See Judas Nazarei, *Vom alten und neuen Gott,* ed. Kück;
also, E. Götzinger, *Joachim Vadian, der Reformator und Geschichtscheiber von
St. Gallen,* Schriften des Vereins für Reformationsgeschichte, Jahrgang 13,
Schrift 50 (Halle, 1895). The little book ascribed to Vadianus enjoyed enormous
popularity; it was reprinted in Vienna, Wittenberg, Strassburg, and Magdeburg,
in Flemish, Dutch, English, Danish, and Latin.

economic as by religious considerations. Correspondence with Cromwell in the spring of 1534 reveals that Marshall printed an English translation, perhaps by Marshall himself, of Marsilius of Padua's once revolutionary political tract *Defensor pacis* (*STC* 17,817). He sent Cromwell two copies of the "Gift of Constantine," which Marshall thought excellent "for defacing the pope of Rome"; the translation, attributed to one B. Picern, was published by Thomas Godfray in 1534 as *A treatyse of the donation gyuen vnto Syluester, pope of Rhome* (*STC* 5641). Marshall hoped Cromwell would "like the translation" of a book on the creed and decalogue by Erasmus, for "It cost me labor and money." This work has been identified as *A lytle treatise on the maner and forme of confession* (*STC* 10,498), which Marshall claimed to have finished before starting to print Turner's book.[2] Marshall also translated from Savonarola ¶ *An exposition after the maner of a contemplacyon vpon the .li. psalme/ called Miserere mei Deus,* which John Byddell printed in 1534 (*STC* 21,795). This work had been published in Venice as early as 1505, and again in Wittenberg in 1523 with a letter of recommendation by Luther, and is "the earliest known printing of this treatise in the English tongue . . . often reprinted in later Primers." Marshall favored prayerbooks compiled by Luther, for his Primer incorporated elements from Luther's catechisms and *Betbüchlein.* Yet Butterworth's conclusion that he "was clearly a staunch Lutheran" seems not to have considered his involvement in the diversity of religious and political tracts here discussed.[3] To his printings from Marsilius, Erasmus, Savonarola, Joye, and Luther, Marshall added in 1535 *A treatise declaryng a. shewing dyuers causes that pyctures & other ymages ar in no wise to be suffred in churches* (*STC* 24,238), translated from a Latin tract compiled by the ministers at Strassburg. Thus, from sources hardly in agreement with Luther, he produced specifically religious pieces, and the majority of his publications, though always anti-papal, sponsored the political theories and interests of

2. Marshall to Cromwell, [April 1, 1534] and [Spring 1534], *LP,* 7, nos. 422–23.

3. Butterworth, *English Primers,* pp. 66–67; the Luther reference is *WA 12,* 245–48.

the humanists. Association with Cromwell in 1534 and 1535 surely brands Marshall a Protestant, but he by no means advanced a singularly Lutheran theology.

More definitely allied with the efforts of Tyndale and his circle was Richard Tracy, about whose father's will Tyndale and Frith had written. A brief treatise of 1533 called *The profe and declaration of thys proposition: Ffayth only iustifieth* (*STC* 24,164: 1540?) is attributed to Tracy. Friend and neighbor of Latimer, Tracy earned his reputation as a radical Protestant by membership in the Reformation Parliament of 1529, and by his struggle against the Church authorities over the burning of his father's exhumed body. Late in Henry's reign his writings were condemned as dangerously Lutheran.

The Scot, John Gau, had in 1533 the distinction of publishing the first Protestant work in Scottish prose, his translation from Christiern Pedersen's *Den rette vey till Hiemmerigis Rige* (Antwerp, 1531) entitled *The richt vay to the kingdome of heuine is techit heir in the x commandis of God/ And in the Creid/ and Pater noster,* printed October 16, 1533, by Hoochstraten in Antwerp under the false designation "Malmö, Sweden" (*STC* 11,686=19,525).[4] This piece drew in part from Luther's *Betbüchlein,* and in part from Urbanus Rhegius.

A tract of Luther entitled *A boke made by a certayne great clerke agaynst the new idole, and olde deuyll* (*STC* 16,962) was anonymously translated, and printed by Robert Wyer in 1534; perhaps the translator was Coverdale, although his earliest literary activity that left its mark for us seems to be a translation, printed at Antwerp in 1534, of Johannes Campensis, *A Paraphrase upon all the Psalms of David.*[5]

A member of Cambridge's "Little Germany," Richard Taverner, who with Frith and others joined the faculty of Wolsey's endowment at Oxford, translated and published religious tracts in the late 1530s. Taverner is perhaps responsible for translating the Augsburg Confession as early as 1530, and to him is attributed the English version of Erasmus, *A ryght frutefull*

4. See Butterworth, p. 282.

5. Mozley, pp. 63, 324, reported that the unique copy extant in 1877 is now lost, and that the work was not listed in *STC.*

epystle in laude and prayse of matrymony, possibly of the same year (*STC* 10,492).

Taken singly or together, all this Protestant miscellany remains minor. Only the book *The Old God and the New* ranks alongside the literary accomplishments of Fish and Roy as presenting a consistent and appealing program for the revision of English Christianity. The other books did little more than invoke famous names to endorse the Protestant program.

HUMANISTIC ADVOCATES OF REFORM

Theologically, the abovementioned works emphasized the themes already standardized by Tyndale and his circle and at the same time confused issues by closely associating Protestantism with the humanistic thought of Savonarola, Erasmus, Marsilius, and others. As early as 1525, Luther had thought it necessary to distinguish the movement he had begun from demands made by Christian humanists for ecclesiastical repristination; therefore, he lustily controverted Erasmus' notion of the freedom of man's will *coram deo.* Luther's effort met less than full success, but he taught his circle at Wittenberg to eschew alliance with humanism's ecclesiology. The English Reformation, per contra, became early and remained a many-sided partnership, open to infusions of humanistic philosophy and moralism, and averse to clear distinction between rediscovered gospel and repristinated religion.

The humanists, not least in this connection Erasmus, spoke ambiguously about religious issues occurring during the reigns of the last four Tudors. The cultural and religious obscurantism that proscribed the vernacular scriptures made it possible as early as 1529 for Roy to enlist Erasmus' *Paraclesis* in the Protestant ranks. Tyndale's own first work as a translator produced an English version of Erasmus' *Enchiridion,* published perhaps as early as 1533 and reprinted frequently. Erasmus, of course, enjoyed fame in England before the Protestants published his work, for the son-in-law of More, Master Roper, translated Erasmus' tract on the paternoster for printing perhaps as early as 1525 (*STC* 10,477). By the end of 1534 some half-dozen works by Erasmus, besides the many already named, circulated in English under the translating sponsorship of persons of diverse and opposing religious views.

The prominence of Church and Crown relations in English life from 1529 on revived interest in England's great humanist of the previous generation, John Colet, the founder of St. Paul's School where Henry himself had studied. About 1530, the sermon Colet had preached before Convocation in 1512, demanding rectification of ecclesiastical abuses and "reform" of religion according to a New Testament pattern, was twice reprinted. Colet never entertained the Protestant idea of man's utter dependence for salvation upon God, but he wanted to remodel the church after a norm which, by his partly enlightened methods, he extrapolated from the epistles of Paul.[6] Similarly, Englishmen turned their interests at about the same time to the thought of Johannes Ludovicus Vives, the Spanish humanist whom Henry had invited to England to lecture, and then had dismissed for opposing the royal divorce. About 1529, one R. Hyde translated from Vives' Latin *A very frutefull and pleasant boke called the instrucion of a christen woman* (*STC* 24,856).

As Henry's opposition to the papacy mounted, the flow of English tracts depicting the papacy as the political and religious enemy of his subjects correspondingly swelled. Translations by Robert Copland, Thomas Swinnerton, Richard Whitforde, and others might be cited to illustrate profusely the fact that, once Henry had seized the reins of the Church in England, which he did with progressive insistence after 1529, proposals abounded as to how he should manage the spiritual side of the realm. These suggestions sprang from many different theological presuppositions, and their diversity indicates the eclecticism of Tudor English religion. Although the royal Church adopted, cautiously after 1529 and with gusto from 1535 to 1540, many humanistic reforms, these translations scarcely attracted the early Protestants in England.

The Battle against Books

Protestant books in English from 1525 to 1535, with all their theological confusion, were produced in quantity. The coun-

6. See my "John Colet and Reformation."

try's reaction during the early 1520s had condemned a sect that was foreign. The later flood of books made it plain that Protestantism had become indigenous, and that its extirpation called for new measures. During the first five years of the conflict, King and Cardinal vigorously displayed the orthodoxy of the English by rejecting newfangled heresies from Wittenberg. Albion detested the mania of Almany as foreign to the faith of the fathers, and, perhaps equally important, as simply foreign. Wolsey burnt Lutheran books and commissioned public services at which Fisher reviled any deviation from Catholic truth. The King harried Luther with the pompous *Assertio,* and then, basking in the glory of the title *defensor fidei,* tried to best him by misrepresenting him as having capitulated. After that, mutual disrespect and distrust marked their exchanges over the question of the King's divorce and of the league of evangelical princes. Fisher's two English sermons against Luther were only a token of his efforts in scholarly Latin to negate the latter's errors. Whatever his part in the King's book may have been, Fisher proved himself an able apologist against Luther by writing three major treatises, the *Assertionis Lutheranae Confutatio* of 1523, the *Sacri Sacerdotii* and the *Defensio Regie Assertionis* of 1525; he produced one of the ablest statements of transubstantiation known to the Reformation generation in *De Veritate Corporis* against Oecolampadius (1527; translated into German by Cochlaeus in 1528). More added his bit with the *Opus Elegans* against Luther (1523) and a Latin reply to Bugenhagen's Letter to the English, both exhibiting a theological sophistication rarely seen in his English works.

Protestantism posed a radically different problem from that met by the early books and acts of Henry, Fisher, More, and Wolsey when, after 1525, it went native, as it were. Although strictly illegal under Archbishop Arundel's old Oxford Constitutions of 1408, a plain text of the New Testament in English was less easy to belittle than plain heterodoxy. Papal agents on the Continent pursued its translators and destroyed the printed books as best they could; they drove Tyndale from Worms and bought all available copies of his translation, yet they failed to stop the flow of Testaments across the channel.

Money spent to buy copies of one printing merely financed another, and by late 1526 or early 1527 English buyers might choose between the small and the great Testaments. Clerics in London were directed to seize all known copies and apprehend those who possessed them, yet the market improved, and, while printers made pirate editions, Tyndale produced guides to the reading and interpreting of scripture. At the end of 1528, heretical books in English might have been counted on the fingers of one hand, but in the following three years they multiplied several times over. These vernacular publications bolstered the market for translated works attacking the existing Church from the various standpoints of the old Lollards, the new Lutherans, and the respected humanists. Henry sought to remedy the vulnerability of the Church to the humanists' demands for purification of abuses by the enactments of the Reformation Parliament of 1529; this started rumors that the King favored the English New Testament and some of the writings of Tyndale, Fish, and their friends. However much Henry liked the *Obedience* of Tyndale and Fish's *Supplication,* religious conservatism ruled him. No matter that Protestant books might interest or amuse him personally; the policy of his realm would nurture an official faith rooted in tradition and guarded by the Crown. Revoking the Pope's headship of the Church in England was accomplished with relatively little difficulty, but when it was proposed that the old religion's view of the mass should give way to modern philosophical and theological teachings, Henry's preference for the faith of the fathers became adamant.

Biblical translations and a variety of English Protestant tracts called for three new lines of defence. As a first measure, specific books in the common tongue were inspected, identified as to author, branded as heretical, and proscribed; as the years passed the lists grew, but were less exhaustive than at the beginning. By 1530, a special commission named the heretical teachings of a number of books, and these were proscribed by royal proclamation June 22, 1530. In 1532, a synod of the ecclesiastical province of Canterbury attempted to list and proscribe the numerous Protestant writings of the intervening years.

As a second measure, sanctions were invoked against authors, printers, sellers, buyers, readers, and possessors of forbidden publications, leading to many ecclesiastical procedures against individuals and small groups of Protestants. These trials forced Protestants to choose one of three courses, abjuration, exile, or martyrdom. Most English Protestant writers on the Continent took the second alternative. Some, like Barnes, abjured; some, like Frith, finally elected martyrdom. Not all could afford or effect exile. The tortuous decision to abjure (with whatever mental reservations), as more strategically advancing the cause than death, confronted many men and women of low and high estate.

Thirdly, the bishop of London appointed an official spokesman to read heretical books and to expose them in the vernacular tongue. This was a great extension of Fisher's task at the book-burning services of 1521 and 1526. It fell heavily upon the already burdened shoulders of Thomas More, layman, liberal humanist, amateur theologian, political philosopher, court official, and successor to Wolsey as chancellor of the realm. The first of these three measures, and the second to the extent that it shows the number and kind of Protestant books in circulation at home from 1525 onwards, are our present concern. More's career as official denouncer of Protestant theology, and his rôle in hunting down Protestants at home, will occupy another chapter.

Of the first banning of the printed English New Testament only somewhat indirect evidence is preserved. In the preface to Henry's English reply to Luther, of about February 1527, the King recorded that, on the advice of the spiritualty, he had determined that the "untrue translations" were to be burnt and appropriate punishment meted out to all who possessed or read the book. The decision seems to have been reached late in August 1526, after Tyndale's complete Testament had been circulating some five months. Tunstall called together the book dealers of his London diocese on October 25, 1526, to warn them against importing Lutheran books, as he had done two years before, now apparently making specific injunctions against the English New Testament. The previous day he had ordered his archdeacons to gather within thirty days all copies of the

vernacular Testament "vnder payne of excommunication, and
incurring the suspicion of heresie" for their owners; the books
were to be delivered to the bishop's vicar-general, and each
archdeacon was to report his activities in this connection
within two months "under paine of contempt." [7] Within a fortnight, William Warham, archbishop of Canterbury, issued the
same order to all suffragans of the province. Little time elapsed
before the Testament was publicly denounced by Tunstall and
burnt at Paul's Cross. In spite of these drastic steps, the flow
of books continued. Attempts were made to dry up the spring
at its sources, not only in Germany, but also in the Low Countries where a small pirate edition had been printed.

The names of several heretical books in English and Latin,
among them writings published as late as 1529, came to be
attached to the mandate issued by Warham November 4, 1526.
The amplified list has been a source of confusion, since it ostensibly indicates a very early date for some books.[8] The English
books, as named in the expanded list, were: "The supplication
of beggars" (by Fish) ; "The revelation of antichrist of Luther" translated by "Richard Brightwell" (Frith) ; "The New
Testament of Tindall"; "The wicked Mammon" (Tyndale) ;
"The obedience of a christian man" (Tyndale) ; "An introduction to Paul's epistle to the Romans" (Tyndale) ; and "A dialogue betwixt the father and the son" (translated by Roy).
Several identifiable Latin titles were followed by an entry, "Luther's exposition upon the Pater noster," possibly referring to

---

7. Tunstall prohibition, October 24, 1526, in John Foxe, *Actes and Monuments*
(London, 1563; *STC* 11,222), pp. 449 f., cited as reprinted by A. W. Pollard, ed.,
Records of the English Bible (Oxford, 1911), pp. 131–35.

8. Wilkins, *Concilia, 3*, 706 f., citing: Exeter Register (Voysey) fol. 62. The
standard study of prohibited books has long been R. R. Steele, "Notes on English Books Printed Abroad, 1525–48," *Transactions of the Bibliographical
Society, 11* (1912), 189–236; this unfortunately was riddled with errors, as
was also H. Reusch, *Der Index der Verbotenen Bücher* (2 vols. Bonn, 1883–85),
1, 87–95, 104 f., 123, 127 and passim, and Reusch, *Die Indices Librorum Prohibitorum des 16. Jahrhunderts* (Tübingen, 1886, reprinted Nieuwkoop, 1961).
The Exeter Register merely recorded Warham's mandate against the English
New Testament, subjoining *"nomina librorum hoc tempore prohibitorum . . . ."*
This same list Foxe, *Actes and Monuments* (London, 1563), p. 450, gave as the
list which Tunstall sent to his archdeacons. While *"hoc tempore"* was much
later than 1526 it need not have been after Tunstall's translation from London
to Durham on February 21, 1530.

some part of Joye's 1529 English primer. The earliest possible date for the entire list is determined by Frith's translation of Luther, printed at Antwerp July 12, 1529. As of that date the list appears to omit only two known English tracts: Roy's *Rede me,* and Roy's translation of Luther's *Exposition of I Corinthians 7.* The latter was printed June 20, 1529, along with Roy's translation of Erasmus' *Paraclesis;* perhaps the possible intent of Roy, to smuggle Luther into the land under the name of Erasmus, briefly succeeded.

The next known official condemnation of Protestant books in English resulted from Henry's studied attempt to align himself with conservative religious elements in the wake of the Reformation Parliament of 1529. The King appointed an ecclesiastical commission under the presidency of Warham, including select persons from the universities, the episcopal bench, and the court. More, then chancellor, Tunstall, now bishop of Durham, and Gardiner as the King's secretary served on the commission; it achieved unanimity despite the presence of four Cambridge liberals, Crome, Shaxton, Thixtel, and Latimer. The committee not only named books but listed the heresies of each. Its findings, reported May 24, 1530, became binding by a proclamation issued by Warham as primate and by a royal proclamation. Fish's translation of *Sum of the Scripture* and Tyndale's *Mammon* and *Obedience* were condemned, along with the following as cited: "the boke of 'The revelation of anticriste,' and . . . the epistle going before" (Frith, *A pistle*); "the book of Beggers" (Fish's broadside), whose heresy was "the greatest infamye that may be . . . to declare . . . that there is noo purgatorie"; "the kalender of the Prymar" and "the Prymar," (Joye's lost 1529 Primer); and, making up for the lapse in the addenda to Warham's mandate, "The ongodly and erroneous saying conteyned in a boke in Englishe inscribed 'An exposition into the sevenith chapitre of the firste epistle to the Corinthians'" (Roy's translation of Luther's exposition; the Erasmian portion was not mentioned). All the heresies explicated by these books contaminated "the translation also of Scripture corrupted by William Tyndall, as well in the Olde Testamente as in the Newe." Lest anything be overlooked, the commission condemned "all other boks in

Englisshe conteynyng such errours." Henry's proclamation
dwelt mainly on the Bible translations, naming *Mammon, Obedience, Supplication for the Beggars, Revelation of Antichrist,*
and *Sum of the Scripture.*[9]

From later in the year 1530, or perhaps very early in 1531,
comes another list that was appended to *A proclamation for
resisting and withstanding of most damnable heresies sown
within this realm by the disciples of Luther, and other hereticks,
perverters of Christ's religion;* Wilkins inserted this document into his collection immediately following the Bishops'
public instrument of May 24, 1530, as drawn from Foxe's
martyrology. This proclamation and its list were published by
Pynson, according to *STC* 7772, in the year 1528. Foxe noted
that the condemned books in this list "be afterwards in the
register more especially named by the bishops; whereof the
most part were in Latin, as are above recited, and some were
in English, as these and others, partly above expressed." The
remark by Foxe has been taken as referring the reader to a very
long list of Latin titles which he took from the Tunstall register,
and thus this list of sixteen English books has been attributed
to the Tunstall register by Foxe's editor Pratt, by Steele, and
by Mozley.[10] While it is possible, or even probable, that the
list of sixteen books did not originally appear with the proclamation, which then may be dated as early as Steele would
have it, or even with *STC* in 1528, the list is on any reckoning
an early one, hardly after the end of 1530, although certainly
after Tunstall became bishop of Durham in February 1530.

The list in question includes most of the books cited in the
earlier public instrument of the bishops, but it contains some
interesting additions and subtractions. The absence of Fish's

9. Wilkins, *3,* 727–39, 740–42; cf. *LP, 4,*3, no. 6487. See Chester, *Hugh Latimer,* pp. 57 ff.

10. Wilkins, *3,* 737–39; *AM, 4,* 676–79, 667–70, 767; Steele listed these books as
"T," that is, condemned by a proclamation from the Tunstall Register issued
prior to March 6, 1529. Cf. R. R. Steele, *Tudor and Stuart Proclamations* (2 vols.
Oxford, 1910), *1,* 13; Mozley, *William Tyndale,* p. 154, apparently followed
Steele but revised his date; Butterworth, p. 15, in discussing these lists sensibly
remarked that "time and strife have blurred the historical details, and
standard authorities are not in agreement over them."

Supplication for the Beggars raises the question of whether Fish actually had abjured, as More said, and thus sanctified his book, or whether the King actually liked it and wanted it stricken from the list. The safer surmise would appear to be the latter. Tyndale's Genesis and Deuteronomy were added, specifying the earlier vague reference to his Old Testament translations; but the other three books of the pentateuch were not actually mentioned. Were Genesis and Deuteronomy then printed somewhat before the others, indicating perhaps that Tyndale preferred these books over the others, and thus illuminating his concern for a theology of the law? *Sum of the Scripture* held its place, apparently not then linked with Fish. So did Roy's translation of *Exposition of I Corinthians 7*. Tyndale's *Mammon* and *Obedience* were not listed, but his *Practice of Prelates* of 1530 was included. Joye's first primer was not explicitly mentioned, but its successor, *Hortulus Animae* (1530), was named along with his new translation of the psalter; Butterworth has contended that the 1529 primer was more fully described by this list's entry of "Mattens and Euensong, vij. Psalmes, and other heauenly Psalmes, with the commendations, in Englishe." The earlier oversight of Roy's *Rede me* was corrected by the entry, "The burying of the mass," and his *Dialogue between Father and Son* found recognition as "A disputation between the father and the son." Roy's most recent book, *Dialogue of the Gentleman and Ploughman,* was not named unless it fell under the heading "A.B.C. against the clergy," a title apt enough to make the surmise probable. Perhaps "Godly prayers" was an English title for *Piae precationes.*

After the foregoing identifications have been made, four titles named in this curious list remain. "The examination of William Thorpe, etc." was an edition of two old Lollard tracts which Tyndale had edited and published from Hoochstraten's press in Antwerp in 1530 (*STC* 24,045). The others were "A boke of the old God and new," "The christian state of matrimony," and "The matrimony of Tindall." The last seems unidentifiable, despite Mozley's contention that it refers to the *Exposition of I Corinthians 7,* for none of the early lists of books named *Exposition* and "also called" it Matrimony of

Tyndale.[11] "The Christian State of Matrimony" also eludes proper identification, unless it refers to Erasmus' *A ryght frutefull epystle in laude and prayse of matrymony,* translated by Taverner and published about 1530 (*STC* 10,492). Finally, there is *The Old God and the New.* Turner translated *Vom alten und neuen Gott* for printing June 15, 1534, by J. Byddell in London (*STC* 25,127), and, as we have seen, the work was an important source for such Protestant writers as Tyndale and Barnes. Possibly this work, often attributed to Coverdale, was put into English as early as 1530.

Three other major lists of heretical books having to do with our period may be summarized briefly. In November 1531 one Richard Bayfield, Benedictine monk of Bury St. Edmunds in the diocese of Norwich, was proceeded against as a relapsed heretic. Sentenced, degraded, then burnt at Smithfield, Bayfield had in his possession, according to the articles against him, a veritable library of the writings of such continental Protestants as Luther, Oecolampadius, Zwingli, Bugenhagen, Francis Lambert, Melanchthon, Hegendorph, Brentius, Bucer, Capito, etc. In addition he owned English books which, although some of them had not been condemned by name, taught damnable heresies; these were: *Answer to More's Dialogue,* all five books of the pentateuch, the *Practice of Prelates,* the New Testament, *Introduction to Romans, Mammon,* and *Obedience* (all the foregoing from Tyndale); Frith's *Purgatory;* a work cited as "A.B.C. of Thorpe's"; *Sum of the Scripture,* translated by Fish; Joye's "the Primer in English" and *Psalter;* and the *Dialogue of the Gentleman and Ploughman* edited by Roy. All of Bayfield's books had appeared on previous lists save Tyndale's *Answer to More,* and Frith's *Purgatory,* which were fresh from the press, and perhaps also the *Dialogue* that Roy edited. The "A.B.C." seems to have become confused with Tyndale's *Examination of Thorpe and Oldcastle,* unless yet another "A.B.C." had appeared but is no longer extant.[12]

Bishop Stokesley preached at Paul's Cross on December 3,

---

11. Mozley, pp. 345–46; see my "The Earliest Translations of Luther into English."

12. Bayfield's story was recounted by Foxe, and the list of books given, *AM,* 4, 684 ff.

1531, and named thirty heretical books. This list seems original
with Stokesley; while it summarizes earlier ones, it correlates
nicely with no other list. The old standbys were included: Tyndale's New Testament, *Introduction to Romans,* and the pentateuch, along with *Mammon, Obedience, Practice of Prelates,*
and *Answer to More;* now also appears his translation of
Jonah. There were Roy's "Burying of the Mass" (*Rede me*),
*Dialogue between Father and Son, Exposition of I Corinthians
7, Dialogue of the Gentleman and Plowman,* and "A.B.C.
against the Clergy"; but listed separately was "A Book make
by Friar Roye against the seven Sacraments," even though the
Dialogue between Father and Son was previously cited. *Sum
of the Scripture* was named, and Fish's *Supplication for the
Beggars* also; perhaps after his death the supposed royal protection no longer covered the *Supplication.* Frith's *Antichrist*
and *Purgatory* were there, as were Joye's *Primer, Psalter,* and
Hortulus. So was the Lollard tract on Thorpe and Oldcastle
that Tyndale edited. This list introduced a new title, naming
"A Book against St. Thomas of Canterbury"; Jerome Barlowe
confessed to have composed and issued such a book, but we
cannot link it with any extant writing. The "Matrimony of
Tyndale" appears again, but with no clue as to its identity. The
list includes three Latin titles; what it called "Precaciones"
and "Economica Christiana" are familiar, but it adds "Liber
qui de veteri et novicio Deo inscribitur"—was the translation
of that work not yet accomplished? [13]

Still another list from about 1531 has been preserved in an
undated British Museum manuscript. Wilkins assigned it to
1529, but Steele attributed it to a provincial council, presumably of Canterbury, held, he thought, in 1532. The document
in question was headed *Statuta et ordinationes praelatorum in
concilio provinciali edita.* Most titles were given in Latin and
are familiar; the few which were named in English are here
placed in quotation marks, and an asterisk marks each title
specified as in the vernacular: *Mammon, Obedience,* Tyndale's
New Testament*, *Revelation of Antichrist, Dialogue between*

---

13. Stokesley Register in Lambeth Library ms. 306, fol. 65, reprinted *LP, 5,*
appendix 18, p. 768; cf. F. J. Furnivall, ed., *Political, Religious, and Love Poems,*
Early English Text Society, Original Series 15 (London, 1903), p. 62.

Father and Son, The Burial of the Mass*, *Introduction to Romans, Practice of Prelates,* "A.B.C. to the Prelacy," *Defence of the Peace, Dialogue of the Gentleman and Plowman, Against St. Thomas of Canterbury, Answer to More's Dialogue*,* "The disputation of purgatory," *Matrimony of Tyndale, Roy Against the Seven Sacraments.* The list then named titles by Luther, Oecolampadius, Zwingli, Bugenhagen, Francis Lambert, Melanchthon, Hegendorph, Brentius, Bucer, and Justus Jonas. Tyndale, Fish, Roy, "Richard Brightwell," and a number of continental Protestants were named as heretical writers. Then more Latin and English titles were cited: *De veteri et novitio Deo, Piae precationes, Oeconomia christiana, Processus consistorialis martyrii Johannis Husse,* "The prologue into the fifth boke of Moyses, called Deuteronomy," "The firste boke of Moyses, called Genesis," "The prologue into the thirde booke of Moyses, called Leviticus," "The prologe into the fourthe boke of Moises, called Numeri," "The prologe into the seconde boke of Moises, called Exodus," "The somme of Scripture," "The exposition into the seventhe chaptre to the Corinthians," *Hortulus animae*, Complanationes in Isaiam, Complanationes in Hieremiam, Capita in Osiam, Capita in Abacuc, Unio dissidentium,* and *Confessio Augustae.*[14]

This last list could not have been made before 1531, and it sheds new light for us on very few items. The "A.B.C. to the Prelacy" seems to be that edited by Roy with his *Proper Dialogue,* but again Roy's book against the sacraments is mentioned separately from the *Dialogue between Father and Son.* Once again *The Old God and the New* was cited in Latin with no suggestion of an English edition. "Defensorium pacis" seems to refer to a Latin edition—one had appeared in Basel in 1522 —rather than to Marshall's translation, the earliest extant copy of which was published by Wyer in 1535. Barlowe's writing against Thomas Becket reappears, as does *Matrimony of Tyndale,* this time with a peculiar first name: "Matrimonium Johannis Tindall." To the "John" we can attach little significance, however, since Tyndale's *Answer to More* carried the

---

14. Wilkins, *3,* 717-21; Steele, "Notes," p. 214; cf. Butterworth, p. 15 n. The *Statuta et ordinationes* have been attributed also to the committee of bishops assembled in May 1530; cf. *LP, 4,3,* no. 6402.

same error. Joye's *Hortulus* seems to have replaced the 1529 *Primer*. *Sum of the Scripture* still was not connected with Fish. The books of the pentateuch were cited according to the title pages of each of the five booklets, but in a peculiar order.

While these and later lists of forbidden books throw some light on the Protestant movement, the problem of identifying and dating several of the lists seems insoluble. Later lists, like these early ones, tended to be cumulative, and rarely dropped allusions to books even when they duplicated more exact entries. The Church authorities, of course, meant to suppress and destroy these books, not to provide later generations with bibliographies. They tended to condemn certain writers by name and reputation, then as a non sequitur to condemn all books linked with that writer. That had been the style since the beginning of the Reformation, and was not invented by English heresy hunters.

During the years in which English indices were compiled, a number of persons were arrested and tried for possessing, reading, buying, selling, and distributing certain books, both proscribed and unproscribed. Already in February 1528 Thomas Garrett of Oxford was charged with possessing and selling a veritable library of continental Protestant theology whose extent would set a high standard for modern British university libraries' holdings of contemporary continental theology. People like Bayfield, whose trade was specifically in books by the English Protestant writers, fell again and again under the hammer of the authorized Church, especially after More became, first, the official anti-Protestant polemicist, and then lord chancellor. Their inventories included as a rule at least a few continental Reformation treatises, always the English New Testament, and more or less complete catalogues of the printed works of Tyndale, Roy, Frith, Joye, and Fish. Barnes' writings were notably absent from the lists of books condemned by Church officials and possessed by booksellers; his *Supplicatyon* was certainly in circulation by the beginning of 1532, and was revised late in 1534, but it appeared on banned lists no earlier than the ones that Foxe published as having been set forth in 1539, 1546, and 1555. This is a further indication that Barnes never identified himself with the Protestants irrevocably, and thus never abandoned his aspiration to become counselor and negotiator for his prince.

The frequency with which new lists of forbidden books were drawn up reflects not only the crescendo of Protestant literary activity after early 1529, but also the ready and widespread reading these books had in England. Repeated proscriptions testify eloquently to the mounting strength of the Protestant movement among merchants, the lowly Brethren, some university folk, and a few men of means and position. Henry's mild plans for a purified Church were endorsed by the Reformation Parliament late in 1529, and the redoubtable Wolsey had no place in the new scheme of things. To judge by the volume and range of Protestant writings circulating in the realm, however, these purgations failed to satisfy the demands of a considerable body of people. Finally, printing came under the regulation of the Crown with the formation of the Stationers' Company and with a proclamation allowing books to be printed only under royal privilege. By that time, Henry was head of the Church of England, More and Fisher were out of the picture, and the reactionary Gardiner had devised the scheme by which Henry might rule as local pope over a national, conservatively Catholic, Church. The 1529 regulation of printing hardly amounted to official censorship, since the new arrangement neither screened the contents of books for which printers asked privilege, nor gave official endorsement to books issued *cum privilegio regali*. Thus by 1535 a welter of Protestant books bore English colophons, and a new phase of the English Reformation was inaugurated.[15]

THE EMERGENCE OF ENGLISH REFORMERS

Out of Cambridge's "Little Germany" there arose men who, as exiles on the Continent, wrote Protestant tracts and translated scriptures and the works of continental theologians, and men who, under hard laws demanding Catholic religious uniformity in England, either abjured or died for their convictions. Still other men found ways to reconcile their Protestant convictions with the changing character of the Henrician Church. These men became great reformers of the Church of England,

15. Cf. Reed, "The Regulation of the Book Trade," pp. 157-84.

who met their opportunities and responsibilities by judicious reliance upon the Protestant writings and theological developments here described. These were king's men under Henry; only after their heady successes under Edward VI did the papalism of Mary Tudor force an unwonted choice between royal headship of the Church and their religious convictions. They had helped Henry to the ecclesiastical headship that actualized an English Reformation, and they lived to see the same ecclesiastical headship under Mary repudiate all the English Reformation had achieved. Thus the rope of their own braiding became the hangman's noose for Ridley, Cranmer, and Latimer.[16]

By 1529 the Cambridge Protestants had lost Stafford by death and Barnes by imprisonment; Bilney was broken by his troubles with the Church authorities.[17] Into the vacuum stepped Latimer to undertake the risky rôle of leadership; he was a chief advocate at home of the vernacular Bible, and was to become the most distinguished Protestant supporter in the English clergy. It is possible that Latimer's first public plea for scriptures in the common tongue occurred in sermons preached early in 1528, just when Wolsey was working most ardently against that cause. Along with men who were selling and distributing Tyndale's New Testament, Latimer was summoned before the Cardinal to give an account of his activities. At this time unready to suffer curtailment of career or death for his convictions, Latimer subscribed to the articles of faith proposed by Wolsey and escaped with an admonition. Maintaining his office as university preacher in Cambridge, Latimer cautiously went on advocating reform of ecclesiastical abuses, and patiently awaited opportunities to plead authorization of an English Bible.[18]

16. The works of Ridley, Cranmer, and Latimer were included in the Parker Society series. Reliable modern studies are G. W. Bromiley, *Thomas Cranmer* (New York, 1956); Chester, *Hugh Latimer;* Muller, *Stephen Gardiner and the Tudor Reaction;* J. A. Muller, ed., *The Letters of Stephen Gardiner* (Cambridge, 1933); J. G. Ridley, *Nicholas Ridley* (London, 1957) and *Thomas Cranmer* (Oxford, 1962). An excellent study of recent Cranmer literature is P. N. Brooks, "Cranmer Studies in the Wake of the Quartercentenary," *Historical Magazine of the Protestant Episcopal Church*, 31 (1962), 365–74.

17. J. B. Mullinger, *The University of Cambridge from the Earliest Times to . . . 1535* (Cambridge, 1873), 609.

18. For Latimer's early career see Chester, pp. 33–102.

The speculation necessarily surrounding his 1528 sermons, which are not extant, disappears when we turn to Latimer's famous "Sermons on the Card," preached in Advent 1529. Wolsey reigned no longer over England's Church, and Latimer was already numbered among protagonists of the King's divorce. At St. Edward's Church, in Cambridge, Latimer popularized Reformation doctrine by the homiletical device of dealing cards for the popular game of "triumph": the cards figured Christ's dealing of spiritual triumphs to repentant sinners. Theologically, the sermons combined Reformation belief that man stands worthless before God with the renaissance ecclesiology that wanted to cleanse the penitential system and eliminate cultic superstition. Relying upon Luther's insights in the dogmatic form given them by Melanchthon, Latimer displayed keener interest in the practical affairs of ecclesiastical purity than in sinful man *coram deo*. He used Luther's teachings to amplify Colet's plea for a corrected church. Like Luther and Colet, Latimer stood for primacy of scripture in principle, but his application of the principle favored the biblical-humanist concern for proper religion over the Protestant emphasis on a God who took the initiative in all dealings with man.

Having made that choice, Latimer turned handily to the kind of moralistic preoccupation with Christ and his followers that we have seen emerge in Tyndale's writings at this juncture. He understood Christ's words less as the promises of a merciful God to spiritually helpless creatures than as rules of right living for men who, once enlisted into Christianity through baptism, would be enabled to live rightly. The sermon on the mount became for Latimer, as for Tyndale, the charter of Christian ethics, not, as for Luther, the absolute intensification of divine law as God's "strange work"—*opus alienum*—proleptically related to his "proper work"—*opus proprium*—of offering free justification to faithful trust in his promises. It is not improbable that it was Latimer's original combination of Protestant reform and humanistic repristination that interested Tyndale. Certainly Latimer's "Sermons on the Card" proposed just such an eclecticism to the Cambridge community. Controversy, hot and immediate, ensued, until Edward Fox, King's almoner and provost, notified the vice-chancellor that the arguments were to cease and that Latimer was not to be dealt with harshly. Frequently, during the crucial years 1529–35, men of Protestant sympathies suffered little if they endorsed causes dear to the King. Latimer ranked with Cranmer, Gardiner, and Fox, all illustrious scholars who condoned dissolution of Henry's marriage to Queen Catherine.

By the end of 1530, Latimer's position seemed secure enough for him to write a polemical letter heavy with pleas for a vernacular Bible. This famous letter of December 1, 1530, bore an address to the King, but probably circulated as a broadside among the Brethren rather than as a direct memorial to the court. All his arguments for scripture in the common tongue, however, accorded with his submission to the royal will. Latimer cleverly hinted that authorization of an English Bible lay within the King's own prerogative, thus linking together royal headship over the Church with the Protestant insistence on reformation of the Church. Seven turbulent years later the two ideas were fused just as he had suggested. Latimer spent these years rather quietly as rector of a country parish in Wiltshire, whence recurrent endorsements of Church reforms stopped short of thrusting him under suspicion as a heretic. Once he went too far, in a sermon preached in London at St. Mary Abchurch in the fall of 1531. During the last days of More's chancellorship, ecclesiastical courts were especially severe upon heretical utterances, and Latimer was summoned to appear before Bishop Stokesley of London in late January 1532. Defending his statements as attacks upon abuses but not upon Catholic teachings and usages, Latimer finally submitted to making a confession of his indiscretion. Having abjured, he was careful not to relapse while the King's great matter was solved by Convocation's declaring the marriage to Catherine illegal. In the process, Cranmer became archbishop of Canterbury, and in mid-1533 licensed Latimer to preach anywhere in the province. Early in January 1535 rumor marked Latimer for a bishopric. By the day of his consecration as bishop of Worcester, September 26, 1535, Latimer held an unsullied record of following where the royal will led. Always he had urged reform of ecclesiastical abuses, but he had never inclined toward a theological revolution.

As a learned humanist divine prompting and following his King toward his own goal of a purified Church, Latimer rivals even Cranmer. Cranmer won the widely coveted authorization of a vernacular Bible, and was the literary architect of common English worship. He believed in Protestant doctrine as subserving the goal of a national church using the language of the people. He excelled in the art of combining general Protestant sympathies with adherence to royal headship of the Church as a theological principle—above him stands only the Elizabethan divine, Richard Hooker. Brought into royal favor by his fellow humanist Edward Fox, Cranmer rose swiftly from an inconspicuous fellowship at Jesus' College, Cambridge—forfeited once by marriage but regained at the death of his first wife—to the archbishopric of Canterbury. Modestly, effectively, and without theological qualm he labored to make the King the real primate of the Church of England; he employed his own office to bring about such Protestant and humanistic reforms as the Crown's religious policy, fickle indeed between 1533 and 1553, would allow. In the end, Cranmer, like Latimer and Ridley, suffered burning at the stake rather than allow royal headship of the Church to be surrendered by Queen Mary to the Pope of Rome; so fundamental was that spiritual authority that the monarch who bore it might not, in their view, relinquish it!

Cranmer's recorded theology emerged as there arose opportunities and demands for him to defend actual reforming activities undertaken after 1535. From an earlier time came a learned treatise arguing the nullity of the King's marriage to Catherine, but, in spite of its appeal to scripture above canon law, it remains an ad hoc work, hardly indicating definite theological inclinations. Without doubt he learned from the discussions of Luther that took place in Cambridge's White Horse Tavern, but his regard for scripture matched more closely Colet's than Luther's. No man pleaded more powerfully than he for authorization of the English Bible, yet after the point had been won Cranmer worked toward supplanting the version embodying Tyndale's work. Among European reformers, conservative peacemakers like Osiander and Bucer attracted him more than the theologically explosive—if ecclesiologically cautious—Luther. Cranmer's participation in important religious affairs revolved around the King's matter from his first public involvement in 1529 until he became archbishop in March 1533; after that came more Kings' matters to command his attention. Cranmer conscientiously maintained the implicit condition of his archiepiscopal appointment, denial of papal supremacy. He brought about churchly preferment of Protestants largely as such preferments lubricated Henry's negotiations with Protestant royalty on the Continent. Cranmer's patience was as evident as his loyalty to the Crown. During the late 1530s, royal policy allowed significant and, as time would tell, irreversible Church reforms, such as authorization of an English Bible and suppression of the monasteries; even Mary Tudor proved able to repeal the authorization only temporarily and the suppression quite unsuccessfully. After 1540, when Gardiner became a formidable adversary of Cranmer's by advising Henry to keep Catholicism as England's religion in a Church controlled by the Crown, Cranmer argued theologically for reforms which now advanced only haltingly. If Cranmer as Protestant theologian was conceived in Cambridge's Little Germany in the 1520s, he was born only in Lambeth Palace in the 1540s.

Edward Fox was another Cambridge man who, like Latimer, ascended the episcopal bench after displaying dogged loyalty to the King throughout his difficulties with the papacy. From his first involvement in the divorce question in 1528, Fox remained a king's man until his untimely death in 1538. Fox published the opinions of the universities of Italy and France on the King's matter in April 1530 as *Grauissimæ totius Italiæ et Galliæ Academiarum censurae* (*STC* 14,286), a work which appeared the following year in translation, possibly by Cranmer, as *The determinations of the moste famous Universities of Italy and Fraunce* (*STC* 14,287); no Protestant theology there! Fox's other literary endeavor, printed in 1534, was an anonymous *Opus eximium, de vera differentia regiæ potestatis et ecclesiasticæ* (*STC* 11,218), translated in 1548 at the beginning of Edward VI's reign by Henry, Lord Stafford, as *The true differens betwen the regall power and the ecclesiasticall power* (*STC* 11,220). As thoroughly as the former work was canonical, the latter was political. Fox's activities, if not his writings, bore a Protestant stamp more definite than the activities of the early Cranmer, but less plain than the activities of Latimer during our period. He negotiated for his King with German princes, befriended Joye and helped him return home after his first exile, and worked with Barnes to establish good relations between Henry and the Wittenberg theologians. He died before those circumstances arose that brought to the fore the Protestantism of his influential friends at home.

A considerable roster of divines active during our period who later became reformers of the English Church might be assembled, but they furnish scant evidence for the character of the English Protestant movement from 1520 to 1535, and even that evidence is ex post facto. That such heroes of the later Reformation in England as Cranmer and Latimer were peripheral to the movement of early English Protestantism indicates how early and how important was the work of Tyndale and Frith, Barnes and Joye, and their less notable fellows. Their writings found sympathetic reception at home by commoners and a few learned men, and only later by prominent ecclesiastics. The early English Protestant movement itself was determined by exiles. They were fascinated at first with the thought of the great Luther, they were determined always to produce a Protestant English Bible, and they were given most devoutly to the articulation of a theology productive of morality. Their program won its way at home by means of books that appealed to the people; they found few advocates among men in powerful Church positions. As their theology focused increasingly on morality, it coalesced the concerns of popular Lollardy and sophisticated biblical humanism. Yet their theology lacked the only motive power by which English Church reform under Henry might proceed—the principle of royal headship of the Church.

15. Thomas More, *Defensor Fidei*

THOMAS Wolsey as prelate and person symbolized ecclesiastical abuse in the minds of the early English Protestants. Yet every known Protestant writer owed life and career to Wolsey's gentleness and good humor in dealing with accused heretics. Thanks to his humane qualities, Protestants and their sympathizers were mercifully handled, as the records of many processes attest. Under him, abjuration and self-exile were the rule, execution the very rare exception. The elevation of Thomas More to the chancellorship swiftly changed all that, for then "a theological zealot sat in the seat of secular power." [1] His *Dialogue* left no doubt that he regarded deviation from the established Church as a crime against God, conscience, and society; certain that the offender's soul would burn, it mattered little to More that the body should burn first.

More as layman and chancellor had legal right neither to examine persons accused of heresy nor to determine the punishment of those convicted. Yet he made it his business to search for and present to the spiritualty those men whose opinions, teachings, and actions subverted the Catholic Church. Heretics were placed in his custody. He deliberated with bishops and divines in the examination of Protestant books. He employed elaborate devices to gain information about Protestants, and there is reason to believe that he used an agent provocateur to trap Frith. Since More has become a subject for hagiography, he has not lacked defenders to point out that his rôle as chancellor left him no choice but to execute the judgment of ecclesiastical courts. Before and while he was chancellor, however,

1. Mozley, *William Tyndale,* p. 217.

he was also the agent of the bishop of London officially designated to read and refute in English the writings of the Protestants, a task which he took so seriously as to make himself a veritable inquisitor. The fact that there were two sides to his character and career gives no warrant for interpreting one side by reference to the other. More was a genial family man and a delightful, learned humanist, but these qualities did not soften his duty to the high position at court that he enthusiastically occupied.

Whether coincidentally or coefficiently, persecution and execution of English Protestants became commonplace after More replaced Wolsey in the chancellorship. If any bishop of the realm thought—apparently many had done so under Wolsey—of Lutheranism as, at worst, a mild danger to the internal life of the English Church, More quickly taught them that in its mildest form it was the worst danger. Regardless of limitations on his technical jurisdiction over heretics, he became a potent if unofficial spokesman to bishops and to populace of the royal policy; he demonstrated emphatically that the King as captain of the ship of Catholic state had named a first officer who would keep the bilges clean. To change the figure, the Protestants who rejoiced that the house was swept clean by the downfall of Wolsey, soon knew that seven devils had rushed in with More's elevation. More reserved his tender spirit for family and friends. No Protestant ever glimpsed it.

HUNTER OF HERETICS

Thomas Bilney, moving spirit of the Cambridge circle of Lutherans, espoused evangelical ideas in conversations with Latimer. From documents reflecting his religion, little beyond a fervent regard for scripture can be discerned. How he fared through the investigation at Cambridge early in 1526 is uncertainly known, but toward the end of the following year he was ordered to appear with Thomas Arthur and Joye to defend himself against accusations of heresy. Joye escaped that trial, but Bilney faced his examiners day after day, answering some thirty-four specific interrogations having to do, for the most part, with minor ceremonial and discipline. When on December 4, 1527, Bilney refused to recant, he was formally

pronounced a heretic by Tunstall, bishop of London. Again
he refused to recant. After declining to abjure for the third
time, Bilney announced on December 7 that he would submit.
Next day he performed the penance, bearing a fagot on his
shoulder at St. Paul's and standing "before the preacher at
Paul's Cross all the sermon time." Forgiven by the Church,
"little Bilney," as Latimer called him some two years later,
could not forgive himself, and began with all the more vigor
to preach the doctrines he had renounced. In 1531, accusations
of Bilney as a relapsed heretic came before More, who pressed
them assiduously.

Foxe, who relished all available details of the story, regarded More's acts toward Bilney as typifying his rôle vis-à-vis
the English Protestants from 1529 to 1534. More was "a man
otherwise of a pregnant wit, full of pleasant conceits; also for
his learning above the common sort of his estate"; Foxe
thought More "esteemed no less industrious in his studies, than
well exercised in his pen." It would have been better "if he had
kept himself within his own shop, and applied the faculty, being
a layman, whereunto he was called, and had not overreached
himself to prove masteries in such matters wherein he had little
skill, less experience, and which pertained not to his profession"; so More should have "deserved not only much more
commendation, but also a longer life." The judgment, if not
generous, was just.

Bilney's fate was to be condemned before More as a heretic.
Examined before one Dr. Pelles of Cambridge, he was degraded by a suffragan bishop and committed to the secular arm
for execution. The sheriff of Norwich, one Thomas Necton,
Bilney's friend, carried out the judgment, much to his personal
dislike. At the Lollard's Pit, outside Norwich, he was burnt.
Foxe, of course, considered Bilney a martyr, and recounted his
story hagiographically, but Foxe was usually a careful narrator
who exercised critical judgment on his sources. Although Foxe
let More appear more directly concerned with Bilney's execution than the lord chancellor either was or could have been, the
tone of his story rings true. The typical procedure with heretics
under Wolsey's chancellorship had left unexplored no avenue
toward abjuration, with whatever secret reservations. Under

More's regime, proceedings ran swiftly to condemnation and burning.[2]

Bilney's story exemplifies the plight of earnest Protestants after the sudden paradoxical turn in English ecclesiastical policy marked by the Reformation Parliament and by the ascendancy of More. As such, it demands attention, although many another martyrdom might as fairly represent this new effort of English Catholicism to protect itself against reformation. The flow of books was extensive despite careful measures taken by King, chancellor, bishops, and divines. In the long view, More's attack upon English disseminators of heretical books and heterodox teachings must be judged an all too tardy reversal of Wolsey's easy way with dissenters. As loyal servant of a prince occupied with his own power, and stubbornly anti-Protestant, More labored to get rid of this particular pestilence. He was effective if not successful. Whereas Wolsey's agents on the Continent, though appointed to apprehend Tyndale and Roy, served only to harass the translators of the New Testament, the program of the bishops during More's tenure was aimed at the means by which readers at home were getting books. More kept the Protestant writers in Antwerp off balance, a fact that helps to explain their sailing off in various directions, physically and theologically, during 1530 and 1531. It was More who for a time caused the failure of the English New Testament to win dominance over English religion, and this failure influenced Tyndale's theological development. More's attitude toward Protestants stemmed the tide of good favor which they and their Testament had previously enjoyed, at least in the universities and in parts of London society. To minimize or apologize for More's persecution of heretics would rob him of one of the great, if temporary, achievements of his career. Tragically, he was hoist on his own petard. Having taught Henry that uniformity of religious opinion could be

2. *AM, 4,* 619–56, told the tale of Bilney; for the quotation, p. 632, and for the estimate of More, p. 652. Unlike many modern writers on More, Foxe professed his hagiographical interest. A long tradition of impugning Foxe's accuracy has been corrected and grievances against him redressed by Mozley, *John Foxe.* More always exerted a similar care for accuracy in recording the events of his own day. For a compilation of data regarding Bilney's career, see M. L. Loane, *Masters of the English Reformation* (London 1954), pp. 3–41.

achieved by sternness, More was forced by his own conscience
to refuse acknowledgment of the religious principle making
Henry head of his Church, and had to suffer the punishment
that the King's sternness meted out to dissenters.

More bowed before Henry's vagaries when he must, as in
the case of the King's fondness for the person and writing of
Fish, against whom More had written one of his more brilliant
polemical tracts in defense of purgatory. According to accounts
preserved by Foxe, Fish produced satisfactory surety, and was
immune to More's investigations and attacks, though More
explained the matter in terms of Fish's submission to the
dogmas of the Church. But Fish's wife, during her husband's
stay on the Continent, achieved some reputation as a trader
in Protestant books. Then, after Fish's death, she married one
James Bainham, gentleman, son of a knight of Gloucestershire. Bainham, who had studied law, became the friend and
defender of people who suffered for their Protestant beliefs.
After marrying the widow Fish he became suspect, and More
accused him. He was arrested and taken from the Middle Tem-
ple to More's home in Chelsea as a free prisoner while More
attempted to bring him to full obedience to the Church. As
Foxe had it, Bainham's refusal to submit led More to "cast
him in prison in his own house," and to have him whipped, then
sent to the Tower "to be racked: and so he was, sir Thomas
More being present himself, till in a manner he had lamed
him, because he would not accuse the gentlemen of the Tem-
ple of his acquaintance, nor would not show where his books
lay." When, on December 15, 1531, Bainham was examined
in Chelsea by Stokesley, bishop of London, the interrogations
dealt with purgatory, praying to saints, auricular confession
and priestly absolution, church and scripture, monastic vows,
and sacraments. He confessed to having, after the King's proclamation, the English New Testament, *Mammon, Obedience,
Practice of Prelates, Answer to More's Dialogue* (all by Tyndale), Frith's book against purgatory, and "the Epistle of
George Gee [Joye], alias George Clerk." Next day, Bainham,
before Stokesley in More's house, was offered the choice of
abjuring or burning. Bainham temporized with pleas of ignorance, and was held for further trial. In February 1532 he

submitted, but halted in reading the sentence of abjuration, pleading for mercy, then finally abjured—all this before More as chancellor—and did his penance. On February 17 he was dismissed, but within a month "bewailed his fact [i.e. deed] and abjuration; and was never quiet in mind and conscience until the time he had uttered his fall to all his acquaintance, and asked God and all the world forgiveness, before the congregation in those days, in a warehouse in Bow-lane." Next Sunday, Bainham in church openly prayed for forgiveness, "with the New Testament in his hand in English, and the Obedience of a Christian man in his bosom." The same resolution he wrote to the bishop and others, and was soon arrested and imprisoned in the Tower. Tried in late April, Bainham stuck fast to his Protestant convictions, and was condemned. Then "for almost the space of a fortnight, he lay in the bishop's coal-house in the stocks, with irons upon his legs. Then he was carried to the lord chancellor's, and there chained to a post two nights." Finally, on May Day 1532, he was burnt at the stake, praying forgiveness for himself and for More, having declared that he had been "accused and condemned for an heretic, sir Thomas More being both my accuser and my judge." [3]

Foxe's account of Bainham sided with Bainham against the authorities, yet its authenticity of times, places, and main events is reliable. To charge More with cruelty, or with illegal treatment of the accused, would be as wrong-headed as to defend him against these charges with the encomiums of later generations.[4] The office of lord chancellor was hardly constitutionally limited. More was not a cruel man. Heresy, however, constituted a gross offence against nature, man, and God, and required radical measures, however cruel they may seem to a

3. *AM, 4,* 698, 700, 702, 705.
4. Chambers, *Thomas More,* pp. 274 ff., cited Jonathan Swift to testify to More's virtue, after exonerating More from Foxe's charges. Chambers was interested in discrediting Foxe's account of More as persecutor of the Protestants by casting him wholly in the rôle of the Church's and Crown's prosecutor. My judgment that this distinction is anachronistic has been verified by R. C. Marius, "Thomas More and the Heretics" (unpublished dissertation, Yale University, 1962), especially pp. 125–37; although this detailed work became available to me too late to use in the study of More here reported, it is gratifying to discover that Dr. Marius' main lines of interpretation agree with mine.

modern world trained to regard religion as inviolably private. More treated Protestant heretics relentlessly in order to preserve the unity of the realm. Religious uniformity was the bond of society in Henry's England just as it was in Innocent III's Europe, Calvin's Geneva, and Luther's Saxony. In the light of that fact, More saw and performed his duty better than Wolsey had done.

CHANCELLOR

More was by no means involved in all the charges and convictions of heresy during his chancellorship. Men and women whose means and influence dignified the Protestant cause naturally attracted his attention. In the one thoroughly sordid case of the era, that of the burning of William Tracy's exhumed remains, More seems to have played no part whatever, however much the Protestants at home and abroad celebrated the incident. Tracy's will offensively brandished Protestant convictions; More, however, incurs no responsibility for the circumstances that created the grievance for Tracy's son. The bishop with jurisdiction was an absentee who held his see as reward for diplomatic services rendered to Wolsey and Henry. When the vicar-general carried out the archbishop's instructions, and, exceeding the orders, had Tracy's body burnt, the Protestants made a legitimate protest against the rough execution of a relentless policy. The policy was More's, but not its bad administration.

More's chancellorship spanned the two-and-one-half-year period of the most strenuous application of canonical and civil laws against Protestant opinions and publications. While the cases that ended in burning during his tenure have been best remembered, they were outnumbered many times over by cases settled by abjuration and apparent cessation of Protestant activities. Only afterwards did men of Protestant leanings ascend the high ranks of the hierarchy, as when Cranmer became primate in 1533. More did not have all things his own way; under Henry VIII nobody did. While More was chancellor, the star of Thomas Cromwell began to rise, and for the latter half of his tenure that clever lawyer was privy councillor.

More's chief interest in heresy cases was in carrying out the terms of the King's proclamation of June 22, 1530, which he understood to have "vtterly forboden all englysshe prented bookes to be brought into thys lande from beyonde the see." More's efforts checked sharply the flow of these books. The Brethren were reduced to making, as More put it, "many shorte treatyses, whereof theyr scolers may shortly write out copyes"; this resort demanded economy of expression such as would "put as mych poyson in one wryten lefe, as they prented before in fyftene," and the manuscript copies sometimes eluded detection altogether.[5] These manuscript treatises made More's task extremely difficult. Probably after his resignation as chancellor, he acquired a manuscript copy of a sermon of the Brethren, reported to have been preached twice openly, on the text "He made vs by the trouth of hys worde" from the first chapter of James. In half-Lollard, half-Lutheran fashion it argued that the "word" by the agency of which God created was the word of the scripture; therefore, long before there was a church the scripture was written in the hearts of men; therefore scripture preceded and gave birth to church. The sermon, which More summarized in his *Apology* of 1533, was based upon Tyndale's *Answer to More's Dialogue*.[6] More sought for these manuscripts, as well as for books, and for the distributors of both, using every means at his disposal, not in order to bring persons to trial for heresy, but to stop the circulation of Protestant teaching in the realm.

Partial and temporary success rewarded attempts, during More's chancellorship and immediately afterwards, to hunt down Protestants and bring them to abjuration or execution under the law of the land. The program crimped the Protestant movement, and the circle of Protestant writers in Antwerp reconsidered both their strategy and their theology. The setbacks cannot be attributed to More alone, but they coincided with his tenure and gave his program the glow of success for a time. Tyndale and Joye went on translating portions of the Old Testament, but no longer as warmly cooperative partners. Frith went to England to reconnoiter, returned to report,

---

5. More, *A letter . . . impugnynge . . . Fryth . . .* , a.ii^{r-v}; cf. *Correspondence*, pp. 440 f.

6. More, *Workes*, pp. 851 f.; PS *3*, p. 24.

printed his book on purgatory and Tyndale's reply to More's *Dialogue,* then returned to England to assume active leadership of the distressed Brethren; More achieved his arrest, imprisonment, and death. Tyndale pondered the failure, partly due to More's efforts, of the vernacular scriptures to commend themselves at home, wondered at the relation between the Old and New Testaments, and arrived at the new notion of the divine-human encounter as a contractual arrangement inaugurated by God but as binding upon Himself as upon mankind. Barnes had to be the messenger of bad news to Henry when he presented Luther's letter on the divorce question, and, fearful of falling into the spider's web that More wove for Protestants, fled once again to Germany to await another possibility of entering the King's service as religious counselor and negotiator. Meanwhile, Barnes reshaped his own theology to distinguish his position from Luther's and to make possible the desired preferment. In England, Protestant books circulated only with great difficulty and danger. Thanks to More, the books were efficiently and officially proscribed by Crown as well as Church.

When More was no longer chancellor, the Protestants heaved sighs of relief. Once again their message went rapidly if surreptitiously about the country, and arrests on suspicion of heresy became once again the exception rather than the rule. Had Henry's whims continued Catholic in the sense that More took the term, More could have continued as chancellor, and the Protestant movement might have died aborning in England. But that was not to be. More resigned as chancellor, but kept the episcopal commission to read and refute heresies which the Crown, with Cranmer as archbishop of Canterbury, no longer would prosecute relentlessly. The King whom More dutifully served repudiated the Pope whom More spiritually obeyed. His fate was not a pretty one. More finally learned, the hard way, the power of a bound conscience; when it had been pleaded by Luther and Tyndale he had ridiculed the claim as vaunting private judgment over due authority and as leading to anarchy. That Henry bore the title "Supreme Head of the Church" posed in itself no insuperable obstacle, since the saving clause proposed by Fisher, "so far as the law of God allows," was appended. Henry took that to mean very far, but neither to More nor to Fisher did it allow any breach from the one body of Christendom presided over by the Pope. Luther might well have said, after Worms, what More wrote after his trial: "But I thanke our Lorde," reads one of his last letters, "that the thinge that I doe is not for obstinacie but for the saluacion of my soule, because I cannot induce myne owne mynde otherwise to thinke than I doe concerninge the othe." [7] Substitute "scripture" or "faith" for "othe," and you have the conviction of Frith, Bilney, Bainham, and of many another Protestant martyred under More's administration as chancellor.

POLEMICIST

The sagacity, and consequent near success, of More's campaign against English Protestantism was founded on his meticulous study of the heretics' vernacular writings. His commission from Tunstall and Stokesley as official reader of these books resulted in a chancellor sensitive to the dangers and plans of the enemy. Yet the literary results of the commission, for all their quantity, were equivocal. For Tunstall to have chosen a layman and belle-lettrist for the difficult task of showing English readers the falsity of vernacular Protestant writings seems at first a stroke of genius. More, friend of Erasmus and successor of the recondite Fisher, now ranked as dean of England's humanists. He brought the weight of learning to bear against the cause espoused by the second-rate minds of Tyndale and his associates. As amateur theologian and as leading social theorist, More might avoid the obscurities of technical theology while training on the foe the weapons of a practical philosopher. Yet, in the end, More had effectively lost and tacitly conceded the victory.

Tunstall wrote More on March 7, 1528, lamenting the spread of Lutheran books; "lest the catholic faith perish utterly" More was invited to "meet the danger by quickly putting forth sound books in the vernacular on the catholic side." Tunstall thought the layman able to "play the Demosthenes both in English and Latin," and licensed him to read Protestant

7. More to Master Leder, January 16, 1535, *Correspondence*, p. 549.

books in both languages to "learn the habits of these serpents, where they lurk, by what shifts and turns they seek to escape when grasped, and what they hope to achieve." The labor promised fame on earth and merit in heaven.[8]

More utilized his abilities as scholar and author by a dubious strategy. All the ammunition of the polemicist—logic, ridicule, personal calumny, vulgarity, wit, a popular style, intellectual agility—was in his arsenal. But he indulged in such ample citation of heretical writings that a reader might gain a liberal and current education in English Protestant thought from More's books. He portrayed the heretical adversary as automatically in error by virtue of being heretical and adversary. He made again and again the claim that the official Church could not err. He discredited opponents where their logic faltered, he gloried in their inconsistencies and disagreements, he scorned their persons and actions as despicable, and he seized every available argumentum ad hominem. Tyndale erred because he led a heretical party; Frith wrote only lies because he was young and no doctor of divinity; Barnes was perversely unorthodox because he repudiated the articles of his abjuration. More always argued that the Church taught truth, the Protestants opposed the Church, ergo the Protestants taught lies.

All the while those whose faith More guarded might legitimately learn from his books what they were forbidden to read otherwise—the precise nature of the Protestant attack upon the established religion. More's point-by-point refutations forfeited the initiative to his opponents, and invited multiplication of Protestant books in reply to his own. Thus he virtually cultivated what he most deplored, and set his truth on the defensive. To refute Protestant theology for the benefit of the simple-minded, More was forced into the position of describing and defending Catholic religious practice as the simple-minded understood and practiced it, and thereby he forfeited the winsome appeal of the typical Christian humanist from an ignorant to an educated religion. Since the Protestants regarded the simple-minded as capable of a mature Christian faith, not

8. Tunstall to More, March 7, 1528, in Mozley, *William Tyndale*, p. 213, citing: Tunstall Register.

as religiously infantile children of ecclesiastical fathers, More
persistently insulted the jury before which he was commissioned to plead. Nonessentials cut away, his prescription was:
believe what the Pope and his Church command and you will
receive what the Pope and his Church promise—it is all available to you through your priest. That was hardly more appealing than: believe what God and his Christ command and you
will receive what God and his Christ promise—it is all written
for you in the Bible.

More's first attack upon the English New Testament only
energized and increased his adversaries, while by the nature
of his task he stood virtually alone. The attack gave Tyndale
an excuse to abandon the magnanimity of his translations and
earliest biblical prefaces and to resort to vituperation in libelli.
Volunteering as Tyndale's seconds—regardless of his approval—were the versifiers Roy and Barlowe, the theologically
astute Frith, the energetic Joye, the layman Fish, and Barnes,
a doctor of divinity. To More's side rushed only his kinsman
by marriage, John Rastell, whose faith, like his learning,
proved inadequate. Distracted only by the need to maintain
personal safety and earn a livelihood, Tyndale and his seconds
fought their battle as a life-consuming vocation, while More
led the busy life of chancellor, pater familias, social leader,
litterateur, and knight, and wrote theological tracts as an extra-
curricular chore dutifully but wearily done.

Duties of the chancellorship slowed More's pen considerably. The *Dialogue* and *Supplication of Souls* had been printed
before he entered the office in October 1529; the next work, the
first three books of the *Confutation of Tyndale's Answer,*
though written in 1531, was not published until 1532. Moreover, his chancellorship outlasted the King's full confidence in
him. Although he occupied the office until May 16, 1532, he
was already at odds with Henry when the King became titular
head of the Church in England in February 1531. Most of his
polemical writing was done during the later and less influential
—but more demanding—phase of his work as lord chancellor.

Despite his many other occupations and distractions, More
produced a vast quantity of verbiage against the Protestants.

In the closely printed, two-column, folio edition of his English writings edited by William Rastell in 1557, these tracts occupy more than a thousand pages. The *Dialogue* took one hundred and eighty-four pages, *Supplication* only fifty-one. After the first part of the *Confutation* (as long as *Dialogue*), there followed the brief letter against Frith on the sacrament of the altar (twelve pages), written by December 7, 1532, but published in the following year. The year 1533 was most prolific of all: by about Easter *The apologye of syr Thomas More Knyght* (*STC* 18,078), ninety-four pages in the collected works, was finished; before the year was out *The debellacyon of Salem and Bizance* (*STC* 18,081), of the same length, had been published, as well as *The second parte of the confutacion of Tyndals answere* (*STC* 18,080), comprising books four through nine, and running to three hundred and eleven pages in the unfinished form in which Rastell preserved them. Also written in 1533, but published early in 1534, was the *Answer to the Poisoned Book* (one hundred and four pages). During 1534, More turned to devotional writings with a spirit wholly different from that which inspired the polemics. His last writings, like the letters to family and friends, shine with the noble sentiment, profound thought, and complete religious dedication of the private man. Yet it was only toward the young and attractive Frith that the public More allowed humaneness to temper his hatred for heretics, and even there he failed to distinguish between the heretic and his heresy.

Much difficulty arose from the unavoidably negative character of More's work as a Catholic propagandist. The very fact of his being licensed to read the Protestants, and commissioned to refute them, implied "a confession of the defeat of the repressive methods" employed by the Church in facing the challenge of the Reformation.[9] The consummate dreariness of More's libelli has been attributed to the nature of his task, to write as a religious, rather than intellectual or literary, man, and to the specification that he "write for the vulgar, *simplicibus et idiotis hominibus*"; for these reasons More "was not allowed to fly very high in theology" although it is difficult to

9. Reed, "Regulation of the Book Trade," p. 173.

judge "how high he could have flown if free." [10] Tedium of
form and matter seldom found relief, and then only in long
paragraphs of personal abuse in which More could exercise
his great literary flair. Simple minds would hardly be won from
or inoculated against heresy by logical minutiae cast in a turgid
style which makes the reading of these works as severe a penance as one suspects the writing of them to have been. Even
the more lively invective by More suffers by comparison with
that of Frith and Tyndale—even with that of the lumbering
Barnes—who sometimes rose above the nicely turned phrase
to real wit.

Theologically monotonous, More sang with gusto only one
chorus: he believes aright who believes the Pope's Church.
The first two anti-Protestant tracts, *Dialogue* and *Supplication of Souls,* deserve credit for humor and literary form, but
theologically these, like the rest, on balance leave More's
cause damaged. C. S. Lewis rightly diagnosed the root of the
difficulty as an attempt "to show in every chapter that every
heretical book is wrong about everything." Quick to capitalize
the blunder, his adversaries taunted More for condemning even
those few points which supported the papal position. The tragedy of the whole affair lay in the fact that More, obeying "his
conscience . . . spent what might have been the best years of
his literary life on work which demanded talents that he lacked
and gave very limited scope to those that he had," as Lewis
put it. The same commentator, judging More's little treatise
on "The Four Last Things," wrote, "In the true late medieval
manner More forgets that to paint all black is much the same
as not to paint at all." That sentence fairly summarizes the
theological significance of all the vernacular writings against
the Protestants.[11]

RELIGIOUS THOUGHT

More's English theological works demand and deserve ad-
verse judgments. Fuller justice to and appreciation for the man

---

10. Lewis, *English Literature in the Sixteenth Century,* p. 171. Lewis' meta-
phor opens itself to the question whether, as theologian or writer, More the
polemicist was ever airborne.

11. Ibid., pp. **174, 176.**

and his motives warrants emphasizing that his circumstances hardly allowed him any alternative. More's honor bound him to refute rather than to assess whatever the foe put forward. That the task appears to have been in large measure self-defeating does not mean that More's dedication to it flagged. Religiously, More was still thinking in the terms of the middle ages, and the religious dimension of his social theories remained bound to tradition. The utopia envisioned by More allowed no multiform religious expression; founded as it was upon natural law and reason, social cohesion depended upon religious uniformity, after the pattern that had prevailed in Europe for a millennium and seemed rooted in the nature of things. What the Protestants proposed was that limbs be torn from the corpus christianum. That, to More, was anarchical. In taking this line, More the social philosopher, More the polemicist, and More the martyr maintained complete consistency. Against subscribing the oath to the Act of Succession demanded by Henry, his basic scruple was that, "sith all Christendom is one corps," no member might "withowt the comen assent of the body departe from the comen hede." [12] Within six weeks after writing those words More was imprisoned in the Tower for refusing to take the oath. As More saw it, neither papal primacy nor conciliar authority, but the corpus christianum was the nub of the issue. By his own profession he had never held to papal primacy on principle until he had read and helped revise Henry's *Assertio,* in the course of which the King rejected the moderate papalism that More suggested and showed More new reasons for the dogma of primacy. During the time that he wrote against the Protestants, he claimed to have found unanimity in all the fathers and doctors, Latin and Greek, on papal supremacy. Toward the end he refused to insist on the point dogmatically, allowing that a general council might speak with authority to a Christendom sundered by the Reformation. But he defended papalism as instituted by the Church to prevent schism.

More's inconsistency lay in failing to reconcile his ecclesiastical universalism and his political territorialism; theoretically, the problem was not very important, but when it actually pre-

12. More to Cromwell, March 5, 1534, *Correspondence,* p. 498.

sented a choice More literally staked his life on the former. His allegiance to the authority of church councils, and his hope for a general council in his own day, failed to solve the difficulty, therefore he lost his life to save his soul. In polemics More also held stubbornly to the authority of the Pope and the inerrancy of the Church. The position of his adversaries he badly mistook, intentionally or not, as that of the radical reformers, like Anabaptists and spiritualists, who would place individual spiritual experience above all concerns of temporal authority and secular order. The early English Protestants believed in ecclesiastical as well as political territorialism, repeatedly imploring and exhorting the King to plant and nurture the gospel (as they understood it) in his realm. More made them out to be far worse than they were, and on the particular issue of ecclesiastical territorialism it was the Protestants with whom Henry eventually sided.

A philosophical gulf separated More from his Protestant opponents. To one degree or another all the English Protestant writers shared the metaphysics of the Ockhamist school of thought, or, more accurately, of the early sixteenth century representatives of the via moderna. In his theological tracts, More followed the Scotist line. This difference showed itself with particular clarity in the question of the capacity of a finite creature to be in many places at once—a crucial point in the arguments over the mass: might the creaturely body of Jesus, however transfigured at the resurrection, reside at once in heaven and on many altars? Sheer folly, thought the Protestants; Frith and Joye were especially emphatic. More preferred the late scholastic device of proving the actual as arising from the possible. He contended that God might have created one man and nothing else in the beginning, in which case that man would have been everywhere at once as a finite creature; God might at any time create a new spirit to fill the whole world, but that spirit's universality need not imply infinitude; therefore God might provide Jesus with a body capable of a multiple residence that would not contravene its creaturehood. Such speculations were to Frith and Joye vain, as they were blasphemous to Luther, in that they refused to let things be as God made them. Against Joye, in the present connection, More put his most telling point on purely logical grounds: Joye erred in arguing from the impossibility of a body's occupation of *all* places at once to the impossibility of a body's residing in *many* places at once. More argued for a ubiquitous creaturely body, carefully distinguishing his conception from the apparently similar notion of the arch-heretic Luther. Then More modestly contended that the body of the Lord was actually present only where the blessed sacrament was. The last point derived its truth, however, not from the metaphysics in the context of which it was explained, but from the authority of the Church that dogmatized it. The metaphysical conception over which More and his opponents differed actually accounted for little when More came to clinch his case, yet he allowed himself to be drawn into a long and unedifying description of it. And in fact, although More never acknowledged the fact, divergent metaphysics made it almost impossible for the disputants to communicate.[13]

Whenever More caught his adversaries disagreeing among themselves he made the most of it. Tyndale alone, on the other side, wanted unanimity, yet even he indulged in personal attacks on members of his supposed coterie. Gleefully, More perceived that Barnes and Frith and the writer of *The Souper of the Lorde* were not in agreement on the manner of the presence of Christ in the Supper, but the actual contentions mattered less than the opportunity for scorn and ridicule. More imputed to his opponents the necessity of theological and dogmatic unanimity, whereas continental Protestants' disagreements were no secret, and, in fact, Tyndale's low estimate of Roy and Barlowe had been public since the publication of *Obedience*. Even while gloating over difference of opinion among the English Protestants, More held them responsible for agreement with certain diverse, even contradictory, continental theologians. Luther, Lambert, Oecolampadius, Zwingli, and Melanchthon were Protestants; Barnes, Tyndale, Joye, Frith, and Roy were Protestants; but every shade of variant opinion gave the lie to all of them, as More presented the case. More scored an occasional point, for example when he accused Tyndale of borrowing from Melanchthon the distinction between

13. More, Answer to the Poisoned Book, *Workes*, pp. 1121 ff. and passim.

historical faith and feeling faith; but More passed up the opportunity to comment on the basic theological problem, namely, Tyndale's (and Barnes') distinction between faith as justifying before God and works as justifying before man. To More's mind the two kinds of faith comprised a false teaching because the distinction was new!

To the objections that simple men at home lodged against his theological writings, More showed an almost touchy sensitivity. The Brethren thought his books overly long and tedious, his arguments weak and often well-refuted by popular sermons and tracts, his treatment of his adversaries' persons unfair and discourteous, his defence of the Catholic clergy one-sided and uncritical, his attacks carping at easy points, his bold promises of convincing and thorough treatises unfulfilled. More recorded these objections, acknowledging in his *Apology* that his duty asked more than he brought to it. Wistfully he wrote "it might much better haue becomen me to let the matter alone, then by wrytinge to presume anye thyng to meddle therwith." Most unfairly, in his view, critics alleged that he misquoted or partly quoted his opponents' words. Rising to his own defence, he noted that his reader might, by overlooking his comments, find the whole substance and almost the whole words of Tyndale, and that if any doubt remained, the reader might find Tyndale's books aplenty among the Brethren to check the quotations! In protecting himself against his accusers, More publicized the wide circulation of heretical books in England, conceded that the Protestants were very numerous, and confessed that their doctrines were preached freely.[14] So fully had the self-defeating nature of his enterprise dawned upon him. Yet he plunged doggedly ahead, returning in the *Apology* to the same familiar style of argument.

A petulance bred of early evidence of defeat crept in upon More with the first books of the *Confutation of Tyndale's Answer,* which marked off the great bulk of the polemical writings from the earlier and more brilliant tracts. The *Dialogue* and *Supplication of Souls* (1529) show More in his best argu-

14. Apology, *Workes,* pp. 845 ff.; cf. Answer to the Poisoned Book, *Workes,* p. 1085.

mentative form and in high good humor, fresh and vigorous. To Fish he retorted. To Joye and Frith and the later Tyndale he only reacted. The constant factor was verbosity. Fish's tiny pamphlet drew some thirty-five thousand words of refutation. Although William Rastell could not find part of the final (ninth) book of the *Confutation* to reprint in 1557, the parts preserved contain a third of a million words. In *Supplication of Souls* More had spoken cleverly. In the name of all the souls in purgatory he pleaded that prayers and masses for the relief of their misery not cease, and that nobody still on earth should allow disbelief in purgatory to send his soul to hell. More derided the *Supplication of the Beggars* as having "gathered these goodly flowres [of the evils of the clergy] out of Luthers garden almost word for word without any more labor but onely the translating oute of the latine into the englishe tonge." [15] He justifiably attacked Fish's dubious statistics, chiding his opponent for having forgotten a recent revaluation of English money. With genuine zest, More's *Dialogue* defended the worship of relics and images, praying to saints, and making pilgrimages.

The contrast between the sparkle of the 1529 tracts and the lackluster tedium of the later ones cannot be explained simply by reference to a weary author and a lusty opposition. The early books dwelt on religious practices, and the later ones on religious belief. Cultic matters fascinated More and charmed the unsophisticated; the commission and the commissioned fitted the task. Later on More turned to doctrine; by contrast, creedal matters lacked excitement. More had shown proficiency and a certain brilliance at doctrinal disputation in Latin, especially in view of his amateur standing. By 1532 he posed as a professional—indeed the official—anti-Protestant English theologian. Admiration for the man's character cannot restrain the judgment that the waters of technical theological polemics were over his head, and he never learned to swim. As to the English writings in which he debated important doctrinal matters, More must be counted as having tried but failed.

Close to the heart of the issue between Catholicism and Prot-

15. Supplication of Souls, *Workes*, p. 295.

estantism in England between 1525 and 1535 was the question of the authority of Church, scripture, tradition, and hierarchy. All the Protestant writers dealt with this matter, some, like Frith and Tyndale, originally and intelligently. Their probings touched on important broad questions such as the conception of history, the weight to be given to irrefutable historical data, the mission of the Christian movement, the diversity of scriptural testimony, and so forth. All this More either failed to understand or deliberately misunderstood, harping as he did on the one string of the self-evident veracity of whatever the official Church taught, and contending that the determination of the official Church's teaching was easily settled by reference to the papacy. Henry's *Assertio* had chosen to rest the question of religious authority on the proposition that teachings contained in scripture were augmented by unwritten traditions thought to have been secretly transmitted by Jesus to the apostles to the succession of popes, for example, the perpetual virginity of the mother of Jesus. These traditions took precedence over plain meanings of scripture, and required the papacy to authorize divine truth for each generation; so Henry had argued. More proudly adverted to that argument as the last word on the question of authority. Catholic scholars and theologians of the early sixteenth century proposed contesting views of religious authority, some of which qualified the appeal to secret traditions over scriptural teachings. Whether More knew nothing or cared nothing about these views, his English writings do not reveal. Appeal to unwritten tradition lodged ultimate authority in the papacy; to question this appeal was to question the papacy. Therefore, whatever the official Church taught, More upheld as divine truth, and whatever the Protestants suggested, he derided as horrible error and heresy. Scriptural contradictions seemed at worst superficial, for the supreme religious authority of the papacy, if given absolute credence, would eliminate the appearances of contradiction. By turning at every juncture away from the arguments of his opponents to the blindly uncritical assertion of papal authority, More demeaned his own cause and avoided serious theological disputation. He thought that his premise made his case secure, whatever he might assert. So committed to a single premise, More in his English polemical works always remained an inconclusive theologian.[16]

Personal calumny of enemies was common in all early sixteenth century religious polemics; what moderns consider vile language was a la mode in More's day. His concern that the pleading for and practice of clerical marriage by Protestants be seen as flagrant immorality which, apart from every other consideration, nullified their teachings, amounted almost to a preoccupation. More had determined his own vocation as layman rather than cleric because the gift of chastity was not among his many endowments. That others—most notably Luther, but, through guilt by association, all who religiously allied themselves with Luther—should have broken vows of celibacy was their ultimate and unforgivable sin. The pretense of marriage, as he saw it, between a former monk and a former nun, constituted the most sordid surrender to the temptations of the flesh, the most debased profligacy. He tainted all his antagonists with this crime, even Barnes who denied that he had ever married and who called various witnesses to testify in his behalf. The vilification thus intended by More proceeded, in fact, only from his own presuppositions, which were not necessarily shared by his desired readers. More alleged his foes' sexual promiscuity and immorality, apparently never asking whether he helped or hurt his cause, much less whether the charges were true.

Sifting personal calumny from More's vernacular writings for the Church leaves much that is religiously instructive but little that is theologically edifying. He warmly commended participation in cultic observances as exhibiting salutary obedience to the Church. He risked no real doctrinal assertions beyond ascribing to the Church inerrant and absolute authority. He never considered the thought of his opponents as deserving engagement. More's high reputation as a religious

16. *Workes,* pp. 852, 1083, 1128 and passim. For an interesting discussion of the doctrine of tradition which More espoused as deviating from the best contemporary Catholic doctrine, see G. H. Tavard, *Holy Writ or Holy Church* (London, 1959).

thinker has been won by the earnestness of his labors, despite the exceeding modesty of his achievements in contesting early English Protestantism.

RETREAT FROM HUMANISM

More gave five crucial years unstintingly to holding English religion within the bounds of papal Catholicism. Failure to achieve the goal is attributable not to him personally but to the whole Church, especially its English hierarchy. More became the champion of Catholicism in England by suppressing the importation, publication, and circulation of Protestant books, by finding and bringing to statutory justice Protestants and their sympathizers, and by a voluminous literary production refuting whatever the Protestants said. More received his summons to the task just as the King's great matter of divorcing his Queen rent the ostensibly solid body of episcopal opinion. The wise counsel and diplomacy of Warham and Fisher had built an episcopal bench with genuine unanimity never rivaled under Wolsey. From 1529, when More became chancellor, until the middle of 1532, when he resigned the office, the hierarchy progressed steadily to a unity of thought and action capable, it would seem, of quelling any uprising by the meager Protestant forces. The very threat to which More called attention united the Church for battle.

Gradually the King articulated the ecclesiastical headship to which personal and political affairs made him aspire. The Submission of the Clergy in May 1532 marked the end of More's chancellorship and the beginning of his most ardent anti-Protestant polemics. A year later Henry was excommunicated at Rome, and there ensued the measures by which a conservative episcopacy was forced toward the surrender of its power by the Act of Succession of March 1534, and the requirement of the oath attendant thereto. More and Fisher resisted, and they were executed in the early summer of 1535 under charges of treason.[17] More was forced to choose between his humanism and his ardent Catholicism. He walked as his God willed.

17. J. J. Scarisbrick, "The Conservative Episcopate in England 1529–1535," (unpublished dissertation, Cambridge University, 1955–56), is an interesting summary of the movement seen from the Catholic side; see especially pp. 246 ff.

During these years, More was helped only slightly by professional theologians in his literary efforts for a conservative Catholicism. Longland, bishop of Lincoln since 1521, had published sermons occasionally during the 1520s. About 1527 there appeared an English translation of his *Tres Conciones* (*STC* 16,790); a Latin exposition of the five penitential psalms (*STC* 16,792) came from the press of Robert Redman about 1532. But Longland eventually followed King against Pope, and at the battle's noisiest he fell silent. Edward Powell, Oxford doctor of divinity, stood firm against the divorce and the Lutherans. He was, like Fisher and More, condemned for treason when he refused the oath of succession in 1534, but was spared until 1540. Then, ironically, Gardiner's policy made him fellow martyr with Barnes. In the heat of controversy, Powell did little to echo his 1523 Latin tract, *Propugnaculum summi sacerdotii euangelici aduer. M. Lutherum* (*STC* 20,140). Thomas Abell maintained steady loyalty to Queen Catherine, whose chaplain he had been, and printed from deKeyser's press in Antwerp, in 1532, his *Inuicta veritas. An answere that by no maner of lawe it maye be lawfull for Kinge Henry the Ayght to be diuorsid* (*STC* 61). He was put in the Tower for his impertinence. Two years later, he was accused in a bill of attainder of being Catherine's accomplice, but his life was spared until the reaction of 1540. John More, Thomas' son, published, from Rastell's press, in Lent 1533, his translation of a eucharistic sermon by Fredericus Nausea, bishop of Vienna (*STC* 18,414). The aging Fisher wrote little during the period, although his earlier sermons against Luther guided More's work. Fisher occasionally printed devotional pieces, exhorting conscientious practice of Catholic religion, but these dwindled between 1532 and 1535.

It was in just these years that many books by humanists, both for and against the old religion, were translated into English. On balance, the Protestants employed these dubious allies far more effectively than the Catholics did. Erasmus' occasional writings—repudiating the crudeness of the monastic intellectual tradition, arguing for a vernacular scripture in every land, and praising the estate of matrimony—favored the new order. More, once the friend of foreign humanists and

leader of the new learning at home, found himself pressed by
events to turn against the very enlightenment for which he
had labored. Humanism's alliance with Protestant attacks upon
the Church was nowhere complete, but to More's ears, at least,
certain strains of the humanists' cry took on overtones of
heresy. His writings from 1529 until his death evidence a drift
and then a march from the ideal of *libertas humanitatis* toward
the ideal of personal and intellectual security in the bosom of
Mother Church.

More's retreat from humanism became manifest when he
refuted the enlightened but implicitly anti-ecclesiastical writings of Christopher Saint-German, barrister and legal contro-
versialist. By 1528, Saint-German had published, through the
press of More's kinsman William Rastell, *Dialogus de fundamentis legum Anglie et de conscientia* (*STC* 21,559).[18] This
work had many editions and revisions, especially in its more
popular English translation as dialogues between a doctor of
divinity and a student of law. About 1532 he published anonymously *A treatise concernynge the diuision betwene the spirytualtie and temporaltie;* probably the first edition was from
the press of Robert Redman in London (*STC* 21,586). More,
smarting under the accusation (as he took it) by the Brethren
that this book displayed "suche a goodlye milde maner, and
suche an indyfferent fasshyon" as far excelled his own works,
devoted to its refutation four-fifths of the chapters and three-
fourths of the verbiage of his *Apology*.[19]

Without advocating Protestantism, Saint-German, on
grounds of jurisprudential theory and legal procedure, had complained about the manner in which persons were punished under
accusation of heresy. Case by case, More defended the temporalty's duty to execute the judgment of ecclesiastical courts.
Of greater significance is the *Apology's* conception of society

18. *DNB* dated the work 1523, calling it "a handbook for legal students,
which was not superseded until the appearance of Blackstone's 'Commentaries'."
19. Apology, *Workes,* p. 869; the refutation occupied chapters 11–50, pp.
869–928. The controversy will receive detailed discussion by J. B. Trapp in his
forthcoming edition of the Apology (the Yale edition of the works of St.
Thomas More). Mr. Trapp has kindly called my attention to Pearl Hogrefe,
"John More's Translations," *Papers of the Bibliographical Society of America,*
49 (1955), 188–89.

as requiring for its own stability that heretics be identified by Church courts and extirpated by the secular arm. Although More's reluctance to pursue Protestant reforms, and his final opposition to reforms demanded by Henry, harmonized with the social theories expressed in *Utopia,* the *Apology* represents a clear retreat from the ideal of an enlightened society of earnest saints on earth, toward the safety of a society so regulated by earnest saints as to include nobody but themselves.[20]

In the *Apology,* More did not revise the polemical strategy by which his refutation furnished the reader a nearly complete account of the adversary's argument, for he reprinted much, and the most telling parts, of Saint-German's *Division.* Already out of the King's favor and removed from the inner circle of counselors, More failed to perceive Henry's blurring of distinctions between Church and State, even then well begun. He confidently predicted that the King would "mayntayne and assist the spiritualtie in executyng of the lawes, euen those that are already made agaynst heresies, and commaund euery temporall officer vnder hym to dooe the same for his parte, though ther wer neuer moe newe lawes made therefore."[21] At the conclusion of the treatise he expressed again the same confidence that Church and State relations as he knew them would not soon be changed and could never be improved.

More's favorite invective in the *Apology* as elsewhere was to label foes as "those that vnder the name of matrimonye, lyue in sacrilege and incestuous lechery, as frere Luther dothe, and frere Lambert, and frere Huskyn."[22] He elaborated the offense of each enemy into an accusation against all. Again he said that the authentication of the Church's teaching arose from the fact that it was the Church's teaching. Still the incessant, repetitive, uninspired verbiage flowed, infrequently punctuated by humor. One new note he added. Humanist aspirations for a hierarchy checked by princes and an increas-

20. Chambers, pp. 99–156 and 256–67, defended More's consistency on the basis of the *Dialogue* but not of the *Apology,* and merely mentioned the important controversies with Saint-German.

21. *Workes,* p. 919.

22. Ibid., p. 889.

ingly educated populace—aspirations shared by More in earlier days—now loomed as attacks upon an embattled Church.
Vernacular scripture, territorial churches, conciliar checks on
papal prerogatives, the merging of temporal and spiritual
authority and law, and religious practices cleansed of their
grosser superstitions now seemed to More to foster the plans
of the Protestant heretics. In his retreat from new learning
to old religion, More branded the humanists' repristinism
with heresy by association.

Saint-German, not subdued, replied swiftly and deftly with
A Dialogue betwixte two Englysshe men—called Salem and
Bizance—anonymously published from Berthelet's press in
London in 1533 (*STC* 21,584), to which *The addicions of
Salem and Byzance* (*STC* 21,585) was added the following
year. More's reply was ready before the end of 1533. Always,
for More, whatever the Church taught was verified by the
fact that the Church taught it. Now, whatever the spiritualty
did was substantiated by the fact that the spiritualty did it.
More carefully blockaded all avenues of thought and action
toward the reform of the established religion. The defender
of Catholic doctrine became apologist for the status quo ante.
The thread running through the *Apology* had been autobiographical, for More defended and explained the manner in
which specific heretics had been dealt with by ecclesiastics
and secular magistrates during his tenure as chancellor. In
answering Saint-German, he exonerated his administration of
the office on jurisprudential and sociological grounds. In *The
Debellacyon of Salem and Bizance* More forswore any intention of ever having wished to propose or allow any reformation of either part of the realm, spiritual or temporal.[23] If
any feature of the status quo worked injustice to a small number of the commonalty, More argued, then any change in the
law predictably would work greater injustice to a greater
number. The wisest course was the traditional course. More
recognized that Saint-German religiously preferred Catholicism over Protestantism, but since his legislative proposals
comforted the Brethren and helped the heretics, they must be
repudiated. *Debellacyon* reasoned calmly, with terrible serious-

23. See especially ch. 2, ibid. pp. 934–36.

ness, almost wistfully, for a stable society and a strong church, unchallenged and unquestioned.

Save for a last vindictive libellus against Joye on the mass, More's *Apology* and *Debellacyon* against Saint-German mark a transition from the task for which Tunstall had chosen him in 1528 to the final phase of his thought and literary endeavor—the beautifully tender meditative and devotional pieces of 1534 and 1535. The security of the Church as warden of civilization had satisfied only the exterior searchings of More's great spirit. Another step awaited him, that of interior wholeness granted—or earned—through personal suffering. He had served the spiritualty and the temporalty without stint. When they clashed, allegiance to the Church proved higher and deeper than allegiance to the throne. Yet beyond that choice, terrible as it was to make, More found haven for his soul in an intensely personal involvement in the mystical piety known to many Catholics of the late middle ages. King's servant he had been. Pope's man he had become. Transcending both of these there came a claim, as More took it, from God himself. Prayer, confession, and the mystery of the mass served their best purpose for More only when he felt and understood his own soul to be united with his God.

Late in life, therefore, More reverted to the devotional writing which, next to his familial letters, best displayed the docile, mystical, and profound religiosity of the man. The little treatise *To Receive the Blessed Body of our Lord, Sacramentally and Virtually Both,* written in 1534, stands in full contrast to his polemical works, especially those against Frith and Joye on the sacrament. As official defender of Catholic teachings, More had been verbose in rhetoric, trite in thought, and personally vindictive. As the King's prisoner he became the noble Catholic, urging by graceful words and pious conviction a holy respect for the sacrament. Even then he was less than a profound theologian, allegorizing as he did scripture and nature, surrendering as gratefully to the certainty of his faith as to the reality thereby apprehended. But the rancor was gone as More bespoke his dedication to Catholicism's most potent miracle. By this time he stood religiously where the detested Luther had stood at Worms and afterwards. When he

was manacled by conscience to the old religion, as Luther was
to the word of God, More's religious stature showed itself
best. Protestant theologians on the Continent quickly forgot
his excoriation of them and stood in horror of Henry's wanton
execution of More; this measured their stature more accurately
than did their diatribes against More's polemics.

More's last letters from the Tower were addressed, his
final affection poured out, to family and friends. Against dangerous heretics, he had bartered humaneness for harshness.
From humanistic hopes he had retreated to ecclesiastical and
social traditionalism. At the end, finding a merciful God, More
received a gift that transcended humaneness and humanism,
for he became serenely human.

16. Epilogue

O judge by palpable tokens of success, the joint efforts of Barnes and Frith, Tyndale and Joye, Roy and Fish toward Church reform between 1520 and 1535 achieved little more than two score banned books, only a handful of them truly constructive theological writings. Yet, although none of these men acquired fame as a church reformer, together they blazed many trails along which English Christianity was led during the ensuing generation by men like Cranmer, Latimer, and even Jewel and Parker. Moreover, they established also the theological and religious platform of biblical moralism that eventually opposed the official Church of England. Theirs were no mean accomplishments. The genius of King Henry, rather than the yearnings of these or any other clerics, must receive credit for the fact that the very England which, in 1520, displayed a fiercer papal loyalty than any contemporary European principality, had, by 1535, unilaterally revoked these ties. But when the national Church, then and later, searched out a doctrine, discipline, and worship as unique as its royalist polity, many of the ideas and some of the words of these early Protestants, along with those of Marian martyrs, came to be regarded as the faith once delivered to the saints, and found a resurrected life that their authors never dared hope for. And an even greater legacy was left by these men to the long, loyal, but stubborn Puritan opposition to the Elizabethan and Stuart Church.

The earliest English Protestant ranks counted some men of mediocre to moderate talents, and one or two figures blessed by genuine but limited genius, but nobody of virtuosity comparable to that of a Luther, Calvin, or even a Melanchthon, Bucer, Cranmer, or Hooker. But their self-sacrificing conviction and persistence drew strength from oppression and compensated for the modesty of their abilities. They wrote boldly and published increasingly. Their most ambitious single project, to print the entire Bible in English, was accomplished after a decade of awful difficulties. They nurtured their devotees at home, few but steadfast, at every cost, including that of life itself. To match wits with the brilliant they pooled their learning, and by sharing their stamina they defied the mighty. They listened to a multitude of Protestant voices from Germany, Switzerland, France, and the Low Countries, reading widely in the profusion of Reformation pamphlets that circulated during their exile, and from these conflicting sources they forged a consistent if not unanimous interpretation of Christianity to present to their countrymen. Out of their thinking sprang fundamental insights, of course imperfectly explicated, around which were polarized later Puritan and Anglican positions that kept English-speaking Christianity in conflict for a century and a half.

THE ENGLISH BIBLE

Ten years after Tyndale and Roy had published their translation of the first gospel from Cologne, Coverdale published the first complete printed English Bible: *BIBLIA The Bible/ that is, the holy Scripture of the Olde and New Testament, faithfully and truly translated out of Douche and Latyn into Englishe (STC* 2063). That achievement crowned the work and fulfilled the aspirations of his predecessors, whose individual translations he knew well and freely employed. By the end of 1534, Convocation, under Cranmer, petitioned the King to authorize a translation of scripture, encouraging Coverdale to proceed with his project in October 1535. Want of royal approval hindered his Bible as it had impeded the English New Testament. Almost two more years were to elapse, and Tyndale was in his grave, before the willful Henry, persuaded by Cromwell and Cranmer, finally allowed the "Matthew Bible" to circulate with his approbation. But if the delayed authorization postponed Tyndale's, Frith's, and Roy's posthumous success, the acceptance of the Bible edited by John Rogers in 1537

ironically magnified the victory, for it contained far more of
Tyndale's prized verbiage, and more of Joye's rendition of the
Old Testament, too, than Coverdale's version had included.

However justly celebrated may be the very fact of an authorized English Bible, the influence of these men upon English
Christianity must be measured by the character of the Bible
that Henry and succeeding monarchs allowed. Quite beyond
any legitimate expectations that might have accompanied Convocation's 1534 request, the approved Bible of 1537 was a
thoroughly Protestant book. Had More been alive, he might
have claimed again that this was no true Bible, but Tyndale's
or Luther's or Coverdale's. For Rogers, who signed the dedication to Henry VIII "Thomas Matthew," relied wherever
possible on the work of previous translators, and thus presented
most of Tyndale's New Testament and pentateuch. Rogers
himself only finished the apocryphal books. Although by 1541
Cranmer, who once preferred this book, sponsored an edition
of the more eclectic and humanistic "Great Bible," nevertheless
Tyndale more than any other man chose the words in which
subsequent generations of English readers were to learn the
word of God. Moreover, prefaces and explanations by Tyndale,
and by Erasmus through Roy, interpreted the more prominent
sixteenth-century editions of English scripture, and Joye's
renderings of scriptural passages often used in worship left
indelible tracings on subsequent Bibles and liturgies.

But the men who first made the modern English Bible had no
taste of success, unless one reckons as success the large demand
for New Testaments that prompted printings and revisions in
the early 1530s—and even that came only after several years.
On the Continent, vernacular Bibles quickly stirred and strictly
controlled religious reform, but when in England the light of
scripture shone, the darkness almost comprehended it. Whereas
on the Continent scripture generated reformation, in England
the prize and goal of reformation was the Bible—a prize
finally bestowed not by Church but by Crown. Then the jealously
guarded books were chained to the lecterns in church and venerated at home. The very difficulties that impeded the progress
of the English Bible during our period determined the way
in which the book came to be read and understood and revered.

First proffered as the free gospel for all the people, the original printed Testaments were burnt by the Church. Next presented as a balanced diet of socially conservative law and religiously liberal promises, major portions of both Testaments encountered royal opposition. Finally interpreted as a contract made between God and everyman, the whole Bible won its way into Church and domestic life by royal leave. The progression was toward an ever more insistent, definite, and confining interpretation of the Bible's central meaning and of Christianity's fundamental character.

Achieving their goal cost the English Protestants not only enormous personal sacrifices but also ominous theological adjustments. The book that evoked stiff opposition demanded particular advocacy. No other branch of Protestantism so early or so necessarily as the English engaged in forensic pleadings for the divine word. English Protestant leaders devised various briefs; Tyndale's contract notion and Frith's adiaphora idea, when explicated, represent sharp divergences. Tyndale's view prevailed, and cohered nicely with certain tenets of the biblical humanists and the Lollards; his introductions and marginal comments were neatly complemented by Roy's translation of Erasmus' *Paraclesis*. Not accidentally, these introductory and explanatory writings set guidelines for most sixteenth-century English Bible introductions, exemplified by Coverdale's and Cranmer's, and reflected in Matthew Parker's preface to the "Bishops' Bible" of 1568 (*STC* 2099). The earliest English Protestants not only produced Bible translations that have indirectly but powerfully guided revisions down to our own time, but they also established the hermeneutical compass points which readers have used to make their way through the holy scriptures.

STRATEGIC SUCCESSES

But one need not look to the years after 1535 to find significant Protestant successes in England. Already, with the appearance of the first pages of the New Testament at Cologne in 1525—pages which the inquisitorial Cochlaeus bought and destroyed as thoroughly as possible—the papal Church was assuming a defensive stance toward the spread of the new teaching in England, and Protestants took every advantage of this defensiveness. By mid-1526 the Church in England had publicly burnt the word of God, testifying its fear of any translation as well as its condemnation of a particular translation. The brilliant Fisher, who preached at the book-burning gala on Quinquagesima Sunday that year, unwittingly reversed the earlier policy of affirming Catholicism, not defending it—a policy he had helped to sustain, a policy defensible because it was not merely defensive. Symbolizing England's initial reaction to Luther, the *Assertio* bearing the King's name really asserted all the Church's seven sacraments. Then Fisher and More wrote affirmatively Catholic tomes in Latin. But after the new Protestant aggressions of 1525 and 1526, Catholic defenders tended merely to negate their foes, affirming nothing more than the categorical (and implicitly negative) inerrancy of every Catholic thought and deed.

When Tunstall commissioned Thomas More to refute the Protestants in English, the exiles implicitly scored another success, for this move forced the argument over Church reform into their favorite medium, the vernacular tongue, and they secured for the debate a friendly jury in the simple men and women who already inclined toward reform. More's commission was effective when he wrote the impressive *Dialogue* and the clever *Supplication of Souls*. But Protestants answered vehemently and voluminously, taunting More to cite them accurately. Conscientiously performing his commission to the letter, an overburdened More during his chancellorship published books that legally spread the enemy's illicit propaganda by his use of citations. Then the Protestants, by forcing upon him a superhuman volume of work if he attempted to answer each of their books, finally elicited his tacit admission of defeat and an expressed yearning, in the face of dwindling royal support, that he had never undertaken his task.

More pursued his rigorous policy against heretics as long as he kept the seal, and allowed Protestants no opportunity to capitalize the successes they scored against him. But they pilfered his richest reserves when they called to testify for them the very biblical humanists whose program for reform the younger More had embraced. The intellectual vigor and popular appeal of the learned transferred to the Protestants when, for example, Tyndale translated Erasmus' *Enchiridion of a Christian Knight,* and Roy conjoined Erasmus' plea for the vernacular Bible with Luther's attack on clerical celibacy. By 1535, the publishers Turner and Marshall virtually alternated their printing activities between Protestant tracts or primers and humanist writings calling for church reform. The alienation of More from the humanists, thus effected in the minds of his readers, became an actual disaffection in More's mind before his death.

Church authorities trying to abolish heretical books carefully discriminated between humanistic and Protestant writings, even to the point of damning the Lutheran but not the Erasmian part of Roy's conjoined translations. The indices of heretical writings made by Church authorities prior to 1534 were astonishingly thorough, notwithstanding their neglect of Barnes. But apparently, even in those times, to be banned increased a work's popularity and inflated its value. When they could, the Protestants turned this to their advantage, financing another New Testament edition with money the Church had paid to buy up and destroy a previous edition.

In England, as in all Europe, the actual spread of the sixteenth-century Reformation would have been unthinkable without the new craft of printing; but the fact remains that in England between 1520 and 1535 the Protestants, whose writers lived in exile, poverty, and danger, and whose books were proscribed, took greater advantage of printing than did the Catholics, whose religion was established and whose resources were vast. Theological tomes by Europe's Church reformers circulated widely in the universities from 1520 onward, and as some of these appeared in translation along with original works by English Protestants, London supported a brisk import trade in contraband publications. Certainly Protestant literary activity provided the occasion, if not the formal cause, for transferring power over publishing from Church to Crown. Until the royal proclamation of 1538, the regulation of reading in England remained largely an ecclesiastical prerogative, and when, for example, London printers grew lax, it was the bishop who brought them into line. The policy of licensing books *cum privilegio regali,* which Henry proclaimed in 1529, began to shift control to King and privy council, and during the ensuing decade there was much confusion until, in 1538, the King insisted that this slogan of privilege be qualified by the words *ad imprimendum solum.* This change in the supervision of printing paralleled many another royal assumption of prerogatives formerly exercised by the Church, but in fact this one climaxed an era during which the Church had ardently tried to suppress Protestant writings and biblical translations, and had failed. In fact, if not in the King's intent, royal regulation of printing signaled a certain success of the literary endeavors of the early English Protestants.

SOURCES

Throughout Europe in the early sixteenth century, printed books made effective religious propaganda. Therefore, while Englishmen in exile tried to shape the destiny of their Church at home, they read widely in a vast array of signed, anonymous, pseudonymous, original, pirated, and translated continental theological polemics—a fact that makes identification of the English writings bristle with difficulties. From a variety of these books the Englishmen found inspiration, ideas, and terminology. They translated those that they considered most directly applicable to home circumstances, and the thoughts and expressions of many others supplied themes and paragraphs in what passed for their original compositions.

None of the early English Protestants, for the moment discounting Barlowe, finished his career without having translated into English either a book or a long passage by Luther. Their interest in him extended throughout our period. Despite that fact, however, Luther's thought by no means determined the theological and religious character of the Englishmen's writings. Among them, only Frith continued to adhere to the theocentric mode of Luther's thinking, and even Frith's application of that thinking to specific religious problems owed more to Oecolampadius than to Luther. While the Englishmen repeatedly paid lip service to Luther's side in his controversy with Erasmus on free will, they yet remained more enamored of Erasmus than Luther ever was, and they owed much of their program for Church reformation to the Hollander. The gospels and epistles seemed to Tyndale and Barnes to be the *fontes* of true Christianity, as they had seemed to Colet and still seemed to Erasmus. Spiritual meditation upon the future life, more than the Lutheran motif of forgiveness, colored the thinking of the English circle, including Frith, just as it did the theology of Erasmus in our period and that of Calvin later on. The Englishmen regarded infinite realities as generally incapable of embodiment in or of communication through finite objects—a point of view shared by Zwingli and the Christian humanists.

The Englishmen's affinity for Erasmian patterns of thought led them to stronger theological and religious affinities with Swiss than with Saxon reformers. If each of them translated Luther, yet each was in debt to Rhineland thinkers such as Bucer, Zwingli, Oecolampadius, and perhaps Vadianus and Farel. To be sure, Bugenhagen, at Wittenberg, wrote a letter to the English that Tyndale probably translated, and he helped guide Barnes' early writings; and Bugenhagen, at Hamburg, probably aided Tyndale and Coverdale when they were translating the pentateuch. But the chief English handbook of Protestant beliefs to appear before 1535 was the *Sum of the Scripture,* certainly a reformed, not an evangelical book, and probably Genevan in provenance. Barnes' major literary and intellectual source before 1535 was *Unio Dissidentium,* possibly Bucer's, and he also relied heavily, as did Tyndale, upon *Vom Alten und Neuen Gott,* possibly by Vadianus. Joye first chose Bucer's Latin as text for his English psalter, then Zwingli's seemed the better one; he used some catechetical material of Luther's in his primers, but he took his tract on *The Souper of the Lorde* largely from Zwingli. Frith openly professed his borrowings from Oecolampadius. Roy translated the *Proper Dyaloge* because he admired its control of the religious life of the Strassburgers under Bucer's leadership.

Granted the heavy debt to Rhenish Reformation thought, early English Protestants maintained a certain independence when they recommended ways of purging their own Church, at least to the extent that their familiarity with late Lollard predilections transmuted and overruled ideas learned from

southern Protestants on the Continent. Similarities between
Tyndale's contract theology and Rhineland Reformation
doctrine account for the development of his seminal idea less
directly than does his wrestling with the temporary failure of
the vernacular Bible to recommend itself to English Christians.
Each cohort brought his own originality to his thinking and
writing. Though they all were epigonous craftsmen dependent
upon the continental Reformation's early creative masters, none
was only a slavish apprentice. Their works followed customary
forms, but Joye employed his own flair for stimulating private
devotion, Tyndale's own idiom regulated English Bible revisions for centuries, Fish's propaganda bore the imprint of
the able lawyer, Barnes developed an adeptness at turning
the Church's canons against the papacy, Frith's young genius
was no transplant, and even Roy's "railing rhymes" were
original.

Though in style and religion the pupils of Luther, these men
had a prior commitment to biblical humanism and a growing
preference for Swiss reformers. Yet each cultivated his own
endowments and employed his own genius in proposing that
England follow the rediscovered gospel into a spiritual religion
and a biblically regulated Church. Continental thinkers as
diverse as Erasmus and Luther and Zwingli contributed to their
theology, but their impact upon English-speaking Christianity
was their own.

IMPACT

The early English Protestants strove to frame concepts
in their native tongue so as to change their own Church. As they
imbued a movement with an idiom, they marked English religion in ways that have been perpetuated down the centuries.
Thereby they joined such men as Tertullian, who, by first
writing Christian theology in Latin, left western Christianity
his eminent practicality and slogan-mindedness; or as Jerome,
who, by compiling medieval Christianity's Latin Bible, bequeathed to a millennium his own monkishness; or as Luther,
who, by first stating the rediscovered gospel in modern German,
impressed religious poignancy and theological meticulousness
upon the tradition that bears his name. These few Englishmen,

by first coining the language and choosing the emphatic concerns of English-speaking Protestantism, left marks not yet erased by religious and cultural upheavals.

Their interest ran more to morality than to theology. To be sure, each member of the circle took Luther's cardinal teaching on justification by faith as axiomatic. But, whereas for Luther faith and justification primarily denoted the humble posture of forgiven sinners in the presence of a compassionate God, the Englishmen construed justification by faith as initiating a morally blameless life characterized by observing God's laws in one's daily deeds. For Luther, faith resulted in a trust that could sin bravely, while for the Englishmen faith resulted in an obedience that could eschew sin.

Making religion ancillary to morality encouraged impatience with theology as an intellectual discipline. For these men, the act, however admirable in itself, of honoring God with the mind by affirming his merciful majesty and by appreciating his marvelous creation, fell short of and tended to usurp the primary function of reflecting the love of God toward mankind by performing the deeds of love commanded by divine law. They made the initial choice that placed England in the camp of re-formed rather than evangelical Christianity. It has proved an irreversible choice, as later generations have successively rein-forced this alliance between religion and morality. Long before the Reformation, Christianity in Britain inclined toward theo-logical voluntarism and away from intellectualism, as witnessed by its two great scholastic thinkers, John Duns Scotus and William of Ockham. Lollardy had demonstrated popular readiness for stiff moral sanctions derived from religion, as clearly as it demonstrated a desire for church reform. The progenitors of the English Reformation maintained continuity with a distinct moralistic tradition, but it was their choice to place good works at the summit of the Christian endeavor even while confessing that only faith might initially impel the believer toward that summit.

More specifically than that, however, the individual work of these men directly influenced certain aspects of English religion. Church reform under the crown's aegis by dissolution of mon-asteries, authorization of scripture in the common tongue, and

prohibition of episcopal oaths of allegiance to the Pope—a
fair summary of important Henrician reforms after 1534—
had been suggested in detail by Fish as early as 1528 or 1529
in his inflammatory *Supplication for the Beggars*. Barnes
attuned his political theory to the times, implored his prince to
assume direct control over ecclesiastical authority, and also
sketched the outlines of what was to become a typical Anglican
appeal to right interpretation of scripture by using a supposed
consensus of the early Church fathers as criterion.

Frith similarly argued that the central eucharistic question
of the meaning of the words of institution must be settled by
patristic consensus. Frith borrowed that solution, as well as
the selection of relevant patristic sentences, from Oecolampadius, but his pleading in the final controversy with More expressed his own constructive thought. Although Cranmer joined
other members of the episcopal bench in condemning Frith
as a heretic for precisely these views, the Archbishop, in later
drawing up the authorized English liturgy, adopted the emphasis upon spiritual presence that Frith had wanted to control
eucharistic doctrine. Thus Frith became, after his death, the
"mid dealer"—to use his own phrase—of sacramental teachings
between Basel and Canterbury.

Joye sharply influenced the common worship that was prescribed under Edward VI even before Joye died, for the first
two printed primers in English that he edited and published
stand in direct continuity with the offices of daily morning and
evening prayer that Cranmer devised for the 1549 and 1552
prayerbooks. Moreover, Joye wrote into English Reformation
thought the eucharistic emphasis of Zwingli upon memorial
aspects of the Supper, a prominent feature in the mind of
Cranmer and in the liturgies he compiled.

Nor was Cranmer the only Reformation leader to adopt
teachings first expressed in English by the early Protestant
exiles, for John Jewel, bishop of Salisbury and the theologian
whom Elizabeth I commissioned to distinguish Anglican from
papal Christianity, taught precisely what Barnes, Tyndale,
Frith, and Joye had taught regarding spiritual authority. Jewel
lodged the power of clergy, including bishops, in the preaching of the word of God; for him precisely and only that activity

turned the keys of the kingdom and bound or loosed the souls of men and women. From the same sources, Jewel took his notion of appeal to scripture through the fathers. Barnes' essay on the true keys is the English historical and literary source of Jewel's teaching on that subject.

John Foxe's estimate of Tyndale, Barnes, Frith, Joye, Roy, and Fish as founding fathers of English Protestantism demands no qualification unless it is misconstrued to attribute little importance to men who—like Cranmer, Latimer, Ridley, Parker, Jewel, and Hooker—later wrought changes in Church doctrine and practice. Foxe read history correctly when he located the principles of English Protestantism under Elizabeth I in the writings of Protestant exiles before 1535, for these men defined much of the content of English Church reform. They were bold men, ready to embrace Protestant views even at great personal cost. Less daring men upheld their King as spiritual head of the Church even while they effected changes based on the tenets that not long before had led to martyrdom.

The primacy of the Bible over all religion, issuing in moral living, however, could not be reconciled with the primacy of the Crown over all religion, issuing in uniform worship. All the earliest English Protestant writers, even those who suggested that Henry assume control over the hierarchy, taught that the word of God, understood as holy scripture, must regulate all things, even the manner in which a prince would guide the Church whose head he might become. Fisher's so-called saving clause, "so far as the law of God allows," saved nothing until one defined the law of God and qualified royal headship in terms of some particular definition of that law. Even Barnes, the most avid king's man among the exiles of our period, insisted that the law of God was to be found only in the Bible. Tyndale taught that whatever scripture said (excepting ceremonial regulations) must be acceded to as God's law. Therefore, even while these exiles influenced many details of reform approved by Henry, Edward, or Elizabeth, their first rule of Christianity and their general understanding of it actually formed the basis of Puritan opposition to the established Tudor Church.

Cranmer, Latimer, Ridley, and Hooper could serve the

royal head of the Church as long as Henry and Edward exercised that office in a generally Protestant—anti-papal—way, but when Mary Tudor abdicated that headship in favor of Tridentine papalism, these men died for their conviction that the law of God prohibited papal Catholicism. After Elizabeth's settlement, Jewel had no quarrel with royal headship as Elizabeth exercised it; in a Protestant succession she was "supreme governor," but under the saving clause Jewel could refer strictly religious questions strictly to scripture. Hooker, Elizabeth's anti-Genevan polemicist, found the law of Christ in Bible, fathers, and human reason, thus investing the Crown with an ecclesiastical authority far more philosophically grounded than any to which Henry ever pretended. But no reforming Tudor monarch placed his sovereignty over Church or temporalty under the rule of the Bible as *lex dei*.

England's earliest Protestants, especially Tyndale, read scripture as God's law, and taught that God bound himself to the terms of biblical law so strictly that only scripture might be God's law. Their biblical, covenantal, moral Christianity logically and actually conflicted with the royal, hierarchical, liturgical Christianity that Ecclesia Anglicana, even under Henry, adopted. But the original English Protestantism can with accuracy as well as convenience be called by the later term, Puritan. The royal, hierarchical, liturgical version of English Protestantism was a reaction against the Puritan dependence in all details of English life, religious and common, on the Old and New Testaments. Tyndale founded English Puritanism as the theological, religious, and moral system that univocally regarded scripture as God's law for everyman, binding everyman and God together in a contract that enjoined and rewarded strict morality. This theologically legalistic and religiously moralistic system, when made explicit, as it increasingly was, struggled relentlessly against official Anglican ecclesiasticism. During the sixteenth century it never prevailed, but neither did it surrender. In the seventeenth century it resorted to regicide, its logical answer to divine right monarchy. After the "Glorious Revolution," it won its right to exist as legalized nonconformity. During the oppression of a century and a half, it had become the religion of the common man throughout what, by 1689, was already an incipient English-speaking "world." Always, its chief advocate has been the English Bible, conceived as a book that tells the faithful man what God would have him do, how God would prosper the obedient, and how God would punish both faithlessness and disobedience. It was the early Protestants, most clearly Tyndale, who caused that Bible to speak that message.

One of the earliest English Protestant writers had attempted to present to England another version of Christianity, neither royal-hierarchical-liturgical nor biblical-covenantal-moral, although it had certain affinities with the latter. Frith had pleaded a pervasively theological Christianity, concerned first and last with the presence of a merciful God to the inner life of the humble believer. Spiritualistic in tendency, Frith's theocentrism regarded all external religion, whether concerned with creed, cult, or conduct, as indifferent in comparison to a forgiven life of trusting faith in a merciful God. Thus, for Frith, both the laws of ecclesiastical polity that preoccupied the later Anglicans, and the laws of biblical morality that preoccupied the later Puritans, were laws that did not ultimately matter for the believer who walked humbly *coram deo*. Before he could explicate his understanding of Christianity as theologically crucial but religiously indifferent, Frith's life ended. Ever since, English-speaking religion has preferred the battle between royal churchly worship and biblically moral living over a theological and spiritual struggle for faith.

Bibliography

SINCE this study deals mainly with certain Englishmen who, in addition to writing original compositions, translated and edited works composed by other writers, this bibliography ascribes such publications—even biblical ones—to their English translators or editors. Places, publishers, and dates are given for early printed books whenever possible, even in cases where these matters are uncertain and under dispute.

In the bibliography, C stands for entries in the masterful but increasingly outmoded *Short-Title Catalogue* compiled in 1926 by Alfred William Pollard and others; in the text and notes these entries have been indicated by *STC*. N stands for the more recent and more authoritative *Nederlandsche Bibliographie van 1500 tot 1540* by Wouter Nijhoff and Maria Elizabeth Kronenberg, referred to in text and notes as *Ned. Bibl.* A few titles show entry numbers designated as DG, for the *Gesamtkatalog der Preussischen Bibliotheken,* published during the 1930s but reaching barely into the second letter of the alphabet. "N.pl." indicates that place or provenance is not known, "n.pr." that the printer is not known, and "n.d." that the date is not known. In the first section, subsidiary sources and editions are marked by asterisks to distinguish them from primary sources.

For other abbreviations, see pp. vii–viii.

I. SOURCES

Abell, Thomas, *Inuicta veritas. An answere that by no maner of lawe it maye be lawfull for kinge Henry the Ayght to be diuorsid,* Antwerp, M. deKeyser, 1532. C-61. N-2224.

[Anonymous] *The xv. Oos in Englysshe with other prayers,* London, R. Copland, 1529. C-20,196.

[Anonymous] *Here begynneth a lytell boke that speaketh of Purgatorye,* London, R. Wyer, ca. 1536?. C-3360X (Huntington Library).

[Anonymous] *The institution of a Christen man,* London, T. Berthelet, 1537. C-5163.

[Anonymous] *Summa totivs sacrae scripturae. Bibliorum veteris & noui testamenti,* Antwerp, J. Grapheus, 1533. N-1970.

[Anonymous] *La Summe de lescripture saincte/ et lordinaire des Chrestiens enseignant la vraye foy Chrestienne,* Basel, T. Wolff, 1523.

Bale, John, *Acta Romanorum Pontificum, a dispersione discipulorum Christi,* n.pl., n.pr., 1559.

———— *Illvstrivm Maioris Britanniae Scriptorvm,* Ipswich, J. Overton, 1548. C-1295.

———— *The pageant of Popes, contayning the lyues of all the bishops of Rome,* London, T. Marshe, 1574. C-1304.

———— joint author, see Barnes, Robert, *Scriptores . . .*

Barlowe, Jerome [or William?], *A dyaloge descrybyng the orygynal ground of these Lutheran faccyons,* London, W. Rastell, 1531. C-1461.

———— joint author, see Roy, William, *A proper . . .* and *Rede me . . .*

Barnes, Robert, *Bapst trew Hadriani iiij vnd Alexanders III,* foreword (and translated?) by Martin Luther, Wittenberg, J. Clug, 1545.

———— *Bekantnus dess Glauben,* foreword by Martin Luther, Wittenberg, Nickel Schirlentz, 1540.

———— *Bekantnus dess Glaubens,* Augsburg, M. Ramiger, 1540.

———— *Fürnemlich Artickel der Christenlichen kirchen,* foreword (and translated) by Johann Bugenhagen, Nürnberg, J. Petri?, 1531. DG-11.7404.

———— *Furnemlich Artickel der Christlichen kirchen,* foreword (and translated) by Johann Bugenhagen, Nürnberg, J. Petri?, 1531. DG-11.7403.

*———— and John Bale, *Scriptores duo Anglici coaetanei ac conterranei de vitis Pontificum Romanorum,* edited and continued by Johannes Martinus Lydius, 3 vols. in 1, Lugduni Batavorum, Georgius Abrahami A. Marsse, 1615.

———— [*pseud.* Antonius Anglus] *Sentenciae ex doctoribus collectae, quas papistae ualde impudenter hodie damnant,* preface by Johann Bugenhagen, Wittenberg, J. Clug, 1530. DG-11.7400.

———— *A supplicacion vnto the most gracyous prynce H. the .viii.,* London, J. Byddell, 1534. C-1471.

———— *The supplication of doctour Barnes vnto the moost gracyous kynge Henrye the eyght,* London, H. Syngelton [1550?]. C-1472.

———— *A supplicatyon made by Robert Barnes doctoure in diuinite vnto the most excellent and redoubted prince kinge henrye the eyght,* Antwerp, S. Cock, 1531. C-1470. N-2372.

————— *Vitae Romanorum Pontificum, quos Papas vocamus, diligenter & fideliter collectae,* foreword by Martin Luther, Wittenberg, J. Clug, 1536. DG-11.7405.

————— *Die weyl yetz so grosse spaltung in allen Christen ist,* n.pl., n.pr., 1533. DG-11.7394. [See also DG-11.7395-11.7399.]

*————— joint author, see Tyndale, William, *The Whole workes . . .* and *Writings . . .*

*Benrath, Karl, editor, *Die Summa der Heiligen Schrift. Ein Zeugniss aus dem Zeitalter der Reformation für die Rechtfertigung aus dem Glauben,* Leipzig, L. Fernau, 1880.

Bodius, Hermannus, *pseud., Certein Places gathered ovt of .S. Austeus* [sic] *Boke intituled de essentia diuinitatis,* London, W. Hill, 1548. C-919.

————— *pseud., Vnio dissidentium,* Cologne, n.pr., 1522. [See N-2523-2525, 4127, 4313-4315, 01,293.]

*————— *pseud., Vnio Dissidentivm, Libellvs omnibvs vnitatis ac facis amatoribvs vtilissimus . . . selectus,* Basel, N. Bryling, 1551.

*Bomelius, Henricus, *Bellum Trajectinum,* edited by B. J. L. Geer van Jutphaas (Werken uitg. door het Historisch genootschap, gevestigd te Utrecht, Nieuwe reeks, 28), Utrecht, Kemink and Zoon, 1878.

*————— *Het oudste nederlandsche verboden Boek. 1523. Oeconomica christiana. Summa der godliker Schrifturen,* edited by Johan Justus van Toorenenbergen (Monumenta Reformationis Belgicae, *1*), Leiden, E. J. Brill, 1882.

————— *Oeconomica Christiana in rem christianam instituens,* Strassburg, n.pr., 1527.

————— *translator, Summa Der godliker scriftvren Oft een duytsche theologie,* n.pl., n.pr., ca. 1523? N-3910. [See also N-1968, 3911.]

*Bradshaw, Henry, *A half-century of notes on the Daybook of John Dorne, bookseller in Oxford, A. D. 1520,* Cambridge, F. Madan, 1886.

Brinkelow, Henry, joint author, see Fish, Simon, *A supplication . . .*

Bugenhagen, Johann, *A compendious letter which Jhon Pomerane . . . sent to . . . Englande,* n.pl., n.pr., 1536. C-4021.

————— *De coniugio episcoporum et diaconorum, ad uenerandum Doctorem Wolfgangum Reissenbusch,* Nürnberg, J. Petri, 1525.

*————— *Dr. Johannes Bugenhagen Briefwechsel,* edited by Otto Vogt, Stettin, Léon Saunier, 1888.

————— *Epistola J. Bugenhagii Pomerani ad Anglos,* Wittenberg, N. Schirlentz, 1525.

*Bullinger, Heinrich, joint author, see Zwingli, Huldreich, *Zwingli*
. . .
Cochlaeus, i.e. Johannes Dobnek, *Epistola Johannis Bugenhagii Pom-erani ad Anglos. Responsio.* N.pl., n.pr., 1526.
Colet, John, *The sermon of Doctor Colete made to the conuocation at Paulis,* London, T. Berthelet, 1520?. C-5550.
Coverdale, Miles, *translator, Biblia the bible that is the holy scrypture,* n.pl., n.pr., 1535. C-2063.
*———— *translator, The Holy Scriptures, Faithfully and truly trans-lated By Myles Coverdale, Bishop of Exeter, 1535. Reprinted from the Copy in the Library of His Royal Highness the Duke of Sussex, for Samuel Bagster,* London, for Samuel Bagster, 1838.
———— *translator,* Johannes Campensis, *A Paraphrase upon all the Psalms of David,* Antwerp, 1534 [not extant].
Cranmer, Thomas, *translator?,* Edward Fox, *The determinations of the moste famous Universities of Italy and Fraunce,* London, T. Berthelet, 1531. C-11,218.
———— editor, *The byble in Englyshe. With a prologe by Thomas archbysshop of Cantorbury,* London, E. Whytchurche, 1540. C-2070.
*Dearmer, Percy, editor, *Religious Pamphlets* (The Pamphlet Library, edited by Arthur Waugh), London, Kegan Paul, Trench, Trübner, 1898. [Contains Simon Fish, *A Supplication for the Beggars.*]
*Dorne, John, "Day-book of John Dorne, bookseller in Oxford, 1520," edited by Falconer Madan, Oxford Historical Society *Collectanea,* First Series, *1* (1885), 71–177.
*Ellis, Henry, editor, *Original Letters Illustrative of English History,* First Series, 3 vols. London, Harding, Triphook and Lepard, 1824.
[England, Proclamations], *A proclamation for resysting heresyes,* Lon-don, R. Pynson, 1528. C-7772.
*Erasmus, Desiderius, *Opera omnia,* edited by Jean LeClerc, 10 vols. Lugdunum Batavorum, Petri Vander Aa, 1703–1706.
*———— *Opus Epistolarum Des. Erasmi Roterodami,* edited by P. S. Allen et al., 11 vols. Oxford, Clarendon Press, 1906–1947.
———— *Paraclesis,* Basel, J. Frobenius, 1520.
———— editor, *Nouum Instrumentum omne, diligenter . . . recog-nitum & emandatum,* Basel, J. Frobenius, 1516.
*Fish, Simon, et al., *Four Supplications 1529–1553 A.D.,* edited by J. Meadows Cowper, re-edited by Frederick J. Furnivall (Early Eng-lish Text Society, Extra Series, 13), London, Kegan Paul, Trench, Trübner, 1871; reprinted 1891, 1905.
———— *Klagbrieff oder Supplication der armen dürfftigen in Engen-landt an den König daselb gestellet,* n.pl., n.pr., 1529.

———— *A supplicacyon for the beggers*, Antwerp, J. Grapheus?, 1528. C-10,883. N-3032.

*———— [Simon Fish, of Gray's Inn, Gentleman], *A Supplication for the Beggars* [Spring of 1529], edited by Edward Arber (The English Scholar's Library, 4), London, Edward Arber, 1878.

———— and Henry Brinkelow [*pseud*. Roderyck Mors], *A supplication of the poore Commons, whereunto is added the Supplication of beggars*, London, n.pr., 1546. C-10,884.

———— *Supplicatorius Libellus pauperum, et egentium nomine, Henricho VIII*, n.pl., n.pr., 1530.

———— translator, *The summe of the holye scripture and ordinarye of the Christen teachyng*, Antwerp?, J. Hoochstraten?, 1529. C-3036. N-3912. [See also C-3036a-3041.]

Fisher, John, *Assertionis Lutheranae Confutatio*, Cologne, P. Quentell, 1523.

———— *Contio in Ioh. xv.26. versa in latinum per R. Pacaeum*, Cambridge, J. Siberch, 1521. C-10,898.

*———— *Defence of the priesthood*, translated from the original *Sacri sacerdotii defensio contra Lutherum*, by P. E. Hallett, London, Burns, Oates and Washburn, 1935.

———— *Defensio Regie assertionis contra Babylonicam captivitatem . . . ad maledicentissimum Martini Lutheri libellum*, Cologne, P. Quentell, 1525.

———— *De veritate corporis et sanguinis Christi in Eucharistia . . . Aduersus Iohannem Oecolampadium*, Cologne, P. Quentell, 1527.

*———— *English Works*, edited by John E. B. Mayor (Early English Text Society, Extra Series, 27), London, N. Trübner, 1876; reprinted 1935.

———— *Hereafter ensueth two fruytfull sermons*, London, W. Rastell, 1532. C-10,909.

———— *Sacri sacerdotii defensio contra Lutherum*, Cologne, P. Quentell, 1525.

*———— *Sermon against Luther*, the first part, "A defence of the papal authority"; reprinted from the first edition (1521), Ditchling, St. Dominic's Press, 1935.

———— *A sermon had at Paulis by the commandment of . . . my lord legate . . . vpon quinquagesom sonday concernynge certayne heretickes*, London, T. Berthelet, 1528?. C-10,892.

———— *The sermon of Iohan the bysshop of Rochester made agayn ye pernicyous doctryn of M luuther*, London, W. de Worde, 1521?. C-10,893. [See also C-10,894–10,897.]

Fox, Edward, *Grauissimae totius Italiae et Galliae Academiarum censurae,* London, T. Berthelet, 1530. C-14,286.

———— *Opus eximium, de vera differentia regiae potestatis et ecclesiasticae,* London, T. Berthelet, 1534. C-11,218.

Foxe, John, *Actes and monuments of these latter and perillous dayes,* London, J. Day, 1563. C-11,222.

———— *Actes and monuments . . . Newly reuised and . . . augmented, and now the fourth time agayne published,* 2 vols. London, J. Daye, 1583. C-11,225.

*————, *The Acts and Monuments of John Foxe,* edited by Josiah Pratt, 4th ed. 8 vols. London, The Religious Tract Society, 1877.

———— *De non plectendis adulteris,* London, H. Syngelton, 1548. C-11,235.

———— *The first (-second) volume of the Eccesiasticall history contaynyng the Actes and Monumentes . . . Newly . . . inlarged by the Author,* 2 vols. London, J. Daye, 1570. C-11,223.

Frith, John, *A boke made by Iohn Frith prisoner in the Tower of London answeringe vnto M mores lettur,* "Münster, Conrade Willems" [Antwerp?], 1533. C-11,381. N-3042.

———— and Richard Tracy?, *The contentes of thys Booke. The first is a letter which was wryten vnto the faythfull followers of Christes Gospell. Also an other treatyse called the Myrrour or glasse to know thy selfe. Here vnto is added a propre instruction, teaching a man to dye gladly, and not to feare death,* n.pl., n.pr., n.d. C-11,386.

———— *A disputacion of purgatorye made by Iohan Frith which is deuided in to thre bokes,* Antwerp, S. Cock, 1531. C-11,388. N-3043.

———— *A disputacion of Purgatorye made by Ihoñ Frith whiche is deuided in to thre bokes,* Antwerp, M. deKeyser, 1535. C-11,387. N-0526.

———— *A mirrour or glasse to know thy selfe,* Antwerp?, n.pr., ca. 1533. C-11,390. N-4230.

———— *A myrroure or lokynge glasse wherein you may beholde the Sacramente of baptisme described,* London, J. Daye, 1548?. C-11,391.

———— *An other boke against Rastel named the sybsedye or bulwark to his fyrst boke,* Antwerp, M. deKeyser, after 1537. C-11,385. N-0525.

*———— et al., *Vox Piscis: or, The Book-fish Contayning Three Treatises,* edited by T[homas] G[ood], London, printed for Iames Boler and Robert Milbovrne, 1626. C-11,395.

———— [*pseud.* Richard Brightwell], *translator,* Martin Luther, *A pistle to the Christen reader The revelation of Antichrist. Antithesis,* Antwerp, J. Hoochstraten, 1529. C-15,060. N-3044.

——— *translator,* Patrick Hamilton, *Dyuers frutful gatheringes of scrypture concernyng fayth a. workes,* London?, R. Copland, 1532?, or Antwerp?, 1532?. C-12,732. N-0587. [See also C-12,733–12,734.]

——— joint author, see Tracy, William, *The testament* . . .

——— joint author, see Tyndale, William, *The Whole workes* . . . and *Writings* . . .

*Furnivall, Frederick J., editor, *Political, Religious, and Love Poems . . . from the Archbishop of Canterbury's Lambeth MS. No. 306* (Early English Text Society, Original Series, 15), London, Kegan Paul, Trench, Trübner, 1903.

Gardiner, Stephen, *A declaration of such true articles as George Ioye hath gone about to confute as false,* London, J. Herford for R. Toye, 1546. C-11,588.

*——— *The Letters of Stephen Gardiner,* edited by James Arthur Muller, Cambridge University Press, 1933.

Gardynare, Germen, *A letter of a yonge gentylman . . . wherin men may se the demeanour & heresy of Iohñ Fryth,* London, W. Rastell, 1534. C-11,594.

Gau, John, *translator,* Christiern Pedersen, *The richt vay to the kingdome of heuine is techit heir,* "Malmö, Sweden" [Antwerp, J. Hoochstraten?], 1533. C-19,525.

Gwynneth, John, *The confutacyon of the fyrst parte of Frythes boke, with a dysputacyon before whether it be possyble for any heretike to know that hym selfe is one or not. And also an other whether it be wors to denye directely more or less of the fayth,* St. Albans, J. Hertford for R. Stevenage, 1536. C-12,557.

——— *A declaration of the state wherein all heretickes dooe leade their lives,* London, T. Berthelet, 1554. C-12,558.

——— *A manifeste detection of the falshed of J. Friths boke,* London, T. Berthelet, 1554. C-12,559.

——— *A playne demonstration of J. Frithes lack of witte and learnynge,* London, T. Powell, 1557. C-12,560.

*Hall, Richard, *supposed author, The Life of Fisher,* transcribed from MS. Harleian 6382 by Ronald Bayne (Early English Text Society, Extra Series, 117), London, H. Milford, Oxford University Press, 1921 [for 1915].

*Hamilton, Patrick, *A Most Excelent and Frvitfvl Treatise, Called Patericks Places. Selected and reduced into this volume by I. D.* [*John Day?*], translated by John Frith, London, printed by William White, 1598. C-12,734.

*——— *Patrick's Places. Translated . . . by J. Frith,* London, The Religious Tract Society, 1807.

Henry VIII, *Assertio septem sacramentorum aduersus M. Lutherum*, London, R. Pynson, 1521. C-10,378.

*———— *Assertio Septem Sacramentorum: or, an Assertion of the Seven Sacraments, Against Martin Luther . . . Faithfully Translated into English by T[homas] W[ebster]*, London, Nath. Thompson, 1687.

———— and Martin Luther, *A copy of the letters wherin . . . kyng Henry the eight . . . made answere vnto a certayne letter of Martyn Luther . . . and also the copy of the foresaid Luthers letter*, London, R. Pynson, 1528. C-10,387.

———— and Martin Luther, *A copy of the letters, wherin . . . kyng Henry the eyght made answere vnto a certayn letter of Martyn Luther*, London, R. Pynson, 1526. C-13,086.

———— and Martin Luther, *Literarum, quibus Henricus octavus respondit ad quandam epistolam M. Lutheri*, London, R. Pynson, 1526. C-13,084. [See also C-13,085.]

*———— *Miscellaneous Writings . . . In which are included Assertion of the Seven Sacraments*, edited by Francis Macnamara, Waltham St. Lawrence, Golden Cockerel Press, 1924.

Henry, Lord Stafford, *translator*, Edward Fox, *The true dyfferens betwen ye regall power and the ecclesiasticall power*, London, W. Copland, 1548. C-11,220.

Hyde, R., *translator*, Johannes Ludovicus Vives, *A very frutefull and pleasant boke called the instrucion of a christen woman*, London, T. Berthelet, 1529?. C-24,856.

Joye, George, *An Apologye made by George Ioye to satisfye (if it maye be) w. Tindale*, n.pl., n.pr., 1535. C-14,820.

*———— *An Apology made by George Joy, to satisfy, if it may be, W. Tindale. 1535*, edited by Edward Arber (The English Scholar's Library, 13), London, Edward Arber, 1882.

———— *A compendyouse somme of the very christen relygyon*, London, J. Byddell, 1535. C-14,821.

———— *A contrarye (to a certain manis) consultacion. That adulterers ought to be punyshed wyth deathe*, London, G. Joye, 1541?. C-14,822.

———— [*pseud.* James Sawtry], *The defence of the mariage of priestes*, "Auryk, J. Troost, 1541." C-21,804.

———— *A frutefull treatis of baptyme and the Lordis Souper*, Antwerp, widow Ruremund (Endhoven), 1541. C-24,217.

———— *George Ioye confuteth, Uvinchesters false Articles*, "Wesill in Cliefelande, 1543." C-14,826.

———— *The letters whyche Iohan Ashwell . . . sente . . . Where in the sayde pryour accuseth George Ioye . . . of fower opinyons: wyth the answere*, Antwerp, M. deKeyser, ca. 1531?. C-844. N-3281.

———— *Our sauiour Iesus Christ hath not ouercharged his chirche with many ceremonies*, Antwerp, widow Ruremund (Endhoven), 1543. C.-14,556.

———— *A present consolacion for the sufferers of persecucion for rightwysenes*, London, n.pr., 1544. C-14,828.

———— *The refutation of the byshop of Winchesters derke declaration of his false articles*, London, J. Herford, 1546. C-14,827.

———— *The Subuersion of Moris false foundacion*, "Emdon, Iacob Aurik," 1534. C-14,829.

———— *The unite and Scisme of the olde Chirche*, Antwerp?, n.pr., 1543. C-14,830.

———— translator, *Dauids Psalter diligently and faithfully translated*, Antwerp, M. deKeyser, 1534. C-2372. N-2486.

———— translator, *Ieremy the Prophete, translated into Englisshe*, Antwerp, M. deKeyser, 1534?. C-2778. N-2484.

———— translator, *The Prophete Isaye, translated into englysshe*, Antwerp, M. deKeyser, 1531. C-2777. N-2482.

———— translator, *The proverbes of Solomon newly translated into Englyshe. (Here foloweth the boke of Solomon called Ecclesiastes.)*, London, T. Godfray, 1532?, 1534?, 1535?. C-2752.

———— translator, *The Psalter of Dauid in Englishe purely and faithfully translated aftir the texte of Feline*, Antwerp, M. deKeyser, 1530. C-2370. N-2476. [See also C-2371.]

———— translator, *The psalter of Dauid, whervnto is annexed certayne godly collettes*, London, E. Whitchurch, 1541?. C-2374.

———— [*pseud.* Lewis Beuchame], translator, Philipp Melanchthon, *A very godly defense, defending the mariage of priestes*, "Lipse, Ubryght Hoff" [Ipswich, J. Oswen], 1541. C-17,798.

———— translator, Andreas Osiander, *The coniectures of the ende of the worlde*, London, R. Jugge, 1548. C-18,877.

———— translator, Huldreich Zwingli, *The rekening and declaration of the faith of H. Zwingly*, Antwerp, widow Ruremund (Endhoven), 1543. C-26,138.

———— translator, Huldreich Zwingli, *The Souper of the Lorde*, "Nornburg, Niclas twonson" [Antwerp, S. Cock?], 1533. C-24,468. N-3996. [See also C-24,468a-24,471, N-01,186-01,187.]

———— editor, *The exposicion of Daniel the Prophete gathered oute of Philip Melanchthon, Johan Ecolampadius, &c.*, "Emprinted at Geneue, 1545." C-14,823.

—————— editor, *Ortulus anime. The garden of the soule: or the eng-lisshe primers,* "Argentine, Francis Foxe" [Antwerp, M. deKeyser], 1530. N-4246.

—————— joint author, see Tyndale, William, *An Answer* . . .

—————— joint author, see Tyndale, William, *translator, The new* . . .

Knox, John, [*The first (second and thirde) booke of the History of the Reformation of religioun within the realme of Scotland*], London, T. Vautrollier, 1587. C-15,071.

*—————— *History of the Reformation in Scotland,* edited by William Croft Dickinson, 2 vols. New York, Nelson, 1949.

Latimer, Hugh, *The sermon* . . . *made to the clergie, in conuocation* . . . *now translated* . . . *into Englishe,* London, T. Berthelet, 1537. C-15,286. [See also C-15,287.]

*—————— *Sermons by Hugh Latimer, Sometime Bishop of Worcester, Martyr, 1555,* edited by George Elwes Corrie (Parker Society, 27), Cambridge University Press, 1844.

*Lloyd, Charles, editor, *Formularies of Faith* . . . *during the reign of Henry VIII,* Oxford, Clarendon Press, 1825.

Longland, John, *Expositio concionalis quinti psalmi poenitentialis,* London, R. Redman?, 1532?. C-16,792.

—————— *Tres conciones,* London, R. Pynson, 1527?. C-16,790.

Luther, Martin, *Ad Librvm* . . . *A. Catharini* . . . *Responsio* . . . *De Antichristo,* "Wittembergae" [Basel, A. Petri?], 1521.

—————— *Eyn bett buchlin,* Wittenberg, n.pr., 1522.

—————— *A boke made by a certayne great clerke agaynst the new idols, and old deuyll,* London, R. Wyer, 1534. C-16,962.

*—————— *Luthers Briefwechsel,* edited by Ernst Ludwig Enders, Frankfurt am Main, Schriften-Niederlage des evangel. . . . Vereins (imprint varies), 1884– .

—————— *Contra Henricvm Regem Angliae,* Wittenberg, n.pr., 1522.

—————— *De captiuitate babylonica ecclesiae praeludium,* Wittenberg, M. Lotter, 1520.

—————— *De seruo arbitrio,* Wittenberg, J. Lufft, 1525.

—————— *Enchiridion piarum precationum cum Calendario et passionali,* Wittenberg, J. Lufft, 1529.

—————— *In septimum primae ad Corinthior caput, Exegesis,* translated by J. Lonicerus, Strassburg, J. Schott, 1525.

—————— *Operationes* . . . *in Psalmos,* Wittenberg, J. Grünenberg?, 1519–1520.

*—————— *The pope confounded and his kingdom exposed, in a divine opening of Daniel VIII.23–25* . . . *Now first* [*!*] *translated into*

English, by the Rev. Henry Cole [translation of *Ad librum A. Catharini responsio*], London, J. Nisbet, 1836.

*———— *Reformation Writings of Martin Luther,* translated by Bertram Lee Woolf, 2 vols. London, Lutterworth Press, 1952–1956.

*———— *Luther's Reply to King Henry VIII (1522) Now First Englished after the Lapse of Four Centuries,* translated by E. S. Buchanan, New York, privately printed by E. S. Buchanan, 1928.

———— *Eyn Sermon von dem vnrechten Mammon Lu. xvi,* Wittenberg, J. Grünenberg, 1522.

———— *Das siebend Capitel S. Pauli zu den Chorinthern,* Wittenberg, Cranach and Dörning, 1523.

———— *Von weltlicher Oberkeit, wie weit man ihr Gehorsam schuldig sei,* Wittenberg, N. Schyrlantz, 1523.

*———— *D. Martin Luthers Werke. Kritische Gesammtausgabe,* edited by J. K. H. Knaake, G. Kawarau, E. Thiele, et al.; *Werke,* vols. 1 ff. in process since 1883; *Die Deutsche Bibel,* 12 vols.; *Tischreden,* 6 vols.; *Briefwechsel,* 11 vols. Weimar, H. Böhlau, 1883– .

———— joint author, see Henry VIII, *A copy . . . ,* and *Literarum*

Marshall, William, *translator, Desiderius Erasmus, A lytle treatise on the maner and forme of confession,* London, J. Byddell, 1535?. C-10,498.

———— *translator,* Marsilius of Padua, *The Defence of Peace,* London, R. Wyer, 1535. C-17,817.

———— *translator,* Girolamo Savonarola, *An exposition after the maner of a contemplacyon vpon ye .li. psalme,* London, J. Byddell, 1534. C-21,795.

———— *translator, A treatise declaryng a. shewing dyuers causes that pyctures & other ymages ar in no wise to be suffred in churches,* London, for W. Marshall, 1535. C-24,238.

———— [*pseud.* B. Picern], *translator, A treatyse of the donation or gyfte and endowment of possessyons gyuen and presented vnto Syluester pope of Rhome by Constantyne,* London, T. Godfray, 1534. C-5641.

Melanchthon, Philipp, *Passional Christi und Antichristi,* n.pr. [Erfurt, 1521].

More, John, *translator,* Fredericus Nausea [*pseud.* Eusebianus], *A sermon of the sacrament of the aulter,* London, W. Rastell, 1533. C-18,414.

More, Thomas, *The answere to the fyrst parte of the poysened booke, whych a namelesse heretyke hath named the souper of the lorde,* London, W. Rastell, 1534. C-18,077.

————— *The apologye of syr Thomas More knyght*, London, W. Rastell, 1533. C-18,078.

————— *The confutacyon of Tyndales answere*, London, W. Rastell, 1532. C-18,079.

*————— *The Correspondence of Sir Thomas More*, edited by Elizabeth Frances Rogers, Princeton University Press, 1947.

————— *The debellacyon of Salem and Bizance*, London, W. Rastell, 1533. C-18,081.

————— *A dyaloge of syr T. More*, London, W. Rastell, 1529. C-18,084.

————— [*pseud.* William Ross], *Ervditissimi viri . . . opus elegans*, London, R. Pynson, 1523. C-18,089.

————— *A letter . . . impugnynge the erronyouse wrytyng of Iohñ Fryth*, London, W. Rastell, 1533. C-18,090.

*————— *Omnis, quae hucusque ad manus nostras peruerunt, Latina Opera*, Louvain, J. Bogardus, 1566.

————— *The second parte of the confutacion of Tyndals answere*, London, W. Rastell, 1533. C-18,080.

————— *The supplycacyon of soulys*, London, W. Rastell, 1529. C-18,092.

*————— *The workes of Sir Thomas More Knyght, sometyme Lorde Chauncellour of England, wrytten by him in the Englysh tonge*, edited by William Rastell, London, Iohn Cawod, Iohn VValy, and Richarde Tottell, 1557. C-18,076.

Murner, Thomas, *Ob der Künig usz Engelland . . . ein Lügner sey oder der Luther*, Strassburg, n.pr., 1522.

*Nazarei, Judas, *pseud.*, Joachim Vadianus, supposed author, *Vom alten und neuen Gott, glauben und lehre.* (*1521.*) *Mit abhandlung und kommentar herausgegeben von Eduard Kück* (Flugschriften aus der reformationszeit, 12), Halle, M. Niemyer, 1896.

————— *pseud.*, Joachim Vadianus, supposed author, *Vom alten und neuen Gott, Glauben und Lehre*, Basel, A. Petri, 1521.

Oecolampadius, Johann, *De Genuina Verborum Domini, Hoc Est Corpus Meum, iuxta vetustissimos authores, expositione liber*, Hagenau, n.pr., c. 1525; Basel, n.pr., 1525.

————— *Dialogus quo Patrum sententiam de Coena Domini bona fide explanat*, Basel, C. Waldkirchus, 1530.

————— *In Iesaiam prophetam Hypomnematōn, hoc est, Commentariorum*, Basel, Cratander, 1525.

————— translator, *Das Testament Ieus Christi das man bissher genennt hat die Messz*, n.pl.?, n.pr.?, 1523.

Parker, Matthew, editor, *The . holie . Bible . conteynynge the olde Testament and the newe*, London, R. Jugge, 1568. C-2099.

Parsons, Robert, *A treatise of three conversions of England from Paganisme to Christian Religion,* (in three parts), St. Omer, n.pr., 1603. C-19,416.

Paynell, Thomas, *translator, The assaute and conquest of heuen,* London, T. Berthelet, 1529. C-862 = 19,491.

Pedersen, Christiern, *Den rette vey till Hiemmerigis Rige,* Antwerp, W. Vosterman, 1531. N-1687.

*Pollard, Alfred William, editor, *Records of the English Bible. The Documents Relating to the Translation and Publication of the Bible in English, 1525–1611,* Oxford University Press, 1911.

Powell, Edward, *Propugnaculum summi sacerdotii euangelici aduer. M. Lutherum,* London, R. Pyson, 1523. C-20,140.

Rastell, John, *A new boke of Purgatory, whiche is a dyaloge betwene Comyngo & Gygemyn,* London, J. Rastell, 1530. C-20,719.

Redman, Robert, *translator, Prayers of the Byble taken out of the olde testament and the newe,* London, R. Redman, 1535.

*Richmond, Legh, editor, *The Fathers of the English Church; or, A Selection from the Writings of the Reformers and Early Protestant Divines of the Church of England,* 8 vols. London, J. Hatchard, 1807–1812.

Rogers, John [*pseud.* Thomas Matthew], editor, *The byble which is all the holy scripture,* Antwerp, M. Crom? for R. Grafton and E. Whitchurch, 1537. C-2066. N-2497.

Roy, William [or Jerome Barlowe], *A proper dyaloge betwene a Gentillman and an Husbandma*n *eche complaynenge to other theyr myserable calamyte through the ambicion of the clergye,* Antwerp, J. Hoochstraten, ca. 1529?. N-4215.

———— [or Jerome Barlowe], *A proper dyaloge, etc.,* Antwerp, J. Hoochstraten, 1530?. C-6813. N-2775.

*———— [or Jerome Barlowe], *A Proper Dyaloge betwene a Gentillman and a Husbandman . . . A Compendious Olde Treatyse,* reproduced in facsimile with an introduction by Francis Fry, London, Willis and Sotheran, 1863.

———— and Jerome Barlowe, *Rede me and be nott wrothe For I saye no thynge but trothe,* Strassburg, J. Schott, 1528. C-21,427.

*———— and Jerome Barlowe, *Rede me and be not wrothe, For I saye no thinge but trothe . . . A Proper Dyaloge betwene a Gentillman and a Husbandman . . . A compendious olde Treatyse,* edited by Edward Arber (English Reprints), London, Edward Arber, 1871; Westminster, A. Constable, 1895.

———— *translator, A Brefe Dialoge bitwene a Christen father and his stobborne Sonne,* Strassburg, J. Schott, 1527.

*————translator, William Roye's Dialogue between a Christian Father and his Stubborn Son. Nach dem Einzigen auf der Wiener K. K. Hofbibliothek befindlichen Exemplare, edited by Adolf Wolf, reprinted from Sitzungsberichte der phil.-hist. der kais. Akademie der Wissenschaften, 76 (1874), 391–476, Vienna, for Karl Gerold's Son, Adolf Holzhausen, 1874.

———— translator, Desiderius Erasmus, An exhortacyon to the dylygent study of scripture, London, R. Wyer, 1540?. C-10,494. [Huntington Library 24,482, 62,017, both listed as C-10,404, vary t. p.-verso.]

———— translator, Desiderius Erasmus and Martin Luther, An exhortation to the diligent studye of scripture made by Erasmus Roterodamus. And translated in to inglish. An exposition in to the seventh chaptre of the first pistle to the Corinthians, Antwerp, J. Hoochstraten, 1529. C-10,493. N-2982.

———— translator, The true beliefe in Christ and his sacramentes, set forth in a Dialoge betwene a Christen father and his sonne, preface by Gwalter Lynne, London, for W. Lynne, 1550. C-14,576.

———— editor, A compendious olde treatyse shewynge howe that we ought to have ye scripture in Englysshe, Antwerp, J. Hoochstraten, 1530. C-3021. N-3980.

———— joint author, see Tyndale, William, The Beginning . . .

———— joint author, see Tyndale, William, translator, The new . . . and New . . .

Ryckes, John, The ymage of loue, London, W. de Worde, 1525. C-21,-473.

Saint-German, Christopher, The addicions of Salem and Byzance, London, T. Berthelet, 1534. C-21,585.

———— Dialogus de fundamentis legum Anglie et de conscientia, London, W. Rastell, 1528. C-21,559.

———— Salem and Bizance. (A dialogue betwixte two Englysshe men.), London, T. Berthelet, 1533. C-21,584.

———— A treatise concernynge the diuision betwene the spirytualtie and temporaltie, London, R. Redman, 1532?. C-21,586. [See also C-21,-587.]

Standish, John, A lytle treatise agaist [sic] the protestacion of Robert Barnes at the tyme of his death, London, R. Redman, 1540. C-23,209.

Sutcliffe, Matthew, The subuersion of R. Parsons his worke entituled, A treatise of 3 conuersions, London, for J. Norton, 1606. C-23,469.

Swinnerton, Thomas [pseud. J. Roberts], A mustre of scismatyke byshoppes of Rome, London, W. de Worde for J. Byddell, 1534. C-23,-552.

Taverner, Richard, translator, Desiderius Erasmus, A ryght frutefull *epystle in laude and prayse of matrymony,* London, R. Redman, 1530?. C-10,492.

Tracy, Richard?, *The preparacyon to the crosse, wyth the preparacion to death,* London, T. Petyte, 1530?. C-11,392.

————? *Of the preparation to the crosse,* London, T. Berthelet, 1540. C-11,393.

———— *The profe and declaration of thys proposition: Ffayth only iustifieth,* London, R. Grafton, 1540?. C-24,164.

———— *joint author,* see Frith, John, *The contentes . . .*

Tracy, William, John Frith, and William Tyndale, *The testament of master Wylliam Tracie esquier, expounded both by W. Tindall and J. Frith,* Antwerp, J. Hoochstraten, 1536?. C-24,167. N-3997.

Turner, William [*pseud.* W. Wraghton], *The huntyng and fynding out of the Romishe fox,* "Basyl" [London?], n.pr., 1543. C-24,353.

———— [*pseud.* W. Wraghton], *The Rescuyng of the Romishe fox, the second course of the hunter at the Romishe fox,* Zürich?, C. Froschauer?, 1545. C-24,355.

———— *translator,* Judas Nazarei, *pseud.* [Joachim Vadianus, supposed author], *A worke entytled of ye olde god & the newe,* London, J. Byddell, 1534. C-25,127.

Tyndale, William, *An answere vnto Sir Thomas Mores dialoge,* Antwerp, S. Cock, 1531. C-24,437. N-3988.

*———— and George Joye, *An Answer to Sir Thomas More's Dialogue, The Supper of the Lord . . . and Wm. Tracy's Testament Expounded,* edited by Henry Walter (Parker Society, 44), Cambridge University Press, 1850.

———— *A briefe declaration of the sacraments,* London, R. Stoughton, ca. 1548. C-24,445.

———— *A compendious introduccion vnto the pistle to the Romayns,* n.pl., n.pr., n.d. C-24,438.

*———— *Doctrinal Treatises and Introduction to Different Portions of the Holy Scriptures,* edited by Henry Walter (Parker Society, 42), Cambridge University Press, 1848.

———— *An exposicion vppon the .v.vi.vii. chapters of Mathew,* Antwerp, J. Grapheus, ca. 1533. C-24,439, 24,440?. N-3839.

———— *The exposition of the fyrste Epistle of seynt Ihon,* Antwerp, M. deKeyser, 1531. C-24,443. N-3990.

*———— *Expositions and Notes on Sundry Portions of the Holy Scriptures, Together with the Practice of Prelates,* edited by Henry Walter (Parker Society, 43), Cambridge University Press, 1849.

———— *The obedience of a Christen man and how Christen rulers ought to governe*, Antwerp, J. Hoochstraten, 1528. C-24,446. N-3991. [See also N-3992.]

*——— *The Obedience of a Christian Man*, edited by Richard Lovett (Christian Classics Series, *5*), London, Religious Tract Society, n.d.

——— [*The parable of the wicked mammon*], Begin. *That fayth the mother of all good workes iustifieth vs*, Antwerp, J. Hoochstraten, 1528. C-24,454. N-3993. [See also N-3994.]

——— *A pathway into the holy scripture*, London, T. Godfray, 1534?. C-24,463.

——— *The practyse of Prelates. Whether the Kinges grace maye be separated from hys quene be cause she was his brothers wyfe*, Antwerp, J. Hoochstraten, 1530. C-24,465. N-3995.

*——— John Frith, and Robert Barnes, *The Whole workes of W. Tyndall, Iohn Frith, and Doct. Barnes, three worthy Martyrs . . . collected and compiled in one Tome togither*, edited with a preface by John Foxe, London, printed by Iohn Daye, 1573 [1572]. C-24,-436.

*——— and John Frith, *The Works of the English Reformers: William Tyndale, and John Frith*, edited by Thomas Russell, 3 vols. London, printed for Ebenezer Palmer, 1831.

*——— John Frith, and Robert Barnes, *Writings of Tindal, Frith, and Barnes* (The British Reformers, *2*), London, The Religious Tract Society, n.d.; Philadelphia, Presbyterian Board of Publications, 1842.

——— translator, *the fyrst boke of Moses called Genesis*, Antwerp, J. Hoochstraten, 1530. C-2350. N-2477.

——— translator, *The first boke of Moses. Newly correctyd by W. T.*, Antwerp, M. deKeyser, 1534. C-2351. N-2488.

——— translator, *The seconde boke of Moses called Exodus*, Antwerp, J. Hoochstraten, 1530. C-2350. N-2478.

——— translator, *The Thyrde boke of Moses called Leviticus*, Antwerp, J. Hoochstraten, 1530. C-2350. N-2479.

——— translator, *The fourthe boke of Moses called Numeri*, Antwerp, J. Hoochstraten, 1530. C-2350. N-2480.

——— translator, *The fifth boke of Moses called Deuteronomye*, Antwerp, J.Hoochstraten, 1530. C-2350. N-2481.

*——— translator, *William Tyndale's Five Books of Moses, Called the Pentateuch, Being a Verbatim Reprint of the Edition of M.CCCCC.XXX. Compared with Tyndale's Genesis of 1534 . . . with Various Collations and Prolegomena*, edited by Jacob Isidor Mombert, New York, Anson D. F. Randolph, 1884.

——— translator, *The prophete Ionas with an introduccion before teachinge to vnderstonde him,* Antwerp, M. deKeyser, 1531?. C-2788. N-2483.

―――― and William Roy, *translators,* [*The New Testament;* sig. A-K only], Cologne, P. Quentell or H. Fuchs?, 1525. C-2823.

*―――― and William Roy, *translators, The Beginning of the New Testament Translated By William Tyndale 1525. Facsimile* [*of STC 2823*] *of the Unique Fragment of the Uncompleted Cologne Edition,* introduction by Alfred William Pollard, Oxford, Clarendon Press, 1926.

―――― and William Roy, *translators,* [*New Testament*], Worms, P. Schoeffer, 1526. C-2824.

―――― and William Roy, *translators,* [*The New Testament in English;* reprintings of the 1526 edition in Antwerp, 1526 to 1534, before Tyndale's or Joye's 1534 revisions]: N-0170, C. van Ruremund (Endhoven), ca. October 1526. N-0171, H. van Ruremunde?, 1527. N-0172, H. van Ruremunde?, 1529. N-0173, C. van Ruremund (Endhoven), ca. 1530. N-0174, Antwerp?, n.pr., 1532. N-0175, C. van Ruremund (Endhoven), 1534. N-0176, M. deKeyser, 1534.

*―――― *translator, The First Printed English New Testament,* edited by Edward Arber, London, Edward Arber, 1871.

*―――― *translator, The New Testament of Our Lord and Saviour Jesus Christ: published in 1526 . . . Reprinted verbatim: with a memoir of his life and writings, by George Offor. Together with the proceedings and correspondence of Henry VIII, Sir T. More, and Lord Cromwell,* London, S. Bagster, 1836.

―――― *translator, The newe Testament dylygently corrected and compared with the Greke,* Antwerp, M. deKeyser, November 1534. C-2826. N-2487.

*―――― *translator, The New Testament Translated by William Tyndale 1534. A Reprint of the Edition of 1534 with the Translator's Preface & Notes and the variants of the edition of 1525,* edited for the Royal Society of Literature by N. Hardy Wallis, Cambridge University Press, 1938.

―――― *translator,* and George Joye, editor, *The new Testament as it was written and caused to be written by them which herde yt,* Antwerp, widow Ruremund (Endhoven), 1534. C-2825. N-2485.

―――― *translator,* and George Joye, editor, [*New Testament*], Antwerp, widow Ruremund (Endhoven), January 9, 1534. C-2827. N-2490.

―――― *translator, The newe Testament yet once agayne corrected by Willyam Tindale,* Antwerp, M. deKeyser [for G. van der Haghen], 1534–1535. C-2830. N-2489.

────── translator, [*The New Testament in English;* reprintings of the 1534–1535 revision in Antwerp in 1535–1536] : C-2828–2828a = N-2491, J. Steels?, 1535?. N-2492, M. deKeyser, ca. 1535. C-2829 = N-2493, M. Hillen van Hoochstraten?, ca. 1535?. C-2832 = N-2494, M. Croom?, 1536. C-2833=N-2495, M. Croom?, 1536. C-2834= N-2496, M. Croom?, 1536.

────── translator, Desiderius Erasmus, *A booke called in latyn Enchiridion and in englysshe the manuell of the christen knyght,* Salisbury?, W. de Worde for J. Byddell, 1533. C-10,479.

────── translator, Desiderius Erasmus, *Enchiridion militis christiani, whiche may be called in englysshe, the hansom weapon of a christen knyght,* London, W. de Worde for J. Byddell, 1534. C-10,480. [See also 10,481–10,487.]

────── editor, *The examinacion of Master William Thorpe, preste . . . The examinacion of syr Ihōn Oldcastell,* Antwerp, J. Hoochstraten, 1530. C-24,045. N-3007.

────── editor, *The praier and complaynte of the ploweman vnto Christe,* Antwerp, M. deKeyser, 1531. C-20,036. N-3763.

────── joint author, see Tracy, William, *The testament . . .*

*Vergilius, Polydorus, *The Anglica Historia of Polydore Vergil 1485–1537,* edited by Denys Hay, London, Camden Society, 1950.

Villa Sancta, Alphonsus de, *De libero arbitrio, aduersus Melanchthonem,* London, R. Pynson, 1523. C-24,728.

────── *Problema indulgentiarum,* London, R. Pynson, 1523. C-24,729.

*Wilkins, David, editor, *Concilia Magnae Britanniae et Hiberniae, a Synodo Verolamiensi A.D. 446 ad Londinensem A.D. 1717,* 4 vols. London, R. Gosling, F. Gyler, T. Woodward, C. Davis, 1737.

*Wittenberg, University of, *Album Academiae Vitebergensis ab A. Ch. MDII usque ad A.* [*MDCII*] *Ex Autographo,* edited by Carl Edward Foerstermann, 3 vols.: *1,* Leipzig, Karl Tauchnitz, 1841 ; *2–3,* Halle, Maximilian Niemeyer, 1894–1905.

*Wriothesley, Charles, *A Chronicle of England during the reigns of the Tudors, from A.D. 1485 to 1559,* edited by William Douglas Hamilton (Camden Society, New Series, *11*), London, Camden Society, 1875.

*Zwingli, Huldreich, and Heinrich Bullinger, *Zwingli and Bullinger,* edited and translated by Geoffrey William Bromiley (Library of Christian Classics, *24*), Philadelphia, Westminster Press, 1954.

II. SECONDARY WORKS

Books

Alcock, Deborah, *John Frith* (Six Heroic Men), London, Religious Tract Society, 1909.

Anderson, Christopher, *Annals of the English Bible,* 2 vols. London, Pickering, 1845.

Baskerville, Geoffrey, *English Monks and the Suppression of the Monasteries,* London, Cape, 1937.

Batley, James Yorke, *On a Reformer's Latin Bible, Being an Essay on the Adversaria in the Vulgate of Thomas Bilney,* Cambridge, Deighton, Bell, 1940.

Bornkamm, Heinrich, and Robert Stupperich, *Martin Bucers Bedeutung für die europäische Reformationsgeschichte* (Schriften des Vereins für Reformationsgeschichte 169, Jahrgang 58, Heft 2), Gütersloh, C. Bertelsmann, 1952.

Bromiley, Geoffrey William, *Thomas Cranmer, Theologian,* New York, Oxford University Press, 1956.

Brooks, Peter N., "Thomas Cranmer's Doctrine of the Sacraments," unpublished dissertation, Cambridge University, 1960.

Bushell, William Done, *The Church of St. Mary the Great, the University Church at Cambridge,* Cambridge, Bowes and Bowes, 1948.

Butterworth, Charles C., *The English Primers, 1529–1545; Their Publication and Connection with the English Bible and the Reformation in England,* Philadelphia, University of Pennsylvania Press, 1953.

—— and Allan G. Chester, *George Joye 1495?–1553, a Chapter in the History of the English Bible and the English Reformation,* Philadelphia, University of Pennsylvania Press, 1962.

—— *The Literary Lineage of the King James Bible 1340–1611,* Philadelphia, University of Pennsylvania Press, 1941.

Cameron, Alexander, editor, *Patrick Hamilton, First Scottish Martyr of the Reformation; a Composite Biography by Several Authors,* Edinburgh, Scottish Reformation Society, 1929.

Campbell, William Edward, *Erasmus, Tyndale, and More,* London, Eyre and Spottiswoode, 1949.

Chambers, R. W., *Thomas More,* New York, Harcourt Brace, 1935.

Chester, Allan G., *Hugh Latimer, Apostle to the English,* Philadelphia, University of Pennsylvania Press, 1954.

—— joint author, see Butterworth, Charles C. *George Joye . . .*

Cleaveland, Elizabeth Whittlesey, *A Study of Tindale's Genesis Compared with the Genesis of Coverdale and of the Authorized Version,* New York, H. Holt, 1911.

Cooper, Charles Henry, *Memorials of Cambridge. A New Edition*, 3 vols. Cambridge, William Metcalfe, 1860–1866.

Cooper, William Barrett, *The Life and Work of William Tindale*, Toronto, Longmans, Green, 1924.

Dallmann, William, *Robert Barnes*, St. Louis, Mo., Concordia Publishing House, after 1917.

Darby, Harold Seager, *Hugh Latimer*, London, Epworth Press, 1953.

Deanesly, Margaret, *The Lollard Bible and Other Medieval Biblical Versions*, Cambridge University Press, 1920.

Demaus, Robert, *William Tyndale. A Biography. A Contribution to the Early History of the English Bible*, London, Religious Tract Society, 1871.

Dickens, A. G., *Lollards and Protestants in the Diocese of York 1509–1558*, London, Oxford University Press, 1959.

Doernberg, Erwin, *Henry VIII and Luther. An Account of Their Personal Relations*, Stanford, Calif., Stanford University Press, 1961.

Dugmore, Clifford William, *The Mass and the English Reformers*, London, Macmillan, 1958.

Ellis, James J., *William Tyndale* (Men With a Mission. New Series of Popular Biographies), New York, Thomas Whittaker, n.d.

Fisher, Norman Hawley, "The Contribution of Robert Barnes to the English Reformation," unpublished thesis, University of Birmingham, 1950.

Fulop, Robert Ernest, "John Frith (1503–1533) and His Relation to the Origin of the Reformation in England," unpublished dissertation, New College, University of Edinburgh, 1956.

Götzinger, Ernst, *Joachim Vadian, der Reformator und Geschichtschreiber von St. Gallen* (Schriften des Vereins für Reformationsgeschichte, Jahrgang 13, Schrift 50), Halle, Verein für Reformationsgeschichte, 1895.

Goldschmidt, Ernest Philip, *The First Cambridge Press in its European Setting*, Cambridge University Press, 1955.

Greenslade, S. L., *The English Reformers and the Fathers of the Church*, Oxford, Clarendon Press, 1960.

——— *The Work of William Tindale*, London, Blackie & Son, 1938.

Gruber, L. Franklin, *The First English New Testament and Luther. The Real Extent to which Tyndale Was Dependent Upon Luther as a Translator*, Burlington, Ia., Lutheran Literary Board, 1928.

Harris, Jesse W., *John Bale: A Study in the Minor Literature of the Reformation*, Urbana, Ill., University of Illinois Press, 1940.

Herford, Charles Harold, *Studies in the Literary Relations of England*

and Germany in the Sixteenth Century, Cambridge University Press, 1886.

Hildebrandt, Franz, *From Luther to Wesley,* London, Lutterworth Press, 1951.

Hopf, Constantin, *Martin Bucer and the English Reformation,* Oxford, Blackwell, 1946.

Hughes, Philip, *The Reformation in England,* 3 vols. London, Hollis and Carter, 1950–1954.

Hume, Anthea, "A Study of the Writings of the English Protestant Exiles, 1525–1535," unpublished dissertation, University of London, 1961. [Permission to examine this work withheld by author.]

Innes, Arthur D., *England Under the Tudors,* 10th ed., revised by J. M. Henderson, (A History of England, *4*), London, Methuen, 1932.

Jacobs, Henry Eyster, *The Lutheran Movement in England During the Reigns of Henry VIII and Edward VI and Its Literary Monuments,* Philadelphia, G. W. Frederick, 1890; revised 1894.

Knappen, Marshall Mason, *Tudor Puritanism, a Chapter in the History of Idealism,* University of Chicago Press, 1939.

Leeuw, Cateau de, *William Tyndale, Martyr for the Bible* (Heroes of God Series), New York, Association Press, 1955.

Lewis, Clive Staples, *English Literature in the Sixteenth Century Excluding Drama* (The Oxford History of English Literature, *3*), Oxford, Clarendon Press, 1954.

Loane, Marcus Lawrence, *Masters of the English Reformation,* London, Church Book Room Press, 1954.

Lorimer, Peter, *Patrick Hamilton* (Precursors of Knox, *1*), Edinburgh, Thomas Constable, 1857.

Manschreck, Clyde Leonard, *Melanchthon, The Quiet Reformer,* New York, Abingdon Press, 1958.

Marius, Richard, "Thomas More and the Heretics," unpublished dissertation, Yale University, 1962.

Martyn, Mrs. S. T., *The English Exile; or, William Tyndale at Home and Abroad,* New York, American Tract Society, 1867.

Moore, W. G., *La Réforme Allemande et la Littérature Française* (Publications de la Faculté des lettres de l'Université de Strasbourg, fasc. 52), Strassburg, La Faculté des lettres de l'Université, 1930.

Mozley, James Frederick, *Coverdale and His Bibles,* London, Lutterworth Press, 1953.

——— *John Foxe and His Book,* London, Society for Promoting Christian Knowledge, 1940.

—— *William Tyndale,* London, Society for Promoting Christian Knowledge, 1937.

Mullinger, James Bass, *The University of Cambridge from the Earliest Times to the Royal Injunctions of 1535,* Cambridge University Press, 1873.

Muller, James Arthur, *Stephen Gardiner and the Tudor Reaction,* London, Society for Promoting Christian Knowledge, 1926.

Paul, Leslie Allen, *Sir Thomas More,* London, Faber and Faber, 1953.

Pollard, Albert Frederick, *Wolsey,* London, Longmans, Green, 1929.

Pollard, Alfred William, *Shakespeare's Fight with the Pirates and the Problems of the Transmission of His Text,* 2nd ed., Cambridge University Press, 1920.

Porter, H. C., *Reformation and Reaction in Tudor Cambridge,* Cambridge University Press, 1958.

Prüser, Friedrich, *England und die Schmalkaldener, 1535–40,* Leipzig, M. Hesenius, successor to Eger & Sievers, 1929.

Ridley, Jasper Godwin, *Thomas Cranmer,* Oxford, Clarendon Press, 1962.

—— *Nicholas Ridley A Biography,* London, Longmans, Green, 1957.

Rupp, Ernest Gordon, *The Righteousness of God; Luther Studies,* London, Hodder and Stoughton, 1953.

—— *Six Makers of English Religion, 1500–1700,* New York, Harper, 1957.

—— *Studies in the Making of the English Protestant Tradition,* Cambridge University Press, 1947; reprinted with corrections 1949.

Scarisbrick, J. J., "The Conservative Episcopate in England 1529–1535," unpublished dissertation, Cambridge University, 1955–56.

Smith, Herbert Maynard, *Henry VIII and the Reformation,* London, Macmillan, 1948.

Smithen, Frederick James, *Continental Protestantism and the English Reformation,* London, James Clarke, 1927.

Smyth, Charles Hugh Egerton, *Cranmer & the Reformation under Edward VI,* Cambridge University Press, 1926.

Strype, John, *Ecclesiastical Memorials, Relating Chiefly to Religion, and the Reformation of It . . . Under King Henry VIII. King Edward VI. and Queen Mary I,* Oxford, Clarendon Press, 1822.

—— *Memorials of the Most Reverend Father in God Thomas Cranmer,* new edition, with additions, Oxford, Clarendon Press, 1840.

Stupperich, Robert, joint author, see Bornkamm, Heinrich.

Sykes, Norman, *The Crisis of the Reformation* (The Christian Challenge Series), Cambridge, J. Heritage, 1938; reprinted 1946.

Tavard, Georges Henri, *Holy Writ or Holy Church; the Crisis of the Protestant Reformation,* London, Burns and Oates, 1959.

Thompson, Craig R., *The Bible in English 1525–1611,* Washington, Folger Shakespeare Library, 1958.

Tjernagel, Neelak Serawlook, "Dr. Robert Barnes and Anglo-Lutheran Relations, 1521–1540," unpublished dissertation, State University of Iowa, 1955.

Westcott, Brooke Foss, *A General View of the History of the English Bible,* 3rd ed., revised by William Aldis Wright, New York, Macmillan, 1905.

Williams, Ronald Ralph, *Religion and the English Vernacular; a Historical Study Concentrating upon the Years 1526–53,* London, Society for Promoting Christian Knowledge, 1940.

Willoughby, Harold Rideout, *The First Authorized English Bible and the Cranmer Preface,* University of Chicago Press, 1942.

Wingren, Gustaf, *Luther on Vocation,* translation of *Luthers Lehre vom Beruf* (Munich, C. Kaiser, 1952) by Carl C. Rasmussen, Philadelphia, Muhlenberg Press, 1957.

Articles

Bowes, Robert, "Biographical Notes on the University Printers from the Commencement of Printing in Cambridge to the Present Time," *Cambridge Antiquarian Society Communications, 5* (1886), 283–362.

Brooks, Peter N., "Cranmer Studies in the Wake of the Quarter-centenary," *Historical Magazine of the Protestant Episcopal Church, 31* (1962), 365–74.

Butterworth, Charles C., "Robert Redman's *Prayers of the Byble,*" *The Library,* 5th ser. *3* (1949), 279–86.

Cargill Thompson, W. D. J., "The Sixteenth-Century Editions of *A Supplication unto King Henry the Eighth* by Robert Barnes, D. D.: A Footnote to the History of the Royal Supremacy," *Transactions of the Cambridge Bibliographical Society, 3* (1960), 133–42.

—— "Who Wrote 'The Supper of the Lord'?" *Harvard Theological Review, 53* (1960), 77–91.

Chester, Allan G., "Robert Barnes and the Burning of the Books," *Huntington Library Quarterly, 14* (1951), 211–21.

Clebsch, William A., "The Earliest Translations of Luther into English," *Harvard Theological Review, 55* (1963), 75–86.

—— "John Colet and Reformation," *Anglican Theological Review, 37* (1955), 167–77.

―――― "More Evidence That George Joye Wrote The Souper of the Lorde," *Harvard Theological Review, 55* (1962), 63–66.

Coates, John R., "Tyndale's Influence on English Literature," *Tyndale Commemoration Volume,* edited by R. Mercer Wilson (London, Lutterworth Press, 1939), 241–56.

Copeland, James R., Jr., "The Place of the Five Books of Moses in the Career of William Tyndale Translator and Reformer," unpublished research paper, Episcopal Theological Seminary of the Southwest, 1960; typescript in the possession of William A. Clebsch.

Gray, George John, "Fisher's Sermons Against Luther," *The Library,* 3rd ser. *3* (1912), 55–63.

Gruber, L. Franklin, *The Truth about the So Called "Luther's Testament in English"―Tyndale's New Testament,* reprinted from the *Lutheran Church Reveiw,* October 1916, and April–May 1917, St. Paul, Minn., Ernst Mustang, 1917.

Guppy, Henry, "William Tindale: Scholar and Martyr, 1536―6th October―1936," *Bulletin of the John Rylands Library Manchester, 20,* (July–August 1936), 258–67.

Hogrefe, Pearl, "John More's Translations," *Papers of the Bibliographical Society of America, 49* (1955), 188–89.

Kronenberg, Maria Elizabeth, "Notes on English Printing in the Low Countries (Early Sixteenth Century)," *The Library,* 4th ser. *9* (1928), 139–63.

Madan, Falconer, "Supplementary Notes to Collectanea I, part 3, Day-Book of J. Dorne, Bookseller in Oxford, 1520. (Including 'A Half-Century of Notes . . .' by Henry Bradshaw)," Oxford Historical Society *Collectanea,* Second Series (1890), 453–78.

Pineas, Rainer, "William Tyndale's Use of History as a Weapon of Religious Controversy," *Harvard Theological Review, 55* (1962), 121–41.

Reed, Arthur W., "The Regulation of the Book Trade Before the Proclamation of 1538," *Transactions of the Bibliographical Society, 15* (October 1917 to March 1919, published 1920), 157–84.

Rogers, Elizabeth Frances, "Sir Thomas More's Letter to Bugenhagen," *The Modern Churchman, 25* (1946), 350–60.

Schwiebert, E. G., "The Reformation from a New Perspective," *Church History, 17,* 1 (1948), 3–31.

Smith, Preserved, "Englishmen at Wittenberg in the Sixteenth Century," *English Historical Review, 36* (1921), 422–33.

―――― "German Opinion of the Divorce of Henry VIII," *English Historical Review, 27* (1912), 671–81.

—— "Luther and Henry VIII," *English Historical Review, 25* (1910), 656–69.

Steele, Robert Reynolds, "Notes on English Books Printed Abroad, 1525–48," *Transactions of the Bibliographical Society, 11* (October 1909 to March 1911, published 1912), 189–236.

Thomas, Alfred, "The Life and Martyrdom of William Tyndale," *Essays by Divers Hands Being the Transactions of the Royal Society of Literature of the United Kingdom,* New Series, *15,* edited by Hugh Walpole (London, Humphrey Milford, Oxford University Press, 1936), 107–33.

Trinterud, Leonard J., "The Origins of Puritanism," *Church History, 20,* 1 (1951), 37–57.

—— "A Reappraisal of William Tyndale's Debt to Martin Luther," *Church History, 31,* 1 (1962), 24–45.

Weiss, N. "Le Premier Traité Protestant en Langue Française La Summe de l'Escripture Saincte, 1523," Société de l'Histoire du Protestantisme Française *Bulletin Paraissant Tous les Trois Mois Etudes, Documents, Chronique littéraire, 68* [5th ser., *16*] (1919), 63–79.

Catalogues, Lists, Encyclopaedias

Barnes, G., joint author, see Jenkinson, F.

Blok, P. J., joint author, see Molhuysen, Philip Christiaan.

Bowes, Robert, *A Catalogue of Books Printed At or Relating To . . . Cambridge, 1521–1893,* Cambridge, Macmillan and Bowes, 1894.

British Museum, *The British Museum Catalogue of Printed Books, 1881–1900,* 58 vols. Ann Arbor, Mich., J. W. Edwards, 1946.

Cambridge University Library, *Early English Printed Books in the University Library, Cambridge (1475 to 1640),* 4 vols. Cambridge University Press, 1900–1907.

Cooper, Charles Henry, and Thompson Cooper, *Athenae Cantabrigiensis,* 3 vols. Cambridge, Deighton, Bell, et al., 1858–1913.

Cooper, Thompson, joint author, see Cooper, Charles Henry.

Crawford, James Ludovic Lindsay, *Bibliotheca Lindensiana. Collations and Notes No. 7. Catalogue of a Collection of Fifteen Hundred Tracts by Martin Luther and His Contemporaries, 1511–1598,* Aberdeen, privately printed, Aberdeen University Press, 1903.

Davies, Myles, *Athenae Britannicae: or A Critical History of the Oxford and Cambrige* [sic] *Writers and Writings, with those of the Dissenters and Romanists,* 6 vols. London, printed for the author, 1716.

Fry, Francis, *A Bibliographical Description of the Editions of the New Testament, Tyndale's Version in English,* London, Henry Sotheran, 1878.

―――― *A Description of the Great Bible, 1539, and the Six Editions of Cranmer's Bible, 1540 and 1541,* London, Willis and Sotheran, 1865.

Great Britain, Public Record Office, *Calendar of Letters, Despatches, and State Papers Relating to the Negotiations between England and Spain,* 17 vols. London, Longmans, et al., 1862–1896.

―――― *Letters and Papers, Foreign and Domestic, of the Reign of Henry VIII,* edited by J. S. Brewer and James Gairdner, 21 vols. London, imprint varies, 1862–1908.

Jenkinson, F., S. C. Roberts, and G. Barnes, *List of Books Printed at the Cambridge University Press: 1521–1800,* Cambridge University Press, 1935.

Kronenberg, Maria Elizabeth, joint author, see Nijhoff, Wouter.

Kuczynski, Arnold, *Thesaurus Libellorum Historiam Reformationis Illustrantium,* Leipzig, T. O. Weigel, 1870; reprinted with supplement, Nieuwkoop, B. de Graaf, 1960.

Lamb, John, *A Collection of Letters, Statutes, and Other Documents . . . Illustrative of the History of the University of Cambridge, during the Period of the Reformation,* Cambridge University Press, 1848.

Laurence, Richard French, *A General Index to the Historical and Biographical Works of John Strype,* 2 vols. Oxford, Clarendon Press, 1828.

Lee, Sidney, joint author, see Stephen, Leslie.

Molhuysen, Philip Christiaan, and P. J. Blok, *Nieuw Nederlandsch Biografisch Woordenboek,* 10 vols. Leiden, A. W. Sijthoff, 1911–1937.

Nijhoff, Wouter, and Maria Elizabeth Kronenberg, *Nederlandsche Bibliographie van 1500 tot 1540,* 3 vols. 's-Gravenhage, Martinus Nijhoff, 1923–1961.

Pollard, Alfred William, G. R. Redgrave, et al., *A Short-Title Catalogue of Books Printed in England, Scotland, & Ireland and of English Books Printed Abroad 1475–1640,* London, The Bibliographical Society, 1926.

Preussischen Staatsbibliothek, *Gesamtkatalog der Preussischen Bibliotheken mit nachweis des Identischen besitzes der Bayerischen Staatsbibliothek in München und der Nationalbibliothek in Wien,* 14 vols. Berlin, Preussische Druckerei- und Verlags-Aktien-gessellschaft, 1931–1939.

Redgrave, G. R., joint author, see Pollard, Alfred William.

Reusch, Heinrich, *Der Index der Verbotenen Bücher. Ein Beitrag zur Kirchen- und Literaturgeschichte,* 2 vols. Bonn, Verlag von Max Cohen & Sohn, 1883–1885.

———— *Die Indices Librorum Prohibitorum des 16. Jahrhunderts,* reprinted from Tübingen edition of 1886, Nieuwkoop, B. de Graaf, 1961.

Roberts, S. C., joint author, see Jenkinson, F.

Steele, Robert Reynolds, *Tudor and Stuart Proclamations 1485–1714,* 2 vols. Oxford, Clarendon Press, 1910.

Stephen, Leslie, and Sidney Lee, *Dictionary of National Biography,* 63 vols. London, Smith, Elder, 1885–1900.

Venn, J. A., joint author, see Venn, John.

Venn, John, and J. A. Venn, *Alumni Cantabrigiensis,* 10 vols. Cambridge University Press, 1922.

Wright, Thomas, *Three Chapters of Letters Relating to the Suppression of Monasteries. Edited from Originals in the British Museum* (Camden Society Publications, 26), London, Camden Society, 1843.

Index